BERNARD SHAW AND THE BBC

L.W. CONOLLY

Bernard Shaw
and the BBC

UNIVERSITY OF TORONTO PRESS
Toronto Buffalo London

© University of Toronto Press Incorporated 2009
Toronto Buffalo London
www.utppublishing.com
Printed in Canada

ISBN 978-0-8020-8920-5

Printed on acid-free paper

Library and Archives Canada Cataloguing in Publication

Conolly, L.W. (Leonard W.)
  Bernard Shaw and the BBC / L.W. Conolly.

Includes bibliographical references and index.
ISBN 978-0-8020-8920-5

1. Shaw, Bernard, 1856–1950. 2. British Broadcasting Corporation – History.
3. Public broadcasting – Great Britain – History. 4. Radio broadcasting – Great
Britain – History. 5. Television broadcasting – Great Britain – History. 6. Radio
plays, English – History and criticism. 7. Broadcasting policy – Great Britain –
History. 8. Radio personalities – Great Britain – Biography. 9. Dramatists,
Irish – 20th century – Biography. I. Title.

PR5366.C66 2009   822'.912   C2008-905072-X

University of Toronto Press acknowledges the financial assistance to its publishing program of the Canada Council for the Arts and the Ontario Arts Council.

This book has been published with the help of a grant from the Canadian
Federation for the Humanities and Social Sciences, through the Aid to Schol-
arly Publications Programme, using funds provided by the Social Sciences
and Humanities Research Council of Canada.

University of Toronto Press acknowledges the financial support for its
publishing activities of the Government of Canada through the Book
Publishing Industry Development Program (BPIDP).

For
Ella, Michela, Amy, and Luca,
With love

Contents

Illustrations follow p. 104

Illustrations

Preface

Two weeks after Bernard Shaw's death on 2 November 1950 Val Gielgud, Head of Drama at the British Broadcasting Corporation (BBC), wrote a tribute to Shaw in the BBC's weekly magazine and program guide, the *Radio Times*.[1] Gielgud recognized Shaw's impact as a 'radio personality,' whose presence produced 'an unforgettable effect ... entertaining, whimsical, witty and wise,' with a voice 'beautiful in itself' and handled by Shaw 'with the virtuosity of an accomplished musician in words and vocal tone.' Shaw at the microphone 'fulfilled every imaginative expectation. He spoke to the individual and not to a hypothetical mass meeting. To listen to him was a joy.'

Shaw's 'greatest impact' on radio listeners was not, however, Gielgud acknowledged, through his several talks, lectures, and debates, but through the broadcasts of his plays. Between the unauthorized broadcast on 1 December 1923 of excerpts from *Man and Superman* and Shaw's death, over twenty of Shaw's plays were given full productions on radio and televison by the BBC, and excerpts from several of the others were included in other broadcasts.[2] A short editorial piece in the *Radio Times* on 2 May 1930 about Shaw was headed '*Greatest Radio Playwright*': 'GBS is the ideal radio dramatist. His brilliant, strongly characterized dialogue, uncomplicated by trivial "action," is even more telling by way of the microphone than on the stage.' A few months earlier the same *Radio Times* (13 September 1929) had ranked Shakespeare as 'Our Best Radio Dramatist,' and a week later (20 September 1929) had also published an article by Richard Church elevating Shakespeare to the '*World's* [my emphasis] Greatest Radio-Dramatist.' But however mixed up the *Radio Times* got about the respective merits of Shaw and Shakespeare as radio dramatists, they were both, from the BBC's point of view, prime assets in the new medium's early (and ongoing) efforts to attract listeners.

The BBC was free, of course, to do what it liked in Shakespearean production – and frequently did. A heavily cut *Hamlet*, for example, was broadcast on 22 November 1928 as *Hamlet in Black and White*: 'The production,' boasted the *Radio Times* (26 October 1928), will 'strip from the tragedy ... that veil with which two hundred years of mannered acting have obscured it, to bring out, stark and vivid, the conflict of a neurotic mind which it was the dramatist's intent to picture ... Where scenes are omitted the space will be filled by a narrator, whose words will further stress the psychological aspect of the drama.' Shaw, ever sensitive to his professional and legal rights, was more of a challenge, though it wasn't long after the first daily radio transmissions began in Great Britain in November 1922 that Shaw – the social activist as well as the playwright – began to appreciate the enormous potential of radio. While theatre managers fretted about radio drama taking audiences away from live theatre, Shaw drew attention to the advantages of home entertainment:

All I can say is that if I could see and hear a play from my fireside I would never enter a theatre again ... [Radio drama] is cheaper; it is more comfortable for those whose homes are at all fit to live in; it is available in town and country and can, in fact, be carried about; to many people it has made the theatre and the trouble of getting there as intolerable as the motor car has made the railway train ... I shall not prophesy, but I again remind our managers that theatre-going is very dear, very inconvenient, and horribly stuffy and promiscuous; unless they overcome those disadvantages by the overpowering fascination of good plays, good acting, and theatres that are like enchanted palaces instead of hotel smoking-rooms, broadcasting will knock them out.[3]

This positive view of radio drama was shared by some other theatre professionals, including, for example, influential actor-manager Nigel Playfair, who saw 'a wonderful opportunity for playwrights and others who will direct their abilities to the production of material specially suitable for broadcasting' (*RT*, 14 December 1923). Playfair was supported by other theatrical heavyweights such as Sybil Thorndike, who extolled the power of radio drama to revivify and inspire the imagination (*RT*, 3 July 1925), and Madge Kendal: 'I do not exaggerate when I say that through wireless the drama is entering upon a new phase which is, at the same time, the beginning of a new vitality' (*RT*, 28 October 1927).

The first drama transmission by the BBC took place on 16 February 1923, consisting of scenes from *Julius Caesar, Henry VIII,* and *Much Ado About Nothing.* The first play written specifically for radio – *Danger,* by Richard Hughes – was broadcast in January 1924, and by September 1925 over one hundred and forty plays had been produced by the BBC, involving actors such as Lewis Casson, Sybil Thorndike, Madge Kendal, and Gertrude Elliott (Briggs, *Birth of Broadcasting* 280–2).

Shaw, of course, also looked beyond the *theatrical* implications of radio's potential. 'Do you realize ... what the wireless has done for the education of the masses?' he asked a visitor to Ayot St Lawrence in 1949. 'When I came to live in this village some forty years ago, almost no one had been more than five miles away. One old chap had been to London and was considered a world traveler. But the wireless quickly changed all this. It brought the world into little hamlets such as this' (Evans 6). Shaw's point was reinforced by a listener who wrote to the *Radio Times* (8 November 1929) to thank the BBC 'for making rural life more endurable for those whose interests extend a little beyond the plough and the beer parlour.' The listener (from East Yorkshire) was especially pleased with the 'heavenly-inspired series' 'Points of View' (see below pp. 62–3): 'To be able to hear men like Dean Inge [Dean of St Paul's], H.G. Wells, and the one and only GBS in the comfort of one's own armchair, and this for the princely sum of ten shillings per annum, is a privilege indeed.'[4] More specifically, Shaw quickly understood the *political* importance of radio. It allowed speakers like himself to reach 'millions of people instead of hundreds' – and 'without the risk of interruptions, missiles, stink bombs, patriotic songs, suffragettes, or having the platform rushed by a lynching mob' (Shaw, 'Telltale Microphone' 465). Shaw also believed – naively, perhaps – that the microphone ('Mike the Detective' he called it) was an effective antidote to political charlatanry: 'Already several front bench celebrities, unaware of the magic of Mike the Detective, have tried their rousing election speeches and their dollops of solemn postprandial humbug on the millions of sober fireside listeners, only to be laughed at, slept through, or switched off' (ibid.). Because the microphone was such a 'ruthless detective' ('I can tell by listening what the speaker has had for dinner'), Shaw predicted (in 1936) that broadcasting 'will raise the moral level of public life,' and his advice to the public was 'never listen to great statesmen or great churchmen except through your wireless set' (Shaw, 'Truth by Radio' 24).

It is worth emphasizing Shaw's point about the capacity of radio to reach millions of people. Since the means of financing BBC broadcasts (which were, and for the most part are, non-commercial) was through a licensing system – each household was required to buy a licence to receive BBC broadcasts – it is possible to trace fairly accurately the potential size of audiences for BBC programs. When Shaw performed *O'Flaherty V.C.* on radio in November 1924 (playing all the roles himself) just over one million licences had been issued, representing, the BBC calculated, a potential audience of about 4.6 million people. The estimated actual audience for the *O'Flaherty* broadcast was three million (*NYT*, 21 December 1924). Shaw's first radio debate (with Hilaire Belloc on 9 June 1925) could have been listened to by over six million people. And when Shaw chaired a broadcast debate between Lady Rhondda and G.K. Chesterton on 27 January 1927 he told his audience that eight million people were listening (*NYT*, 13 February 1927). By the time of the first radio performance of a complete Shaw play – *The Man of Destiny* on 28 March 1928 – some 2.5 million licences were held, representing over ten million listeners (about one household in five, or about a quarter of the total population of Great Britain).[5] Even allowing for those who chose not to listen to Shaw, the numbers are staggering compared to regular theatrical or political audiences. And, of course, they grew significantly during Shaw's lifetime. By the end of 1947, for example, over eleven million households held licences (Coase 199). Shortwave broadcasts to the United States and the BBC's Empire Service (launched in 1931) further increased the size of Shaw's radio audiences, and the introduction of regular television service in the early 1930s (suspended during the Second World War) gave Shaw another medium through which ever-larger audiences could be reached.

It is not surprising, then, that Shaw should have been enamoured of broadcasting. But there are some puzzles and complexities about Shaw's relationship with the BBC, a relationship, important though it was to both Shaw and the BBC, that has never been thoroughly explored.

Why, for example, did Shaw never write a play for radio? – a situation that was 'nothing less than a tragedy, both for broadcasting and for the causes which Shaw had at heart,' in Val Gielgud's judgment (*RT*, 17 November 1950). Why did it take over six years for the BBC to persuade Shaw to allow a production of one of his big plays (*Saint Joan* in April 1929)? What caused Val Gielgud, in the otherwise eulogistic article referred to above, to draw attention to 'the Shaw problem'–'one of the most consistent and baffling of headaches to beset the [BBC] Drama Department'? What caused the almost constant tension between the BBC and Shaw, virtually until the day he died? Why, in the words of one BBC official, did Shaw 'keep on being as nasty as possible'?[6] Why was it, in short, that Shaw became known as the BBC's 'Grandest Inquisitor' (*RT*, 17 November 1950)?

One quick, though not entirely superficial, answer is that in Shaw's view the BBC was too important to be left to the BBC. The BBC enjoyed, it must be remembered, a monopoly on broadcasting in Britain.[7] Ultimately accountable to government through its board of directors, to whom the BBC's Director-General reported, but at least nominally (if not always actually) free from political control, the BBC exercised enormous authority over anyone in Great Britain – including, of course, writers and artists – who wanted access to the benefits of broadcasting. The benefits encompassed the tangible (financial remuneration) as well as the intangible (the opportunity to shape public opinion). Both were of considerable interest to Shaw. About three years before his death Shaw was interviewed by the *Radio Times* about his views on broadcasting (which, said the *Radio Times*, 'are little known'). To the question: 'If broadcasting had existed at the time you were making your name as a dramatist would you have written plays specifically for radio audiences?' he answered, 'Yes, of course' (*RT*, 7 November 1947). Both the question and answer beg another question. Why didn't Shaw write plays for radio *after* he had made his name as a dramatist? The answer might have been that all the time and energy that Shaw felt disposed to allocate to the BBC was taken up with badgering and advising them on how to live up to the onerous responsibilities that the government had bestowed on them, including responsibilities to the world's most famous living playwright, whose plays, though written for the theatre, were, as drama critics frequently pointed out, eminently suitable for broadcasting (thus obviating the need, in Shaw's view, for tailor-made radio plays). The endeavour of keeping the BBC up to the mark, so far as Shaw was concerned, was infinite, and, sometimes, necessarily confrontational. But at the same time – to the credit of both Shaw and the BBC – confrontation led to some significant achievements for both sides. The BBC helped Shaw reach his millions, while Shaw's presence on the airwaves, albeit not as pervasive as the BBC would have liked, not only helped the BBC reach *their* millions, but also, behind the scenes, helped the Corporation become a better and more responsible broadcaster.

The story of the relationship between Shaw and the BBC is not replete with harmony, cooperation, and mutual understanding. The BBC's sense that it knew what was best for its listeners was established very early on by the redoubtable Scottish Presbyterian John Reith, the BBC's first Director-General, who believed that the BBC had a responsibility 'to carry into the greatest possible number of homes everything that is best in every department of human knowledge, endeavour and achievement, and to avoid the things which are, or may be, hurtful.' Reith's response to those who criticized him and the BBC for presuming to know what the public wanted or needed was that 'few knew what they want, and very few what they need' (Reith, *Broadcast* 34). As one biographer of Reith has put it, 'To offer [the public] what *they* wanted would have turned the BBC into a spiritual whore-house, himself into a cultural pimp' (Boyle 151). Shaw admired Reith's sense of purpose and single-mindedness, but was not about to be dictated to by the BBC on what or how he might contribute to its pursuit of the mission established by Reith. Conflict between two hugely self-confident (and sometimes self-righteous) mindsets was inevitable. Like two boxers, the BBC and Shaw sparred over many rounds in the nearly thirty years of their relationship, with Shaw usually the more aggressive, throwing many powerful punches, though never delivering a knockout blow. Indeed, it was not in the best interest of either of these two great cultural heavyweights of the twentieth century to end the fight, for they both benefited from staying in the ring, as did the spectators – in this case the vast worldwide audiences of the BBC.

Acknowledgments

I am grateful to the editors of *Theatre Notebook, SHAW: The Annual of Bernard Shaw Studies,* and the *Independent Shavian* for permission to publish material that appeared in earlier forms in those journals. I also gratefully acknowledge permission from the following institutions to quote from materials held in their collections: the British Library; the Harry Ransom Humanities Research Center, the University of Texas at Austin; the British Broadcasting Corporation; the William Ready Division of Archives and Research Collections, McMaster University; and the Bernard F. Burgunder Collection of George Bernard Shaw, Division of Rare and Manuscript Collections, Cornell University Library. Library staff at all these institutions have been unfailingly helpful and courteous. It is a particular pleasure to express appreciation for the support provided by staff at the BBC Written Archives Centre at Caversham Park, Reading, and at Cambridge University Library. Staff at Archival and Special Collections at the McLaughlin Library, University of Guelph, and at the Inter-Library Loan Office at Trent University have also provided valuable support.

It is a pleasure to acknowledge the friendship and encouragement of Jeremy Crow, Head of Literary Estates for the Society of Authors, who, on behalf of the Estate of Bernard Shaw, kindly gave permission to quote from Shaw's correspondence, plays, and other works throughout this book.

Anonymous reviewers for the University of Toronto Press and the Canadian Federation for the Humanities and Social Sciences made many helpful suggestions for which I am most grateful. Jill McConkey, Daniel Quinlan, and Barb Porter at UTP have provided consistently helpful editorial support and guidance, and I have once more been fortunate to have John St James as my copy editor at UTP. Joan Eadie provided invaluable help with the index.

I express appreciation as well to colleagues at Robinson College, Cambridge, whose patience has been sorely tested by many discourses on Shaw and the BBC in Senior Common Room conversations. Colleagues in North America who have stoically endured similar discourses include Michael Peterman, Eugene Benson, Michel Pharand, and many fellow members of the International Shaw Society. Special thanks are due to Richard Dietrich, President of the ISS, and to Don Wilmeth, former Vice-President. Members of the Shaw Society in England generously gave me an opportunity in May 2007 to address them on Shaw and the BBC. The late Barry Morse, then President of the Society, graciously shared with me his own vast experience of BBC and Shavian acting.

And, once more, I thank my immediate and extended family for overlooking my many and various delinquencies and transgressions while I again neglected them for GBS. My wife Barbara, my children James and Rebecca, and their spouses Lucy and Aldo lightened my labours with a formidable range of practical and psychological support mechanisms, for which they have my heartfelt thanks.

And the inspiration that comes from four very young and very precious people is reflected in the dedication of this book.

A Chronology of Bernard Shaw and the BBC

For the BBC components of this chronology I am indebted to the far more extensive one in Briggs, *The BBC: The First Fifty Years* 363–401.

1922	18 October	Founding of the British Broadcasting Company (a consortium of radio manufacturers)
	14 November	First BBC daily transmissions
	14 December	J.C.W. Reith appointed general manager of the BBC
1923	8 January	First outside broadcast (part of *The Magic Flute* from Covent Garden)
	12 February	First outside broadcast of a play from a theatre (*Cinderella* from the London Hippodrome)
	28 May	First full-length play broadcast (*Twelfth Night*)
	28 September	*Radio Times* first published
	1 December	First broadcast of a Shaw play (excerpts from *Man and Superman*)
1924	20 November	First broadcast by Shaw (reading *O'Flaherty V.C.*)
1925	9 June	Shaw's first BBC debate (with Hilaire Belloc)
1926	13 January	First full-cast Shaw play broadcast (*Passion, Poison, and Petrifaction*)
	11 July	Shaw joins the BBC's Advisory Committee on Pronunciation
	26 July	The government bans Shaw's seventieth-birthday speech
	31 December	The British Broadcasting Company dissolved
1927	1 January	The British Broadcasting Corporation established by Royal Charter, with a monopoly on broadcasting in Great Britain

	28 October	Broadcast debate between Shaw and G.K. Chesterton
1929	16 January	*The Listener* first published
	25–6 April	*Saint Joan* broadcast over two evenings
	30 September	First experimental television broadcast
	16 October	Broadcast of *Captain Brassbound's Conversion* condemned by Shaw
1930	14 July	First television broadcast of a play (Pirandello's *The Man with the Flower in His Mouth*)
	28 October	Shaw's broadcast 'Toast to Einstein'
1932	19 December	Beginning of BBC's Empire Service
1934	20 August	Shaw joins the BBC's General Advisory Council
1936	2 November	Beginning of regular television service from Alexandra Palace
1937	8 July	First television broadcast of a Shaw play (*How He Lied to Her Husband*), with live post-production comments from Shaw
1938	22 April	Shaw writes and broadcasts new prologue for *The Dark Lady of the Sonnets*
	30 June	Reith resigns as director-general, succeeded by F.W. Ogilvie
1939	28 July 1939	Last pre-war television broadcast of a Shaw play (*The Man of Destiny*)
	1 September	Television service suspended
	3 September	Prime Minister Neville Chamberlain broadcasts declaration of war
1940	9 June	The government bans Shaw's commissioned talk on the war
1942	27 January	R.W. Foot and Cecil Graves appointed joint directors-general
	28–9 June	Broadcast of *The Millionairess*, adapted for radio by Shaw
1944	31 March	W.J. Haley appointed director-general
1945	29 July	Beginning of the Light Programme
1946	7 June	Television service resumed; opening programs include *The Dark Lady of the Sonnets*
	23 June	First televison production of *Saint Joan* (with Ann Casson as Joan)
	26 July	Radio and television broadcasts by and about Shaw on his ninetieth birthday

	29 September	Beginning of the Third Programme on BBC radio
	1 October	Third Programme broadcast of the full *Man and Superman*
1947	19 January	Launch of five-play 'Shaw Festival' on the Third Programme (*Mrs Warren's Profession, The Devil's Disciple, The Doctor's Dilemma, The Shewing-up of Blanco Posnet, The Apple Cart*)
1948	8 February	First television production of *Pygmalion* (with Margaret Lockwood as Eliza)
1950	2 November	Home Service and Light Programme broadcast obituaries of Shaw

Abbreviations

BL   The British Library
Burgunder   The Bernard F. Burgunder Collection, Cornell University
CL   Bernard Shaw, *Collected Letters*. Ed. Dan H. Laurence.
                4 vols. London: Reinhardt, 1965–88
CP   Bernard Shaw, *Collected Plays with Their Prefaces*. Under
                the editorial supervision of Dan H. Laurence. 7 vols.
                London: Max Reinhardt, The Bodley Head, 1970–4
HRC   The Harry Ransom Humanities Research Center at the
                University of Texas at Austin
NYT   *New York Times*
RT   *Radio Times*

BERNARD SHAW AND THE BBC

1 In the Beginning, 1923–1928

First Things First: Copyright

It is unclear precisely when the BBC first approached Shaw to broadcast, but a letter of 12 May 1923 from Shaw to Herbert Thring, secretary of the Society of Authors, shows that Shaw was by then involved in discussions with the BBC about what to do for them and how much to charge (*CL* 3:825). He wasn't quite sure what the amount should be ('Hang me if I know,' he said to Thring), but Shaw's assumption from the beginning of the BBC was that the broadcasting of plays constituted performance under the terms of the 1911 Copyright Act. No plays still in copyright could be performed, therefore, in part or in whole, without permission of the copyright holder. The only question was the fee – not an easy question given the newness of the broadcast medium. Shaw was anxious, under the auspices of the Society of Authors, with Thring playing the lead role, to get this sorted out in negotiations with the BBC.

But before any real progress had been made on this issue two problems arose. The first occurred in December 1923. It has generally been accepted that the first Shaw play to be broadcast by the BBC was *O'Flaherty V.C.*, read by Shaw himself on 20 November 1924. But this understanding has to be modified (at least partially) in the light of a short letter from Blanche Patch, Shaw's secretary, to Herbert Thring, of 18 January 1924: 'Mr Bernard Shaw desires me to say that the broadcasting on the 1st December was unauthorized, and that he will be glad if the Society will ask the British Broadcasting Company what they mean by it and what they intend to do about it.'[1]

This is puzzling because no Shaw broadcast before *O'Flaherty V.C.* has previously been noted, and the *Radio Times* list of programs for

1 December 1923 contains no reference at all to Shaw. A subsequent letter, this time from Shaw himself to Thring, throws some light on the situation. Unusually for Shaw, the letter is undated, but it is stamped as having been received at the Society of Authors on 30 January 1924, so a dating of 29 January 1924 seems reasonable. The letter addresses 'this broadcasting affair,' and after referring to the 'Il balen' song from Verdi's *Il Trovatore* and Antony's oration speech from *Julius Caesar* (i.e., self-contained extracts from longer works, each extract 'a work of art by itself') goes on:

> Anyhow, the speech from Man and Superman *now* in question is precisely in the position of Antony's oration or of an operatic solo; and its copyright must be defended on that ground and not on the ground of length. I take it that the copyright of the whole covers the copyright of the parts; and that when the parts are complete in themselves and separately valuable for performing purposes, reasonable quotation means reasonable quotation of passages in the parts, and not reproduction or performances of the whole part.[2]

This makes it clear that the unauthorized broadcast that Shaw was objecting to was an extract from *Man and Superman*, but when was it broadcast and by whom? Although the *Radio Times* listings for 1 December (the date given by Blanche Patch) are inconclusive, there was a broadcast that evening (10:00–10:15 pm, confirmed by program information in the *Birmingham Post* for that day) from the Birmingham regional station of the BBC of 'Impressions of famous Actors in famous Parts' by Fred Pardoe (presumably an established Midlands entertainer). No further information is provided. Granville Barker, Robert Loraine, or Esmé Percy as Tanner? Loraine or Percy as Don Juan? Was this the broadcast that exercised Shaw? There is no way of knowing for sure (at least with the evidence currently available), but the fact that it seems to have taken over six weeks for Shaw to hear about it does argue for a regional rather than a London broadcast.

In any event, Shaw wanted action in the form of BBC recognition of his copyright on the *Man and Superman* speech, and payment for its use. The money, however, was not the main issue. In his letter to Thring, Shaw refers to a letter he has received from the BBC (not found, but presumably one responding to a complaint from him) in which the BBC expresses concerns that Shaw's financial demands 'are likely to be unreasonable.' Not so, Shaw tells Thring: 'I will accept in this case any payment from a farthing upward, provided it be made in a form which constitutes an acknowledgment of the liability of the BBC.'

Thring immediately took the matter up with the Society of Authors' London solicitors, Field, Roscoe & Co. His letter to the solicitors has not been found, but by 2 February he had received a reply (headed *'Bernard Shaw & British Broadcasting Co.'*), advising him that the question raised by Shaw 'was of some little difficulty ... one upon which there is no legal authority to show the way.' But after some legal rambling the solicitor, C.D. Medley, offered a cautious and qualified conclusion: 'Upon the whole, I think that the Court would not be favourable to permitting the Broadcasting Co. to publish and perform in this way substantial and important passages from a man's work, and I should press for recognition of the claim, and if necessary I should be inclined to proceed. My impression is that the Broadcasting Co. will not allow the matter to go to that extent.'[3] He was right. There was some further exchange of correspondence, with Shaw continuing to insist that the BBC must pay, since, as he put it in a letter to Thring on 12 February 1924, 'the act of payment is an admission of the claim, and a proof that the person making payment does not claim a right to broadcast without a license from the author.'[4] A month later (15 March) he was still saying the same thing: '[T]hey must not ... be allowed to think that they can perform again without authorization, and then pay what they please afterwards.'[5] There is only one more extant letter on the subject – Medley to Thring, 18 March 1924[6] – in which the discussion seems to have moved into a post-settlement phase: changes that should be made to the Copyright Act to clarify this issue. No evidence has survived to confirm the resolution of this first skirmish between Shaw and the BBC, but it looks very much as if Shaw (and the Society of Authors) won this one, ensuring thereby that the BBC could not pillage plays and deny copyright obligations.

But a bigger copyright issue loomed. The BBC was ready, it seems, to concede defeat in the battle about extracts, while preparing for a full copyright war. Without consulting the Society of Authors, the BBC negotiated an agreement with the Society of West End Theatre Managers and other theatre management organizations concerning the broadcasting of stage plays or extracts from plays live from theatres or in studio productions. The agreement was intended to 'remove those elements of friction hitherto encountered in securing from the stage items suitable for broadcasting' (*The Times*, 6 June 1925), frictions arising from the anxiety of theatre managers that box-office returns would be jeopardized by

competition from the BBC. Theatre managers agreed to cooperate with
the BBC under certain conditions – no first-night broadcasts, no broadcasts of plays during the first twelve months of provincial tours, a maximum of twenty-six broadcasts a year of excerpts from stage plays,
broadcasts restricted to Friday and Saturday nights ('as far as possible')
and for a maximum of thirty minutes ('normally'). A joint committee
was established to resolve any differences that might occur. On behalf of
the Society of Authors, Herbert Thring objected to the exclusion of its
members from the negotiations and announced that 'if any of the property of the dramatists is broadcast without their knowledge and sanction,' the Society would 'take such actions as may be legally possible
to defend the property of their members' (*The Times*, 20 June 1925). On
22 June 1925 the BBC fired back the response (through *The Times*) that
while 'the arrangement with the theatres was made without prejudice or
reference to copyright interests,' in its view 'there is no legal criterion for
copyright in broadcasting.' Magnanimously, however, the BBC 'have
been careful not to take advantage of this fact. Our policy is to consider
all copyright claims on their merits and to compensate owners on a basis
of moral justice.' This attitude of what author A.A. Milne very gently
called 'kindly condescension to the author' (Bonham-Carter 2:210) was,
of course, totally unacceptable to the Society of Authors, and Thring immediately challenged it – again through the good offices of *The Times*
(23 June 1925): 'Authors do not desire to accept charity from the British
Broadcasting Company,' Thring stated. He insisted that the 1911 Copyright Act applied to broadcasting and that the Society of Authors was
prepared to test this in the courts 'on the first opportunity that the British
Broadcasting Company creates.' That upped the ante, and while
Thring's firmness prompted John Reith, the BBC's Managing Director, to
enter discussions with the Society, no agreement could be reached. Reith
claimed to have been influenced 'by the moral aspect' of copyright, but
he conceded only 'a *feeling* [my emphasis] that payment should be
made,' and then only 'on certain classes of matter used, though not on
everything' (Reith, *Broadcast over Britain* 94–5). There is no evidence to
indicate that Shaw was a participant in these discussions, though it is
hard to imagine that he kept a low profile. In the absence of a mutually
satisfactory arrangement between the BBC and the Society of Authors,
the copyright question was discussed by the Broadcasting Committee
established by the government in 1926 to consider the future of broadcasting in Britain. The major recommendation of the committee – accepted by government – was to establish the British Broadcasting

Corporation, but the committee also addressed the copyright issue. Its views on this were equivocal – writers whose work was used for broadcasting 'should be adequately rewarded,' hardly a resounding endorsement of authors' rights. But that, it seems, was enough to cause the BBC to abandon its imperious 'moral justice' approach to copyright obligations, and the Society of Authors (and Shaw) could henceforth rest easy on this issue (Bonham-Carter 2:209). But not, for sure, on others.[7]

And Then the Money

Establishing copyright was one thing. Figuring out a reasonable fee for broadcasting a play (or part of a play) was another. The stakes on both sides were high. Any agreements reached in the early years of the BBC's operations would inevitably set the basis for subsequent negotiations and settlements, significantly impacting on professional incomes for playwrights and on the BBC's budget. Shaw was in the thick of things from the beginning, sometimes on his own behalf, sometimes – in association with the Society of Authors – on behalf of fellow professionals. His carefree 'Hang me' attitude metamorphosed into a whimsical calculation based on a shilling per listener, 'which on a reckoning of 200,000 listeners was £10,000,' a BBC executive subsequently calculated.[8] Another early speculation was with Cecil Lewis (see below, 'Courtship'), who gave Shaw his first tour of BBC studios (Shaw having turned up unexpectedly) and some information about audience size. Lewis then listened to Shaw do some calculations: 'An audience of a hundred thousand people at, say, five shillings a head, £25,000. Assuming that I take 20 per cent royalty, that works out at £5000. Can you afford that?' (C. Lewis 82). But the realities of hard-nosed business dealing soon took over. The BBC's 'maximum fee' of five guineas for reading a play on air 'is not enough to overcome my inertia,' Shaw told Thring, 'to say nothing of the fact that I could make considerably more by a reading in the ordinary manner' (CL 3:828). Shaw's initial asking price for a reading seems to have been an ambitious hundred guineas.[9] And when the BBC was offered a production of The Dark Lady of the Sonnets in late 1923 or early 1924, the manager's asking price of £50 – a figure recommended by Shaw – was too much.[10] A few weeks later the BBC was to get permission (through the Society of Authors) for a broadcast of How He Lied to Her Husband from the Bournemouth regional station. Thring wrote to Shaw on 21 May 1924 that the BBC was offering two guineas an act, and reminded Shaw – as if he needed reminding – that 'it is, of course, open to members to ask any higher terms they may think fair, though I have not found the B.B.C. prepared to pay anything beyond the minimum rates.' Two days later Thring had Shaw's response: 'I object strongly, because the broadcasting of an inadequate reading by unknown performers might do me considerable harm professionally. I must have the same guarantees as to the quality of the performance as would be offered me as a matter of course by any theatrical management. Also the fee is not sufficient in view of the size of the audience.'[11] The BBC responded by telling Thring (27 May 1924) that they would like to broadcast *How He Lied to Her Husband* from London, and wondered 'what Mr. Shaw would consider an adequate fee for it.' They also asked Thring to enquire whether Shaw would lecture on the BBC, and for how much.[12]

Nothing came of the plans for *How He Lied to Her Husband*, and it was a year before the first Shaw BBC lecture occurred. In the meantime, two guineas an act emerged as the figure that both the BBC and the Society of Authors thought reasonable, though it was never acceptable to Shaw. The Society formally proposed to the BBC on 10 June 1924 that 'a minimum fee of £2.2. per Act, Canto or Division be paid by the British Broadcasting Company for a single performance provided that such an Act, Canto or Division exceeds 200 lines in length.' The proposal was accepted by the BBC on 1 July 1924 'for the next twelve months.'[13] There followed a series of (usually) annual negotiations, with regular but unspectacular increases. Thus it was that a fee of two guineas was paid for a broadcast of the first act of Synge's *Deirdre of the Sorrows* in 1926, while in 1927 three scenes from John Drinkwater's *Abraham Lincoln* cost the BBC five guineas. By 1930 the standard fee had risen to three guineas an act. The majority of playwrights accepted the standard terms, though a few demanded – and received – more. John Galsworthy, for example, was paid £50 in 1930 for two broadcasts of his full-length play *Strife*.[14]

Shaw was in a different league, far and away the BBC's top priority among British playwrights, and the BBC knew that they would have to pay significantly above the norm to get him. He took everyone by surprise, however, by charging absolutely nothing for his first appearance on the BBC, his reading of *O'Flaherty V.C.* He explained his decision to a puzzled and, no doubt, concerned Herbert Thring two nights after the broadcast. If Shaw would appear for free, what chance had other Society of Authors members of charging a fee?

It is quite true that I did not broadcast professionally. If I had I should have charged £105 at least. But I have never given a *personal* performance of any kind for money, though I have been offered prodigious sums by the Americans. When it came to the point I could not overcome my repugnance to breaking this record; and I told the BBC that I would do it for fun as an experiment, which naturally relieved them enormously, as they were expecting me to open my mouth very wide indeed. Fortunately for us the experiment was a very great success. The testimonies are overwhelming as to the superiority of a good reading to a performance by invisible actors; and now is the time for those of our members who can read effectively to make hay while the sun shines. Far from intending to create a precedent of broadcasting for nothing, I wanted to test the market; and any member who is confronted with 'Shaw did it for nothing' can reply 'Then there is all the more left for me. Shaw is not a professional reader, and I *am*.'[15]

Shaw held to his principle of not charging for personal performances (and lectures) throughout his long relationship with the BBC, but if the BBC thought that Shaw would allow subsequent productions of his plays 'for fun as an experiment,' they were to be disappointed. (Shaw also, fortunately, abandoned the peculiar notion that a *reading* of a play was superior to a *performance*.) It was well over a year before another Shaw play was broadcast, but this time Shaw not only charged, but charged well above the odds. He got ten guineas – five times the going rate – for the one-act *Passion, Poison, and Petrifaction*, broadcast from London and picked up by most regional stations on 13 January 1926.[16]

Thereafter it was a matter of negotiation. It took nearly two years to reach agreement for the broadcast of another Shaw play – *The Man of Destiny* in March 1928 – progress being impeded, in the BBC's view, by Shaw's intransigence. The terms for *The Man of Destiny* broadcast are unknown, but despite large figures being discussed internally by the BBC (in the thousands of pounds for a package deal – see below, p. 31), Shaw eventually accepted a modest fifty guineas for the April 1929 broadcast of *Saint Joan*, the same amount paid for *Captain Brassbound's Conversion* in October 1929 and another broadcast of *The Man of Destiny* in May 1930.[17]

It was evident that Shaw's level of confidence in the BBC's ability to do justice to his plays was not sufficiently high to make a commitment to any more than one broadcast at a time, however attractive a long-term, multiple-play deal the BBC might try to tempt him with. The

BBC, like it or not, would not be able to escape the vexation of dealing with Shaw on a broadcast-by-broadcast basis. If they wanted his plays – as they most certainly did – it would have to be on his terms: financial and artistic. That was the way it was in the theatre; that was the way it would be on radio.[18]

Listening In

A good way for Shaw to keep himself informed about what the BBC was doing was, of course, to listen to the programs. In her memoirs, Blanche Patch recalls that Shaw became an avid radio listener. His tastes were, as she puts it, 'catholic': school broadcasts, the news ('Both Charlotte and he invariably switched on for the nine o'clock news, and at six o'clock too during the war'), the Third Programme (the station set up by the BBC in September 1946 for classical music, drama, and talks) – but also lighter fare such as comedian Wee Georgie Wood and singer Gracie Fields. After Charlotte's death in 1943 the radio became even more important to Shaw; he would have it on during and after dinner, 'perhaps not turned full on but always there in the background until the programme closed down' (Patch 227–8).

It took a while, though, for Shaw to get into the listening habit. Cecil Lewis invited him in May 1923 to listen to the set in his London home, but Shaw replied that 'my evenings in town are so occupied for the moment that I am afraid I cannot avail myself of your kind invitation.' Shaw thought, however, that he might look into a 'listening arrangement' at the Royal Automobile Club, the London club where he used to take regular morning swims (CL 3:828). He listened only intermittently during the whole of 1923 and 1924, though by 1924 his friend Sidney Webb had a set; he found it 'amusing,' Shaw told Lewis. Shaw also told Lewis that he had done some listening on his summer holidays in Scotland. 'What I heard was hideous' – it is not clear whether the judgment refers to program content or technical quality (one suspects the former). Shaw thought, however, that his 'domestics in the country might like it.'[19]

By spring 1925, however, thanks to Charlotte, the servants, and 'a wireless-mad doctor,' Shaw could no longer avoid the inevitable:

Dear Captain Lewis
My wife, to amuse the servants, wants to buy a receiving set at Vickery's, where she buys pretty things mostly.

Is there any danger of buying the wrong thing? Are Burndept's Etho-phones (say 4 valve) all right?

Don't tell me that the B.B.C. will put in a set for me. I must not incur the smallest obligation to anyone in connection with the thing: I should have to pay too dearly. I appeal to you as a private man to give me any tip that may save me from wasting my money through blank ignorance when I buy for myself. You have not long to live: nobody could survive many months of radio (I have been listening in through a crystal set shoved on me one day by a wireless-mad doctor for nothing; and the aerial is up) and I want the solemn truth.

Money – in reason – is no object ...

faithfully

G. Bernard Shaw[20]

Despite his profession of 'blank ignorance,' Shaw had obviously done some research on radios: the set that he mentions was one of the top-of-the-line models among dozens regularly advertised in the *Radio Times* and other magazines and newspapers. Lewis confirmed this fact, and a set was duly installed at Ayot on 23 June 1925.[21] Shaw was never again without a radio.

Courtship: Cecil Lewis

The BBC had limited success in persuading Shaw himself to broadcast in the early years or to allow his plays to be broadcast. They were re-buffed more often than accommodated, let alone embraced. That didn't stop them trying. One of the earliest BBC executives to court Shaw was Cecil Lewis, who served in various capacities – Deputy Di-rector of Programmes, Organiser of Programmes, Chairman of the Pro-gramme Board – from the very beginning of the BBC until his departure in 1926. Lewis also wrote, produced, and directed radio plays, and adapted novels for broadcasting. He subsequently enjoyed a successful career in film, directing, among other things, Shaw's *How He Lied to Her Husband* (1931) and *Arms and the Man* (1932), both for Wardour Films. During the First World War he had seen distinguished active service as a fighter pilot.[22] Dealing with Shaw – as Lewis did from as early as 1923 – was perhaps not quite as dangerous as flying primitive airplanes, but it required the kind of perseverance, determi-nation, and evasive action that Lewis no doubt found valuable in dog fights with the Germans.

Lewis's first effort to get Shaw on the radio was a request that he introduce the BBC's first series of Shakespeare plays, directed by Nigel Playfair. Lewis should have known better than to expect Shaw to play second fiddle to Shakespeare and he got turned down, of course: 'Shakespear by himself is all right and so am I. But the mixture would be a bore and a failure' (C. Lewis 81). When Shaw did eventually make his BBC debut, he made sure that he had the whole occasion to himself.

The initial suggestion for a broadcast of *O'Flaherty V.C.* came from Shaw himself in a letter to Lewis on 24 June 1924 – 'There is a short play – about forty minutes – called O'Flaherty, V.C. which never fails when I read it; and I should like to make my first experiment with it.'[23] It took some time to agree on a date for the broadcast (Shaw visited Lewis at the BBC studios at least twice in October 1924),[24] but it was finally announced to listeners in the *Radio Times* on 14 November 1924 that on 20 November Shaw would read the play 'and explain the situations and the dialogue in exactly the same way as he would to a company of actors who were going to undertake the play in production.' What they weren't told – perhaps because the BBC didn't know – is that Shaw would also sing a few bars from the popular First World War song 'Tipperary.' Shaw went to the BBC studios at Savoy Hill, just off the Strand, for the live broadcast, which was aired between 8:30 and 9:20 pm, relayed across all regional stations except Belfast (where mockery of the Irish, even by an Irishman, and however gentle, was probably considered inappropriate, especially so soon after the partition of Ireland in 1921 and ongoing discussions of border definitions with Northern Ireland).[25]

Lewis, to put it mildly, was impressed by Shaw's performance. 'Everybody I have met so far,' he wrote to Shaw, 'is unanimous in the opinion that it was the best thing that has ever been broadcast ... People seem to think that it is uncanny that a playwright should be actually able to sing *Tipperary* and assume three or four different voices as well. I think they are right. In any case the ease and intimacy which you achieved without any practice or rehearsal leaves us, the regular broadcasters, gasping.'[26] Shaw himself deemed the broadcast 'a very great success'[27] – at least initially; some months later he included his own performance among those drama productions on radio that convinced him that there was 'no hope' for the medium.[28] And clearly there *was* no hope if the future of radio drama lay with playwrights reading their own work. In a perceptive article on radio drama on 21 December 1924 the *New York Times* quoted a British critic (unidentified) on the *O'Flaherty* reading:

It was an object lesson in how not to broadcast a play. In their eagerness to please, the British Broadcasting Company lost sight of the basic principle governing the sending of plays by wireless. This is that there must be as many actors as there are parts. If they wanted their audience to hear Shaw they should have asked him to read one of his own prefaces, recite a popular poem or sing a well-known ballad. If they wanted their audience to hear a Shaw play, they should have engaged actors for the job. To combine the two aims was impossible. Bernard Shaw knew this as well as anybody, and made a brave attempt to get out of the difficulty by changing his voice to suit the different characters he was trying to impersonate. But no play can stand this kind of treatment. Even a trained ventriloquist would make mincemeat of it.

O'Flaherty, then, was not a great beginning, but Lewis kept the pressure on Shaw, including a request in May 1925 that Shaw do a promotional broadcast for Nigel Playfair's production of Chekhov's *The Cherry Orchard* at the Hammersmith Theatre – a strange request considering the non-commercial nature of the BBC. Lewis justified it as being 'in the interests of dramatic art generally'; he conceded that such a broadcast would 'give a leg up' to Playfair's production, but suggested that there need not be 'specific reference' to it. 'Impossible,' was Shaw's prompt reply. 'There would be no end to this sort of thing if I began it.'[29] He was right, of course.

He was right as well, surely, to stay clear of another Lewis idea. On 19 October 1925 Lewis wrote to Shaw to ask if was 'interested in mass telepathy.' If so, Lewis continued, 'would you be drawn into a plot?' He then went on to describe what must rank as one of the most witless proposals ever to come Shaw's way:

> We are going to turn the brains of the whole British public (!) on to half-a-dozen simple things, such as a colour, a well known tune, a number, etc. one evening by telling them, over the microphone, to think of each in turn for a minute. A few bold spirits (among which I hope to number you as one) will be invited as guests to dinner at a private room at the Savoy, and when the public starts thinking of the various items, will put down the impression they receive (if any!). Of course the effect of the combined intelligence of the British public concentrated on a few people in one room might cause us to burst, go mad, or anything, but more probably will leave us quite unmoved.[30]

It certainly left Shaw unmoved – there is no record of any response from him – so Lewis came up with some other ideas for Shaw-BBC

collaboration, this time more successfully. He secured the agreement
of Shaw (and others) for the broadcast of a debate with Hilaire Belloc
on 9 June 1925 (see below, pp. 18–20). Shaw was 'splendid,' Lewis told
him the next day, taking the opportunity to offer a little more flattery
in the hope that a bigger prize – the broadcast of a Shaw play (on a
grander scale than *O'Flaherty*) – might be within reach. Lewis was
also clearly a bit peeved that Shaw had ignored some earlier requests
– 'I have written [to] you many times about this but I expect you have
been too busy to reply or have not thought about it seriously' – and
also irritated that some of Shaw's plays had been broadcast in the
United States (without authorization, Shaw later explained). 'I need
hardly say,' Lewis pointed out, 'that your type of work with its brilliant dialogue is most suitable for our medium.' The BBC's 'dramatic
transmissions,' he argued, have passed the 'experimental stage' and
have now 'reached a high standard.' Moreover, Lewis added, 'we
will concur in any stipulation you like with regard to cast, production, etc.' and 'I think we ought to be able to agree about terms.' 'I do
wish you could settle this for us now,' Lewis pleaded.[31]

To no avail. Shaw seems not to have replied to this letter either, so
Lewis telephoned him a month later (10 July 1925). It was not a productive conversation. Lewis told Reith about it in a memo. The account
is worth quoting at length as evidence of Shaw's early recalcitrance
about the broadcasting of his plays:

> I spoke to [the] great man this morning after having written him several
> times asking him whether we could have permission to broadcast some of
> his plays.
>
> He has recently installed a Burndept 4 valve set and loud speaker. His
> opinion of the plays we broadcast was expressed in the one word 'damna-
> ble.' When I asked him if he thought it was really as bad as that, he said
> he thought it was even worse. I then suggested to him that possibly our
> plays seemed dull to him owing to the poorness of the dialogue, and that
> his work, which was so unique and pre-eminently noted for the brilliance
> of its dialogue, would probably come over very well. He said that that
> was a nice thing to say to a stage dramatist who relied on visual surprises
> as much as on anything else.
>
> In the course of further conversation G.B.S. said he considered that I
> should take playwriting very seriously and give up broadcasting, because
> if I did not stop broadcasting soon, he was quite certain I should go mad.
> I told him I was already going mad. I finally reverted to the question of

plays and suggested doing a private test, to which he would listen, as an experiment to see if it was as bad as he thought it would be. He asked how much we would pay him for this and I replied by asking him how much he wanted. He said the least sum he could possibly consider would be £50,000.

After further irrelevancies I asked him if he was entirely adamant in his feeling about broadcasting plays, and he said that the word 'adamant' did not adequately express his state of mind. I mentioned the fact that some of his plays had been broadcast in America and he said that this was done without his consent and his lawyers would be put on to it.

I am afraid, therefore, that for the moment we shall not be able to do anything more in this direction.

He is writing a book on Socialism and asked if we would like to broadcast that – I said we would see.[32]

Perhaps it took some time for Lewis to recover from this conversation, but, war veteran that he was, he didn't give up. He did, however, lower his sights. If he couldn't get Shaw to agree to a big broadcast, he would go – again – for a little one. Thus it was that the second Shaw play to be broadcast by the BBC – and the first with a full cast – was *Passion, Poison, and Petrifaction, or The Fatal Gazogene; A Brief Tragedy for Barns and Booths*. It wasn't quite what Lewis had in mind, but it was, presumably, better than nothing. He had been considering the play 'for some time,' he told Herbert Thring in a letter on 27 November 1925[33] – the consideration presumably beginning at some point after his frustrating summer telephone conversation with Shaw. Lewis first contacted Thring about it in October 1925. Thring sought guidance from Shaw on 30 October.[34] Shaw replied on 3 November, reminding Thring that he had already made arrangements for the Society of Authors to authorize performances of the play and that fees for any performances should go directly to the Actors' Orphanage. Shaw also told Thring that his 'general objection to broadcasting does not apply to this particular tomfoolery.' 'If you can drive a bargain with Lewis to broadcast it for the benefit of the Orphanage, by all means do,' Shaw continued, 'provided it is not announced in the Press lists and Radio Times as a serious work, and Lewis undertakes to say a word or two when introducing it to explain that it is one of the Regent's Park series, to which all the most distinguished authors have contributed, and in which our most famous actors have appeared.'[35] Lewis complied without a murmur over the conditions,[36] and Shaw gave him and Donald Calthrop, the director, 'a free hand to vary the stage directions and so on, to make it suitable for broadcasting.'[37] The broadcast of *Passion, Poison, and Petrifaction* was announced in the *Radio Times* on Christmas Day 1925, the BBC counting itself 'particularly fortunate to have secured this play for production over the microphone.' Readers might have wondered how the BBC got the date of the broadcast wrong (they announced it for 12 rather than 13 January 1926, when it was actually broadcast)[38] and why no cast members were given. More important, they might also have wondered why, of all the great Shaw plays written to that point, the BBC had managed to broadcast only two of the obscurest. A.B. Walkley, theatre critic for *The Times*, while conceding that he was 'no fan of Shavianism,' also questioned the wisdom of broadcasting such a slight work as *Passion, Poison, and Petrifaction*: 'More dismal fooling it would be difficult to imagine. It is no discredit to [Shaw] to fail in the "tomfool" business, at which hundreds of inferior hands succeed every day. But it *is* rather hard on him that the BBC should broadcast his mistakes to every listener in the kingdom, as though to demonstrate that we are none of us infallible, not even "celebrities"' (*The Times*, 20 January 1926).

Lewis kept trying. He wrote a long letter to Shaw on 4 January 1926, discussing some of his own work, and also making sure that Shaw, who was on holiday in Cornwall, would have access to a radio to hear *Passion, Poison, and Petrifaction* on the 13th. He also renewed his efforts to get a well-known Shaw play on radio. His approach this time was inventive, but it still didn't work. Lewis had been working on one of his own plays with the actress Gwen Ffrangçon-Davies, familiar to Shaw through her performances at the Birmingham Repertory Theatre (she was in the British première of *Back to Methuselah* at the BRT in October 1923) and London. She had, Lewis told Shaw, 'a great idea – that she and you might do the Sphinx from "Caesar and Cleopatra," and as there is practically no action (!) and we can do the noise of the "voice of Caesar" very well, it seems this would come over splendidly if you could only be persuaded to relax your ironclad attitude. Do consider it. I think Gwen is mischievously tickled at the thought of calling you "old gentleman."'[39] Shaw's reply has not survived, but he didn't take to the idea, and Gwen Ffrangçon-Davies was left to do her mischievous tickling with someone else. And so Lewis, soon to quit the BBC, was left with not much to show for his three years of courtship of Shaw: a reading, a debate, and a tomfoolery of a play.

BBC English: 'the purity of our spoken language'

A less difficult negotiation than usual between Shaw and the BBC was concluded shortly after Lewis left the company. Indeed, it seems that the negotiation, such as it was, consisted simply of an exchange of letters between John Reith and Shaw, though the task that Shaw (and a few others) took on had far-reaching implications for how the English language was to be spoken throughout Great Britain and, indeed, the world, for generations to come. As the BBC's transmission capabilities improved and it became possible for its broadcasts to reach large areas of the country, Reith and his colleagues decided that the BBC had a responsibility 'in the matter of setting a standard of spoken English by means of the speech of their announcers' (*RT*, 16 July 1926). How were foreign names to be pronounced? And technical terms? What about that 'vast number' of words for which there were variable or alternative pronunciations, 'even among educated speakers'? Who, if not the BBC, was going to maintain 'the purity of our spoken language'? Doing nothing meant allowing announcers (e.g., those reading the BBC news bulletins) to decide for themselves how to pronounce a word. That way, it was concluded, would lead to 'confusion,' so 'uniformity has to be attempted.' But who would determine how a word should be pronounced? The answer to this question was the BBC Advisory Committee on Pronunciation.

The BBC initiated discussions with Poet Laureate Robert Bridges, Sir Johnston Forbes-Robertson, distinguished actor-manager with impressive Shavian connections (Caesar and Dudgeon, for example), and pronunciation expert Professor Daniel Jones of London University. The three agreed to form a committee to advise the BBC on pronunciation issues. Logan Pearsall-Smith (American-born) from the Society for Pure English and A. Lloyd James, Lecturer in Phonetics at the London School of Oriental Studies, also agreed to join the committee. Its first meeting, chaired by the poet laureate, was held on 5 July 1926. At that meeting the committee was asked to advise on the pronunciation of several words, most of them submitted by announcers. A partial list was published in the 16 July issue of the *Radio Times*, the problem word followed by the committee's recommendation:

acoustics	a-coó-sticks
gyratory	jyratory
courtesy	cúrtesy
gala	gáhla

idyll	iddil
obligatory	oblígatory
Northants	Nórth-ámptonshire
Southampton	Soúth-hámpton
char-à-banc	shárrabang
garage	garage (French), *not* garridge
Mozart	Moze-art
Marseilles	Marsáles
Rheims	Reams

At the 5 July meeting the committee also decided to invite Shaw to join them. He responded, positively, to Reith's invitation on 11 July 1926 (*CL* 4:24), and added six new words to the problem list: cowardice, facile, fertile, isolate, Jacobean, and exemplary. According to BBC executive Roger Eckersley, Shaw quickly found himself at odds with the chair of the committee. The pronunciation of 'acoustics,' said Bridges, wasn't a problem. 'Up jumped Bernard Shaw ... The one wanted the ou to rhyme with "cow," and the other with "coo." I forget which wanted which' (Eckersley 109).

Shaw's appointment to the Pronunciation Committee was announced in the *Radio Times* on 23 July 1926. He continued to serve on the committee until it was dissolved in 1939, when its responsibilities were taken over by BBC staff members. After the death of Bridges in 1930 Shaw served as chair of the committee until 29 January 1937.[40] During its thirteen years of operation the committee published seven pamphlets with 9000 pronunciation recommendations, pronunciations that in nearly all cases became standard English usage.

The Debates

The one Shaw debate that took place during Cecil Lewis's stewardship of BBC programming was broadcast from the Savoy Theatre, London, on 9 June 1925 from 5:30 to 6:30 pm. The debate was with essayist, novelist, critic, and historian Hilaire Belloc on the subject 'What Is Coming?' Belloc was a well-known public figure who had debated Shaw before and had also participated in the series of debates Shaw had had with G.K. Chesterton (with one more to come – see below, pp. 21–2). Shaw, who spoke first, realized that it was going to be tough to generate much interest in a debate between two men whose views on almost every subject under the sun were already familiar to many people: 'If there are two men living on the face of the earth about whom you may be perfectly sure what they are going to say because they have said it so often before and never say anything else, it is Mr. Hilaire Belloc and Mr. Bernard Shaw.' Shaw was perhaps thinking more about the audience in the Savoy Theatre than the thousands of listeners for whom Shaw and Belloc were not such everyday names, but to introduce some freshness into the debate Shaw cleverly, though rather circuitously, managed to bring in William Jennings Bryan, then in the news on both sides of the Atlantic for his opposition to the teaching of evolution in American schools. This opposition culminated in the famous trial in July 1925 of John T. Scopes, the biology teacher prosecuted for teaching evolution in Tennessee. Prosecuting counsel Bryan (Clarence Darrow defended Scopes) won the case, but died five days after the end of the trial. In the debate with Belloc, Shaw declared himself to be an evolutionist, someone who believes that 'there is something coming that is different from what has been, and higher than what has been, and which lives more intensely than before.'

> And if I had Mr. Bryan here instead of Mr. Belloc, there would be no confusion between our ideas, and I would quite frankly tell him that what he called Fundamentalism I called Infantilism, in the pathological sense, and that I regarded the holding back of the knowledge of modern evolution from the children as a gross violation of the rights of the children, and that I regard the desire to do that as part of the dogma of a blockhead.[41]

But Shaw didn't have Bryan there, and despite his instinct that a Shaw-Bryan debate would have been a lot more fun than this Shaw-Belloc debate, he had to do his best, as he put it to his audience, to 'provoke' Mr. Belloc, and 'say things that are most likely to bring him out in his best controversial form.' Since Belloc was a well-known Catholic, religion was Shaw's chosen provocation, more particularly the Church – both Catholic and Protestant. He spent a good part of his allotted thirty minutes excoriating the Church for its history of violence and intolerance, seeing little hope for change:

> The Catholic Church has a few wonderful men. I know some of them, and I get on with them perfectly. But I also know what the ordinary average priest is like. I know what the ordinary rector is in a Protestant country, and so do you. We find that we have everywhere a little nucleus of saints; but the great mass of things which we call 'the' Church is a church of people

who are at the best very tiresome, very snobbish, very stupid and often downright scoundrels. Therefore the world gets tired of them, and I am afraid that is going to bat the Church. We are tired of the parson and the priest.

And then – with a nice rhetorical flourish – Shaw concluded his remarks on a positive note (and got back as well to both the evolution and American themes):

Provided, however, that the theory of evolution is kept alive, and men march on to be super men, I don't care twopence if all the churches that ever existed crumble and fall. Our souls would still go marching on, as the American says.

That gave Belloc a splendid entrée, but, disappointingly, he failed to respond to the provocation, sticking closely to the set topic for the debate and expounding only on the limp thesis 'We do not know what is coming.'

You do not know what is coming. You have no idea what the world is going to be like in 50, 100 or 200 years' time. You do not know what you yourself will be like in a few hours from now. Something may happen to one, to change one altogether.
  This is my thesis; that is all I have to say, and if you ask me how I can say it for the next twenty-four minutes, wait and listen.

Those who waited and listened were not rewarded. Belloc offered a couple of meandering anecdotes and then concluded, to his own evident satisfaction, 'I am perfectly glad I have not the least idea what is going to happen in any direction whatsoever.' Radio listeners may have been spared the excitement of Belloc's conclusion because it appears that the debate was cut off when it ran longer than the hour that the BBC had programmed.[42]

Lewis was no longer with the BBC when Shaw next agreed to participate in a broadcast debate. In some ways it is surprising that Shaw did agree, given his displeasure at the government's directive to the BBC not to broadcast his speech to the Parliamentary Labour Party on his seventieth birthday in July 1926 (see below, pp. 23–9). But two things probably attracted him to the invitation to chair a debate between the Viscountess Rhondda and G.K. Chesterton on 27 January 1927 from London's

Kingsway Hall on the subject of 'The Menace of the Leisured Woman.' The first was that it promised to be an altogether livelier occasion than his debate with Belloc; the second was that it afforded him an opportunity to hit back at the government and the BBC for their intransigence about his birthday speech. Since broadcasts were live, the BBC had no way of controlling what Shaw might say, so he took full advantage of the opportunity to be controversial – which is what the BBC feared from the birthday speech – and to ridicule both the BBC and the government for their sensitivity about controversial broadcasts.

The BBC billed Shaw's role in the Rhondda-Chesterton debate in the *Radio Times* (21 January 1927) as merely ensuring 'fair play,' but they could hardly have expected him to leave it at that – especially with an es-. timated eight million listeners in Britain alone, plus Shaw's first North American radio audience (excerpts from the debate were relayed across the Atlantic). In its report of the debate, the *New York Times* (13 February 1927), while recognizing the eminence of the debaters – Viscountess Rhondda, a successful businesswoman, journal editor, and prominent political activist, was a worthy match for veteran debater, essayist, novelist, and critic G.K. Chesterton – nonetheless conceded that the contestants 'merely served as foils for the Chairman, Mr. Shaw.' The central issue of the debate was clear enough: Lady Rhondda argued for getting more women out of the home and into business and professional life ('If the trades and professions are good enough for men, then I think they are good enough for women'); Chesterton thought women were fortunate to be able to stay in the home, 'the only place left where there is any liberty, and individuality and creative power, and possibility of human personalities counting as such.' In his far from impartial summing-up Shaw said that the problem wasn't just the leisured woman, but the leisured human being. 'We have to make up our minds to destroy the idler, that we won't have the idler under any circumstances. It ought to be a capital crime to idle.'[43] It is hard to know what Lady Rhondda – with whom Shaw's sympathies presumably lay – would have made of that.

But Shaw was even feistier in his introduction than his summing-up, free as he was in the introduction from any encumbrance of what the speakers might actually say. It took him only half-a-dozen sentences to get to his beef against the government. 'Now the condition on which broadcasting is conducted in this country is that nothing of a controversial nature must be spoken from the platform or anywhere else, except by members of the Government.' The first part of the statement was substantially true, the second arguably true – government ministers had access to the BBC for official announcements, though not for overtly partisan speeches. What was palpably untrue was Shaw's subsequent comment: 'I myself individually and personally am not to be allowed to broadcast on any terms whatever.' What he meant was that he was not allowed to broadcast if the government feared he would say something controversial – which is why the BBC refused to carry his birthday speech. But now – in a live broadcast – he had the BBC and the government at his mercy. He began by mocking the Postmaster General, the minister responsible for the BBC. 'His horror is probably growing with every sentence that falls from my lips. How am I to be stopped. How are the speakers of the evening to be stopped if they become controversial? Well, I don't know, but it is evident to me that the Postmaster General may call out the Guards.' Shaw then offered the seductive but unlikely prospect of totalitarian state action: 'an energetic force of military and police breaking into this hall, shattering the microphone, and leading me away in custody.' And in those circumstances should the audience in the hall rise up to defend the champion of free speech? No; 'I must ask you not to offer any resistance. Your remedy is a constitutional one: you must vote against the Government at the next election,' the first time in the history of British broadcasting that such advice had been offered. But what of those who already intended to vote against the government? Then – and here Shaw included 'the eight millions of people who are listening-in' – 'I suggest to you that if every one of you writes a letter to the Postmaster General telling him what you think of him ... you will make it absolutely certain that no Postmaster General in England will ever [again] attempt to interfere with freedom of speech in England.' Shaw continued to enjoy himself, making sure in his remaining introductory remarks that the issue of the leisured woman was linked to birth control (fewer children = more 'leisure' for women), a subject the BBC would have rather avoided, especially in a program featuring such a prominent Roman Catholic speaker as Chesterton.

Suppression of free speech; images of totalitarianism; anti-government sentiment; harassment of government ministers; birth control. These were not on the list of the BBC's preferred topics (not in a British context, anyway). Shaw subsequently told the *Daily Express* (6 March 1928) that he had 'deliberately set out' to challenge the ban on controversial subjects on the BBC. It's a wonder, then, that they invited him back. But they did – in part, perhaps, because it was his impression, as he told Beatrice Webb in a letter on 13 February 1927, that the BBC was 'at its wits end for attractions' (Michalos and Poff 213).

It was another debate with Chesterton, a platform opponent of long standing. Their first debate had taken place in Cambridge on 29 May 1911 on the topic 'The Religion of the Future.' Their last was to be the one broadcast by the BBC on 28 October 1927 from 8:00 to 9:00 in the evening. Their subject this time was 'Do We Agree?' The debate, chaired by Belloc, was held again in the Kingsway Hall, amid great public interest. 'Tumultuous crowds struggled in the corridors,' says Michael Holroyd (2:20), 'burst open the doors, flowed round the building like hot lava.' And there were some interruptions during the debate as well. Shaw wasn't far into his opening remarks before he had to pause, 'interrupted by persistent knocking at the doors by ticket-holders who had, through some misunderstanding, been locked out.'[44] 'Persistent knocking' might be an understatement. The account of the evening in the *Manchester Guardian* (29 October 1927) speaks of irate ticket-holders 'hammering and shouting at the door.' Laughter and mild heckling occurred during the debate, but the debate did not in the end sparkle, theatrically or intellectually. Shaw persisted with a familiar theme – 'the obviously monstrous and anomalous misdistribution of wealth under what we call the capitalist system.' Chesterton responded by emphasizing the problems of any kind of state-controlled system of wealth distribution, with power resting in the hands of 'a few oligarchs or a few officials who ... control all the means of production.' Shaw said he didn't believe in democracy; Chesterton accused him of propagating 'a bewildering welter of fallacies.' Personal ownership, said Chesterton, is 'infinitely more healthy' than nationalization. Shaw advocated a coherent and consistent 'political philosophy'; Chesterton was more interested in dealing with 'human beings.' And so on. It was all rather routine, perhaps not surprising from two men who really liked each other too much to get genuinely animated, and who knew each other's opinions too well to be taken by surprise by anything that either of them might say. Belloc's sardonic conclusion, that wherever industrial civilization might lead 'you will all be dead' before significant change occurs, seemed somehow apposite in the circumstances.

The Birthday Speech Row:
'Does nobody see the gravity of the issue?'

Perhaps in an effort to generate a more exciting discussion than Shaw achieved with Chesterton, the BBC (through Roger Eckersley) asked Shaw on 14 June 1928 if he would care to discuss on radio his just-published *Intelligent Woman's Guide to Socialism* – 'provided,' Eckersley said, that 'a worthy protagonist [*sic*] can be found for you.' Eckersley thought that Dean Inge might be suitable, but also gave Shaw the opportunity to suggest other names. Eckersely promised 'a comfortable chair, complete freedom of speech, and a fee at an agreed figure.'[45] Shaw would certainly have been sceptical about that commitment to free speech, but what seems to have upset him most about Eckersley's proposal was the talk of a fee – not just for himself, but also, presumably for his opponent. Shaw instructed Blanche Patch to respond, which she did – succinctly and bluntly – on 18 June 1928: 'The BBC must not bribe anyone to challenge him: he is not a professional prize-fighter, and would object to forfeit his amateur status by meeting a paid antagonist.' In any case, the note concluded, after three years' work on the *Guide* 'he is heartily tired of it.'[46]

More than a year passed after the debate with Chesterton before Shaw was on the air again, this time giving a talk at the theatre of the Royal Academy of Dramatic Art (RADA) on Malet Street, Bloomsbury, on 7 December 1928 in support of RADA's building fund (*The Times*, 3 December 1928). This was the first solo Shaw talk the BBC had broadcast. Shaw told his audience that 'the government is always very nervous, for some reason or other, whenever I speak in public,' and he might have said the same about the BBC as well. But although Shaw teased that he was going to speak 'on one of the most controversial subjects in the world' ('whether a member of a family should go on the stage or not'), he was at his genial best, entertaining his audience for the forty-five minutes the BBC had allotted with stories and reminiscences about theatre ancient and modern and about GBS ('I cannot deny that I have got the tragedian and I have got the clown in me; and the clown trips me up in the most dreadful way') before concluding with some serious observations about the 'very conspicuous public service' that theatre provides.[47] The BBC had gambled that on this occasion Shaw would be on good behaviour, and the gamble paid off.

The BBC had not been prepared to gamble, however, on the occasion of a dinner held in honour of Shaw's seventieth birthday, 26 July 1926, thereby provoking Shaw's harshest criticism to date of state-controlled broadcasting. The birthday was a cause for celebration, and the Labour Party of Great Britain, then the official opposition under the leadership of Ramsay MacDonald (former and future prime minister), arranged a dinner in Shaw's honour at the Hotel Metropole on Northumberland Avenue, just off Trafalgar Square. Shaw, of course, would speak, and the BBC naturally felt inclined to broadcast such an auspicious occasion. But could Shaw be trusted to be non-controversial, particularly at an event hosted by a political party? The BBC (in consultation, according to Shaw, with Prime Minister Stanley Baldwin)[48] thought it prudent to seek an undertaking from Shaw that he would avoid controversy, a request as naive as it was futile. They approached Shaw through Labour MP (and Fabian) Harry Snell. Shaw's response was blunt and to the point:

> Tell the B.B.C. and the 'authorities' what they know very well already: that my speech, like all my speeches, will consist from beginning to end of violently controversial arguments on questions of public policy, and that the only undertaking I will give is to use my own best judgment as to what I ought or ought not to say. If any authority pretends to be a better judge, the public will be glad to know his or her name.
>
> Should I abuse the right of free speech, the authorities have their legal remedy. That is the only security to which they are entitled.[49]

That was more than enough to cause the BBC to refer the matter to the government. The Postmaster General directed the BBC to cancel their plans for the broadcast, and Shaw had to make do with a dinner audience of 120 rather than a radio audience in the millions.[50] When word of the ban got out there were questions in the House of Commons, responded to by the Postmaster General, who explained that he 'would have been glad to have given permission for the broadcast of Mr. Shaw's speech if an assurance could have been obtained that argumentative political controversy would be avoided. Such an assurance could not be obtained, and permission was accordingly refused' (*The Times*, 28 July 1926). The account of the Postmaster General's remarks in *The Times* indicates that they were interspersed with laughter, presumably from the government benches, but for Shaw it was no laughing matter, and he refused to let the dispute rest there. There were, in his judgment, major issues raised by the ban, issues that were at the core of the BBC's mandate and its relationship to government.

Shaw's first opportunity to retaliate was, of course, the speech itself. His main topic was capitalism, particularly as practised by Baldwin's Liberal government. 'We are producing eighty horse-power motor cars when many more houses should be built. We are producing most extravagant luxuries while children starve.' Ultimately, Shaw said, 'we must honestly confess the truth: that is, that this great industrial and financial machine on which the country depends is like a motor car that is running away. It is quite evident that our Government does not know how to drive it. As a matter of fact, there is no steering wheel in the car yet.'[51] This, of course, was not the point of view that the government wanted aired on the BBC. Nor would they have been happy at Shaw's many jibes against government ministers, particularly Winston Churchill, then Chancellor of the Exchequer. Or Shaw's praise of Trotsky ('our talented friend'), and Marx ('Karl Marx made a man of me'), and Mussolini ('that remarkable statesman'). And, naturally, time had to be found to condemn the BBC ban. Ramsay MacDonald prepared the way in toasting Shaw's health at the beginning of the evening: 'Owing to the smallness of mind of the Government and an incapacity to gauge what was in the hearts of the people Mr. Shaw was not being broadcast that night,' *The Times* (27 July 1926) reported MacDonald as saying. Shaw picked up on this by drawing unflattering comparisons between Baldwin's Britain and Mussolini's Italy: 'I don't know whether Signor Mussolini has ever laughed, but I cannot help thinking that when next our Liberal newspapers reproach him for his suppression of freedom of speech he will smile. I think that the laugh will be distinctly on his side, and it will be a laugh against England – not merely against us in this room, but against the traditions of England.' Shaw also reminded his audience of the political importance of the new broadcasting medium, and of the implications of government controlling it for its own ends: 'I hope that everyone here will do all he can to make the seriousness of the matter known' (*NYT*, 15 August 1926).

Shaw took his own advice and continued to do all he could to embarrass the BBC and the government. He drew attention, for example, to the contrasting British and German reactions to his birthday. Germans were effusive in their compliments to Shaw. In addition to numerous private communications – including an album of tributes from leading musicians, writers, and scientists (Einstein, Mann, Spengler, Hauptmann, Schnitzler, Richard Strauss, and Schönberg among them) – the German foreign minister, Gustav Stresemann, sent official congratulations through the German ambassador in London, Friedrich Sthamer. Shaw's letter of thanks to Sthamer – copied to the press[52] – was, Shaw told his German translator Siegfried Trebitsch, likely to be 'more popular in Germany than in England' (Weiss 272).

> The public honour done me by the message of the German Minister of Foreign Affairs ... is the sort of thing that would never occur to a British Foreign Secretary, because, as you well know, we are a barbarous nation in matters of culture. We have a genuine dread of intellect in any form,

and a conviction that Art, though highly enjoyable clandestinely, is essentially immoral. Therefore the sole notice taken of my seventieth birthday by the British Government was its deliberate official prohibition of the broadcasting of any words spoken by me on that occasion.

The letter goes on to credit Germany with creating 'such European sense as exists of the importance of thought and dramatic poetry, and the value of lives devoted to them. Therefore, a tribute from Germany confers on me a distinction that no other nation in the world could give me.'

As Shaw expected and hoped, these comments set the cat among the pigeons – Britain had been at war with Germany only eight years earlier – but he was probably surprised that even the left-of-centre *Manchester Guardian* came to the BBC's (and the government's) support against his 'cantankerous' attitude. 'In the perfectly intelligible interests of a service which is not a political agency, speeches which may be controversial in the political sense are not distributed,' the paper's editorial argued on 2 August 1926. The embargo on Shaw's birthday speech was not directed at Shaw personally: 'it is a general embargo against controversial politics in the middle of an ordinary wireless entertainment.' Shaw knew an intellectually flabby argument when he saw it, and as soon as the *Guardian* editorial reached him in Italy (where he was vacationing with Charlotte) he let fly at its 'shattering, staggering, swoon-inducing' position in a long letter to the *Guardian*.[53] Shaw's point was that far from being free from controversy, many BBC broadcasts dealt directly with some of the most politically contentious issues of the day, including, for example, the 1926 General Strike – but only from the government's point of view. The church and politics, pacifism versus imperialism, the League of Nations, Anglo-Italian relations: on these and other issues, on 'every controversial topic of the moment,' Shaw pointed out, the prime minister and his cabinet colleagues had enjoyed access to the BBC and its millions of listeners 'without the smallest restraint.'

'Does nobody see the gravity of the issue?' In the newspapers, in parliament, in election campaigns, the government could be challenged, criticized, questioned. But when it comes to the BBC, Shaw pointed out, 'Mr. Baldwin seizes me by the throat and says, "I and my friends shall address the five millions as we please; but you shall not address them politically at all, except on conditions dishonourable to yourself, and not only impossible to be observed, but not binding on me and my supporters."' Why had the *Manchester Guardian*, of all papers, 'lain down under the Government steam roller like any other doormat in Fleet Street?' A 'general embargo against controversial politics'? 'The plain truth is that it is not a general embargo: it is an embargo on criticism of the Government. It is waived automatically in the case of members of the Government and their friends, and specially applied to the Labour Opposition and its friends. It is a shameless abrogation of the British right of free speech, and is, for any other purpose, blank nonsense.'

The *Guardian* – stung perhaps by the vigour and validity of Shaw's criticism – responded in an editorial in the same issue (17 August 1926). The General Strike wasn't a good example of government abuse of its control of the BBC because although 'Ministers certainly delivered controversial speeches,' it was 'a time of grave emergency' and therefore it was appropriate that 'the whole broadcasting service' be at the disposal of government. And if only Shaw wouldn't be so 'extravagant' in his arguments! 'If he had said that members of the Government, although the strict theory is for "no controversial speeches by wireless," allowed themselves in the occasional broadcasting of their addresses from banquets and other functions, rather more latitude than they allow to other people, we should have been inclined to agree.' Apart from the fact that Shaw could never have come up with a sentence quite that tortuous, or expressed a thought in such a mealy-mouthed way, the *Guardian*'s timorous approach was hardly likely to cause tremors at the BBC or in Whitehall. Interestingly, though, the *Guardian* could, when they thought about it, recall instances of other complaints about the BBC's 'no controversy' rule and 'it is now understood that the rule will be relaxed and that "a moderate amount of controversial matter, provided that it is of high quality and distributed with scrupulous fairness," will be permitted when the new governing body of our British broadcasting service comes into existence.' No credit for this change, however, was due to the 'perverse rather than persuasive' Shaw and his 'self-destructive cunning.'

Shaw was more interested in real reform than empty credit, but despite the *Guardian*'s prediction, the new BBC structure established in January 1927 (on the recommendation of a committee chaired by the Earl of Crawford and Balcarres) did not herald a new era of free speech on radio. Nor did Shaw expect it to. In an article in the *Radio Times* on 26 March 1926 Shaw had acknowledged the Crawford Committee's view that 'a moderate amount of controversial matter might be admitted,' but given the report's 'uninterrupted flow of amiable obscurities,' it didn't look as if any serious thinking had gone into it. And indeed in

January 1928 Shaw – this time supported by the independent Listeners' Advisory Committee – was still hammering away at the government ban on controversy, and perhaps even beginning to make some headway. It was, at least, the view of the *Evening Standard* (12 January 1928) that 'opinion is steadily growing that greater latitude should be given to the B.B.C. in the dissemination of controversial matter.' Not that there was unanimous support for the removal of the ban. The *Morning Post*, for example, fretted in an editorial on 9 January 1928 that removal of the ban would open up 'a vista of horrible possibilities.' In the *Post's* view, 'the average man or woman, when at leisure and peace with the world, has not the slightest desire to be plunged into disputes.' Shaw wrote to the paper on 13 January 1928 saying that he awaited with interest 'the first non-controversial number' of the *Morning Post*.

But some relaxation of government restrictions on the broadcasting of controversial material was in the works. Baldwin announced in the House of Commons on 5 March 1928 that the prohibition on 'matters of political, religious, or industrial controversy' was to be 'withdrawn forthwith' (*The Times*, 6 March 1928). The BBC was expected, however, to exercise its 'discretionary power' to stay within the 'spirit' of the Crawford report, which called for controversial material to be 'of high quality' and distributed with 'scrupulous fairness.' The *Guardian*'s prediction had, after all, some substance.

Opinion among BBC listeners about the new freedom was divided (radio gives access to the 'unvarnished truth of the politics and proposals of different parties'; 'I am dismayed at the prospect that on some inclement night I shall draw to the fireside only to find the political asses braying on my hearth' – *RT*, 8 March 1929) and whatever progress was made during the 1930s was reversed on the outbreak of war in 1939. When Shaw, at the BBC's request, submitted a talk on the war in June 1940 – what *were* they thinking of? – it was summarily rejected as being altogether too critical of the government (and sympathetic towards Hitler). (See below, pp. 106–12.)

Vicarious Shaw

While radio audiences in the 1920s enjoyed only limited and occasional opportunities to hear Shaw's plays or Shaw in person, they did have other access to him and his work through articles that he wrote for the *Radio Times* and through broadcasts *about* him. The first of Shaw's articles for the *Radio Times* was the one mentioned above about the Crawford Committee report, and another followed on 18 March 1927 when he wrote a lengthy essay on Beethoven in celebration of the centenary of his death. On this occasion, Shaw was introduced to readers as 'the author of that perverse and amusing book, *The Perfect Wagnerite.*'

The first of many BBC talks over the years about Shaw was given by T. Wilkinson Riddle on 16 February 1926 from the Plymouth station. The title of the talk was 'Bernard Shaw, A Puritan Self-Revealed at Last.'[54] This was followed on 24 January 1927 by a talk by Cecil Lewis in a series called 'Famous Writers of Today.' The *Radio Times* blurb on Shaw this time (21 January 1927) described him as 'the most brilliant of our contemporary playwrights, one of the most formidable of controversialists, and an eternal enigma to the critics.' Lewis's talk, however, was not well received by the BBC brass: 'His panegyric (for that was all it was) on Bernard Shaw was second-rate journalism and, if the adjectives had been cut out of it, surprisingly little would have been left' (internal BBC memo).[55] Esmé Percy, already an experienced Shaw actor and director on stage, and soon to play several broadcast roles, gave the talk 'Bernard Shaw (from the Actor's Point of View)' from the Liverpool studios on 30 May 1927, and a more academic talk was given by A.E. Morgan, founding principal of University College, Hull, on 5 July 1927 on Shaw's place in modern English drama. Later in 1927, on 18 November, Irish playwright and critic (and, subsequently, Shaw biographer) St John Ervine began a series of six talks called 'The Modern Drama.' Shaw – along with Shakespeare, Marlowe, Sheridan, Galsworthy, Pinero, and Barrie – was among the playwrights named by the *Radio Times* (4 November) as Ervine's 'points of reference.' And Shaw even made it onto the BBC as a fashion icon, featuring in a talk from Cardiff on 20 August 1928 (by 'Antoinette') on clothes and personality. 'No public character,' said the 17 August 1928 issue of the *Radio Times* (below a photograph of Jaeger-clad Shaw), 'better expresses his individuality in his clothes than Mr. Bernard Shaw.' Sadly, no script of Antoinette's sartorial insights has survived.

Breakthrough

The GBS–BBC relationship was in a sorry state after the birthday-speech row. There were no further broadcasts by Shaw during the remainder of 1926, and in 1927 he made only two appearances on radio – chairing the Chesterton–Viscountess Rhondda debate on 27 January, and debating with Chesterton on 28 October. Part of the difficulty from the BBC's point of view was the loss of Cecil Lewis in April 1926. Lewis didn't have enough clout to override any BBC or government directives about keeping the political Shaw off the air, even had he wanted to intervene, which is unlikely. But in the three years or so that the two had known each other since the founding of the BBC, a mutual respect had developed. As Lewis tells it, he had been the only BBC senior staff member to take the trouble to welcome Shaw to the studios for the broadcast of *O'Flaherty V.C.* in November 1924. After the broadcast, Lewis walked back with Shaw to his flat in Adelphi Terrace, dropping in at the Tivoli Theatre to take in a show. 'From that day on,' Lewis says, 'he allowed me a certain intimacy' (C. Lewis 83). The only other person at the BBC for whom Shaw developed a similar respect (though not intimacy) was Director-General John Reith, but that was still some years in the future. For now Shaw had to deal with the less interesting and less understanding bureaucrats who replaced Lewis.

They tried hard, particularly Roger Eckersley, the BBC executive who took main responsibility for trying to make the breakthrough of persuading Shaw to agree to a production of a major play – Lewis, despite his good relationship with Shaw, having achieved only *O'Flaherty* and *Passion, Poison, and Petrifaction*. Eckersley's approach was to offer Shaw a lucrative package deal. After the arid 1927, there was new energy in BBC approaches to Shaw in 1928. In an internal memo dated 20 February 1928 (marked 'private'), and following a meeting with Shaw on 17 February,[56] Eckersley initiated discussion around a potential offer to Shaw of £1000 for the broadcast rights to six plays, with perhaps an initial offer of £200 for an 'experimental' production. On 7 March 1928 a colleague proposed seven, rather than six, plays 'because probably Shaw would want to change one or another': *Saint Joan, Captain Brassbound's Conversion, Arms and the Man, Fanny's First Play, The Devil's Disciple, Caesar and Cleopatra*, and *Candida*. Three short one-acts were also suggested as plays that the BBC might 'find useful': *The Shewing-up of Blanco Posnet, The Dark Lady of the Sonnets*, and *The Man of Destiny.* Armed with this advice, Eckersley 'had a long talk' (probably by telephone) with Shaw, and although Shaw was, apparently, 'very non-committal,' Eckersley sought the Director-General's approval on 12 March to offer Shaw £150 for 'one of his plays as an experimental start' and a further £800 'for a further series of six if the experimental one is a success' – at the same time cautioning Reith that Shaw 'may want a good deal more.'

Shaw didn't make it easy. The internal memo quoted above (p. xiv) – 'He keeps on being as nasty as possible' – is dated 6 March 1928, and has the additional comment: 'I don't think we should rush after him.' Eckersley, however, was persistent, and his determination paid off just a few days later when Shaw finally agreed to another broadcast of one of his plays. On 16 March he sent a simple postcard message to the BBC:

> Gentlemen
> The proposed broadcast of my play, The Man of Destiny, by Mr Charles Macdona's Company on the 28th March next, has my approval; and, as the sole proprietor of the performing rights, I hereby license the B.B.C. to carry it out on the terms arranged with Mr Macdona.
>
> Faithfully
> G. Bernard Shaw[57]

Eckersley was pleased, as were his colleagues at the BBC. He passed on the postcard to R.E. Jeffrey, Director of Drama, who initialled it and wrote 'Good.' Reith also initialled it, and commented 'A satisfactory licence.' The BBC promoted the agreement with Shaw as something of a coup, announcing the production in the *Radio Times* (23 March 1928) as 'an event of outstanding interest and importance.' The announcement also claimed that 'for the first time, George Bernard Shaw, whose name stands pre-eminently for British Drama in every country of the world, has given permission for a play of his to be broadcast.' That, of course, was not true, but perhaps the excitement at the BBC over *The Man of Destiny* caused a loss of memory about *O'Flaherty V.C.* and *Passion, Poison, and Petrifaction*.

Esmé Percy, Margaret Macdona, George C. Bancroft, and George de Lara – all experienced stage actors – were the cast of the production of *The Man of Destiny* broadcast from London on Wednesday 28 March 1928 from 9:45 to 11:00 pm. Shaw rewrote those parts of the play 'which are unintelligible without visible action,'[58] but despite the textual revisions and the efforts of the experienced cast the production didn't please either Shaw or the BBC. On 7 May 1928 Eckersley checked with Jeffrey to see if there had been any word from Shaw or Macdona about further productions. Jeffrey sent an encouraging note back to Eckersley to the effect that he had indeed heard from Macdona, and that Macdona was 'hopeful' that he could get Shaw to agree to a broadcast of the last act of *Fanny's First Play*.[59] A further memo from Jeffrey to Eckersley on 18 May confirmed that while Shaw had told Macdona that he was 'quite disappointed' with *The Man of Destiny* broadcast he was willing to 'have another experiment.' That 'quite disappointed' must have been toned down by Macdona; Shaw told Trebitsch on 8 May that the production was 'abominable' (Weiss 288), and on 24 July he wrote to Norman Veitch at the People's Theatre, Newcastle-on-Tyne, that the production had convinced him that 'the broadcasting of theatrical performance (except of an opera) is a mistake. It was very disagreeable to listen to; and people who did not know the play could make neither head nor tail of it' (Laurence, *Theatrics* 180). Undeterred, Jeffrey was now willing to think in terms of £5000 for rights to broadcast Shaw plays 'over the next five or seven years.'[60] However, while financial issues remained important to both parties, it was quickly becoming clear that an equally important issue had to be resolved before Shaw and the BBC could get beyond the 'experimental' stage.

Stage versus Microphone: The 'invisible drama'

In the 18 May 1928 memo to Eckersley just quoted, Jeffrey also said this: 'I do not think success with the transmission of Shaw plays lies in the direction of Mr. Macdona unless (as I mentioned to him) he will allow us to choose our own artists and to produce for the microphone in our own way. I think the last transmission prejudiced rather than improved our chances.' Four years earlier, Shaw had urged Cecil Lewis to recognize the difference between stage and microphone performances. His advice to Lewis on this key issue is worth quoting at length.

> As to broadcasting plays, I think you are on the wrong tack about it. You are in the position of the railway companies when railways were new. They persisted in making up trains to resemble as much as possible a string of mail coaches, just as the motor cars of 1896 were built like gigs and phaetons. You want to broadcast plays; and instead of recognizing that the invisible play is a new thing, and cannot be done in the old way, you persist in asking handsome actresses like Miss [Cathleen] Nesbitt and well known pictorial producers like Mr [Lewis] Casson to get up ordinary theatrical performances and allow the public to overhear the dialogue. That is absurd. What use is Miss Nesbitt's beauty or Mr Casson's stage pictures to people who cannot see them?
>
> What the B.B.C. have to do is to set to work to form a company of good dramatic readers, regardless of their age and appearance and memory, but very particular as to their voices and powers of expression and characterisation, with a good uncle to read the necessary explanations and directions, and keep this company as a permanent dramatic staff. This

uncle should be clever enough to study the conditions of the invisible drama, and to make the requisite suggestions to the author when some modification of the dialogue – for instance, make the characters address one another by name more frequently – is needed to supply the lack of vision. Many actors and actresses who have lost their place on the stage through losing their youth, their good looks, and their memory, could do admirable work for broadcasting. Queen Victoria had a beautiful voice and first rate delivery at an age when she could not have played any part on the stage presentably except the nurse in Romeo and Juliet. And there are plenty of young people whose appearance is destructive to romance, but who speak very well, just as there are movie heroes and heroines of surpassing beauty with impediments in their speech or impossible accents. A well selected company taking advantage of its own invisibility would soon develop a special art of broadcasting and enable you to do at least one play a week better for your purpose than you will ever get it done by sending to the theatre for a performance.[61]

This was cogently argued, and it is surprising (the BBC not having followed his advice to establish a permanent company of actors)[62] that Shaw didn't insist on the BBC's hiring specialist radio actors for the broadcast of *The Man of Destiny.* The BBC thought there might have been a misunderstanding about Macdona's rights in the contract for the production. On 11 July 1928 Eckersley wrote to Shaw to clear up a few matters and to try to move things towards another production. Eckersley had seen a letter (now lost) that Shaw had recently written to a Mr Burnett, a BBC employee in Scotland, who had asked Shaw if the BBC could broadcast some of his plays to schoolchildren (one doesn't need Shaw's letter to know what the response was). In the letter, Shaw had, it seems, complained to Burnett about using theatrical companies for radio plays. Eckersley expressed his 'sympathy' with that point of view. Moreover, he continued,

I would venture to say in self-defence that when we broadcast 'The Man of Destiny' the cast was not really of our choosing. We understood from Mr Macdona that it was part and parcel of the contract that his players should be used for this transmission, and though we have nothing but praise for their stage work, we could not guarantee by means of a few rehearsals to turn people whose entire experience was a stage one into broadcast specialists.

We have for a long time been aware of the disabilities which pertain to those who have not had thorough experience of the microphone, and for that reason we have been specialising more and more using people whom we have been specially training for this type of work. We would, from our point of view, have much preferred to have these specialists when broadcasting your play, but as I have said it was understood at the time that it was your wish that the Macdona Players should be used.[63]

Eckersley went on to describe to Shaw a new BBC project, a series called 'Twelve of the World's Greatest Plays,' and hoped that Shaw would allow *Heartbreak House* to be included.[64] The cast 'would be entirely chosen for their ability for microphone drama,' and Shaw would be welcome to participate in planning discussions and to attend rehearsals. Eckersley even offered a private pre-broadcast performance for Shaw, but to no avail. Shaw's reply (13 July 1928, through his secretary Georgina Musters – Blanche Patch was on holiday) made two points: the use of the Macdona Players for *The Man of Destiny* wasn't a misunderstanding – 'one must give the stage people their chance, and not turn them down on pure theory' – and he didn't want to make a commitment about *Heartbreak House*, 'which depends for its queer atmosphere on visible effects. And it is very long.' Shaw did make it clear, however, that he liked the project, 'provided it is carried out by B.B.C. specialists and not by West-End theatrical casts.'[65]

Saint Joan

The BBC and Shaw were coming tantalisingly close to seeing eye to eye, though there still wasn't a commitment from Shaw for the broadcast of another play. Eckersley wrote to Georgina Musters (he called her 'Masters') on 18 July 1928 to let her know that he was taking a holiday in Devonshire and that his deputy, C.G. Graves, would be looking after things Shavian in his absence. A week later Graves wrote to say that Eckersley had in mind *Candida, Arms and the Man*, and *You Never Can Tell*, but also wondered if Shaw had any suggestions for the next production. Nothing had been concluded by the time Eckersley got back from his holiday, so he wrote again (this time to a correctly spelled Blanche Patch) to remind Shaw, through Miss Patch, that they really were in full accord about the need for specialist radio actors – 'we are not dependent on ordinary theatrical companies for our productions, but are working as closely as we can to the policy he suggests – that is, training people to be broadcast specialists' – and to seek a meeting with him. Nothing happened, so Eckersley wrote again on 7 December 1928, but now there was a new idea, one that finally sparked Shaw's interest:

a BBC production of *Saint Joan* to commemorate the '500th anniversary of Joan of Arc.'[66]

Eckersley finally got his meeting with Shaw on 13 December 1928. It was an entirely satisfactory occasion, as Eckersley explained to Jeffrey in the most positive internal memorandum that had yet circulated in six years of Shaw discussions at the BBC.

> I saw Bernard Shaw to-day[67] and as a result of our interview I have come away with the impression that he will not raise any difficulties in regard to our producing 'Saint Joan' when we want to. Furthermore, if this is successful I think we shall probably be able to arrange to broadcast other plays of his. I emphasised that we were at one with him in regard to choice of performers, and that we, just as much as him, had not liked the performance given by the Macdona Players. He seemed to have forgotten that it was his own wish that they should be engaged.
>
> He thinks the outcome of our work must necessarily envisage the formation of a Repertory Company.
>
> However, in order to get the matter settled while it is fresh in his mind, I would like you to draft me a letter to send to him referring to 'Saint Joan' in a more detailed manner and offering him a concrete fee for the broadcasting rights. You might discuss this with Howgill,[68] but I imagine we might be able to get somewhere in the neighbourhood of £50.
>
> Incidentally, he said he thought Sybil Thorndike might play her original part, and he also asked me whether Dorothy Holmes Gore had ever broadcast as he thought she would be a useful acquisition in this play.
>
> The interview in general was very satisfactory, and he definitely is not really anti broadcasting in any sense; he just wants things done properly, or rather what he likes to think of as properly. I told him we should be delighted to see him at a rehearsal, and I think he might follow this up.
>
> Did you know that 'Saint Joan' had been done from Hilversum in Dutch with his consent?[69]

The draft requested by Eckersley was quickly prepared, and the formal offer went to Shaw on 18 December 1928. The fee was increased from £50 to 50 guineas, which was far lower than figures previously bandied about at the BBC. Shaw accepted it, however, demonstrating again that money was not his major concern.[70] The *quality* of the BBC's work was equally, if not more, important to him, and he would have been pleased at Eckersley's willingness in this letter to involve him in the preparations for the production. Shaw was invited to rehearsals and encouraged to make suggestions. Moreover, Eckersley had already followed up on Shaw's interest in Dorothy Holmes Gore: 'I discovered,' Eckersley told Shaw, 'that Dorothy Holmes Gore has broadcast a number of times and her voice comes over particularly well. She has an easy, natural style, not too much coloured by theatre conventions.' Eckersely considered her a better radio performer than Sybil Thorndike, but 'special rehearsals' could be arranged if Thorndike were cast.[71]

Eckersley and his colleagues had handled things well, and Shaw – so far – had been accommodating. There were still many problems to solve about the production – who would direct? who would be in the cast? how could the length of the play be fitted in to the BBC's programming schedule? what textual revisions would be necessary? – but it was evident that a new phase of the GBS–BBC relationship was emerging, a phase that for the next decade saw Shaw as a regular and prominent feature of BBC broadcasting. The struggles of the first six years of the relationship were about to pay off for both parties.

2 *Saint Joan*, 1929

By early 1929 the prospects for what would be the BBC's highest-profile drama production yet, and what for Shaw would be by far the largest audience one of his plays had ever reached, looked promising. With a potential audience of some ten million listeners,[1] the proposed production of *Saint Joan* that Roger Eckersely had discussed with Shaw in December 1928 (see above, p. 36) would be a landmark occasion for both Shaw and the BBC, but pulling it off wasn't going to be easy.

The goodwill that seemed to have developed between Eckersley and Shaw was crucial to the negotiations that ensued from the December meeting, for there were some sensitive and difficult issues to resolve. The principal players were Eckersley, Cecil Lewis (selected in early February 1929 as director for *Saint Joan*), Val Gielgud (new Director of Drama at the BBC), and, of course, Shaw himself, who was not going to leave such an important production under BBC control. Lewis was one of the original BBC senior executives, and had been the key BBC link to Shaw until he left the Corporation in 1926. During that time he earned Shaw's trust and respect, and the relationship continued as Lewis pursued his career in film, theatre, and broadcasting. Gielgud, however, was an unknown to Shaw. Brother of actor John Gielgud, Val Gielgud had joined the BBC in May 1928 as assistant editor for the *Radio Times*, and succeeded R.E. Jeffrey as Director of Drama in January 1929 (a position he would hold with great distinction until his retirement in 1963). The modus operandi adopted by Eckersley was to deal with Shaw himself – consulting BBC Director-General John Reith as needed – while Gielgud worked closely with Lewis on the nuts and bolts of the production.

Shaw had made it clear in his discussions with Eckersley in December that he expected to be consulted about the casting of *Saint Joan*, and lest anyone should forget that condition he reminded Eckersley of it early in January – *before* confirming his agreement.[2] Initially, Eckersley, who was about to leave on a European vacation, asked Gielgud to handle the problem by writing to Shaw with some casting ideas. He then thought better of it – rightly so, considering Gielgud's lack of experience with Shaw and considering also that there really hadn't yet been any serious discussion of casting by anyone at the BBC. On 3 January, and again the next day, Eckersley tried to reach Shaw's secretary, Blanche Patch, by telephone. That didn't work, so he wrote to her instead, explaining that 'in regard to the suggested cast for Saint Joan, we had not really got down to a close consideration of this as we were waiting for Mr. Shaw to give us his permission to go ahead.' Eckersley realized, however, that he had better do something about it before he left on vacation, especially since he hoped to schedule the production for February (an unrealistic expectation as things turned out). He told Blanche Patch, then, that he would 'see to it that this is done before I leave for the Continent on Monday [7 January].' At least, that's what the draft letter reads; Eckersley then altered 'is done' to read 'is put in hand.'[3] There is no record of how exactly it was 'put in hand' in Eckersley's absence – perhaps Gielgud had to deal with it after all. In any event, whatever was done was done quickly, and whatever it was satisfied Shaw.

It is unclear exactly when Shaw gave the BBC formal approval for the *Saint Joan* production. The first extant evidence of his approval is in a letter to Charles Macdona dated 10 January 1929, which was the Thursday after Eckersley left for vacation on Monday the 7th. Shaw told Macdona that the BBC broadcast of *The Man of Destiny* had convinced him that stage actors do not necessarily make good radio actors: stage actors 'depend on their faces, their make-up and their business to make the effects instead of with the voice alone.' Shaw had, therefore, he explained to Macdona, 'told the BBC that unless they formed a company of fine speakers of their own (age and ugliness no drawback) I would not authorize any more wireless performances.' Identifying and using 'fine speakers' was in fact (as Shaw acknowledged) exactly what the BBC had been trying to do, and wanted to do. In these circumstances, Shaw continued, 'I have consented to let them have a go at Joan next month to see whether the result is tolerable, with Dorothy Holmes Gore and some of the old Thorndike cast.'[4]

Clearly, then, between the Monday when Eckersley left on vacation and the Thursday when Shaw wrote to Macdona, there had been communication between Shaw and (presumably) Gielgud about casting, and agreement had been reached on Dorothy Holmes Gore as Joan and on using 'some of the old Thorndike cast'– that is, the cast of the English premiere that opened at the New Theatre on 26 March 1924 with Sybil Thorndike as Joan. There were still huge uncertainties about the casting, but evidently Shaw was willing to move ahead. An internal BBC memo written by Gielgud on Monday 14 January 1929 confirmed that 'we have obtained Mr. Shaw's definite permission to broadcast *St. Joan*,'[5] and on 17 January Eckersley, back from his holiday, congratulated himself and his colleagues (in a memo to Reith) for 'rather a good bit of work in getting Bernard Shaw to let us have the broadcasting right of *St. Joan* for £50.' It should, he thought, be 'a peak' in BBC programming.[6]

Perhaps so, but the peak would not be reached easily. It had already occurred to Gielgud that they had secured Shaw's agreement for the production without even considering, let alone resolving, an 'extraordinary difficulty' – the length of the play, and how to fit it into regular BBC schedules. The regular evening broadcasting schedule had already settled into a structure that was circumscribed by news and weather bulletins at 6:15 and 9:00. *O'Flaherty V.C.* had aired from 8:30 to 9:20 pm on 20 November 1924, before the news and weather bulletins had settled into their regular time slots, and both *Passion, Poison, and Petrifaction* (13 January 1926) and *The Man of Destiny* (28 March 1928) were short enough to be accommodated *after* the nine-o'clock news (*Passion* from 9:25 to 10:00, and *The Man of Destiny* from 9:45 to 11:00). Gielgud had calculated that he needed at 'the very least' three and three-quarter hours for *Joan*, and he absolutely didn't want 'such items as news bulletins and shipping forecasts' interrupting a play set in the Middle Ages: this 'would destroy the atmosphere and jeopardize the success of the play.' Such a 'handicap' could cause 'a possible fiasco,' and in those circumstances Gielgud thought it better 'not to do the play at all.'[7]

This surely is not what Eckersley and Reith wanted to hear, especially from a novice BBC administrator. Gielgud, to his credit, offered two possible solutions to the dilemma. One, he knew, was a long shot. That was to break the BBC veto of broadcasting plays on a Sunday. Gielgud suggested that they could run the play between 2:30 and 6:30. 'Our listeners,' he thought, 'might not be averse to spending a Sunday afternoon in hearing *St. Joan*, particularly at this time of the year when they are not likely to be attracted to the joys of the open road.' Knowing full well, however, that the decision to allow drama on Sundays would be Reith's and Reith's alone, and being aware of Reith's strict Scottish Presbyterian beliefs (antithetical to perceived frivolities on the sabbath – Sunday programming was restricted almost exclusively to church services and serious music), Gielgud also thought it worthwhile reminding his superiors that *Saint Joan*, 'apart from its being a fine classic drama,' also 'deals directly with religion.'

But Gielgud really had a better idea than challenging Reith to secularize BBC Sundays. It was a risky idea, though, because it seemed very likely to upset Shaw. Gielgud suggested doing the play on two successive weekday evenings, 'cutting the play in half at the end of the Rheims coronation scene.' 'If we could obtain Mr. Shaw's permission for it to be done in this way,' Gielgud said, 'I should favour it, as I think that to demand that our listeners should concentrate upon even the best classic for over three hours is something of a risk.' Gielgud was not optimistic that Shaw would allow the BBC to 'bisect his work in this way,' hence his alternative Sunday proposal, and if Reith vetoed that, then it would be better to abandon the project altogether. (The BBC's method of dealing with long Shakespeare plays was simply to cut them down to conform to BBC scheduling. Thus, the *King Lear* broadcast on 11 September 1928 was only two hours long.)

Given Shaw's well-known antipathy towards adaptations and alterations of his plays, Gielgud's pessimism was understandable, but Reith's reaction to Gielgud's memo was needed before any approach to Shaw could be made. As soon as Eckersley got back from his holiday, he cautiously expressed his views to the Director-General: 'Supposing Shaw is unwilling for us to perform [*Saint Joan*] in two halves as Gielgud suggests, do you not think as a special case we might include it on a Sunday afternoon? I am not sure myself that bisection is artistically sound.'[8]

Reith's response, handwritten on Eckersley's typewritten memo, and dated 18 January, is worth quoting in full:

> I don't think it's desirable at all on a Sunday. Apart from any dramatic embargo on Sundays, to give a long play on one of the most 'popular' times in the week w^d be odd surely. I don't like bisection – impossible I think. I would do it deliberately on a week night & cut out news or anything else if you want to, and make a great feature of it, & try to get it listened to. I sh^d give resumés between acts & advertise them also so that late diners can come in there. We want a very fine cast. I sh^d go all out for this [as] it might have a big effect on listeners' opinion of radio drama.

And then there is a postscript:

Of course I sh^d *try* for some cuts to get it down if possible to 2 hours –
then it w^d go over better & your other troubles be lessened.

Reith did not volunteer to tell Shaw that *Saint Joan* 'would go over better' if it were cut by about a third, but at least Eckersley and Gielgud still
had some options. The only certain thing was that a Sunday performance wasn't on. Eckersley passed on Reith's comments to Gielgud
with a peremptory note of his own: 'Mr. Gielgud – Please speak.'

And speak Gielgud must have done, but there is no extant documentation of his discussions with Eckersley. There were three options: take
up Reith's offer to do the whole play on a weekday evening, uninterrupted by news and weather bulletins – a generous offer in view of possible complaints by non-Shavian listeners who wanted and expected the
news at its regular time; try to get Shaw to agree to cuts that would allow the play to be broadcast without disrupting the regular schedule
(e.g., 6:30–9:00); or try to get Shaw to agree to spreading the play over
two evenings.

The third option, as we have seen, was Gielgud's preference, but both
Reith and Eckersley had expressed reservations (Reith quite forcefully –
'impossible'). It is disappointing that there is no record of the discussions
that now took place, but the outcome is known, and it's a surprising one.
Gielgud, although Director of Drama, was very much the junior participant in the discussions, but his preference was the one adopted. Even
more surprising, perhaps, is that he had Shaw's support.

On 4 February 1929 Eckersley wrote to Shaw:

Dear Mr. Shaw,
I am glad to say that at last it is possible to put before you a definite date
for the broadcast production of ST. JOAN. We propose, with your consent, to break the play on the first night at the end of the third scene, and
thereby to do it on two successive nights as you suggested to me the other
night. The dates proposed are the 25th and 26th April, the first night's ·
performance to run from 7.30–9 p.m.; the second from 9.30–12.^{9} These periods include a certain amount of incidental music.

I think I mentioned to you that I hope to get Cecil Lewis to produce.
What do you think of these hypothetical arrangements?

Yours sincerely,
[R.H. Eckersley]^{10}

It's an interesting letter. At the meeting (or, more likely, a telephone conversation) Eckersley had with Shaw 'the other night,' who first raised the possibility of breaking the play into two parts? Eckersley makes it sound like Shaw's idea ('as you suggested to me'). Did Shaw also suggest the break after scene 3 (the French victory at Orleans)? This is a different break from the one Gielgud had originally proposed (i.e., after scene 5, the coronation at Rheims). Did Eckersley simply explain to Shaw the dilemma and the options, and let him choose? Whatever happened, Eckersley obviously handled the situation well, and even now did not force the issue, seeking Shaw's reaction to the 'hypothetical' arrangements.

Shaw's reaction was favourable. On 9 February he sent a message to Eckersley through Blanche Patch (perhaps by telephone – there is no written record), which Eckersley acknowledged in a letter on 13 February. While supportive of the proposals in Eckersley's letter of 4 February, Shaw still had two concerns. One was that the broadcast on the second evening would run until midnight. 'We quite agree with you,' Eckersley responded with typical BBC paternalism, 'that as a general rule, people should not be encouraged to sit up till all hours, but we feel that one special occasion will not hurt them, and that our audience will be so interested by the first half of the play in the earlier part of the programme that they will be glad to make a special effort the following evening.' (Normal BBC close-down time was midnight, but the last program of the evening was usually dance music, which, presumably, wasn't thought to encourage listeners to stay up late.) And Shaw also raised again the question of casting, on which little or no work had been done while the scheduling matter was sorted out. 'I am afraid,' said Eckersley, that 'we cannot come to a definite decision about it until the putting of the play into a definite programme is a certainty.' And as a prudent afterthought Eckersley added, 'We will of course send you a list of the cast directly things are a little more advanced.'[11]

Things were falling nicely into place. 'Shaw continues to be a little difficult on small points,' Gielgud reported to Cecil Lewis on 14 February, 'but we have settled on the tentative dates of 25th and 26th April, and he has agreed to let us bisect the play and do it on two successive nights.'[12] This memo was written in the context of negotiations between Gielgud and Lewis about the appointment of Lewis as director of *Saint Joan*. Eckersley had worked effectively with Shaw; now Gielgud had to get Lewis signed on and the casting sorted out. Neither task was straightforward.

Negotiations with Lewis were complicated by plans for broadcasting his own play, *Ultimatum*, Lewis wanting a single fee to cover both projects. The BBC's starting point was 50 guineas for directing *Saint Joan* – the same fee that Shaw was receiving. Then Gielgud got approval to offer Lewis a combined fee of £75 for *Saint Joan* and *Ultimatum*, and did so on 15 February. Lewis's response (17 February) was to ask for £60 for directing *Saint Joan*, with an additional £20 if the play was broadcast a second time. Lewis's justification for wanting a higher fee than offered was that *Saint Joan* 'requires the greatest care in casting and attention to detail in production. It is a masterpiece of great length and in consequence the actual quality of work required will be more than double that of a normal play.' Gielgud could not have been very convinced by this argument, since he raised the offer (22 February) by only £6.10.0, the increase being in the fee for *Ultimatum*, not *Saint Joan* (£50 for *Saint Joan*, £31.10.0 for *Ultimatum*). Lewis agree to the fee on 27 February.[13] (*Ultimatum*, a one-act play, was broadcast on 4 April 1929, repeated on 5 April.)

Gielgud now got seriously down to work on the casting. Although he assured Lewis in a letter on 11 March that he (Lewis) would have 'the last word' in casting, Gielgud also described the task as one of 'finding a cast that will both suit us and not irritate Shaw,'[14] which was hardly giving Lewis a free hand. And in any event Gielgud had by then exchanged ideas directly with Shaw, and on 6 March had sent Lewis a 'hypothetical' cast that Shaw had 'approved as far as it went.'[15] This was the list Lewis received:

Joan	Dorothy Holmes Gore
Dunois	Andrew Churchman
Stogumber	Michael Hogan
Inquisitor	O.B. Clarence
Archbishop of Rheims	Marcus Barron
Dauphin	Harold Scott
Warwick	Henry Oscar
Bishop of Beauvais	Eugene Leahy
Brother Martin	Harman Grisewood
Baudricourt	Leslie Perrins

Gielgud also told Lewis that Shaw had also recommended Robert Speaight and Jon Swinley, 'though with no particular application.'

Of the actors included in this partial and preliminary casting, only Dorothy Holmes Gore, Marcus Barron, and Leslie Perrins appeared in the production (all in the roles identified here),[16] so there was still plenty of work to do, with seven weeks to go to the 25 February broadcast. The

BBC announced the play, with dates, in the *Radio Times* on 8 March 1929, describing the occasion as 'a definite landmark in the history of broadcast drama.' Shaw, readers were told, 'is acknowledged as the first contemporary dramatist in Europe,' and *Saint Joan* was his 'masterpiece.' Readers were advised not to miss the broadcast of a play that dealt with 'one of the most fascinating personalities in history,' and explained the historical period with 'brilliant lucidity.' They should not be concerned about the division of the play into two parts – 'necessitated by its more than usual length' – for 'those who hear the first half will be far too interested to miss the second.'[17]

There was no turning back now, but the aura of confidence exuded by the *Radio Times* was not apparent behind the scenes. Lewis was having major problems with the casting. It was too late to do much about Joan, since Dorothy Holmes Gore had Shaw's approval, but Lewis feared that she lacked sufficient 'simplicity and directness' for the part. He would much have preferred the younger, though much less experienced, Alison Leggatt, he told Gielgud.[18] Oscar he thought 'too young' for Warwick. Michael Hogan 'lacks sufficient dramatic power' for Stogumber, 'the most difficult part in the play.' Eugene Leahy 'always talks as if he had too much saliva in his mouth' (though that didn't stop him from playing Cauchon in all three of the New, Regent, and Lyceum productions in 1924, 1925, and 1926 respectively), and 'Shaw's recommendation of Speaight and Swinley isn't much good is it?' – Robert Speaight being busy as he was in R.C. Sheriff's *Journey's End* at the Savoy Theatre, and Ion Swinley 'always playing somewhere or other.' (Swinley appeared in a short run of *Red Rust*, by Virginia and Frank Vernon at the Little Theatre, 28 February–16 March 1929.) On the other hand, Lewis thought O.B. Clarence 'magnificent'; 'it will be a great piece of luck' to get him as the Inquisitor. (He had played the role at the New and the Regent.) And Bruce Winston 'would make a very good Warwick.' Winston had played La Trémouille at the New and the Regent, and Lewis succeeded in getting him as Warwick for the BBC. With Clarence, though, he wasn't so lucky.

Lewis went after – and got – other actors with stage experience of *Saint Joan*: Milton Rosmer played Bluebeard (as at the New and Regent); Douglas Burbidge played Dunois (as at the Lyceum); H.R. Hignett played the Inquisitor (as at the Lyceum); and Lawrence Anderson played Brother Martin (as at the New, Regent, and Lyceum).

Lewis's final cast was a compromise, of course. Gielgud had ostensibly given him the final word on casting, but as soon as Alison Leggatt's name came up Gielgud told Lewis that he thought her 'the most over-rated actress on the English stage ... [H]er voice fills me with horror every time I hear it.'[19] And there was Shaw's preference for Dorothy Holmes Gore to keep in mind. And availability. And budget (see below). And judging whether stage experience could translate into radio success, and whether radio experience could compensate for limited or non-existent Shavian stage experience. The cast published in the *Radio Times* on 19 April 1929 was as follows:

Robert de Baudricourt	Leslie Perrins
A Steward	George Howe
Joan	Dorothy Holmes Gore
Bertrand de Poulengey	Harvey Braban
Archbishop of Rheims	Marcus Barron
La Trémouille	Ambrose Manning
Constable of France	John Reeve
Bluebeard	Milton Rosmer
La Hire	Atholl Fleming
The Dauphin	Russell Thorndike
Duchess de la Trémouille	Barbara Horder
Dunois	Douglas Burbidge
A Page	Peter du Calion
A Chaplain	Arthur Douglas
Cauchon, Bishop of Beauvais	Arthur Clay
Warwick	Bruce Winston
Stogumber	Harcourt Williams
Warwick's Page	Joan Brierley
An Inquisitor	H.R. Hignett
D'Estivet	Francis Beaumont
De Courcelles	George Howe
Brother Martin	Lawrence Anderson
An Executioner	Harvey Braban
An English Soldier	Bertram Brown
A Gentleman	Rupert Bruce

There is no record of when casting was finally determined. Gielgud and Lewis were still discussing it in mid-March, but it seems reasonable to assume that all was settled by the end of the month. In the meantime, the BBC was busy promoting the broadcast. There was another short piece about it in the *Radio Times* on 29 March, this one stressing that although listeners might miss the 'gorgeous colours' of Charles Ricketts's designs for the New, Regent, and Lyceum productions, 'the loss would be more than atoned for by an added ease listening to those static scenes whose only interest [*sic*!] is an intellectual one, and of which *St. Joan* contains one of the bravest examples in all of Shaw.' And there was another explanation-cum-apology for broadcasting the play over two nights: 'to cut it would be unpardonable, and to listen to all of it over the air, without a break, impossible.'

And then on 28 March Shaw received the strangest of letters from *The Listener*, the BBC's 'literary weekly' (still then in its inaugural year). R.S. Limbert, the editor, explained to Shaw that *The Listener* 'publishes regularly a critical article after each broadcast performance of an important play,' and he certainly wanted to carry a 'critique' of *Saint Joan*. No one, he thought, 'would be as well able to do this as the author of the play,' so would Shaw be willing to write 'your own opinion' of the performance for the 1 May issue of *The Listener* for a fee of 25 guineas? Part of Shaw must have been intrigued and enticed by the opportunity to write a review of one of his own plays, but, he told Limbert, 'decency forbids.' 'What will you pay me for NOT criticizing it? ... It is, obviously, just the one performance that I must not criticize.'[20]

Meanwhile, the *Radio Times* was preparing its own special recognition of the broadcast production of *Saint Joan*. The issue of 19 April 1929 carried not only a photograph of Shaw on the front page and an announcement (with times) of the production of Shaw's 'famous play,' but also an announcement of articles in this issue by Hilaire Belloc and Willa Muir. Both Belloc and Muir dealt with the historical Joan, Belloc analysing the spiritual and religious implications of Joan's life (particularly the 'miracles'), while Muir, a well-known feminist, stressed the significance of Joan's achievements in a world – political, religious, and military – dominated by men. There were also illustrations of scenes from the play (artist unknown) and a synopsis of the first three scenes for listeners who missed the first evening's section.

No one could complain that the BBC hadn't worked hard to make the event a success, and no budgetary restraints seem to have been placed on Gielgud and Lewis. Original estimates had assumed a fee of £5 for each actor, but Dorothy Holmes Gore got £20, Bruce Winston £17, Lawrence Anderson £17, and Harcourt Williams £16. Lewis had also decided, 'a few days before the play,' to have some crowd scenes, which cost another 18 guineas for actors. Even so, despite inaccurate estimates and unexpected expenses, production costs exceeded budget by only £18. 7s.[21]

The play was duly broadcast on the evenings of 25 and 26 April. The only problem appears to have been that Bruce Winston became ill and was unable to perform. It may or may not have been widely known at the time, but although the *Radio Times* listed Winston as Warwick, the part was actually played by Val Gielgud – 'at short notice,' as Gielgud explained in a *Radio Times* article some years later.[22] Despite – or perhaps even because of – his unanticipated involvement in the production, Gielgud was well pleased with the outcome. He wrote to Lewis on 27 April to congratulate him on his 'triumph' with *Saint Joan*, adding, 'I don't think there can be the slightest doubt of its complete success, and if you will allow me to say so, I think you handled it superbly well.'[23] Lewis, no doubt, was perfectly prepared to allow Gielgud to say that, but a more objective view could be expected from the press.

Regular reviewing of BBC programs was not yet extensive, but *The Times* was one newspaper that thought a broadcast of *Saint Joan* worthy of attention. It praised both Lewis and Shaw, Lewis for relying on 'the simplest form of production' with 'well-chosen incidental music,' Shaw for his 'consummate skill in character drawing' and for 'the vivifying resources' of the play's dialogue. Shaw's skills, *The Times* thought, 'can be appreciated as well by the fireside as in the theatre,' but the 'pageantry and ceremonial' of the play are 'a clear loss' in a radio production. It falls upon the actors to 'indemnify' listeners for this loss by 'concentration of power and purpose in every word they utter.' In this regard, *The Times* praised Harcourt Williams, Russell Thorndike (Sybil's brother), and (ironically, since he was too ill to perform) Bruce Winston. Dorothy Holmes Gore was successful, too, but 'if she had not occasionally spoken in terms too refined for a country girl, she would have been even more deeply convincing.'

Praise, then, for playwright, director, and actors, but *The Times* did have a problem with the issue that had troubled everyone at the BBC from the start – how to fit such a long play into regular broadcast scheduling. The solution, as we have seen, was to spread the play over two evenings. That, thought *The Times*, was a 'questionable' decision. 'It would have been better boldly to put courage (the producer's and the listeners') to the test and give the complete play on the one evening, with, perhaps, a fairly long interval of music in the middle and possibly the excision of the third scene between Joan and Dunois, in which the play flags for a few moments.' More easily said than done, especially if cuts were required (for which Shaw's approval would have been needed), but only then, *The Times* argued, could the 'accumulative strokes wield their full power and the play be recognized by those unfamiliar with it as the moving masterpiece it is.'

Having failed to engage Shaw to review *Saint Joan*, *The Listener* commissioned G.G. Coulton, whose comments (1 May 1929) had more to do with the play itself than the production. Lukewarm about the play ('propagandism interferes with [Shaw's] art ... his satire is very cheap'), Coulton limited his thoughts on the production to a complaint that extracts from the 'ignorant and foolish' preface were included. Perhaps Shaw regretted that he had not done the review himself.

It would, no doubt, have surprised both Gielgud and Lewis if there had not been some criticism of their production of *Saint Joan*. It had been a huge challenge, and they must have been relieved, above all, that Shaw was supportive and – apparently (though there is no evidence of this one way or the other) – appreciative. Gielgud had done well in his first test as a producer of serious drama at the BBC, and his reputation and influence grew rapidly. And Shaw, at least, had been pleased enough with the BBC that he was on the air again as a lecturer in October, and gave permission for a production in the same month of *Captain Brassbound's Conversion*, his fifth broadcast play on the BBC.[24] Important as it was, then, in its own right, the 1929 production of *Saint Joan* was perhaps even more significant as heralding the beginning of a decade of productive cooperation between Shaw and the BBC, brought to an end only by the outbreak of the Second World War and the BBC's ill-judged request to Shaw for a talk on the war.

3 'Saying Nice Things Is Not My Business': Shaw Talks, 1929–1937

On the morning of Sunday 3 September 1939 Prime Minister Neville Chamberlain addressed the British people on radio to inform them that Britain was at war with Germany. The broadcast reached practically all areas of Great Britain, the installation of regional transmitters throughout the 1930s having greatly extended the BBC's reach. The British public responded to the BBC's expansion initiatives by buying licences and receivers in record numbers. In 1930 more than 1000 new licences a day were issued (over 400,000 for the year), 'unanswerable proof,' observed the BBC, 'of the rapidity with which Broadcasting has sloughed the skins of Novelty and Luxury and taken its place in contemporary life as a fully-fledged Necessity' (*RT*, 9 January 1931). Judged by further significant increases in the number of licences issued in subsequent years, this was no idle boast. The *Radio Times* reported on 24 March 1933 that over five million licences were in use, raising the number of potential listeners at any given time to around twenty million – double the number of five years earlier (see above, p. xiv). By the spring of 1935 there were twenty-eight million listeners (*RT*, 24 May 1935), and by early 1939 some thirty-two million, about three-quarters of the population of Great Britain (*RT*, 10 March 1939), a massive audience for Chamberlain's speech. Those numbers did not include overseas listeners, international broadcasts having become a significant feature of BBC programming with the introduction of regular short-wave service in 1932. And by 1939 the *Radio Times*, still the sole official source of information about BBC programming (though the daily newspapers now carried basic program times) had a weekly circulation of three million (Briggs, *BBC* 114).

In the meantime, Shaw was spending the 1930s writing new plays (*The Apple Cart, Too True to be Good, Village Wooing, On the Rocks, The*

Simpleton of the Unexpected Isles, The Six of Calais, The Millionairess, Geneva, In Good King Charles's Golden Days), travelling (including visits to South Africa and New Zealand, in both of which countries he made radio broadcasts), and forging a productive new theatre alliance with Barry Jackson at the Birmingham Repertory Theatre and the Malvern Festival[1] – not to mention celebrating his eightieth birthday (in 1936) and winning an Oscar in February 1939 for the screenplay of *Pygmalion*. He was also winning many new admirers among those millions of listeners in Britain and overseas who had never heard his voice or seen one of his plays. At the same time, he was provoking, challenging, and, not infrequently, upsetting listeners to the many talks he gave on radio in the politically and socially turbulent 1930s.

'The supreme arbiter on correct pronunciation'

The early years of Shaw's relationship with the BBC were, as we have seen, frequently disputatious. The relationship in the 1930s continued to be disputatious, but the altercations were punctuated by occasions and by periods of relative cordiality, both sides recognizing that self-interest dictated some backing down from entrenched positions – the BBC's to control its broadcasts, Shaw's to control his work. Nor was Shaw averse to going public with beefs against the BBC unrelated to his work, such as the occasion of a letter to *The Times* on 7 July 1938, when he complained on behalf of British 'breadwinners' (who 'rise at 6 or earlier' and 'have to be in bed at 10 to make room for their eight hours' sleep') about the BBC decision to move the evening news from 9:00 to 10:00 pm.[2] But Shaw more typically gave vent to his ire, or offered advice, privately. A personal letter to John Reith on 30 September 1932, for example, urged the BBC to commission a third symphony from Edward Elgar, whose 'financial position is a very difficult one.' Reith accepted Shaw's advice and quickly arranged the commission. Elgar, unaware of Shaw's involvement, thanked Reith – 'I shall always treasure the remembrance of your kindness and consideration' – but died (23 February 1934) before completing the work.[3]

Shaw also spent a good deal of his time advising the BBC in formal (but voluntary) capacities, joining, for example, the General Advisory Council in 1935 (whose mandate was to 'interpret the policy and practice of the corporation to the various sections of the community with which they may be specially associated'),[4] and continuing his work on the Advisory Committee on Spoken English until it was dissolved in

1939. He had first joined this committee in July 1926 (see above, p. 18), and became chairman in 1930, a position he held until his resignation on 29 January 1937. Shaw was always conscientious about attending the committee's frequent meetings, and, particularly as chair, he exercised considerable influence over English pronunciation as the voices of BBC announcers entered an ever-increasing number of British households. Alistair Cooke, who sat in on some meetings of the committee in 1935, noted that while the committee always reached its decisions by vote, Shaw, as chair, could cast the deciding vote when there was a tie, making him, in Cooke's words, 'the supreme arbiter on correct pronunciation' (Cooke 8).

Neither Shaw nor the committee were immune from criticism on issues of pronunciation, Shaw once being taken to task by a BBC listener for his (allegedly) slovenly pronunciation during a talk he gave on *Saint Joan* on 30 May 1931. Shaw 'fell sadly from grace,' charged the listener, for saying (twice, no less) 'I wan chew to remember' (*RT*, 7 August 1931). And some of Shaw's American listeners were offended by his pronunciation of some words in the NBC broadcast of his speech on 'The Future of Political Science in America' from the Metropolitan Opera House in New York on 11 April 1933 (see below, pp. 69–70). What 'goaded his listeners beyond endurance,' reported *The Listener* (26 April), was not so much 'his criticisms of American banking, the American constitution, [and] the Mormons,' but 'his abuse of the American language.' Shaw, it was reported, pronounced 'privacy' 'prívvacy' (rather than 'pryvacy'), 'evolution' 'ēvolution' (rather than ĕvolution), and 'financier' 'fináncier' (rather than 'fínnanséer'). Shaw subsequently conceded (in a letter to *The Times*, 2 January 1934) that the American criticism was justified, especially of his pronunciation of 'privacy,' 'the short i,' he said, being 'much less effective than the long one.'

More serious criticism of the work of Shaw's committee came from prominent British writers such as Scottish poet Hamish Maclaren, who objected to standardization of pronunciation, for 'words are like birds: when free they sing and swoop and often do astonishingly beautiful things; but put them in a cage, and all but a few of the tamer sort pine away and die' (*RT*, 11 October 1929). And English novelist Compton Mackenzie perceived what he described as 'the BBC's pedagogic enthusiasm for a standard pronunciation' as 'nothing more than a camouflage for the attempt ... to make what the BBC calls Southern English the common speech of the whole country, and of Scotland and Wales as well' (*RT*, 24 March 1933), an accusation that must have been particularly irksome to Shaw, who kept his gentle Dublin accent to the end of his life. In response to criticism of this kind, the BBC denied that they wished to 'impose their conventions' on the public, but insisted that, as with the printed word (in spelling, for example), some conventions are necessary (*RT*, 19 October 1934). Nonetheless, in order to represent the interests of 'the general public' as well as 'literary, scientific and artistic people' and 'professional lexicographers, philologists and phoneticians,' the membership of the committee was expanded in 1934 to around twenty-four (from the original five in 1926, six after Shaw joined). Shaw worried that he wouldn't be able to remember all the names ('I am beginning to forget people's names quite ridiculously,' he told Reith),[5] but, more importantly, he advised Reith a few months later that the new committee was 'a ghastly failure.' Generation gaps among committee members caused differences of opinion on pronunciation and 'the young people just WON'T pronounce like the old dons.' There were also differences on issues of principle: 'Are we to dictate to the mob, or allow the mob to dictate to us?' wondered Shaw. The solution, Shaw suggested, only half tongue-in-cheek, was to reconstitute the committee 'with an age limit of 30, and a few taxi drivers on it.' 'I give up,' he concluded, but, perhaps revitalized by the voyage with Charlotte around Africa early in 1935, he carried on working with the committee until its dissolution five years later.[6]

Undeterred by criticism, and confident that 'the extraordinary prevalence of doubt and uncertainty' (*RT*, 19 April 1935) about pronunciation justified its endeavours, the committee continued to grapple with 'uncertain' words and to publish its decisions in the *Radio Times* and in occasional pamphlets. Many of the decisions have stood the test of time: 'Wednesday' is pronounced with two syllables, not three; the stress in 'bureaucracy' comes on the second syllable; 'heinous' is pronounced 'haynus', with the stress on the first syllable. Others didn't make it: 'landscape' hasn't survived as 'lanskip,' and venison eaters order their meal with three syllables, not two ('venz'n').[7] Shaw won some arguments, and lost some as well. He didn't see why the pronunciation of 'polka' should change from 'poalka' to 'pollka,' but it did, nor did he know that some words existed, let alone know how to pronounce them. When he learned, for example, that there was such a word as 'celeriac,' he said he would use 'turnip celery' instead.[8] Give-and-take was the very nature of the committee's work, Shaw argued, and committee members were 'quite frequently obliged to decide unanimously in favour of a pronunciation which they would rather die than use themselves in their private lives.'

He made this point in a letter to *The Times* (2 January 1934) when the committee was facing a barrage of criticism, arguing as well that 'wireless and telephone have created a necessity for a fully and clearly articulated spoken English quite different from the lazy vernacular that is called modd'ninglish.' And as the correspondence continued in *The Times*, Shaw reminded readers that 'pronunciations are always obsolescing and changing,' and would continue to do so (25 January). And in a fit of unaccustomed royal fervour, Shaw in the same letter declared that 'the best English to-day is literally the King's English.' 'Like his Royal grandmother [Queen Victoria] before him King George is the best speaker in the realm; and his broadcasts are astonishingly effective in creating loyalty.'[9]

The BBC and Controversy

Shaw served the BBC diligently and conscientiously on the Pronunciation Committee, but he was far too valuable to the BBC to be kept behind the scenes. Recognizing Shaw's brilliance as a public speaker and his ability to adapt his skills to the medium of radio, and responding to listeners' eagerness to hear him, the BBC did its best to give Shaw a voice on radio as often as possible. From time to time, listeners wrote to the *Radio Times* with lists of their favourite speakers. Shaw frequently appeared on the lists – fourth and third most popular on lists published in the 10 and 24 July issues in 1931; 'top of the poll' in the 12 August 1932 issue for 'this delightful, if provoking, speaker.' And when there was a lull in his appearances, requests for 'more of GBS' (5 August 1932) ensued.[10] A blind listener (Miss Eva Longbottom from Bristol) associated Shaw's voice with colours: 'delightfully yellow,' which, 'on occasion, he exchanges for crimson,' she said (*RT*, 28 April 1933).

But colourful or not, popular or not, Shaw's voice would not be as regular a presence on radio as the BBC might have wished so long as he felt constrained by BBC policies that limited his freedom of speech. After the lifting in March 1928 of the government ban on the broadcast of 'matters of political, religious, or industrial controversy' (see above, p. 29), the BBC loosened restrictions on its speakers, and increased its direct involvement in the political issues of the day. The General Elections of 1929, 1931, and 1935, for example, all featured party political broadcasts, Reith even urging on Winston Churchill in 1931 the idea of freeing speakers from party control as a means of generating greater expression of 'original and provocative points of view' (Briggs, *Golden*

Age 127). Shaw supported this view, but advised the BBC's Director of Talks, C.A. Siepmann, to warn politicians that 'their platform bunk is no use on the wireless.' Politicians, Shaw said, 'are so accustomed to stoking up audiences of excited partisans that they have no notion of how to handle millions of innocent non-politicians sitting quietly by their firesides.' 'Besides,' he added, 'the mike gives away the least insincerity mercilessly.'[11] Churchill himself argued in a *Radio Times* article ('Broadcasting as an Influence in Politics,' 25 May 1934) for the broadcast of 'fair interchange of views, including sharp controversial discussion.' It seemed possible in the summer of 1935 that such a discussion might indeed take place when Siepmann tried to get Churchill and Shaw to debate the proposal 'That free food rather than free education should be provided by the State.' Shaw thought the topic 'excellent,' but didn't want to put Churchill 'in the position of denying food to starving children.' So Shaw suggested that the topic should be announced as 'What is the most immediately desirable extension of British Communism?' He would begin, he told Siepmann, by contending that 'there should be public supplies of bread and milk.' The rest, he thought, could be 'improvised as we go along.' The next step, said Shaw, 'is to sound Mr Churchill on the subject.' Siepmann went to the trouble of doing that personally, but had to report to Shaw after meeting Churchill that he had failed to persuade him: 'He is not concerned to come to the microphone other than on major political issues, and then only as a matter of duty.'[12]

Generally, however, the BBC's kind of controversy was one that existed in an ordered and balanced environment – debates, for example, among those respectful of the established political order, or talks by respected writers such as H.G. Wells, J.B. Priestley, and Arnold Bennett. Shaw's suggestion, on the other hand, that he give a talk in 1931 on 'The Election Viewed from the Extreme Left' got nowhere.[13] Still smarting perhaps from the broadcast ban on his seventieth-birthday speech in July 1926 (see above, pp. 24–5), Shaw was not convinced that the BBC had fundamentally changed, telling Director of Programmes Roger Eckersley in no uncertain terms in a letter of 27 July 1929 that he would not 'take the BBC seriously' until 'the childish absurdity' about 'expressions of opinion being free from argument and controversy' was dropped, 'finally and without compromise.'[14] Shaw was not alone in his doubts. Leonard Woolf argued vigorously in his 1931 essay 'The Future of British Broadcasting'[15] that the BBC had a responsibility and an unprecedented opportunity to develop 'an educated, informed, tolerant and rational public opinion,' but that it could hardly do so while banning controversial issues. The BBC's response to Woolf (*RT*, 22 May 1931) could have done little to alleviate Shaw's and Woolf's anxieties. In the opinion of the BBC, the British public was not yet ready for 'the liberal reception of uncensored opinions.' Its series on 'Russia in the Melting Pot,' for example (beginning on 25 May 1931), would focus on 'the presentation and elucidation of accurate facts,' deliberately avoiding 'controversial aspects of the question' (*RT*, 22 May 1931). A few weeks later, on 7 July, a memorandum marked 'PRIVATE' circulated at the BBC reporting that senior management (the Control Board) had discussed the possibility of inviting Shaw to give a talk on Russia when he returned from his forthcoming trip (18–30 July). 'It was unanimously decided,' the memo stated, 'that Mr Shaw should not be asked to speak to his experiences in that country.'[16] Shaw did subsequently give such a talk, but it was not broadcast in the BBC's domestic services (see below, pp. 67–9). And while allegedly allowing politicians to be 'as controversial as they please' in a weekly series of broadcast talks in the autumn of 1933, the BBC also made it clear that discussion of India (then the subject of contentious constitutional talks that eventually led to independence from Britain in 1947) was proscribed (*RT*, 8 September 1933). This particular decision was made after Churchill had been to see Reith to 'demand to be allowed to broadcast his views.' Reith had been willing to consider the possibility of a discussion on India, but backed off after consulting the government (Reith, *Into the Wind* 151). Generally, though, the BBC was so confident and self-assured in knowing what was best for the British public that it positively boasted about its powers of censorship. 'Plays,' it declared, 'are censored by the Lord Chamberlain, films by the British Board of Film Censors ... Broadcasting is its own censor.' And what's more, the BBC was a 'strict' censor; its 'blue pencils flicker over talks, manuscripts, plays, comedians' patter' (*RT*, 16 December 1932).

By setting itself up as the arbiter of what was or was not in the public interest, and by denying access to broadcasting to those who would seriously challenge orthodoxy, the BBC was, of course, taking a firm political position of its own as defender of the status quo. In this way, as many observers commented, the BBC's power and influence were enormous. *The Era*, which billed itself as the 'Official Organ of Entertainment' in Great Britain, was hardly a neutral witness to the BBC's role, concerned as it was that the increasing popularity of radio was a principal cause of declining theatre attendances. Thus, its claim that 'this vast machine has acquired a comprehensive stranglehold on the national life' has more than a touch of desperate rhetoric about it. And the BBC might have been hard pressed to recognize itself in *The Era*'s description of its power: 'It sways elections, dictates to politicians, lectures Europe, controls the musical profession, castigates screen and stage, and, through its enormously successful publishing business [e.g., the *Radio Times* and *The Listener*], competes with the newspaper industry for the general reader and commercial advertising.' *The Era*'s conclusion from all this was blunt: 'If the BBC is to be an instrument of political propaganda, let us have a plain statement from the Government to that effect, and we shall soon attach the right label to its activities, in the way that we attach a label to other instruments of propaganda' (*The Era*, 18 January 1933).

Public opinion, however, as expressed in letters to the press and newspaper editorials,[17] was generally less harsh on the BBC than *The Era*, and even Shaw – despite his reservations – accepted BBC invitations to broadcast more often than not during the 1930s. Of the dozen or so talks broadcast by Shaw in the decade leading up to the outbreak of the Second World War, five were part of major series in which prominent writers, statesmen, religious leaders, and others were asked to give their views on a major topic or current issue. The remainder were sometimes broadcasts of talks that Shaw had been invited to give by other organizations, sometimes talks commissioned by the BBC itself for broadcast from its own studios. The talks were usually scripted, which was the BBC's preference because the script could then be monitored for length and content, but even so the BBC could not necessarily predict listeners' reactions. A discussion, for example, on film censorship, broadcast on 20 January 1935, gave Shaw the opportunity to talk about films and sex. He argued that the proponents of film censorship are 'obsessed with sex appeal,' a subject that is 'a perfectly legitimate element in all the fine arts that deal directly with humanity.' 'To educate and refine it is one of the most sacred functions of the theatre. Its treatment under the censorship is often vulgar; yet I believe that, on balance, the good that has been done by the films in associating sex appeal with beauty and cleanliness, with poetry and music, is incalculable' (as reported in the *Daily Telegraph*, 21 January 1935). That set the cat among the church pigeons, in part because it ran counter to an initiative by the Archbishop of Canterbury to persuade the government that there should be an enquiry into the (allegedly lax) censorship system run by the British Board of Film Censors, in part because (to add insult to injury) Shaw's views were broadcast on a Sunday. The Lord's Day Observance Society lodged 'an emphatic protest' with the BBC against this 'deplorable' violation of 'the hallowed hours of the Christian Sabbath' (*Daily Telegraph*, 22 January 1935), prompting the BBC to reconsider Sunday programming of current affairs discussions 'in the light of experience now being acquired' (*Daily Telegraph*, 26 January 1935).[18]

Occasional Talks

It was something of an understatement for the BBC to describe Shaw as 'without doubt one of the wittiest and most stimulating speakers of the day,' which is how he was introduced in the *Radio Times* (with picture) for a speech broadcast on 31 January 1930 from a meeting of the British Drama League at the Kingsway Hall in London. The meeting was in support of a National Theatre, a subject close to Shaw's heart. He spoke of the need for 'a monument to justify to the country the dignity of theatrical art,' a state theatre 'to be what St. Paul's and Westminster Abbey are in religion – something to show what the thing can be at its best.' A national theatre should have a site provided by government, together with an endowment to keep ticket prices affordable. Shaw likened a national theatre to the BBC, which was 'spending thousands a year, but the only complaints were that the programmes were too good.'[19]

Later in 1930 Shaw was invited to toast the health of Albert Einstein, who was to speak at a dinner – held at London's Savoy Hotel on 28 October – in support of Jewish charitable fund-raising initiatives. The BBC seized the rare opportunity of having Shaw and Einstein on the same program, and made arrangements to broadcast the occasion live from the Savoy. Shaw, however, quickly became frustrated by the BBC staff assigned to the event, who seemed more concerned with fitting the speeches into a fixed schedule than with giving the two great men adequate broadcasting time. Bristling at the affront, Shaw went to the top, informing BBC Director-General John Reith (in a letter dated 20 October 1930) that to do justice to Einstein's achievements he (Shaw) 'must make a full dress oration about Ptolemy & Aristotle, Kepler & Copernicus, Galileo & Newton, gravitation and relativity and modern astro-physics and Heaven knows what, hailing Einstein as the successor of Newton, and speaking on the largest scale in the name of British culture and science welcoming the foremost natural philosopher of the last 300 years.' 'I cannot do it in 15 minutes,' Shaw told Reith – and 'As to limiting Einstein, it is out of the question: we must be prepared for 2 minutes or

30 at his pleasure.' What the BBC should do, Shaw advised Reith, was to schedule 'an elastic musical program which can be adapted to whatever may happen in the hour following my rising.' And that is more or less what the BBC did, allocating a 9:40–10:10 slot, but not cutting off the speeches as – inevitably – they exceeded the thirty minutes (particularly since Einstein spoke in German, followed by an English translation).[20]

There was, perhaps, some BBC concern as well over what an unvetted speech by Shaw might contain, but apart from an occasional political and religious aside,[21] Shaw focused his remarks on Einstein's scientific achievements, concluding with a tribute that might well be applied to Shaw himself:

> I rejoice at the new universe to which he has introduced us. I rejoice in the fact that he has destroyed all the old sermons, all the old absolutes, all the old cut-and-dried conceptions even of time and space, which were so discouraging because they seemed all so solid that you never could get any further. I want to go further always. I want more and more problems. And our visitor has raised endless and wonderful problems, and has begun solving them.[22]

The Shaw/Einstein combination guaranteed widespread publicity, with major reports of the speeches in the press, including, for example, the *Manchester Guardian* (29 October 1930) and the *New York Times* (29 October), all of which was good publicity for the BBC. In addition, the America public was able, for the first time, to listen to Shaw live on the BBC, courtesy of CBS, which carried the broadcast on shortwave.

Shaw's next solo broadcast of the 1930s – on Joan of Arc – was also carried by shortwave to the United States, one radio enthusiast, James R. Power, writing to Shaw (on 3 July 1931, on the impressive letterhead of The Marshall of the Municipal Court, City of Los Angeles) not only to let him know that 'except for some slight interference' the talk 'came through to Los Angeles very well indeed,' but also to send him a transcript of the talk to prove it. (It was, it seems, Mr Power's hobby to make transcripts of broadcasts, 'which I later discard.')[23]

The talk, commissioned by the BBC to mark the five hundredth anniversary of the execution of Joan of Arc (30 May 1431), was broadcast on Saturday 30 May 1931, from 9:20 to 9:40 in the evening. Mr Power told Shaw that he found the talk 'most interesting'; other listeners expressed their views more colourfully. It was not, on the face of it, a controversial script, but it aroused hostility on both sides of the Atlantic.[24]

In London a Catholic priest condemned the 'impudence – I might almost say criminal folly' of the BBC in allowing 'that irresponsible playboy and mountebank to preach on this solemn occasion a panegyric of a Catholic and national saint' (as reported in the *New York Times*, 1 June 1931). Other British listeners expressed surprise that Shaw 'should have been allowed to insult the intelligence and wound the feelings of tens of thousands of listeners by his attack on their most sacred beliefs' and ridiculed his 'infantile conception' of religious subjects (*Listener*, 10 June). American listeners attacked Shaw for his poor research, likened him to a mountebank 'stand[ing] on his head and kick[ing] his heels to get the attention of the crowd,' and criticized him for being 'irreverent and flip' (*NYT*, 3, 10 June). Shaw had his defenders, too, including the BBC, which, perhaps making a virtue of necessity, congratulated itself on the 'healthy' controversy arising from Shaw's talk and praised its 'vast audience' for being 'capable of listening on occasion to a provocative talk without resenting the fact that its thesis may step beyond the limits of widely-accepted belief' (*RT*, 12 June). Was this, one wonders, the same BBC that had said just three weeks previously that the British public was not yet ready for 'the liberal reception of uncensored opinions' (above, p. 56)? After further protests from prominent Catholics – including a telegram from the Archbishop of Westminster to the BBC saying that Shaw's remarks 'have given grave offence to Catholics both in England and abroad'[25] – the BBC climbed down a notch or two from its principled position, declaring, 'To have caused offence to the Roman Catholic community ... was certainly not the wish of either Mr Shaw or the BBC' (*RT*, 19 June). There is no evidence to suggest that the BBC consulted Shaw before making this statement, and little likelihood that Shaw would have agreed to it – though there is every likelihood that he welcomed being called a playboy (at seventy-four years old) and a mountebank.

The expressions of outrage about Shaw's talk are short on specifics, so it is hard to be sure about what upset their authors. The Joan of Shaw's talk, however, like the Joan of his play, is a human being, not a saint; Shaw compares her experiences and values to those of Leon Trotsky and Sylvia Pankhurst – hardly Joan's peers in the eyes of the Catholic Church. And he reminds his listeners that Joan was 'burnt by a Catholic Tribunal,' and 'killed by the Inquisition.' Shaw's purpose in the talk was not to venerate Joan but to scrutinize her human and historical dimensions and show how she and her circumstances can 'contact with our life and circumstances.'

Less contentious – except, perhaps, to some fellow playwrights – was another British Drama League talk given by Shaw, this one broadcast from the League's annual conference in Edinburgh on 28 October 1933, where Shaw spoke ('as a humble delegate of the Welwyn Garden City Theatrical Society') of the importance of amateur companies – 'who are the very seed from which the drama springs, from which all the taste, the love of the drama, the power to act the drama, the love of seeing it, all come' – and the responsibility of playwrights to support them by treating them as fairly as professional companies are treated, that is by charging fees as a percentage of box office and not the standard flat fee of five guineas when receipts might be as little as fifteen shillings. Shaw regarded the five guinea fee, he said, 'with loathing and disgust,' and advocated abolition of 'this nonsense about amateurism and professionalism.' 'All who are working for love of the drama ought honestly to give the best dramatic performances to the public they can, and are entitled to professional terms.'[26]

A more whimsical radio appearance by Shaw took place on 17 August 1935 during Radiolympia, a trade show for radio manufacturers and a promotional event for the BBC. Shaw – in Malvern for the annual Malvern Festival – wrote a short sketch for a live telephone conversation between himself and Ethel Cain, a telephone operator. The three-minute exchange is based on a humorous misunderstanding about Cain wanting to sell fruit to Shaw, but ends with Shaw offering her a leading part in his next play because she has such pleasant voice. The conversation is peremptorily cut off, however (the Post Office's three-minute time limit having been reached), by an anonymous telephone official before a deal can be made.[27]

There was some whimsy as well in Shaw's broadcast to sixth-form students on 11 June 1937, but also considerable educational substance. The twenty-minute talk was commissioned by the BBC, and completed on 5 June, when Shaw told his producer (Mary Somerville), 'You will probably commit suicide when you read it.'[28] She didn't, but she *was* anxious about some aspects of the script, including 'the violent attack on examinations and examiners,' the comment that 'the 39 Articles do not change, though they ought to,' and 'the fling at Cabinet Ministers,' which she interpreted as 'a fling at Baldwin.' The script was also too long (by about 1000 words), and it was decided that rather than trying to censor Shaw he should be asked 'to do what cutting time demands without reference to the above points in particular.'[29] In the event, Shaw did cut the reference to Cabinet ministers, though he kept the attack on examinations and examiners and the reference to the 39 Articles. Some educators and parents must have squirmed at Shaw's observations and advice. School for him, he said, 'was ... a sentence of penal servitude,' and the 'subjects that educated me were never taught in my schools,' for his schoolmasters were 'utterly and barbarously ignorant of them.' His young listeners, he suggested, would have the same experience when, after leaving school, they realize that their education 'has been very defective.' As regards examinations, 'if you happen to have any original ideas ... you must not air them in your examination papers. You may very possibly know better than your examiners; but do not let them find out that you think so.' One listener at least – a medical student from Liverpool – took exception to this calumny on examiners, soberly pronouncing, 'The examiners in medical examinations are not quite as senile as Mr Shaw imagines.'[30]

The Big Series

The BBC was keen to engage Shaw to give talks whenever an opportunity arose, taking advantage of occasions such as the Einstein dinner or the anniversary of Saint Joan's death. Other talks by Shaw formed part of major series that spread over several weeks and involved other speakers.[31] There were several such series in the formative years of the BBC, one of the earliest occurring in late 1929 under the title of 'Points of View.' There were six weekly thirty-minute talks, beginning on 30 September with G. Lowes Dickinson, a Cambridge philosopher. Other participants were the Cambridge biochemist J.B.S. Haldane, scientist Sir Oliver Lodge, W.R. Inge (Dean of St Paul's), H.G. Wells, and Shaw. The BBC billed the group as 'six of the leading thinkers of the day,' each of whom had been invited to give his opinions on 'the tendencies of the times.' Shaw was described as 'the playwright who has taken the whole of life for his province and whose outspoken opinions still, in his seventy-third year, never fail to grip the world's attention' (*RT*, 27 September 1929). He spoke on 14 October from 9:20 to 9:50 pm. The topic he chose was 'Democracy,' broadcast from the BBC's studio in Plymouth, where Shaw was visiting the Astors.

Shaw didn't paint a pretty picture of democracy – 'sometimes furiously violent ... dangerous and treacherous ... a big balloon, filled with gas or hot air, and sent up so that you shall be kept looking up at the sky whilst other people are picking your pockets ... [W]e are now governed by a civil service which has such enormous power that its regulations are taking the place of the laws of England ... [W]ho can blame

Signor Mussolini for describing it as a putrefying corpse? ... [O]ur present Parliament is obsolete ...' Shaw's point, though, was not to reject democracy as a political process and structure, but to disperse the 'cloud of humbug' that usually obscures discussions of democracy, so that the perils of democracy can be more clearly seen and we can 'provide against them as far as we can.' Specifically, he urged at the end of his talk, 'We need two or three central parliaments and several regional ones to cope with the work and to maintain as much contact as possible between us and the bodies that really govern us.' (Prescient thinking in light of British political restructuring – a Scottish Parliament, a Welsh Assembly – seventy years later.) But as his final thought, Shaw insisted that effective participatory democracy depends on 'the consciences of the governors and the governed,' a forlorn prospect when 'we have been badly brought up, and are full of anti-social personal ambitions and prejudices and snobberies.' Should we not, then, 'teach our children to be better citizens than ourselves?' 'We are not doing that at present. The Russians *are*. That is my last word. Think it over.'[32]

One listener – 'Working Mother' from Burton-on-Trent – did think it over, and wrote to the *Radio Times* (25 October 1929) to say she was 'disgusted' by Shaw's compliment to Russia. 'Why does Mr Shaw make his home in England? Surely Russia should be his place.' Other listeners were more appreciative of Shaw's talk, one saying that he had never heard Shaw 'in better form.' 'It was a memorable talk, simple, original, marvellously well reasoned, and as witty ... a searchlight on the use of the microphone as an instrument of political education' (*The Listener*, 23 October).

Shaw's next appearance was in a series called 'Rungs of the Ladder.' When the series was first announced (*RT*, 15 April 1932), Shaw wasn't included, though the BBC had again attracted some high-profile speakers: press magnate Lord Beaverbrook, theatre impresario C.B. Cochran, and Poet Laureate John Masefield among them. The idea of the series was to hear 'reminiscences' from those 'who have started with few advantages and attained recognition and eminence in various fields of life' (*RT*, 15 April 1932). Shaw was approached early in April by John Reith, but didn't reply (he apologized for the delay) until 2 May. He initially demurred – 'I am afraid that my early experiences and my later conclusions based on them would be scandalously unedifying. If ever there was a man who succeeded in spite of his incompetence for helping himself that man is myself'[33] – but finally agreed to participate. He gave his talk on 11 July 1932 (9:20–9:50 pm), declining an invitation from Siepmann to dinner beforehand because 'dining involves talking, and I must save my voice and my conversational energy for the broadcast.'[34]

Shaw focused in his talk on parents and children, arguing on the one hand that parenting is of such importance that 'it is the business of the State to see that ... parents are well paid for it' – 'At present our statesmen neglect this duty scandalously' – but on the other hand advising parents, 'You had really better give your children no advice at all, but go your own way and leave your children to go theirs and form their own conclusions.' In his own case, he pointed out, 'My parents took no moral responsibility for me. I was just something that had happened to them and had to be put up with and supported.' In any event, he said, it's a 'silly notion' that 'happiness is to be found at the top of a ladder.' 'The moral of my career is down with the ladder! Let us all keep our feet on the ground and see to it that the footing is good.'[35]

Shaw ended his talk, 'Good-bye. Always glad to come and wake you up and set you thinking,' which was his consistent objective in his radio talks, constrained though he was by BBC proprieties. A further opportunity, however, for waking people up arose with the BBC's 'Whither Britain?' series in 1934. Shaw was again in the company of the country's political, cultural, and intellectual heavyweights, including Wells, Winston Churchill, Lloyd George, and Ernest Bevin. Shaw also thought that Oswald Mosely, founder of the British Union of Fascists, should be part of the series – 'He is said to be a very good speaker; and he puts real work into his speeches' – but the BBC did not take up Shaw's recommendation.[36] A total of twelve speakers were invited to give their views on 'the shaping of our national future' (*RT*, 15 December 1933). Shaw's talk, the fifth in the series, was broadcast on 6 February 1934 (8:30–9:00 pm). It was pre-recorded (on 13 January 1934)[37] to accommodate Shaw's preparations for his voyage to New Zealand, beginning (from Tilbury) on 8 February. As it happened, however, Shaw found himself in the BBC studios on 6 February to broadcast the same talk live to the United Sates, the Federal Radio Commission in the United Sates having banned recorded talks (Hibberd 97).

The talk resonates with ideas that Shaw had explored nearly thirty years earlier in *Major Barbara*, whose protagonist, arms manufacturer Andrew Undershaft, claims that he – not the government – runs Britain. After predicting (correctly) that Britain, 'a ship without a pilot' (an image Shaw used also in *Heartbreak House*) is 'as likely to drift into war as into anything else,' and that 'in the next war all the most diabolical means of spreading death and destruction will be ready for use,' and also predicting (incorrectly) that when London 'finds itself approached by a crowd of aeroplanes, capable of destroying it in half an hour ... London will surrender,' Shaw moves to economic matters. Because of the power of money, he argues, and the 'enormous profits' made from transactions in money and from international trade, 'we ... live under a dictatorship of bankers and ship-owners, with cabinet ministers as their puppets and scapegoats.' Because modern warfare – thanks to the Undershafts of the world – no longer kills 'merely ... young soldiers, mostly unmarried,' but also 'women and men indiscriminately,' and so 'means not glory but extermination,' it 'is becoming impossible.' The 'disappearance' (sic!) of war, however, leaves the 'Boss Syndicalism' of capitalism in control, which is 'much worse than the slaughter in old-fashioned war.' Civilization, Shaw concludes, may, therefore 'be in greater danger from peace than from war.'[38]

'Whither Britain?' was a courageous and provocative broadcast, marred, some listeners argued, by errors of detail in its economic analysis, and by its 'tomfoolery' (albeit 'delightful' tomfoolery), according to another listener. *The Times* (7 February 1934) limited itself to a neutral summary of the talk, while a London listener praised the 'dramatically impassioned broadcast.'[39]

The next invitation to Shaw to take part in a major series of broadcast talks came in April 1935. This time Charles Siepmann chose 'Freedom' as the topic, with – in addition to Shaw – speakers such as Chesterton, artist and novelist Wyndham Lewis, and Labour politician Herbert Morrison. Shaw told Siepmann that he couldn't do a talk until after taking 'a voyage of some sort' for the sake of his wife's health.[40] The voyage was to South Africa, from which the Shaws returned in early June, and Shaw then did the broadcast on 18 June (10:00–10:20 pm, and to the United States by shortwave), the week after Chesterton. There was some nervousness around the BBC about the talk because by 17 June no one had seen a script. Attempts were made by telegram and telephone to persuade Shaw to send one, but he let it be known that he would bring the script with him to London (from Ayot) when he came to make the broadcast. 'Are you prepared to let it go at that?' Siepmann was asked by anxious BBC colleagues. 'I suppose we must' was Siepmann's resigned response.[41] Shaw had already alerted Siepmann (in the letter cited above) that he would deal with the topic 'very simply and mostly in the abstract.' Shaw's main point, he told Siepmann, was that 'the first conditions of freedom are leisure and pocket money: people without either cannot enjoy freedom.' Shaw developed the theme in his talk, calling for radical reform to allow freedom to spread, ridding the country of 'the idolatry of the slave class and the arrogance of the master class.' 'We must change our politics before we can get what we want; and meanwhile we must stop gassing about freedom, because the people of England in the lump don't know what freedom is – never having had any.'[42]

Shaw picked up on this theme of the redistribution of wealth in his next broadcast series, this one, in 1937, in the company of Lady Astor, Wells, novelist Hugh Walpole, the classicist Gilbert Murray (the model for Cusins in *Major Barbara*), and others. The series theme, 'As I See It,' again allowed speakers wide latitude for their talks. The series was designed for listeners to the Empire Service of the BBC, and Reith took the unusual step of issuing the invitation to Shaw personally, telling him (by letter, 27 July 1937) that he 'would be assured of a very large audience in all parts of the world.' Shaw did not respond until September, and his response caused some more nervousness at the BBC: 'If it is to be about the Empire and I may let myself go on it I consent.' That 'let myself go' was worrying. What did Shaw have in mind? Perhaps it might be advisable 'to put in some caveat about the monarchy,' one of Reith's colleagues advised; 'I do not think we want to have him saying disrespectful things about the crown.' Reith thought it best to write to Shaw again himself, which he did on 22 September. 'Maybe you misunderstand about the object of the series,' Reith tactfully said. 'It is not necessarily to be about the Empire but addressed to listeners in the Empire outside the British Isles. We are leaving the choice of subject open to speakers, and they may say what they like. We had imagined that they would choose to speak on subjects with which they were most closely connected, but, of course, if you want to talk about the Empire, do so.' However, Reith continued, again tactfully, 'We are sure you will remember that you are talking to a very mixed audience, many of whom are likely to resent too critical an approach to the subject, at any rate where the Monarchy [capital M from Reith] is concerned.' On any other occasion Shaw might have taken serious umbrage with a suggestion that he should go easy on the monarchy, but his reply to Reith (27 September) must have come as a relief. 'After the coronation overdose,' Shaw said – referring to the extensive press and BBC coverage of the coronation of George VI on 12 May 1937 – 'nobody will mention the monarchy [small m from Shaw] again for ten years without producing a universal switch-off: certainly I won't.' What Shaw had in mind for the broadcast, he told Reith, was 'an apparently simpleminded and literal statement of my own predicament up against all the empires and revolutions and movements and nomenclatory bunk of which the newspapers are full. Too personal to sound like propaganda, though of course it will all be propaganda.'[43]

But when the time actually came for the talk on 2 November 1937, Shaw chose 'This Danger of War' as his topic – 'What about this danger of war which is making us all shake in our shoes at present,' he began. And danger there was, as military and political tensions grew in Europe in the late 1930s: 'I have visions,' said Shaw, 'of streets heaped with mangled corpses, in which children wander crying for their parents, and babies gasp and strangle in the clutches of dead mother. That is what war means nowadays.' To stop it, 'we must all become conscientious objectors.' Or, if 'nations had any sense they would begin a war by sending their oldest men into the trenches. They would not risk the lives of their young men except in the last extremity.' The horrors of nations at war, however, were not for Shaw the greatest threat to civilization. That threat came from civil war, which, Shaw said, was inevitable under a social and political structure in which 'millions of laborers die in the workhouse or on the dole after sixty years of hard toil so that a few babies may have hundreds of thousands a year before they are born.' Such a situation 'is stupid and wicked ... and it will smash us and our civilization if we do not resolutely reform it.'[44]

International Shaw

'This Danger of War' was broadcast on the BBC Empire Service (introduced in 1932), but was not aired domestically. It was, however, broadcast to the United Sates, where Shaw's voice was becoming increasingly familiar. Such was his popularity that the CBS network had made arrangements some years earlier, quite independently of the BBC, for an exclusive broadcast by Shaw from London to the United Sates on 11 October 1931. But what 'started as a coup' for CBS ended, it has been observed by one historian of the CBS, 'in fierce controversy,' with the broadcaster 'thrust ... into the unwanted role of sponsor of the famous writer's unpopular views on communism.'[45] Shaw took Russia as his subject, drawing on the experience of his visit there (with, among others, the Astors) in the summer of 1931. Shaw's ten days' of government-arranged sightseeing, receptions, dinners (including one for his seventy-fifth birthday attended by 2000 guests in Moscow's Trade Union Central Hall), and other events (including meetings with Gorky and Stalin) left him with a very positive impression of the country, and he used the occasion of his CBS talk to compare Russia to the United States, Communism to Capitalism.

Shaw began with a cheery 'Hello, all you dear old boobs who have been telling one another for a month past that I have gone dotty about Russia!' He went on to castigate President Hoover, who 'became famous by feeding the starving millions of war-devastated Europe,' but 'cannot feed his own people in time of peace,' and to excoriate capitalism's 'ruined' agriculture, 'collapsing' industries, 'business incompetence, political helplessness, and financial insolvency,' with millions of unemployed and 'degrading poverty for nine-tenths of the population.' Russia, by contrast, Shaw claimed, can boast budget surpluses, full employment, thriving agriculture, 'roaring and multiplying factories,' 'efficient rulers,' and an atmosphere of 'hope and security for the poorest as has never before been seen in a civilized country on earth.' American visitors to Russia, he advised his listeners, will be welcomed, but he cautioned them that they will be received 'with a mixture of pity for you as a refugee from the horrors of American Capitalism, with a colossal intellectual contempt for your political imbecility in not having established Communism in your own unhappy country.' He recognized that in Russia there is still 'a good deal of the poverty, ignorance, and dirt we know so well at home,' but insisted that 'these evils are retreating there before the spread of Communism.' The activities of the Russian secret police, who 'will just liquidate you' for 'your belief in individualism,' were flippantly excused by Shaw on the grounds that 'a well-kept garden must be weeded.' All in all, Russia 'has us fooled, beaten, shamed, shewn up, outpointed, and all but knocked out ... We have rebuked her ungodliness, and now the sun shines on Russia as on a country with which God is well pleased, whilst His wrath is heavy on us and we dont know where to turn for comfort or approval.'

The broadcast was live, and CBS could have cut Shaw off, which probably would have delighted him, and would have added to his case against capitalism. Wisely, CBS chose to let him have his say, but gave air time a week later to an opposing point of view from the Reverend Edmund A. Walsh, vice-president of Georgetown University and an authority on modern Russia. Walsh painted a very different picture, one of 'famine and pestilence, confiscation, terrorism, [and] military dictatorship,' as well as 'successive invasions and violations of rights, liberties, and lives,' and massive imposition of forced labour. Walsh also pointed out – not unreasonably – that Shaw's comparison of the

American and Russian systems was based on a short visit to Russia arranged by the 'skillful window dressers in the Political Bureau of the Communist party' and no visits at all to the United Sates (his first wasn't until March 1933).[46] There were many other letters of protest in the U.S. press, but since the BBC chose not to use the speech, reaction in Britain was negligible.

Nor was there much publicity in Britain of the first radio talk that Shaw broadcast from another country. This was on the Russian trip that he spoke about in his CBS broadcast on the occasion of his seventy-fifth birthday celebration. Shaw spoke from Moscow (in English – but for Russian audiences only) of Lenin's achievements, expressing the view that if 'other countries follow his example and follow his teaching, if this great communistic experiment spreads over the whole world, we shall have a new era in history.'[47] Shaw also broadcast in South Africa while visiting there in 1932, but was much less complimentary to his hosts, urging upon them 'a little more thinking and a little less surf-bathing.' He felt that he was in a 'Slave State,' the 'very worst sort of Slave State' where the slaves ('coloured' people) are 'nominally free,' but 'can be thrown into the streets to starve, without pensions or public relief, when nobody happens to need their services or when they are old and are displaced by the young.' 'I have been asked to say some nice things to you,' he said, 'but 'saying nice things is not my business,' and he went on to condemn, among other things, 'inadequate and obsolete' South African farming methods, and the slums of Cape Town, for which the city 'deserves to be destroyed by fire from.Heaven.'[48]

In his next broadcast outside Britain Shaw followed his principle of not 'saying nice things' about his hosts. His hosts on this occasion were in the United States. His first visit there began in Hawaii in March 1933, but he did not broadcast until 11 April, when he spoke to an audience of 3500 at the Metropolitan Opera House in New York under the auspices of the American Academy of Political Science. The speech was carried over the NBC network. The topic was 'The Future of Political Science in America,' which took Shaw back into the territory of his controversial CBS talk in 1931. He was again unsparing in his criticism of the United States, in a speech that lasted well over an hour, and was received politely but cooly. His targets were at the core of American values – the Statue of Liberty ('a monstrous idol'), Hollywood, the Constitution, Wall St ('nationalize your banks') – but he wasn't happy with his performance ('I'm afraid I bungled a great deal of it,' he told Charlotte), and he was glad to leave America the next day (Holroyd 3:309–13).[49]

There was one more foreign broadcast by Shaw in the 1930s, this one from New Zealand on a visit there in 1934. This time there was no live audience, and his address lasted just under half an hour. It was broadcast by the New Zealand Broadcasting Board (the New Zealand equivalent of the BBC) on 12 April, and relayed as well to Australia. Shaw was kinder to New Zealand than he had been to America, largely because he perceived a political structure that gave a greater role to government. 'Thanks to your communistic institutions,' he complimented his listeners, 'you are to some extent leading world civilisation today. You are second only to Russia.' Conceding that New Zealanders might be a little taken aback that this stalwartly democratic member of the British Empire might harbour 'communistic institutions,' Shaw suggested that while 'leading the rest of the world in Communism' and 'thinking that Communism is a very terrible thing,' New Zealand does not *realize* that it is Communist. 'I am a Communist,' he declared, and then bid his listeners goodnight.[50]

Talks and Articles on Shaw

While radio talks *by* Shaw were provocative and wide-ranging – theatre, politics, culture – those *on* Shaw tended to focus straightforwardly on his plays. The BBC produced many discussion and lecture programs on the arts, and (in the absence of extant recordings or published scripts) it is not always easy to say to what extent Shaw was a subject of these programs. For a talk by Charles Macdona on 'The Theatre' on 27 April 1938, for example, the only information is the listing itself in the *Radio Times* (22 April 1938). But given Macdona's long association with Shaw's plays through his touring company, the Macdona Players, it is hard to believe that he did *not* discuss Shaw in his short talk.

In most other instances, however, we know from BBC publicity and program information that Shaw *was* a topic –⸱especially in talks given by Desmond MacCarthy. Former dramatic and literary editor of the *New Statesman* – and frequent reviewer of Shaw plays – MacCarthy became a regular contributor to the BBC, specializing on modern drama.[51] He gave a major series of six thirty-minute radio talks on modern drama, broadcast weekly from 7 March to 11 April 1930 (all published in *The Listener*). In his first talk MacCarthy spoke briefly of the ways in which Shaw's plays excited and instructed audiences 'through the clash of ideas and points of view,' while regretting that the action of the plays relates to the ideas only 'in an ancillary way' (MacCarthy specifically had in mind *Getting Married*, *Misalliance*, and *The Apple Cart*). His second talk ('Problems of Dialogue') used *Pygmalion* as an example of dramatic dialogue that fails to convince because 'however entertained we may be, we often hear the author ventriloquising rather than the characters themselves speaking.' Doolittle, in particular, 'is not a dustman talking.' Shaw's characters, MacCarthy argues, 'are made articulate, but they do not speak out of themselves so much as explain themselves.' MacCarthy had nothing to say about Shaw in his next three talks, but in his concluding talk ('Diction and Realism') he returned to Shaw – specifically *Getting Married* – once more to offer muted praise. While Shaw 'has written the most exhilarating harangues of our time,' and while he moves 'with such energy and freedom in the world of ideas,' his dramatic diction (as evidenced by a speech by Mrs George from *Getting Married*) ultimately 'falls short of the finest imaginative prose.'

MacCarthy continued his analysis of Shaw's work – this time going beyond the plays – in a talk he gave on 15 August 1932 (published in *The Listener*, 24 August) about the publication of Shaw's works in a new edition from Constable (the Standard Edition, which began appearing in 1931, eventually being completed in 1951 in 37 volumes). MacCarthy still expresses frustration with some aspects of Shaw's work – much of *Doctor's Delusions* (1931), for example, he finds 'an exasperating mixture of good sense and outrageous nonsense' – but there was much in the broadcast that would have pleased Shaw (he was in Malvern at the time and probably did not hear it). Shaw's work, MacCarthy said, 'represents the biggest literary disturbance in the pool of thought which took place in England at the end of the nineteenth and the beginning of the twentieth centuries'; he is 'a moralist of the first importance,' the 'most infectious element' of whose work is 'a rare kind of gay, generous, sensible chivalry.' MacCarthy focused again on the drama in a talk on 23 February 1933, speaking about Shaw and his contemporaries ('Ibsen and After'), but this talk was not published, and no script has survived.

Other talks that included Shaw were given by Sir Barry Jackson, founder of the Birmingham Repertory Theatre and the Malvern Festival, who worked closely with Shaw from 1923 (when Jackson staged the British premiere of *Back to Methuselah* in Birmingham) to the end of Shaw's life. Jackson gave two talks on 'The Drama' on 5 and 12 January 1932. In the first talk, Jackson discussed 'the effect upon the drama of the enlarged outlook and the new values of the present century'; the second had to do with the relationship between drama and social activity (*RT*, 1 and 8 January 1932). Later in 1932 (15 November), a dramatic sketch by Edith Baring (a member of the board of trustees of the Birmingham Repertory Theatre) was broadcast from the theatre's own studio. Set in 'the Memorial Talkiedrome during the Shaw Tercentenary Celebrations in A.D. 2156,' *Back to GBS*, as the BBC put it (*RT*, 4 November 1932) 'is delightful nonsense, based on the idea that in another few hundred years our great GBS will be treated by a certain section of society much as Shakespeare is treated today ... There will be the same old argument as to whether Shaw really wrote his own plays, the same disputes about his religion, his looks, and even what he ate, until the beauty in his teaching is lost and only the superficial praise of his famous name remains.' And then on 14 January 1938, in honour of the twenty-fifth anniversary of the founding of the Birmingham Repertory Theatre, Barry Jackson spoke on 'the significance of the repertory movement in general and its contribution to drama' (*RT*, 4 February 1938). As with the Macdona talk, there is no firm evidence that Jackson discussed Shaw in his talks, though, again, it is hard to imagine that he did not.

Other BBC-commissioned insights into and appreciation of Shaw and his work appeared from time to time in the two major official BBC publications, the *Radio Times* and *The Listener*. Theatre critic Ivor Brown discussed Shaw in articles in the *Radio Times* on 31 October, 14 and 24 November 1930 ('he has restored the dignity of the theatre' and 'made the author a sovereign'), and another critic – M. Willson Disher – reminisced in the *Radio Times* on 10 September 1937 about the 'brilliant' and 'magical' premiere of *Pygmalion* at Beerbohm Tree's His Majesty's Theatre in April 1914. *The Listener* devoted the front page of its 31 December 1930 issue to a review of *The Apple Cart* (published on 11 December) by prominent political scientist Harold Laski, who much preferred the preface ('prose which is the best instrument for its purpose since Swift's') to the play itself ('the second act is still an irrelevant and not very amusing interlude'), and *The Listener*'s 24 August 1932 issue carried an article by Charles Falkland on an imaginary debate between Thomas Carlyle and Shaw ('the dividing of the ways between the nineteenth and twentieth centuries'). Shaw's achievements as a music critic were discussed in articles in *The Listener* on 20 July 1932 by Harvey Grace (a review of the Standard Edition of Shaw's *Music in London 1890–94* – 'genial, well-informed, discursive, and full of gusto'), the *Radio Times* (12 August 1932, another review of *Music in*

London, this time by W.R. Anderson), and the *Radio Times* again on 26 November 1937 (a review by Gerald Abraham of *London Music in 1888–89* – ('he no more helps you to understand music ... than a display of fireworks would help you to read your evening paper').

4 'Radiogenic Shaw': Broadcast Plays, 1929–1939

By the time of the landmark broadcast of *Saint Joan* in April 1929 (see chapter 2), drama was a regular feature of BBC programming. Two years after *Saint Joan*, the BBC had accumulated a 'Play Library' of 3000 scripts, was receiving about 2000 new plays a year for consideration for broadcasting, had about 600 actors in its files, and was producing at least one play a week (*RT*, 3 April 1931). Drama, however, was by no means a universally admired feature of BBC programming. 'I cannot understand,' wrote one listener in 1931, 'why the BBC persists in broadcasting plays. I cannot believe that any listener enjoys them. It is impossible to appreciate any play unless one can see the actors and watch the action and the pose and personality of the players. Dialogue given without any idea of the individuality of the speaker is unmeaning' (*RT*, 22 May 1931). But under the leadership of Val Gielgud, the BBC kept the faith, and the results of a poll conducted by the Research Unit of *The Listener* in 1939 seemed to justify that faith. In a breakdown of BBC program types into twenty-one categories, drama ranked fifth – behind variety, organ music, military bands, musical comedies, and dance music, but ahead of talks and classical music. With age differences taken into account, drama did even better with the under-twenties (fourth, overtaking musical comedies and military bands), but not so well with the over-seventies (seventh, now behind brass bands as well as military bands, and also dropping below talks and discussions). But more significant than the surface results of such popularity polls was the BBC's conclusion from an analysis of the figures that for any given broadcast play there was a potential audience (listeners who 'like plays') of a staggering seventeen million (*RT*, 10 March 1939).

As far as the BBC was concerned, Shaw remained 'the ideal radio dramatist,' his 'brilliant, strongly characterized dialogue, uncomplicated by trivial "action,'" being 'even more telling by way of the microphone than on the stage' (*RT*, 2 May 1930). What successful radio drama depends on, wrote one listener, is not 'complicated sound effects; nor mysterious music surging and dying; nor a background of whispering waves; nor fantastic voyages through time and space; nor the insistent voice of the narrator' – but 'purely, simply, and basically, dialogue and character.' And one need look no further for those qualities than 'our two greatest dramatists' (*RT*, 10 February 1933).

Readers' letters were always welcomed by the BBC, but Val Gielgud took his own more comprehensive soundings to learn about listener preferences. When he invited listeners in the spring of 1934 to send him their views about play selection, he received 12,726 responses. In his report on the letters (*RT*, 20 April 1934) he listed Galsworthy, Ibsen, Eden Phillpotts, and Shakespeare as 'the names that appeared again and again.' Not Shaw. When, however, Gielgud came to select plays for 1935, a selection 'closely related,' the BBC said, to the letters, Shaw was there – although outnumbered three to one by Shakespeare.[1]

From Shaw's point of view, the size of the radio drama audience was obviously attractive, and the income, though relatively insignificant for Shaw by the 1930s (when he was comfortably off) was not unwelcome. In 1929 he had accepted 50 guineas for performances of *Saint Joan* and *Captain Brassbound's Conversion* (see above, p. 9). In the 1930s his fee increased, but not by much. He was paid 35 guineas for *Village Wooing* in December 1934 (a much shorter play than *Saint Joan* and *Captain Brassbound* – a fifty-minute broadcast compared to two hours for *Captain Brassbound* and over four hours for *Saint Joan*) and the same amount for a ninety-minute *Candida* in December 1935. Earlier in 1935 Shaw had asked the League of British Dramatists what the agreed rates were with the BBC. He was advised that £50 was the *minimum* for a full-length play, and that 'unless the Dramatist is one able to dictate terms either because of his standing, or because of the popularity of the play desired, the BBC will not pay much beyond the minimum.'[2] That information seems to have had some impact on Shaw. When the BBC raised with him the possibility of another production of *Saint Joan* in 1936, he suggested a fee of 100 guineas,[3] and he demanded, and got, 35 guineas in October 1938 for the one-act (thirty-five minutes) *How He Lied to Her Husband*.[4] A few extracts from *The Apple Cart* in December 1939 cost the BBC 15 guineas, Shaw reminding them that 'the Government will take most of it. I shant have more than seven guineas of it to live on.'[5] That Shaw was reasonably satisfied by his remuneration from the BBC is shown by his refusal to participate some years later (summer 1947) in a threatened boycott of the BBC by members of the Society of Authors in protest against low rates of pay. He told his colleagues that he wouldn't participate because he had 'nothing to complain of.' The BBC, he said, 'have always treated me well' (quoted in Whitehead 95).

Shaw would also have been aware that radio drama was beginning to be taken more seriously as an art form by the early 1930s. A 'Radio Critics' Circle' – 'an association of prominent journalists engaged in regularly reporting and criticizing the activities of the BBC' – was formed in the spring of 1931, a move welcomed by the BBC as a validation of the importance of its programs (*RT*, 5 June 1931). Radio plays were still only infrequently reviewed in the press, though a substantial article in the *Radio Times* on 5 February 1932 ('Wanted! A Radio Drama Critic,' by Frank Orde) argued strongly for radio drama critics with some experience of the 'machinery'of radio drama production – 'dramatic-control panel, studios, and effects room' – a 'professional listener' rather than someone 'whose critical faculty has been carefully attuned to the consideration of a visual medium.' Orde was taken to task by prominent *Daily Telegraph* theatre critic W.A. Darlington, who argued that a radio play was not deserving of the same attention as a West End opening, and if a radio play did merit critical attention regular drama critics were quite capable of doing the job: 'Let me assure Mr Orde,' Darlington wrote on behalf of his confrères, 'that our critical faculties, such as they are, have more adaptability that he gives them credit for' (*RT*, 19 February 1932). What actually happened was that, over time, the regular theatre critics of the press – particularly *The Times*, the *Manchester Guardian*, and the *Daily Telegraph* – did carry more notices of radio plays, while the BBC's own monthly journal, *The Listener*, developed drama critics who specialized in radio productions.

The 'infamy' of *Captain Brassbound's Conversion*

The radio production of *Saint Joan* in April 1929 had been successful enough to encourage both the BBC and Shaw to move quickly ahead with another production, this one of *Captain Brassbound's Conversion* (the broadcast premiere, 16 October 1929, repeated on 19 October 1929). It was not nearly such a happy occasion.

Written in 1899 as a vehicle for Ellen Terry (in the part of Lady Cicely Wayneflete), *Captain Brassbound* is a curious and comical tale (Shaw subtitled it an 'adventure'), set in Morocco, of the moral conversion of a smuggler sea captain. The radio production, directed by Howard Rose (his first – and last – Shaw play) starred prominent stage actors Gertrude Kingston as Lady Cicely (she had played the role in London in 1912) and Baliol Holloway as Captain Brassbound. A correspondent to *The Listener* (23 October 1929) considered the production 'uneven' – 'Miss Gertrude Kingston was as unlike the Lady Cicely of my imagination as was humanly possible. Were those artificial tones of gentility proper to the resolute traveller in equatorial Africa?' – but praised the play as 'first-rate stuff, lively and eloquent, admirably salted with Shavian commonsense, Shavian iconoclasm, Shavian wit, and the Shavian passion for righteousness.' But there was no reaction from Shaw himself. So Hilda Matheson, Director of Talks, who had recently worked with Shaw on his 'Points of View' broadcast (see above, pp. 62–3) ventured to wonder (in a letter of 22 October 1929) if he had in fact listened to the play. She told him that she had found it 'extraordinarily interesting,' as had 'a great many people to whom I have spoken.'[6] Still no word from Shaw. Then, a week later (29 October 1929), a Shavian blast. After explaining why he was returning his cheque for 'Points of View' broadcast ('I have never accepted payment for my work as a political speaker'), Shaw erupted about *Captain Brassbound*:

> As to the broadcast of Brassbound, its infamy was such that I hereby solemnly renounce, curse, and excommunicate everybody who had a hand in it. Apart from the artistic side of the affair the selection of 9.25 as the hour for raising the curtain, thus deferring the end until midnight, would have been a studied insult if any such thing as study had entered into the wretched business. The way the performers had to gabble through their parts was beyond description. Brassbound, in his highest Restoration Comedy soprano, set a pitch and a pace which probably convinced the listeners-in (before they went to bed towards the end of the second act) that he was the heroine. Lady Cicely's basso profundo provided the necessary contrast and made it clear that she was the pirate. Everything that could be done to make the characters undistinguishable from one-another, and the dialogue unintelligible, was done and done thoroughly. The cockney [Drinkwater][7] had evidently been born a thousand miles from Bow Bells and had remained there until he came to Savoy Hill.[8] The American captain's part [Kearney] was a series of surprises to him: he plunged into his sentences without the least notion of how they were going to end. If the producer [i.e., director] has not already

been shot, I will pay for the cartridges. The second time [i.e., the repeat broadcast on 19 October] was not quite so bad: the hour [7:00–9:00 pm] was a reasonable one; and there were signs that after six more rehearsals the speakers would have begun to guess what on earth the whole thing was about; but the cast was a bundle of misfits; and I doubt whether any-one who listened will ever be induced by love or money to give me an-other trial.

'I note,' Shaw concluded, 'that you declare you found it very interesting. How can you have the cheek—!'[9] Shaw's letter naturally enough pro-voked some internal BBC reaction, which blamed Shaw for any real or perceived problems with the production. 'There can surely be no ques-tion of gabble,' it was said; the play took two hours and ten minutes (in-cluding two short intermissions) 'and at no time did anyone speak faster than normally.' Criticisms that the BBC had received (other than Shaw's) complained that the production was too long, and that was Shaw's fault – 'it is a pity Mr Shaw will not allow us to cut.' The director, it was noted, 'is still alive,' 'but if Mr Shaw cares to send the cartridges along, we will see what can be done.'[10] But those were all comments for BBC ears only. When Eckersley wrote to Shaw on 1 November he merely expressed his disappointment: 'you seem to have been so displeased with the whole business' (which was something of an understatement).[11]

The Aftermath of *Brassbound*

After this debacle, the BBC and Shaw had somehow to reach a rap-prochement if there were to be more Shaw plays on radio. This took less time than might have been expected, mainly because Cecil Lewis was brought back to direct the next play. Lewis had gained a measure of trust from Shaw through his early relations with him as a BBC administrator, writer, and director (he directed the 1929 *Saint Joan*). Lewis's production of *The Man of Destiny* (the second BBC broadcast of this play),[12] with Bruce Belfrage as Napoleon, went on air on 15 May 1930 (with a repeat broad-cast on 16 May), but even with Lewis as director Shaw was unhappy. Seven years later, when the BBC sought his permission to broadcast the play again, Shaw remembered the 1930 production as 'unintelligible, ugly, and unbearable,' which was, Shaw pointed out, 'very bad for me, as it set people saying that my stuff is no good on the mike.'[13] For the 1937 pro-duction (11 January, repeated on 12 January) Shaw said he wanted George Arliss as Napoleon, a suggestion that prompted Gielgud to conclude that

Shaw 'must be absolutely gaga!' (Arliss was nearly seventy, and had acted exclusively in film for the past decade.) In an internal BBC memo,[14] Gielgud went on to say that 'quite apart from the economic impossibility of getting Arliss, he would give a perfectly grotesque performance.' Gielgud advised his staff that while Shaw's suggestions about casting were always welcome, 'we really cannot accept them as though they were a Papal Bull!' In the event, Napoleon was played by the experienced Esmé Percy, who came across, said *The Times* (13 January 1937), as 'a bit of a vulgarian, but otherwise a model of a lesser British General.' There is no record of Shaw's reaction to the production, though *The Listener* (27 January 1937) was not at all impressed by a play whose talk, without the action, was simply 'bewildering.'

In the meantime, the radio premiere of *Village Wooing* was aired, on 3 December 1934 (repeated on 4 December 1934).[15] Broadcast live from the Malvern Festival Theatre, the production featured R. Lindsell Stuart as A, and Phyllis Gill as Z. Stuart also directed. The BBC's view was that *Village Wooing*, with just two characters and 'practically no action,' was even better suited to radio than to the stage. The announcement of the production in the *Radio Times* (23 November 1934) was headed 'Radiogenic Shaw,' and described the play's construction as 'very like some of the most successful radio plays.' 'Can Mr Shaw,' the writer wondered, 'be getting radio-minded?' Hardly – Shaw wrote the play with the performance at Malvern in mind[16] – but it seems to have been well received by listeners, one *Radio Times* correspondent (28 December 1934) comparing it to 'a walk on a cold, frosty day – everything around sparkling and glowing in the winter sunshine,' though the ending 'was more like a dull, stuffy room.' But more Shaw plays, please, the listener pleaded: 'they are the best for wireless listeners; not too long, and they do not need to be seen to be enjoyed, as in this case they mostly depend on conversations between two or more persons.' (Had this listener perhaps missed the broadcasts of *Saint Joan* and *Captain Brassbound's Conversion*?)

By way of contrast to *Village Wooing*, the BBC showed an early (and courageous) interest in *Back to Methuselah*, Shaw's five-part epic that would have needed several evenings of BBC scheduling for a production of the whole play. More modest in its ambitions, the BBC aired a few excerpts from Part I, *In the Beginning*, on 17 June 1933 with Edith Evans as the Serpent, the role she had played in the British premiere at the Birmingham Repertory Theatre in 1923. The *Radio Times* reported

(16 June 1933) that in order to get into the 'feel' of the part in the studio she 'crouched in a chair, with the directional microphone, specially adjusted, pointing down at her.' Another brief passage from Part I was read by Nesta Sawyer – presumably from a more conventional position than the one adopted by Edith Evans – on 7 September 1934 to fill in a five-minute programming gap, but the biggest BBC commitment to *Back to Methuselah* came in 1935 with a full performance of *In the Beginning*. Directed by Cecil Lewis, and starring such heavyweights as Robert Speaight, Gwen Ffrangçon-Davies (Eve in the Birmingham premiere and in this production), and Dorothy Holmes Gore, the production aired on 2 January 1935, with a repeat the next day. The BBC wanted to do Part V (*As Far as Thought Can Reach*) as well, but Shaw let it be known (through Blanche Patch) that while he thought 'the Adam and Eve scenes would go with well contrasted players and a vamp voiced serpent,' Part V 'would be a failure invisible.'[17] Shaw did, however, agree to Gielgud's request that the *ending* of Part V (from the appearance of Adam's ghost, and including Lilith's final long speech) could be included, and the problem of linking the full Part I with the final scene of Part V was solved by Shaw himself. 'To connect the two parts,' the *Radio Times* announced (14 December 1934), 'Mr Shaw has himself written a new link; after all, it isn't anybody who can write a few hundred words summarising four Shaw plays.' The linking passage was read by a BBC announcer:

> We must now ask the listener to make a colossal jump from the beginning of recorded time to the utmost horizon of the future. Not that the author has left the gap unfilled – he has shown us in three intervening plays first, how Adam's choice of a thousand years for a reasonable lifetime became shortened by war, by disease, by unwholesome living of all sorts, until it shrank to our present span of seventy years, which our Insurance Companies will tell you is considerably in excess of the real average duration of human life to-day.
>
> It is at this point that the author gives us a play [*The Gospel of the Brothers Barnabas*] of modern political life to convince you that seventy years is far too short a time to qualify for the work of governing the world wisely. Two brothers, a sociologist and a biologist, decide that a lifetime of three hundred years is necessary if civilisation is to be saved.
>
> Then in another play [*The Thing Happens*] he moves just far enough into the future to show you certain people mysteriously growing older without showing any signs of age and being compelled to conceal their

extraordinary and incredible condition by staging imaginary deaths – mostly sham drowning – and reappearing under false names and false ages: also how the strange people at last find out each other's existence and get together to form a colony of long-livers, who attain the age of three hundred years.

The next play [*The Tragedy of an Elderly Gentleman*] makes a further and much longer leap into the future, showing us these long livers in sole possession of the British Isles, acquiring in their later years such an intensification of their psychic powers that they are consulted as oracles by short livers like ourselves from all the rest of the world in search of advice which the poor creatures are unable to understand or follow. The very presence of a long liver discourages and even kills the short livers unless elaborate precautions are taken.

All this development of the great Methuselah theme brings us to the last play [*As Far as Thought Can Reach*] – the final limit of our famous author's imagination – where thirty thousand years hence we find [ourselves in a world in] which the short livers have long been discouraged out [of existence whilst the long livers] all have returned to Adam's first state of immortality and have acquired powers and knowledge which, compared to ours, may be described as omnipotence and omniscience. We are shown one day's life under these conditions; but when the night falls the spirit of the beginning stirs again in the forest and the voices from the Garden of Eden are heard calling out of the darkness. Listen ...[18]

The radio critic for *The Times* certainly listened, praising the cast for speaking prose 'as Mr Shaw wrote it,' prose that can best be appreciated 'when the eyes are bandaged' (3 January 1935). And listeners liked it too. The BBC 'has amply justified its existence ... by its excellent production of the greatest of all plays,' enthused one correspondent in the *Radio Times* (18 January 1935), while in the same issue another correspondent insisted that the broadcast of *Back to Methuselah* was a 'lesson which must not be forgotten. Dialogue is the most important part of a radio play,' and 'Shaw is without equal.' This listener also urged the BBC to do the 'brilliant' *Apple Cart*, but the first production of that play (and then only extracts) was still more than two years away (August 1937). In the meantime, however, there was the broadcast premiere of *Candida* to enjoy – but only if you lived in the Midlands region.

The idea for a broadcast of *Candida* came from the Coventry Repertory Company, which offered to do the play in a series of productions that ran in the Midlands region every Sunday, usually from 5:30 to 7:00 p.m.

Because it was Shaw, the Programme Director for the Midlands, H.J. Dunkerley, sought the help of the BBC's London office, specifically R.J.F. Howgill, who worried what Shaw's reaction would be to cutting *Candida* to ninety minutes, and demurred in any case at paying Shaw a fee that might amount to £50 for 'such limited radiation' (*sic*). Howgill also reminded Dunkerley that since it was a Sunday broadcast (of a play, to boot, containing religious elements) the approval of the BBC's Director of Religion would be needed.[19] In the event, Howgill need not have worried. There were no objections on religious grounds, and Shaw was cooperative – for a fee of 35 guineas. *Candida* was broadcast on 22 December 1935.

Another proposal for a *Candida* broadcast – this one from theatre impresario Hugh Beaumont – came to nothing. Beaumont wanted to broadcast his production running at the Globe Theatre in the spring of 1937. Shaw thought that a broadcast of the whole play would kill the stage production, but that a broadcast of the first act as an 'appetizer' might work. The idea, however, seems to have been dropped.[20]

A full radio production of *Candida*, for a national audience, was, however, soon to materialize. Gielgud's plans for the autumn 1937 season included a new version of the *Alcestis* of Euripides, Sean O'Casey's *Juno and the Paycock*, and *Candida*. Shaw agreed (for a fee of 35 guineas) on 17 September 1937,[21] and the production was announced in the *Radio Times* on 15 October 1937, with a cast led by Gwen Ffrangçon-Davies. Critic Ivor Brown contributed a full-page article on the play for the same issue of the *Radio Times* ('Candida represents a maternal commonsense in an extreme and adorable form'), and the production duly aired on 17 October 1937 from 6:10 to 7:50 pm. It generated much discussion and varying interpretations of the play and its characters: 'Candida knows better than anyone else that it is the menfolk, those incorrigible and startled idealists, who stir up trouble' (review, *The Times*, 18 October 1937); *Candida* 'exposes, brilliantly, sharply and entertainingly the fact that most of us take refuge in phrases rather than think' (review, *The Listener*, 27 October 1937); 'Eugene is the central character; and his strength is the strength Shaw calls upon us to admire, not Candida's' (letter, *RT*, 29 October 1937); 'Surely the point of the play is to show that the strongest tie which can keep a wife faithful to her husband is the latter's dependence upon her for his life's happiness' (letter, *The Listener*, 10 November 1937). Perhaps it was because the play engaged its listeners so intensely that the drama critic of *The Listener* (Grace Wyndham Goldie) chose the 1937 *Candida* as one of the 'outstandingly successful' radio plays of the year (*The Listener*, 29 December 1937).

Grace Wyndham Goldie was also impressed by a production – its broadcast premiere – of *The Dark Lady of the Sonnets*. A special feature of this broadcast was a new prologue written – and spoken – by Shaw.[22] Starring Robert Donat as Shakespeare and Lena Ashwell as Elizabeth, the production took place on 22 April 1938, timed to coincide with the transfer of the deeds of the proposed site for a National Theatre to the Shakespeare Memorial National Theatre Committee (see below, p. 248n19). Shaw's fee for the production was 30 guineas, though he cautioned the BBC that 'in future, if I am to take part personally, the fee will be a thousand guineas.'[23] For the *Dark Lady* broadcast Shaw was promoted as 'the possessor of one of the most attractive of all microphone voices ... In our belief, it's the "little dash of Dublin" that does it, an incisive burr that can ram a point home so much more firmly than the suave accents of Oxford' (*RT*, 8 April 1938). The prologue ('The play which you are going to hear is all about Shakespear and Queen Elizabeth; but it is really only an appeal for the Shakespear Memorial National Theatre which we have been trying to make the English nation establish for thirty years past') gave some historical context for the action and characters of the play, and Shaw's reading of it was a bonus for listeners.[24] But the production itself was acclaimed. For Grace Wyndham Goldie it 'seized and held the attention as few radio plays do.' Shaw's 'brilliant prose' was delivered with 'super-excellence' by Donat and Ashwell: 'these two players gave us a duet which for sheer quality and virtuosity I have never heard equalled in a radio production' (*The Listener*, 4 May 1938). Not surprisingly, the BBC decided to repeat the performance. It aired on 21 July 1938, but this time without Shaw and the prologue and without Donat, who had to withdraw at the last minute. Donat was replaced by Marius Goring; Lena Ashwell appeared again as Elizabeth.

The relatively smooth relations between Shaw and the BBC at this time were occasionally jeopardized by announcers' forgetful use of 'George,' causing Shaw to remind the BBC that 'I am professionally Bernard Shaw,' and that 'there will be an additional fee of ten guineas' if an announcer called him *George* Bernard Shaw.[25] This warning was occasioned by the use of his full name in a production of *How He Lied to Her Husband* on 6 October 1938. An internal BBC memo reminded everyone involved in the production of the importance of Shaw's sensitivity on this issue.[26]

There was one other major BBC radio production of a Shaw play in the 1930s, another radio premiere, but this time approached a little

differently from the norm. In a short announcement about the new production – the play was *Arms and the Man* – the *Radio Times* (24 March
1939) claimed that 'Shaw will not allow his plays to be cut for broadcasting.' This was not true, but it created the rationale for serializing the production rather than devoting an estimated two hours of uninterrupted
programming time to the play. The 1929 *Saint Joan* had been spread over
two evenings; *Arms and the Man* was to be spread over three.[27] 'The instalment plan,' said the *Radio Times*, 'will probably be a boon to listeners
who like their Shaw but find two hours of brilliance a little dazzling to
the ordinary mind.' The 'brilliance' was enhanced by the presence of
stars Barry Jones (Bluntschli) and Peggy Ashcroft (Raina) in the cast,
and, as Peter Purbeck pointed out in *The Listener* (27 April 1939), the
three acts of *Arms and the Man* 'provide, neatly and naturally, separate
instalments for the microphone.' And for the benefit of those who might
have missed an earlier instalment, brief plot summaries were given before the second and third instalments.

Shaw Snippets

An account of full-length productions of Shaw plays tells only part of
the story of their presence on the BBC during the 1930s. Full productions were supplemented by regular excerpts from the plays, for both
national and regional (and often international) programming. Sometimes the extracts were so slight that Shaw's permission wasn't
needed, though the BBC – having learned from some uncomfortable
tensions in the past – was usually ultra-cautious in contacting Shaw on
all occasions. Thus, they sought permission for using ninety words
from *John Bull's Other Island* for a program in 1937 on Ireland 'seen
through the eyes of poets, writers and musicians' (*RT*, 29 January
1937). On Shaw's behalf, Blanche Patch responded, explaining that
while Shaw 'is quite willing to accept the fee of half a guinea,' he
'thinks that if you consulted the Copyright Act you would find that
you have a statutory right of reasonable quotation, within the limits of
which there is no obligation to consult him.'[28] Shaw was also very
obliging when asked if the BBC could use parts of *The Perfect Wagnerite*
in a broadcast from Covent Garden of *Das Rheingold* in May 1932 –
'Yes, certainly: read as much of it as you darn [well] please as often as
you please,' he replied.[29] But in most instances permission was, of
course, necessary, and sometimes Shaw chose not to give it. He
thought, for example, that a proposed broadcast of the third act of *The*

Millionairess from the Malvern Festival in August 1937 would be 'stupidly unintelligible,' and barred 'anything short of a complete broadcast' of the whole play.[30] He approved, however, the scene between Boanerges and Magnus from act 1 of *The Apple Cart*, the other Shaw play at Malvern in 1937 (broadcast 1 August 1937),[31] and two short extracts (unspecified in the surviving documentation) from the same play for broadcast in the BBC's 'Scrapbook' series on 12 November 1939.[32] Shaw also approved a five-minute excerpt from *Too True to Be Good* for a weekly program called 'In Town Tonight' on 27 February 1937,[33] and act 3 of *Geneva* for broadcast on 25 January 1939.[34]

But the Shaw play that continued to appeal more than any other to the BBC was *Saint Joan*. There had been no broadcasts of the play, or excerpts from it, since the 1929 production, but new initiatives were taken in the spring of 1935. Knowing that Shaw was abroad (in Africa), Howgill wrote to Blanche Patch to let her know that Val Gielgud was interested in directing the play in the autumn with Elisabeth Bergner as Joan. Bergner had enjoyed great success as Joan in Germany and Austria in 1924, but a radio production in 1935 was problematic – as Patch explained to Howgill – because a film version of the play, starring Bergner, was being planned, and so, wrote Patch (25 May 1935), 'I do not think there is the smallest chance of Mr Shaw consenting to a broadcast of the play.' Further enquiries were made, until Patch confirmed on 5 July 1935 that 'Mr Bernard Shaw has asked me to say that he is not free to authorize a broadcast of St Joan until the contemplated Bergner film is released and has had a fair start.'[35] The Bergner film never got made, largely because of fears of an organized boycott by the Catholic Church (Holroyd 3:381–2), so the BBC raised again the possibility of a full radio production, writing to Shaw on 10 August 1936 for authorization to produce the play as part of the coronation celebrations for Edward VIII in 1937, and offering a fee of 50 guineas. Shaw replied on 16 August 1936, asking for 100 guineas (for two performances) and enquiring who would play Joan. 'Can you get Miss Thorndike,' he wondered?[36] But with the abdication of the king in December 1936 neither the coronation nor *Saint Joan* materialized.

Perhaps the two disappointments over a full production of *Saint Joan* dampened the BBC's enthusiasm for the play, for no more pre-war efforts to broadcast the whole play were made. Several extracts were aired, however. Some had been heard on 27 May 1936, read by Sybil Thorndike, and the Scottish Region included an extract in its 'Stage Parade 1924–27' program on 3 March 1937. Also in 1937 (17 October), the Northern Region broadcast part of the Cathedral scene (scene 5) from a production by the Liverpool Repertory Company, Shaw agreeing to a 15 guinea fee for this, endorsing the Cathedral scene as 'much the best for broadcasting.'[37] Extracts from scene 5 were also included in a program about the People's Theatre in Newcastle-upon-Tyne, broadcast on 28 March 1939, for which Shaw also recorded a 'genial and generous speech.'[38] And although BBC listeners were never to hear Elisabeth Bergner in a full production of *Saint Joan*, they did get to hear her in extracts from the 1938 Malvern Festival production of the play, broadcast in the Midland Region on 14 August 1938 as part of a review of that year's Malvern season. Bergner was heard in the Trial scene (scene 6), which was also the BBC's choice a year later, when the complete scene, with Wendy Hiller as Joan, was broadcast (13 November 1939). And in its 1939 New Year's Eve 'Scrapbook' program the BBC turned to the Trial scene in *Saint Joan* again, but this time just for a two-and-a-half minute extract (for which Shaw charged three guineas).[39] *Saint Joan* was also a favourite for BBC Schools programs – though Shaw's view of the use of his plays in school broadcasts is reflected in a terse comment added to his approval to use an extract from *Saint Joan* in 1938: 'Poor kids!'[40]

And although the BBC naturally concentrated on Shaw's plays, someone had the good sense to remember that Shaw had also written short stories. 'The Emperor and the Little Girl,' written (and published) in 1916, was broadcast on 3 May 1937 ('you must not abridge,' Shaw warned)[41] and again on 5 September 1937 and 7 November 1938.

Empire Shaw

The BBC had started experimental shortwave broadcasts to the Empire and British Colonies in 1927, but installing and operating the necessary equipment to do so on a permanent basis was delayed for financial reasons until late 1931, when, 'encouraged by the desire expressed in all parts of the Empire, and in the Crown Colonies in particular,' the decision was made to establish an 'Empire Short-Wave Station' at Daventry in the Midlands.[42] The BBC initiative – encouraged by the government – was transparently political and cultural. The new service, the BBC said, will 'tighten still further the bonds of thought and feeling between the scattered constituents of the Empire,' and it was important, therefore, to provide programming 'to as many listeners as possible, in every corner of the Empire ... at hours when it is most convenient for them to listen,' even if this meant (as it did) 'more or less continuous [service] throughout the twenty-four hours of the day'– a significant factor since normal domestic broadcasting hours at this time ran only from about 10:15 am to midnight. The new service opened on 19 December 1931, and was soon supplemented by a system of sending recordings of BBC programs directly to radio stations in the Colonies and Dominions so that listeners could 'hear British programmes exactly as we hear them at home' that is, without the interference of short-wave static (*RT*, 18 November 1932).

Whatever he may have thought about the political and cultural implications of the BBC's expansionist policy, Shaw's reputation and bank balance certainly benefited. Shaw's plays, or extracts from them, were broadcast frequently in the 1930s throughout the British Empire and Colonies. On 28 May 1936 Shaw approved the BBC's request to broadcast (for an unspecified fee) excerpts from *On the Rocks* and *The Doctor's Dilemma*;[43] interestingly, neither of these plays, in whole or in part, had yet been heard on domestic radio in Britain. Nor had *Heartbreak House* and *The Apple Cart*, extracts from which – featuring Edith Evans – Shaw approved for Empire broadcast on 7 July 1936.[44] And Empire listeners were also the first to hear *Pygmalion*, Shaw agreeing on 13 June 1939 (for a fee of 30 guineas) to a three-part broadcast in July and August 1939.[45] The BBC also dealt with requests that came from Empire and Colonial radio companies to use scripts of BBC broadcasts of the plays for their own productions. On one such occasion – a request from the Australian Broadcasting Commission to use BBC adaptations of *Back to Methuselah* and *The Apple Cart* – the BBC asked Shaw's permission to send scripts abroad whenever requested ('we have frequent requests from overseas broadcasters about radio plays'), the host broadcaster still needing of course to secure Shaw's permission for any ensuing broadcast. Shaw's note back (23 September 1936) was clear: 'May I have a look at the scripts first? The copyright in them is mine. Such is the law. Lend me a copy.'[46] But when a similar request came to the BBC from the South African Broadcasting Corporation in March 1938 for *Candida* Shaw simply replied 'No objection.'[47]

There was a world, as well, beyond the British Empire and its Colonies, and the BBC facilitated broadcasts of Shaw's plays in several European countries – sometimes by sending scripts, sometimes by passing on permission requests to Shaw. When the broadcasts were in a language other than English, Shaw was always sensitive to the translator's rights, reminding Swedish State Radio in 1938, for example (through the BBC), that if they wished to broadcast *The Dark Lady of the Sonnets* in Swedish they would have to consult with Ebba Low, to whom Shaw had assigned Swedish translation rights.[48] There were also regular broadcasts of Shaw's plays in the United States, beginning with the world premiere broadcast of *How He Lied to Her Husband*, directed by Cecil Lewis for NBC radio and its affiliates on 21 January 1930.[49] But another kind of premiere was in store for *How He Lied*, one that heralded a whole new set of opportunities and experiences for Shaw in his relationship with the BBC. On Thursday 8 July 1937 *How He Lied to Her Husband* became the first Shaw play to be televised.

5 'GBS Has Been Very Kindly Disposed': Pre-War Television

Early Days

When, in 1925, responding to a question about the impact of broadcasting on the theatre, Shaw said, 'If I could see and hear a play from my fireside I would never enter a theatre again,'[1] he was still (like everyone in Great Britain) coming to terms with the introduction of radio into British homes. The use of the verb *see* in his response had no immediate application, but it was, perhaps, an unconsciously prescient insight into a situation that was soon to become reality. John Logie Baird had started experiments with television as early as 1923, and advances were such that by 1929 the Baird Television Development Company had reached an agreement with the BBC to begin a series of experimental broadcasts (Briggs, *Golden Age* 506–7). The first transmission was on 30 September 1929 – a thirty-minute broadcast with a few speeches, a comedian, and a singer watched by an estimated thirty people (ibid. 507) – and a few months later, on 14 July 1930, the first play was televised – Pirandello's *The Man with the Flower in His Mouth*, promoted by the BBC as 'by far the most interesting television transmission so far attempted' (*RT*, 11 July 1930). The other televison programs that day consisted mainly of musical concerts – classical and popular – news, children's entertainment, and talks (including one on the forthcoming World Poultry Congress).

When asked some years later – in January 1947 – specifically whether production of plays on television 'will have an adverse effect upon the theatre box office,' Shaw argued that theatre and television were independent of each other: 'Plays are works of art which depend on their own dramatic merits and the histrionic abilities of the performers no matter what their method of presentation may be.' He did, however, repeat the point he had made in 1925, namely, that the box office did, indeed, stand to lose, but only when 'proletarian homes,' now 'mostly uncomfortable, overcrowded, and dull,' become comfortable enough to induce people to stay at home so that they can 'have their fill of drama and music without leaving their firesides, at a negligible cost.'[2] Later on in the interview Shaw was asked for his reaction to the televising of his own plays (there had been several by 1947), but he claimed never to have seen one, and 'I dont possess' a television receiver – nor did he acquire one during the three remaining years of his life.[3] By 1950 Shaw sensed that the combined effect of increasing middle-class comforts, improvements in the technical quality of television transmissions, and expanding numbers of viewers *was* having an impact on the box office, particularly for new plays and for plays – such as his – that 'neither sleep nor die.' He made this comment in a letter to Val Gielgud (now head of television drama as well as radio drama) on 5 May 1950, just a few months before his death, taking the position that 'the better the performance' of one of his plays on television, 'the more surely it will strike the play dead in the theatre box office from which I get my living' (Laurence, *Theatrics* 235). The only play that Shaw was prepared to offer Gielgud at that stage for a television production (Gielgud wanted *Major Barbara*) was *Jitta's Atonement*, 'which nobody will touch' (ibid. 236).[4]

Shaw had, however, been more accommodating in the early years of television. Experimental broadcasts had continued in the early 1930s, though in an uncertain financial and policy environment – how would the service be financed, and who would have editorial control? In 1934 the government established a committee (chaired by former Conservative MP and Postmaster-General Lord Selsdon) to consider these questions. Selsdon's report (1935) took the view that there should be a 'close relationship' between 'sound and television broadcasting' and concluded, therefore, that 'the Authority which is responsible for the former' – the BBC – 'should also be entrusted with the latter.' The BBC had assured Selsdon that it was 'prepared fully to accept this additional responsibility and to enter whole-heartedly into the development of Television in conformity with the best interests of the licence-paying public.' Concerned about the 'growth of vested interests,' the Selsdon Committee rejected the involvement of private enterprise (including advertising) in television broadcasting and urged that the financing come in part from the revenue generated for the BBC through radio licences, in part directly from government. The recommendations were accepted by the government, and confirmed when the BBC's charter was renewed for a further ten years at the end of 1936.[5] By then the BBC had demonstrated its commitment to television by installing a new transmission station at Alexandra Palace[6] in north London, beginning services from there on 2 November 1936.

Even with the new transmitter, television was accessible only to viewers in the London area, and transmissions were in any case initially limited to two hours a day, weekdays only. The two principal programs on the opening day from the Alexandra Palace studios were a variety show (3:30–4:00 pm) consisting of Adèle Dixon ('musical comedy star'), Buck and Bubbles ('comedians and dancers'), the Lai Founs ('Chinese jugglers'), and the BBC Television Orchestra; and a thirty-minute (9:20–9:50 pm) 'Picture Page,' 'the first of a series in which people of interest will be introduced' (*RT*, 30 October 1936). Later in the week there was some ballet and theatre (scenes from a comedy, *Marigold*, then running at the Royalty Theatre), as well as regular 'British Movietone News' bulletins.

The First Televised Shaw Play

It wasn't long before the thoughts of BBC television officials turned to Shaw. Towards the end of June 1937 Shaw was telephoned to see if he would agree to a television production of *How He Lied to Her Husband*. Shaw seems to have had no qualms about this new venture, and quickly agreed to a modest fee of 5 guineas.[7] The broadcast was scheduled for 8 July, for an afternoon performance running from 3:00 to 3:30, and again in the evening from 9:30 to 10:00. Consisting of only three characters, a single set, and one act, *How He Lied* was a cautious but sensible choice for the Shaw television premiere (which also happened to be the broadcast premiere for *How He Lied*, the play not yet having been heard on radio). At least two members of the cast had had previous experience of playing Shaw, Greer Garson as The Patient in a 1932 touring production of *Too True to be Good* (she subsequently went on to a major Hollywood film career) and Douglas Clarke-Smith as Bonnington in a 1926 London production of *The Doctor's Dilemma*. None of the cast had previously broadcast on television or radio. The third cast member, Derek Williams, had stage experience in London and New York, but no Shaw and no radio or television. The director, George More O'Ferrall, had acted and directed professionally in London and the provinces, but had no radio (or Shaw) experience and was, like everyone else, a novice in television. And the broadcast was, of course, live. Twice.

The production was, then, largely a matter of trial and error. Perhaps it was this element of risk that tempted Shaw to accept a BBC invitation not only to visit Alexandra Palace for the production, but also to appear on television himself immediately following the afternoon performance. According to the *Daily Telegraph* (9 July 1937), Shaw watched the play on a television set and then walked into the production studio with Gerald Cock, the first Director of BBC Television. Shaw immediately made some unscripted remarks, reported by the *Telegraph*:

> You might not suppose it from my veteran appearance, but the truth is that I am the author of that ridiculous little play you have just heard. This is a very special occasion because, as a writer of plays, I never come before the curtain and accept a call. But, you see, on this occasion you have not called me. You are not like the unfortunate people in the theatre who, no matter how much they may be bored, cannot get up and go away. You who are still listening show that you are interested by that very fact. I myself very nearly went to sleep during the play.

A photograph in the *Telegraph* shows Shaw looking into the camera, though his verbs ('heard,' 'listening') suggest that he hadn't quite adjusted to the television medium. After his brief comments, he met the cast and the director, a photograph of the occasion not revealing any disgruntlement about Shaw's assessment of the sleep-inducing quality of their performance. Shaw also spoke to the *Telegraph* reporter, L. Marsland Gander, telling him that the production 'ought to be burned' (though there was nothing to burn) and that he wasn't at all impressed by television. Shaw's 'jocular tone,' however, Gander reported, 'neutralised the acidity of his remarks,' and Shaw 'showed great interest in the equipment, transmitters and studio.'

A few days after the production of *How He Lied*, Cock wrote to Shaw to thank him for the visit to Alexandra Palace and for 'so kindly taking part in the programme.' 'We were confident,' Cock continued (apparently without irony) 'that you would do it as to the manner born, and you certainly did. It was a most effective wind up to the televising of your play.'[8]

Encore

Shaw's attendance at the production of *How He Lied*, and his own television debut, deflected attention from the production itself, but the

BBC appears to have been happy with the broadcast, and pressed ahead to get more Shaw plays on television. O'Ferrall was entrusted with approaching Shaw, apparently hoping to get a full-length play that could be cut down to about forty-five minutes, a 'hopeless' expectation, Shaw replied, drawing O'Ferrall's attention to a 'bushel of playlets no longer than How He Lied' that he could use.[9] Undeterred, the BBC tried for a big one again in September 1937 – or at least *part* of a big one, asking if an act of Tyrone Guthrie's Old Vic production of *Pygmalion* (which opened on 21 September with Diana Wynward as Eliza and Robert Morley as Higgins) could be televised and offering a fee of 5 guineas. Shaw, holidaying in Sidmouth, wrote back to say that he hadn't seen the production, wouldn't make a decision until he had, wouldn't give permission if he didn't like the cast, and asked for double the offered fee.[10] The idea was dropped.

There was no way that Shaw was going to be rushed, though the BBC's commitment to serious television drama was increasing. Of the regular two hours of television broadcasting on 15 November 1937, for example, an hour and thirty-five minutes was devoted to drama – an excerpt from the Vaudeville Theatre production of *Ghosts* in the afternoon, and an hour-long version of R.C. Sherriff's *Journey's End* (directed by O'Ferrall) in the evening (*RT*, 12 November 1937).

By the following spring there was still no more Shaw. The next effort came on 11 April 1938 with a suggestion for a May production of *Androcles and the Lion* – two performances for a fee of 25 guineas. 'Why the appalling cut in author's fees?' was Shaw's immediate reaction. 'Is the television audience so small that it runs to £12-10-0 [just under twelve-and-a-half guineas] only?' (Shaw was being paid a minimum of 35 guineas for a radio play in the 1930s.) *Androcles* was available, Shaw said, 'if we can come to terms.'[11] The BBC reply (19 April) pleaded that 'the number of television receivers in existence is still very small,' and that 'the money available for this service is very limited,' but the fee was raised to 35 guineas, which Shaw accepted with a 'Hooray!'[12] An announcement in the *Radio Times* (1 July 1938) indicated that Shaw had 'demanded' that the play be performed uncut, and gave details of the cast, which included Esmé Percy, veteran of many Shaw productions, including as Androcles, the role he took in the television production. The play was duly broadcast on 4 July (9:00–10:00 pm) and on 13 July (3:00–4:00 pm), and was declared by *The Times* to be a 'conspicuous success,' with credit given in particular to Percy's Androcles, 'simply and convincingly played.' All the cast, however, did well, said *The Times*; indeed, so striking was the casting that it 'almost suggested that the author had had a hand in it.' (He hadn't.)

1939: Boom and Bust

By the time of the *Androcles* broadcast, discussions were already under way between Shaw and the BBC about the next Shaw play for television. When Shaw attempted on 16 July 1938 to return a telephone call from his BBC contact on this occasion – R.G. Walford – he got through to the BBC operator, but, as he explained in a subsequent postcard to Walford, 'I could not make out what the young lady was saying (beyond that you were not available) and she could not hear me at all.'[13] It may have been the poor telephone lines that caused some confusion about what Walford was asking. Shaw explained in his postcard that he would 'veto' anything from *Geneva*, 'to which I understood your enquiry to refer,' but, Shaw said, you 'may broadcast anything you like from St. Joan.' The problem with *Geneva* – from Shaw's point of view – was that it was scheduled for its world premiere at the Malvern Festival in August 1938, with an expected transfer to the West End in the autumn, and Shaw always took the point of view that a broadcast – radio or television – would diminish, rather than increase, box-office interest in his plays, though he did subsequently agree to a *radio* broadcast of brief extracts from *Geneva* on 25 January 1939 (see above, p. 85).

As things turned out, however, it was neither *Geneva* nor *Saint Joan* that became the third play of Shaw's to be televised, but another 'playlet,' *The Dark Lady of the Sonnets*. The initial request was sent to Shaw (by letter) on 31 August 1938 at his Whitehall Court address in London, but by then the Shaws were in the Midlands for the Malvern Festival and the Worcester Music Festival. The BBC sent a reminder on 13 September, by which time the original request had reached Shaw at his hotel in Droitwich. He replied – affirmatively ('Go ahead') – on 15 September 1938, accepting the proposed fee of fifteen guineas for a single performance, while adding a comment that 'the last performance was not as good as it might easily have been made' (a reference to the radio broadcast of *The Dark Lady* on 21 July 1938 – see above, p. 83).[14] The television production was initially planned for 9 October, but (for reasons unknown) the schedule was rearranged and viewers saw Arthur Wing Pinero's *Trelawny of the 'Wells'* instead. The new schedule, however, allowed for *two* performances of *The Dark Lady* (on 26 February and 6 March 1939), for which Shaw received 25 guineas. In accepting the offer, Shaw again could not resist giving some advice – 'you will overdo the Dark Lady unless you get two really beautiful voices for it and an Elizabeth with a supermajestic style.'[15] It's hard to know whether Helen Haye – who played Elizabeth – met Shaw's definition of supermajestic, but although Shaw-less and making her broadcast debut, Helen Haye was vastly experienced in the Shakespearean and modern repertory in London and in North America, as well as in film (though she is not to be confused with the more illustrious movie star Helen Hayes) – and she did later (in 1939) play Mrs Higgins in *Pygmalion* at the Haymarket.

There is no record of any grumbling from Shaw about the production of *The Dark Lady*, so he was not ill disposed to other BBC approaches – indeed, as the *Radio Times* put it on 5 May 1939, with some incredulity perhaps, Shaw was showing himself 'very kindly disposed' towards Alexandra Palace, making 1939 a very good year for Shaw enthusiasts among the still small, but growing, British television audience.

There still hadn't been, however, a television production of a major Shaw play. Would Shaw consider *Candida*, asked Hamilton Marr (Head of Copyright at the BBC) in a letter of 6 March 1939?[16] *Candida* had been broadcast on radio twice (22 December 1935 and 17 October 1937), and with its one set and small cast was clearly manageable on television. Marr cleverly invited Shaw to make suggestions for casting (Shaw would have done so anyway). 'We should be very glad to have them,' said Marr. Shaw duly obliged, both by agreeing to the broadcast (35 guineas for two performances) and by recommending actors, principally Phyllis Neilson Terry as Candida and Stephen Haggard as Marchbanks.[17] As it happened, none of Shaw's suggestions were taken up – whether for reasons of availability or BBC preferences is not clear – and the selected cast, led by the experienced actor Marie Ney as Candida[18] – was not altogether successful. A young actor named Peter Osborn played Marchbanks, and the contrast between his 'extreme youthfulness' and the forty-three-year-old Ney (who 'managed to be rather too mature') 'made the situation a little absurd,' according to *The Times* (17 April 1939). But this shortcoming was balanced by 'a really sympathetic' performance by Miles Otway as Morrell, so all-in-all it was, concluded *The Times*, 'a delightful production.' Shaw's views on the production are, alas, not known.

Only four days after the second performance of *Candida* (19 April 1939), a Shaw play was again on television. Having rejected the idea of a television production of *Geneva* in July of the previous year (see above, p. 94), Shaw had subsequently allowed some brief radio extracts to be broadcast on radio on 25 January 1939. He now – at the end of March 1939 – reflected on a letter he received from Roy Limbert (producer of the Malvern Festival and West End premieres of the play).

Limbert was tempted by the BBC's interest in televising the play – or parts of it – because business at the St James's Theatre for *Geneva* was 'flagging,' and 'a Televise [*sic*],' Limbert thought, would be 'of big value.' Shaw wasn't so sure, again expressing the view that a broadcast of the play would damage box office ('kill it dead') rather than improve it. Still, he said, if business doesn't soon pick up, 'it does not greatly matter' if there is a television production or not. Shaw's suggestion was that there be a television broadcast of the third act of *Geneva*, provided that an announcer first give 'the substance of the first two acts in a précis.'[19] The idea was acceptable to Limbert and to the BBC, but who was to presume to summarize the first two acts of the play? Who better, of course, than Shaw himself? And, happily for the BBC, Shaw agreed, and in the most obliging of ways. While declining an invitation to deliver the summary himself, he gave *carte blanche* to whoever was selected to 'adapt this [summary] to your own turn of speech if it comes awkwardly' (*RT*, 5 May 1939). Shaw's synopsis was released to the press before the broadcast, and carried in *The Times* on 22 April 1939, the day before the broadcast (which was on a Sunday evening, directly from the St James's Theatre).[20]

Otherwise unremarkable, the synopsis surprises, *The Times* notes, by conceding the 'need for economy in time' in producing *Geneva* on television ('as the first two [acts] only explain how the famous third act could possibly come about we can save your time by substituting a brief statement of the situation they create,' writes Shaw) and (according to *The Times*) by agreeing with critics 'that the third act is the one that matters.'[21]

Geneva was broadcast only a few weeks before the German invasion of Czechoslovakia, so Shaw's lampooning of European and British political and military leaders in the play (including Hitler and Mussolini) could hardly have been more timely – though there seems to have been little public or press reaction to either the radio or television broadcast. There was also a timely political relevance in the television broadcast of Shaw's 'revolutionary romancelet' (his term), *Annajanska, the Bolshevik Empress*, on 2 May 1939 (repeated on 7 May), with its theme of revolution against autocracy, though the whimsical *Passion, Poison, and Petrifaction*, televised on 9 and 15 June 1939, is free of political ramifications.

The Shaw television boom of 1939 ended with a production of *The Man of Destiny* on 20 and 28 July. A popular play on radio – there had been productions in 1928, 1930, and 1937 – *The Man of Destiny*, with Napoleon as its protagonist, might also be said to have spoken to contemporary as well as historical issues (Germany was preparing to invade Poland), but the events of the final months of 1939 were moving quickly to end not just Shaw's prominence on television, but television itself.

Television Suspended

By 1939 the BBC had a good sense of the size and the interests of its television audience. The *Radio Times* reported in its issue of 7 July 1939 that there were approximately 20,000 owners of television sets.[22] In the early months of 1939, these owners had been invited to complete a questionnaire about their viewing interests. The BBC received 4027 completed questionnaires, from which it was determined that television was not 'a privilege only of the rich,' but that 'labourers' and 'scores of men-in-the-street like confectioners, salesmen, and schoolteachers' owned televisions. And what did they like to watch? 'Musical features' were not very popular, achieving an approval rating of only 12% on the survey, and ballet didn't do well either (25%). At the other end of the scale were 'news reels' and 'plays or variety from theatres,' both scoring 93%. Since plays were lumped in with 'variety,' the 93% figure might be a generous assessment of the popularity of legitimate drama, but plays produced in the studio also did well, short plays receiving a rating of 70%, 'full length' an impressive 83%. Where Shaw fitted into these results is impossible to know, but clearly the BBC had confidence in his plays, and there was nothing in the results of the questionnaire to suggest that the confidence was misplaced.

Nor was there anything to suggest – from the questionnaire or from broader public and political opinion – that the future of television itself, and the BBC's administration of it, were seriously questioned. The BBC could look forward confidently to expanding its commercial-free service, both in terms of the number of hours of broadcasting each day and in terms of its geographical reach beyond the immediate area of London. And Shaw could look forward to further opportunities for television productions of his plays. All that anticipation, however, was thwarted by the outbreak of war in September 1939. Great Britain, boasted *The Times* on 23 August 1939, just days before Neville Chamberlain's declaration of war against Germany on 3 September 1939 (see above, p. 50), 'has led the whole world in the field of television,' but now there were higher priorities both for the country at large and for the BBC. Technical and financial resources had to be redirected to support the war effort, causing television broadcasts to be suspended. The last pre-war television broadcast took place on 1 September 1939; it was a Mickey Mouse film. The next was not until 7 June 1946. The opening program featured, among other items, a repeat of the Mickey Mouse film and Shaw's *Dark Lady of the Sonnets*.

6 'I Won't Have That Man on the Air':
The War Years

The Context

The 1930s have been described as the BBC's 'golden age,' a decade during which the BBC established itself as 'a source of authority over the language, an arbiter of cultural taste, a national impresario and a reinvigorator of national drama and song' (Smith 62). The authoritarian and unashamedly élitist leadership of John Reith had not prevented the BBC from building a massive popular audience. By the time Reith announced his retirement in June 1938 (to become chairman of Imperial Airways, precursor of British Overseas Airways Corporation and, ultimately, British Airways) there were over thirty million listeners in Great Britain. Reith had also overseen the creation and growth of international BBC transmissions, and had successfully argued that television broadcasting, like radio, should also be run as a BBC monopoly. And as BBC operations and staff grew, Reith ensured that there would be adequate space and technology resources by moving BBC headquarters in 1932 from the original location in Savoy Hill (off the Strand in central London) to a new purpose-built ten-storey building – Broadcasting House, still a major BBC facility – between Oxford Street and Regent's Park.

Reith and Shaw were never close, but the relationship was characterized by mutual respect. Shaw appreciated Reith's effective leadership and his commitment to the BBC's role in supporting and promoting the arts. He was particularly appreciative of Reith's assistance to Edward Elgar in commissioning his third symphony (see above, p. 51), and some years after Reith had left the BBC Shaw expressed regret that he had done so ('You cannot deplore your departure from the

BBC more than I did').[1] For his part, Reith was well aware of how important Shaw had been to the BBC as debater, lecturer, pronunciation expert, and, of course, playwright.

Reith's achievements were widely celebrated by the BBC and the national press when he resigned in 1938, leaving his successor, F.W. Ogilvie – former president of Queen's University, Belfast – the difficult task of setting his own mark on BBC policy and values. As if that were not challenging enough in itself, Ogilvie took over (on 1 October 1938) less than a year before Britain went to war with Germany.

One of Ogilvie's major priorities on becoming Director-General of the BBC was to prepare for the war. Considerable thought went into what the role of the BBC would be – should be – in the event of war. The answer came in the issue of the *Radio Times* published just one day after Neville Chamberlain broadcast Britain's declaration of war on Germany. In an article defiantly headed 'Broadcasting Carries On!' the BBC recognized its importance to government as a means of communication ('The Government can speak to the people – news can reach the remotest village – instructions can be issued by the Ministries – warnings can be given of approaching attacks'), but also insisted that it had another function, 'nearly as important' – entertainment. 'Broadcasting,' said the BBC, 'can help to take our minds off the horrors of war as nothing else can.' And so the BBC made a commitment to continue to broadcast plays, musical comedies, features, talks, children's programs, and school programs, in addition to government announcements and regular news broadcasts. Programming would run from seven in the morning until 'after midnight.' Since London was so vulnerable to air attacks, broadcasting facilities were established around the country, and all programming would be limited to a single wave-length.[2]

The BBC's Drama Department had become accustomed to state-of-the-art equipment and spacious studios at Broadcasting House, but now found itself located in makeshift facilities, initially in Evesham in Worcestershire, and then, from November 1939, in Manchester. An article in *The Listener* shortly after the outbreak of war conceded that there would be difficulties in maintaining the range and quality of BBC drama productions, and recognized that radio drama, 'like everything else,' 'must make [its] contribution to the nation's war effort.' That meant, the article continued, producing the kind of drama that can 'stir our national pride and arouse interest in the life, culture and war-effort of our allies,' without, however, 'descending to the level of cheap jingoism.' And classic drama, listeners were assured, 'will not be neglected.'[3]

There were those, however, who worried that the BBC did not appreciate the nature of the raised cultural expectations for which it had itself been responsible, and that, in the words of one newspaper critic, it was content to pour out 'an endless stream of trivialities and sillinesses, apparently labouring under the delusion that in any time of crisis the British public becomes just one colossal moron.'[4] Shaw was very sensitive to the impact of radio on the British public, including members of the armed forces. 'The pre-wireless soldier of 1914–18,' he wrote in a letter to the *Daily Telegraph* on 6 February 1940, 'was incredibly primitive in his tastes.' Soldiers of the last war were 'decent lads,' but 'nine out of ten of them had no artistic culture and had never heard a scientific lecture in their lives.' 'The wireless,' he said, 'has changed all that.'[5]

The issue of BBC values and standards during wartime was important, of course, to Shaw professionally, but on a personal level the BBC had become an increasingly prominent factor in his life. His flat in central London (in Whitehall Court, close to the Houses of Parliament and several major government departments) was not the safest of locations during the war, and he and his wife Charlotte spent much of their time in the relative safety of their home in the village of Ayot St Lawrence in Hertfordshire, where the radio was a constant companion, or, as Shaw's secretary Blanche Patch saw it, 'the bane of my life': 'We have it some days all through lunch & dinner so those days we hardly speak as we live in different rooms at other times,' she complained in a letter to Barry Jackson, one of Shaw's theatrical colleagues and friends (8 December 1940, Conolly 119). In September 1942 Shaw told Nancy Astor that his daily routine at Ayot included listening to the BBC news every evening (Wearing 113), and he was equally fond of classical concerts.

Shaw remained, then, as interested as ever in the BBC, though his age was now a consideration in the extent to which he could actively participate in broadcasts, even when the BBC was willing, as it usually was, to set up broadcast facilities in his home. His response to an enquiry from the BBC's Mary Somerville in February 1941 about the possibility of his involvement in a literary discussion series was that while he would enjoy seeing her again – 'You are still young and beautiful; but I, alas! am no longer so' – he had made a decision on his eightieth birthday (26 July 1936) to 'withdraw from the public eye for ever.' 'All that is left of me,' he continued, 'is a toothless old skeleton, whose artificial teeth drop out when it forgets itself and tries to talk vigorously.'[6] Hardly – actor Joyce Grenfell was not the only one who commented on how well Shaw resisted age: 'He *is* older; but golly he's still incredible for eighty-five. Looks so wonderfully pink and white and so fresh and beautifully dandified,' she recalled after lunch with the Shaws in August 1941. But even on that occasion he told another guest – broadcaster and writer Stephen Potter – that he was too old to do a radio autobiography. Joyce Grenfell told her mother that what Shaw really meant was that 'his teeth don't fit and [they] make rude noises that would be particularly exaggerated on the air and his vanity wouldn't stand for such a thing' (Grenfell 227–8).

But loose false teeth didn't stop Shaw from giving advice to the BBC, whether asked for or not, and throughout the war he continued to write letters and post-cards to various officials or to jot down his thoughts in his neat, firm hand, on letters he received from the BBC before returning them to their sender. In agreeing to the broadcast of a three-to-four minute extract from act 4 of *Man and Superman* in a January 1941 program, Shaw told the producer not to 'hurry' the extract – 'the fee is fixed [4 guineas] and you will gain nothing by gabbling it in two minutes.' Based on recent listening experiences, Shaw postulated that there was someone in BBC drama production who 'is crazy on the subject of Pace, Pace, Pace; and the result is that the broadcasts are now often unintelligible.' There was a particular problem, Shaw claimed, when dialect was involved – 'because this somebody does not know that dialect has to be as carefully articulated as Shakespear and as artistically delivered. Mere imitation is useless, and very irritating.'[7] And when Shaw was asked for his advice on the casting of a September 1941 production of *Saint Joan* he responded with a page and a half of directions on how the roles should be played: 'Baudricourt requires careful handling ... Everything that Joan says to him [in the first scene] takes him aback; and he must convey this by his tone ... De Stogumber is an Edmund Kean part ... [U]nless the actor knows its possibilities and is encouraged to go for them all out, he may underplay it ... In the Loire scene Dunois, pleasant voiced and troubadourish at first, becomes the iron-clad commanding officer when Joan enters, not moving an inch while Joan rages and storms at him ... Joan cannot get her effects unless Baudricourt and Dunois give her these contrasts to play against.'[8]

Much of the correspondence between Shaw and the BBC, as in the past, had to do with fees. In separate correspondence about the *Saint Joan* production, Shaw was offered a fee of 50 guineas, but insisted on 60, 'of which the Government will snatch back £44.2.0 [in tax], leaving me less than twenty.'[9] On the other hand, he was always careful to remind the BBC that short extracts from his works could be broadcast without a fee. A proposal by critic John Palmer, for example, to quote from *Arms and the Man* in a February 1944 talk was judged by Shaw to be within Palmer's 'statutory right of fair quotation.'[10] He also drew a distinction between short performances of his work 'to illustrate a lecture' (such as the one given by Neville Coghill on *Caesar and Cleopatra* in a schools broadcast on 6 July 1945), for which the BBC could claim a statutory right, and performances for 'entertainment,' for which Shaw felt he 'must extort' 'a guinea a minute.'[11] On another occasion Shaw suggested that it might save everyone a lot of time if the BBC simply paid him 'five thousand a year or so for carte blanche over all my works.'[12] There is no record of a BBC response to the suggestion. Interestingly, however, the BBC did propose some years later – in January 1945 – that they buy the rights to 'a number of plays,' which would then be available to the BBC 'in a suitable form' (i.e., usually cut) for broadcasting on radio and television 'at any time in years to come.'[13] This time it was Shaw who chose not to answer.

Blanche Patch, Shaw's secretary since 1920, dealt with many requests from the BBC to Shaw, and she had grown accustomed to the inconsistency of his responses to the BBC. She told BBC producer Lance Sieveking in 1945 that he should drop the subject of building a BBC collection of abbreviated recordings of Shaw's plays because Shaw was in one of his 'obstinate moods,' when 'nothing will make him change his mind.' But 'six months later,' she says, 'he will have forgotten all about the thing he has opposed and take up quite a different attitude.'[14] He could be acerbic and uncooperative, too, whenever the BBC forgot the agreement not to refer to him as *George* Bernard Shaw. He had warned them about this previously (see above, p. 83), but had to do so again in October 1940, and did so in no uncertain terms: 'I absolutely refuse to license any broadcasts of my plays by the BBC until the express agreement that I am to be announced as Bernard Shaw and not as George Bernard Shaw is respected.' That issue was quickly resolved, but his unpredictability was not so easily dealt with. There are, for example, many instances of his cooperation with the BBC in using excerpts from his plays in school broadcasts, but when he was asked in November 1945 if a recording of a 25-minute excerpt from *Saint Joan* that he had approved for a May 1938 schools broadcast could be distributed for use in the BBC's Kenya Service he refused – 'I object,' he said, 'to any association of my plays with schoolwork. They are not intended to be instruments of torture. Cut me out of your school lists.'[15]

It was always hard to predict as well how Shaw would react to requests to make cuts to his plays to fit them into broadcast schedules. He was rarely happy about cuts, but there are many instances throughout his years on the BBC of his agreeing to – and sometimes even suggesting – cuts. This pragmatic approach to the broadcast of his plays is evident in the war years as well, but it is also in these years that Shaw makes some of his strongest statements against cutting his plays. In November 1942 Val Gielgud asked Shaw if would consider condensing *Man and Superman* into two-and-a-half hours for a version that could be broadcast over two evenings. 'Splendid in its entirety, but impossible in two nights' was Shaw's reply, suggesting rather that 'at least four, if not five' nights would be more appropriate.[16] And here is his response to Hamilton Marr, head of program copyright at the BBC, for permission to broadcast an abbreviated version of act 1 of *Arms and the Man*:

> I will not consent to the omission of a single word or comma from the first act of Arms and the Man. You can find 40 minutes for a Church service. You can find 45 minutes for a Brahms symphony. You can find 60 minutes for the most damnable variety muck or for one of your intolerable rechauffés of obsolete drivel from the XIX century. Well, if you want me you must find 40, 50, 60, and if necessary 180 minutes for me, or else do without me. Tell those overseas people that their thirty minute arrangements are not applicable to works of art, but only to tripe, which can be cut up and supplied by the pound.
>
> If that is clear I may remark that the first act of Arms and the Man should take 27 minutes, which allows 3 for fluffing.[17]

Five years later Lance Sieveking was in the line of fire on the same issue, via Blanche Patch. 'Mr Shaw,' she told Sieveking, 'has asked me to say that as the recent broadcasts of Peer Gynt, King John, and Bleak House have convinced him that the present policy of the BBC is to cut and alter every literary masterpiece until it does not contain a line that might not have been written by an average free lance journalist he will permit his plays to be broadcast only on condition that not a syllable of the dialogue shall be omitted or added to, and that the announcer's part shall be written by himself.' Shaw also insisted, Ms Patch said, on 'a decisive choice of the producer [director] and the cast.' Even then 'it is not sure that Mr Shaw will authorize any broadcasts at all, as he was so disgusted with the three broadcasts mentioned that he has lost all confidence in the competence of the BBC to handle first class work.'[18]

The BBC's response to Shaw's complaints about cuts and adaptations was usually that time constraints – especially under wartime broadcasting conditions – made it very difficult to accommodate plays

Shaw, Belloc, and Chesterton: the debate of 28 October 1927. Courtesy the BBC.

Einstein, Lord Rothschild, and Shaw, 28 October 1930. Courtesy the BBC.

Shaw broadcasting from Kingsway Hall, 31 January 1930. From *Drama*, 8.15 (March 1930), courtesy Cambridge University Library.

Shaw broadcasting on *Saint Joan*, 30 May 1931. From *The Listener*, 20 July 1932, courtesy the BBC and Cambridge University Library.

Shaw broadcasting from the BBC studios, early 1930s. Courtesy the BBC.

Front-page *Radio Times* promotion of Shaw's 'Whither Britain?' broadcast, 6 February 1934. Courtesy the BBC and Cambridge University Library.

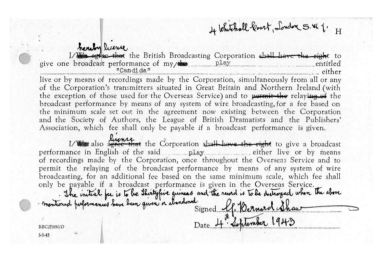

Shaw's agreement with the BBC for the broadcast of *Candida*, 16 October 1943. Courtesy the Burgunder Collection, Cornell University Library.

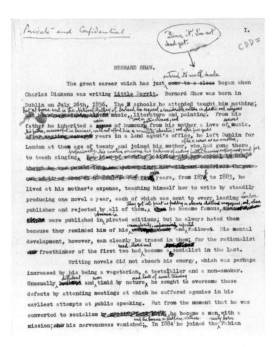

First page of Hesketh Pearson's obituary of Shaw, emended by Shaw, 1946. Courtesy the Harry Ransom Humanities Research Center, the University of Texas at Austin.

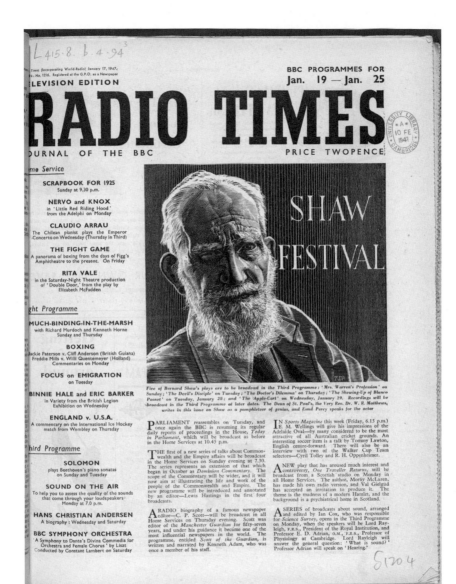

Front-page *Radio Times* promotion of the BBC 'Shaw Festival,' 17 January 1947. Courtesy the BBC and Cambridge University Library.

Scene from the BBC Television Production of *Pygmalion*, broadcast 8 February 1948. Courtesy the BBC.

Scene from the BBC Television Production of *The Devil's Disciple*, broadcast 26 July 1949. Courtesy the BBC.

Scene from the BBC Television Production of *The Man of Destiny*, broadcast 21 March 1950. From *The Listener*, 6 April 1950, courtesy the BBC and Cambridge University Library.

as written. 'We are so much tied down by the time factor,' explained B.H. Alexander from the Copyright Department in May 1945 after Shaw had rejected a request to adapt *Androcles and the Lion* for a thirty-minute broadcast. To which Shaw promptly and caustically replied:

> You cannot be tied down unless you tie yourselves down. Why not loose yourselves?
>
> At the first two performances of Richard Strauss's Heldenleben symphony in London the second, conducted by Henry Wood, took twenty minutes longer than the first, conducted by the composer. Must Sir Adrian Boult finish it in half an hour?
>
> You must either put classics on a separate wave length or drop them altogether. No play of mine will fit your half hour.[19]

Despite these strong words, the record shows that Shaw *was* willing to accommodate the BBC's requests for cuts to and adaptations of his plays, depending on the circumstances (and, as Blanche Patch would have it, his mood). Where he had shown much less willingness to compromise was over the BBC's attitude towards controversial issues. He had fought several battles in the 1920s and 1930s[20] against what he saw as the BBC's timidity about broadcasting programs of a controversial nature, and – not surprisingly – he took a dim view of the BBC's decision in March 1941 to ban from broadcasting actors and musicians who had participated in a recent pacifist convention – 'The whole managing staff of the BBC should be sacked instantly,' he said, for this 'exhibition of British Nazi-ism gone mad.'[21] He worried too that the government-imposed restrictions on war news would be counter-productive, commenting to Nancy Astor that suppression of information about the bombing of Plymouth in June 1943 ('Every day we hear about a tip & run trifle with little damage, a few casualties, and two raiders shot down in a southwest town, when the truth is that Plymouth has been heavily blitzed') 'make[s] us take it easy just when we need a touch of the whip to make us buckle-to' (Wearing 134).

And yet Shaw could on occasion be even more cautious than the BBC. They were prepared to broadcast the final speech from *Too True to be Good* (performed by Esmé Percy) in March 1944, the magnificent speech in which Aubrey expresses deep existential doubts caused by war: 'I am the new Ecclesiastes. But I have no Bible, no creed: the war has shot both out of my hands.' Soldiers have remained strong 'in the old uncompromising affirmations which give them status, duties, certainty of consequences;

so that the pugnacious spirit of man in them can reach out and strike deathblows with steadfastly closed minds. Their way is straight and pure; but it is the way of death; and the preacher must preach the way of life.'[22] The BBC showed itself fully aware of the sensitive nature of the content of the speech at a time when the allies were making inroads in Europe (and D-Day, though few knew it, was only weeks away), but thought an introduction to the speech would neutralize the impact. They drafted the following for Shaw's consideration:

> You must remember that this speech was written for an audience living in 1930; it excited enthusiasm, and also a great deal of animosity, although today we realise that its comments were just. We must hope that after this war our way of life will take all the point and sting from this speech. We hope that it will be thought of as just a speech from a play of 1930 written by George Bernard Shaw.[23]

In his response to the initial request for permission to use the speech, Shaw had told the BBC that it did not strike him 'as a wise selection at this moment ... I do not advise.' But he had nonetheless approved it (for a fee of 5 guineas) and even offered to 'send a line or two for the announcer if I can find the time.'[24] A week later, however, he was adamant: 'This wont do at all. Never cry stinking fish. Better drop it: this is not the moment.'[25]

'The Unavoidable Subject'

The question of the right moment for outspokenness during the war – and outspokenness itself – was easy to disagree about. Such was the case with the speech from *Too True to be Good*, and, surprisingly, Shaw, rather than the BBC, erred on the side of caution in this instance. What Shaw did not know, however, was that at virtually the same time as the *Too True* discussion was taking place, the BBC (through another Department – Overseas Services) was quietly but firmly quashing an initiative by the Australian Broadcasting Commission to arrange an Empire broadcast by Shaw on his next birthday (his eighty-fourth on 26 July 1940). C.J.A. Moses, General Manager of the ABC, wrote to London on 13 March 1940 to suggest a talk by Shaw 'On Being Eighty-Four.' He even offered to contribute twenty-five pounds towards the costs. The response came from R.A. Rendall, Director of Overseas Services, on 17 April 1940 to say that the suggestion had been 'carefully considered,' but that the BBC had 'reluctantly come to the conclusion that the arrangement of such a broadcast would not be opportune in present circumstances.' Rendall went on to explain, 'confidentially,' that 'it is very uncertain whether a world-wide broadcast by GBS, with the inevitable attendant publicity, would be in the national interest.' 'We should not wish to approach him,' Rendall continued, 'unless we were able to give him absolute freedom to speak his mind, so long as the Defence Notices were not contravened.' The problem was that if Shaw were free 'to choose his own ground' there was a good chance that he would choose to say something about the war, in which case, given his involvement in 'public controversy in earlier days of the war[26] ... he might well provide valuable material for the German propaganda machine.'

Moses must have wondered at the distance Rendall's thinking had travelled from a simple request for Shavian birthday reflections to fuelling the German propaganda machine, and had Moses been party to subsequent BBC deliberations about Shaw he would also have marvelled at the BBC's seeming inability to get its act together about what to do with Shaw in the wartime context. For while Rendall was telling Moses that having Shaw on the air would not be 'in the national interest,' some of Rendall's own colleagues in the Overseas Services Department were working strenuously to get Shaw on the air to speak about the war – which was precisely the concern that caused Rendall to keep Shaw *off* the air.

In early January 1940 Shaw was contacted (through a relative, Sir William Wheeler) by a man named Ivo Geikie-Cobb, a physician and surgeon by profession, who had recently joined the BBC's Overseas Services Department as a writer, editor, and broadcaster (using the pseudonym Anthony Weymouth). Weymouth wanted Shaw to give a radio talk on the war to the British Colonies – with no worries, it seems, about the German propaganda machine. But Shaw declined: 'my speciality is keeping my mouth shut when I have nothing to say or at least I think I had better not say it' (*CL* 4:544). Weymouth let that idea drop, but some weeks later he was in touch with Shaw again, this time at the suggestion of Stephen Tallents, Controller of Overseas Services, who was eager to give Shaw an opportunity to elaborate on a recent comment in a newspaper interview that the British 'must fight to the last ditch' in the war against Germany (*CL* 4:563). Weymouth followed up his initial telephone conversation with Shaw with a letter on 30 May 1940, inviting Shaw to give his talk in a BBC series called 'This Land of Ours.' That telephone call and letter set off a chain of events that embroiled Shaw, Tallents, Weymouth, the Director-General of the

BBC, the Minister of Information, and, some thought, even the Prime Minister himself, in intense discussions that culminated in a government ban on the talk that Shaw wrote shortly after he received Weymouth's letter.[27]

The ostensible objective of the series 'This Land of Ours' was 'to reflect characteristic English life and culture ... to show the lives lived by men and women in England, the ideals they cherish, and, in a word, to reflect the British character.' Talks in the series, including Shaw's, would 'no doubt have a war-time flavour,' Weymouth said in his letter, and he regretted that, while quite understanding Shaw's views on censorship, he would have to have the script 'a few days in advance' of the talk. There followed a meeting between Shaw and Weymouth to discuss the talk, a meeting at which Shaw agreed to 'expound his views on the war and why we should fight Hitler.' Shaw also told Weymouth that he quite understood the need for censorship in wartime, but that if that had to happen the 'right person' to do any censoring was Shaw himself. There quickly followed an exchange of correspondence between Weymouth and Shaw about the scheduled time for the talk, but Shaw confirmed that he would do it, and that, indeed, most of the talk was already drafted (this was on 5 June). Shaw also told Weymouth that 'the pepper in it is very red indeed.' Perhaps it was this remark that prompted Weymouth – or, more likely, Tallents – to alert the Ministry of Information, the government ministry responsible for wartime censorship, of the impending talk. The official ministry position at this stage (6 June 1940) was open-minded: 'This Ministry cannot, of course, give any final comments on the general proposal as such. It is easy to imagine a Shavian script which would be most impolitic in present circumstances, but if he were saying the right sort of thing, he might be a good card to play.'

The next day, 7 June, Shaw arrived at Weymouth's office at the BBC to deliver the talk. He was shown into the office 'holding himself very erect and wearing a tweed jacket and knee breeches,' and 'with a smile,' he handed Weymouth a copy of his talk. The title, Weymouth discovered when he took the script from its envelope, was 'The Unavoidable Subject.' Weymouth read the script as soon as Shaw had left, and then shared it with his colleagues. A 'certain liveliness,' as Weymouth puts it in his diary, characterized the discussions among BBC officials about the talk, and there were those who 'feared that some of the opinions expressed might give offence to listeners, especially if taken out of context.' Weymouth was asked to visit Shaw again, this time to 'persuade him to modify or delete certain statements in his script,' a possibility that Shaw had anticipated in his first meeting with Weymouth. Without Shaw's knowledge, however, a copy of the script had been sent to Harold Nicolson, Parliamentary Secretary to the Minister of Information, Duff Cooper, with a covering letter from Weymouth saying that (in his view) parts of the talk, if broadcast, 'would be liable to be used out of their context adversely to the national interest by the enemy, and which would also undoubtedly excite protest from British listeners at home and overseas.' The German propaganda machine was, then, back in the picture, but Weymouth was confident, he told Nicolson, that Shaw would be amenable to dropping the 'objectionable passages.' Two days later (9 June), however, Stephen Tallents told Weymouth that Cooper had telephoned him to say that the talk was 'not to go on the air.' Weymouth's diary recollection is that Tallents reported that Cooper expressed his antipathy even more emphatically: 'I won't have that man on the air.' Tallents confirmed the situation in a memorandum on 10 June and now altered his directive to Weymouth from visiting Shaw to seek changes to the script to telling him that 'after reference to the Ministry of Information, we are obliged, in view of the critical military situation, to cancel the talk.'

Weymouth went to see Shaw the next day (11 June) to explain the situation. He made the difficult wartime journey to Ayot St Lawrence (there were no signposts, and the village of Ayot St Lawrence, then and now, is not an easy place to find) and was rewarded with lunch (on the terrace) with Shaw and Charlotte. Conversation flowed easily about various matters, but it was only over coffee that the subject of the BBC talk was broached. Weymouth – understandably – was nervous. The official explanation that Weymouth had been instructed to give Shaw was that 'Italy's entry into the war and other events in the international field had made [Shaw's] script out of date.' That wasn't actually Cooper's reason for banning the talk, but Italy's entry into the war (Mussolini had declared war on Britain and France on 10 June) eased Weymouth's task. Moreover, Shaw, he said, 'made it easy for me,' and Charlotte helped as well – 'she was as helpful as anybody could possibly be,' Weymouth recalled. On his return from Ayot, Weymouth briefed Ogilvie, who then (12 June) wrote to Nicolson to report that Shaw was 'willing to alter the text at any points which had been felt to give difficulty, and [that] he left Weymouth with the impression that his one anxiety was to serve the national cause.' Tallents then spoke to Nicolson, who was 'all in favour' of further negotiations with Shaw, provided that Shaw understood that the final say would be the Ministry's, and that 'this means leaving out paradoxical remarks liable to misunderstanding.'

Two days after Weymouth's visit, Shaw sent a copy of 'The Unavoidable Subject' ('a very untidy copy') to Beatrice Webb, and told her that it had been banned. It is clear from this letter that Shaw was not hoodwinked by the explanation that the talk had been dropped because it was 'out of date.' 'It may interest you to know,' he wrote, 'that before the Italian news came in, the Ministry of Information had already "cancelled" the broadcast curtly, without giving any reasons.' Shaw also told Beatrice Webb that 'the BBC was inclined to demur' at the government ban, but that 'I persuaded them to drop it, as a broadcast this week without any reference to Italy would have been ridiculous; and the extension of the war from a scrap between the Reich and the Allies to the European scale made my stuff childish' (Michalos and Poff 244–5).

But the BBC hadn't dropped it. Tallents conjectured that what the Ministry would really like was something from Shaw aimed at persuading Americans that 'the war is worth fighting and that the stakes at issue are theirs as well as ours.' He was right. A memorandum from the ministry on 18 June confirmed that the minister 'agrees that if Shaw can be persuaded to say the right thing ... his testimony might well be valuable.' So Weymouth visited Shaw again (on 21 June). There is no record of what was said at that meeting, but Shaw told Weymouth by letter on 24 June that he didn't see much point in revising the talk since 'the Information Ministry wont let me broadcast at all' (CL 4:563). Weymouth wasn't so sure, and so he revised the talk anyway,[28] and Ogilvie personally delivered it to Nicolson on 1 July, stressing in their meeting its 'great propaganda value in America and overseas.' On 5 July, having discussed the script with Cooper, Nicolson got back to Ogilvie, reporting that the minister 'still sees grave objection to any talk of this sort going across.' As Cooper understood the talk, Nicolson explained, 'Shaw's main theme is that the only thing Hitler has done wrong is to persecute the Jews.' However, it was the minister's view that 'millions of Americans and some other people [think] that this is the only thing he [Hitler] has done right.' The minister has concluded, therefore, Nicolson told Ogilvie, that 'the talk would do much harm,' so 'I fear we shall have to drop the whole question and risk the wrath of that strange old man.'

Duff Cooper may have been biased against Shaw from the beginning. Cooper had served (with distinction) in the army in the First World War, and would have known of Shaw's fierce opposition to that war, expressed particularly in *Common Sense about the War* (1914), a book that caused Shaw to be vilified by almost everyone.[29] Cooper was doubtless also just as appalled by some of the views that Shaw expressed in 'The Unavoidable Subject.'[30] The problem was that Shaw wanted to give a balanced and contextualized view of the European situation as he saw it in the early months of the war. 'Mr Hitler did not begin this war; we did. It is silly to revile him as a treacherous wolf pouncing on a nation of innocent lambs,' Shaw declared. 'I have no patience,' he continued, 'with the journalists and the tub thumpers who are breaking our spirits by snivelling about our being the victims of a foul and treacherous aggression.' Shaw could be as enthusiastic a tub thumper as anyone when the issues were clear, but the origins of the war were complex, he believed, and it would be intellectually and morally dishonest to claim otherwise. In addition to Hitler even having 'adopted ... my [vegetarian] diet' (a bit of Shavian whimsy that must have been particularly galling to the bureaucrats), he displayed, Shaw said, 'physical and moral courage' and 'diplomatic sagacity' in the 'triumphant rescue of his country from the yoke the Allies imposed on it in 1918.' What's more, Hitler's mind 'is a twentieth-century mind,' while 'that of our governing class is mentally in the reign of Edward the Third [1327–77], six centuries out of date.' It is only at this point (about half way through the talk) that Shaw says anything critical at all about Hitler, and the criticism focuses almost entirely on the 'pernicious nonsense' of Hitler's anti-Semitism, which Shaw personalizes into the persecution of his friend Albert Einstein (who left Germany after Hitler came to power in 1933 and whose property was seized by the Nazi government the following year): 'We ought to have declared war on Germany the moment Mr Hitler's police stole Einstein's violin.' Shaw concludes the talk by denying that the war is about Democracy (good) against Fascism (bad). Those 'who believe that Fascism is a better system of government than ours, and that what we call democracy is a sham' are 'not altogether wrong.' And there is no point either in appealing to God: 'as most of us believe that God made both Mr Hitler and Lord Halifax [Britain's Foreign Secretary], we must believe that God will see fair.'[31]

In so far as Shaw's talk was intended to convince listeners (at home and abroad, including in the United States) that Britain was engaged in a just and necessary war against an evil adversary, it fell somewhat short of expectations. Nor – as Cooper had pointed out – was Shaw's emphasis on Hitler's anti-Semitism (the full consequences of which had not yet materialized) likely to resonate as much with most listeners as it did with Shaw. In addition, there was the clear risk of the talk being exploited by Germany for propaganda purposes.

Weymouth's well-intentioned efforts to rework the talk to fit more closely with Ministry of Information aspirations lacked conviction. Of the passages quoted above, the BBC deleted only the statement that 'Mr Hitler did not begin this war; we did.' It was too little, too late. At least one member of the Overseas Services Department, Marjorie Wace, believed that the ban on Shaw's talk had been authorized by Churchill (though she conceded that she couldn't be 'absolutely sure' about it).[32] But even that possibility did not convince Weymouth that the matter was entirely closed. He was still trying over a year later – in September 1941 – to get approval for a modified version of the banned talk. 'It seems such a pity,' he wrote to his colleagues, 'that the Empire is not allowed to hear a talk by a man who can write a script like this – and is such a first-class broadcaster.' Ogilvie, however, thought the talk was now 'dated,' and preferred asking Shaw for something entirely new on Russia. 'I will take up again the question of getting permission to approach him anew – but I have no great hope of shifting the Ministerial ban.'[33]

Ogilvie had good reason not to be sanguine about getting Shaw back on the air. R.A. Rendall's ban on the eightieth birthday talk was followed in 1941 by a ministerial ban on a BBC-initiated proposal for a 1942 birthday talk, when Cooper 'positively' declined to agree to the BBC's request.[34] And a few weeks earlier, on 5 June 1941, Tallents had told his colleagues to drop a proposal to ask Shaw to talk on Latin America because it would need 'the personal approval of the Minister,' and it would be 'idle' to seek it – 'at any rate at present.'[35] There was a slight thaw in August 1941 in the ministerial aversion to Shaw when Ogilvie sought and received approval to approach Shaw to participate in a broadcast to Sweden. The idea, Ogilvie explained in his letter to Shaw, was to bring together British winners of the Nobel Prize in a series of messages to the Swedish people to let them know that 'they are not forgotten by civilized people in other parts of the world' and to provide 'a powerful antidote to German *kulturpropaganda*.'[36] Shaw was offered 'between 800 and 900 words' on any subject that 'you consider would interest the people of Sweden.' Ogilvie cautioned, however, that the talk 'would be subject to censorship in respect of any points affecting national security.' Ogilvie's letter was typed, but he added a personal, handwritten note at the end: 'I hope very much that you will be able to accept this invitation.' Shaw returned Ogilvie's letter on 5 September 1941 with his own handwritten note at the foot of it: 'NO. What could we possibly say except the flap-doodle of which everyone is heartily sick? It would bore the Swedes stiff. They would switch off after the first two doses. Dont do it. Anyhow, *I* wont.' The ministry had in any case made it clear to the BBC that approval for Shaw on this occasion 'did not imply sanction for other invitations' to him.'[37]

Ogilvie made his formal request for the ban on Shaw to be lifted in early October 1941,[38] but did not get a response until late November. The news, however, was probably better than Ogilvie had anticipated – Shaw could have 'access to the microphone,' but only for Empire broadcasts (that is, the ban remained in effect for domestic broadcasts).[39] And it would still be necessary to alert the ministry to any BBC proposals for Shaw broadcasts. There were several such proposals in 1942 and 1943 – for a musical talk (on the two hundredth anniversary of the first performance of *Messiah* – but only if Shaw agreed to do 'a serious talk on the subject, not a dissertation on how we might win the war if only Winston Churchill played the fiddle better than Hitler,' the producer said);[40] a talk on Stalin (Wearing 107); an obituary of John Burns, the trade unionist (who died on 24 January 1943); an interview with Leslie Mitchell;[41] a talk on Ibsen (proposed by Eric Blair for the India Service – 'it would obviously be a great scoop,' Blair said);[42] an appearance on the 'Brains Trust' program with Wells, Beerbohm, and Sydney Webb.[43] Shaw turned them all down, either by rejections or by ignoring them. By early 1943 he was clearly getting fed up with being pestered by the BBC; an internal memo at the BBC explained that 'Shaw is rather inclined not to answer letters from the BBC unless they are telegrams signed by the Director General.'[44]

Shaw's opinions were still occasionally to be heard in BBC publications – most notably in a lengthy correspondence in *The Listener* arising from a broadcast by Julian Huxley about Charles Darwin on 28 October 1942[45] – but a combination of government censorship and Shaw's own lack of interest kept the real voice off the air for the duration of the war.

A final aspect – never previously noted – of the 'Unavoidable Subject' affair is worth mentioning. Behind much of the BBC and government anxiety about having Shaw on the air during the war was the possibility first mentioned by R.A. Rendall in his letter to the Australian Broadcasting Commission on 17 April 1940 (above, p. 107), namely, that anything Shaw said might be exploited by 'the German propaganda machine.' During the war most plays from enemy countries were banned in Germany, but two notable exceptions were Shakespeare and Shaw. Propaganda

Minister Joseph Goebbels was personally instructed by Hitler (who was particularly fond of *Caesar and Cleopatra*) to 'protect' Shaw from censorship, and Rainer Schlösser, head of the theatre section of the Propaganda Ministry, stressed the potential of some of Shaw's plays to help the German war effort. It is now known as well that Hitler and Goebbels were fully aware of Shaw's public comments about the threat of war during the 1930s, including those critical of the British government (Symington 173–6). But just how – or even whether – German propaganda radio broadcasts would use Shaw was unknown until the BBC's Director-General decided to investigate. A brief internal BBC memo dated 29 July 1940 is an instruction to provide Ogilvie with a list of 'references to Bernard Shaw on the German wireless' so that he may draw them to 'ministerial attention.' The memo says that Ogilvie 'wants' to do this, not that he has been instructed to do so, so it sounds very much as if this was Ogilvie's initiative. The BBC routinely listened round-the-clock to German (and other international) broadcasts, and provided translated transcriptions for government use. It was a relatively straightforward task for a staff member to go through the transcripts to find any references to Shaw. The list that came back to Ogilvie covered the period May-July 1940 and contained nine references, some in German domestic broadcasts, some in German international broadcasts – to France (in French), South America (in Spanish), England (in English), Brazil (in Portuguese), and Norway (in Norwegian). It is not known whether Ogilvie investigated beyond the basic information that was given him – that is, that Shaw was mentioned in these German broadcasts. But transcripts of the actual broadcasts were (and are) available and show that German propaganda writers did perceive Shaw as useful to the German cause. By quoting and sometimes misquoting, and by taking his words out of context, they made Shaw a friend of Germany and an enemy ('England's Bad Boy No. 1') of British economic imperialism, 'Churchillism' (with its 'crimes and misdeeds'), capitalism (and its betrayal of the working class), and – in particular – Duff Cooper, portrayed (not without some plausibility) as someone determined to gag Shaw. Shaw's banned BBC talk – never broadcast and not published until after the war – would indeed have been welcome grist to the German propaganda mill. (See appendix 3 for full transcriptions of the German broadcasts.)

Wartime Radio Drama

The plays were another matter. Still under the energetic leadership of Val Gielgud, the BBC Radio Drama Department remained committed to regular broadcasting of plays despite difficult wartime conditions. Gielgud had his critics, including the drama critic for *The Listener*, Grace Wyndham Goldie, who took him to task for his ultra-conservative programming during 'Radio Drama Week,' 6–12 October 1940. The wartime situation, Goldie argued, gave the BBC extra responsibilities. 'This, heaven knows,' she wrote in the *Radio Times* (4 October 1940), 'is a moment when we need broadcast drama. With the London theatre wounded,[46] with every kind of theatrical enterprise in desperate straits, with cinemas shut or closing early, it is left to broadcasting to provide that nourishment of the mind and spirit which people do get from fine plays.' Gielgud's selection for 'Radio Drama Week' of plays by Shakespeare (*Hamlet*), D.G. Bridson (*Aaron's Field*), Somerset Maugham (*The Fall of Edward Bernard*), J.M. Barrie (*What Every Woman Knows*), Chekhov (*The Proposal*), P.G. Wodehouse (*The Crime Wave at Blandings*), and Noel Coward (*Cavalcade*) lacked imagination – 'Where are all the new plays that London managements would be staging this winter if London managements were staging anything?' – and why, in any case, have a 'Drama Week'? 'What we want is not one week of mixed and often mediocre drama, but at least one first-rate play with a first-rate cast on a fixed night at a fixed time every week of the winter.' And, Goldie added, 'why not matinées? ... The nightly trek to the shelters makes evening listening difficult for so many.' Another correspondent, a Mr Bourne, was less polite about Gielgud's programming: 'He has missed a grand opportunity to assist the hard-hit dramatist and to keep drama progressive and representative of the times ... No drama, or anything else for that matter, can live on revivals – the lines of last resistance and the funk-holes of the unenterprising' (*RT*, 25 October 1940).

Gielgud was brusque in his response to Mr Bourne – 'I was brought up to believe that argument which employed personal scurrility was probably based on ignorance. Mr Bourne's letter confirms this view' (*RT*, 8 November 1940) – but he was more forthcoming in his response to Grace Wyndham Goldie's criticisms, pointing out (*RT*, 4 October 1940) that the selection of plays for 'Radio Drama Week' was in direct response to listeners' requests, that it is 'impossible ... to conjure original plays out of the air in order to put them on the air,' and that he would welcome a secure and predictable weekly spot for plays – if only the BBC program planners could squeeze all the 'quarts' of requests into 'the pint pots of existing programme time.'

Debates about radio drama continued throughout the war. Grace Wyndham Goldie in particular kept the pressure on Gielgud until she left *The Listener* in January 1942. Her parting shot was a wish that 'the figures of Listener Research will not act as too violent a brake upon radio's advance' (*The Listener*, 1 January 1942).

Gielgud had to balance what the Listener Research Unit told him about listener preferences with his own sense of the appropriate mix of new and established plays, and he had to worry as well about production quality, no easy matter when so many actors, directors, and technicians were serving in the armed forces. One of Gielgud's great successes of the war years was, in fact, the creation of a BBC Repertory Company, established at the beginning of the war, and four years later numbering forty-nine actors (*RT*, 17 September 1943). Almost twice that number had gone through the ranks of the company in the four years, and of the original thirty members only five remained. Still, there was a body of experience and expertise that, along with Gielgud's experience (he had been Head of BBC Drama since 1929), gave a degree of continuity from which all productions benefited. And as the war drew to a close Gielgud could take some satisfaction in learning (again from the Listener Research Unit) that the radio play had now become – in BBC parlance – a 'majority programme item' (*RT*, 19 February 1945).

Shaw's War Plays

Given the prevalence of war during Shaw's lifetime it is not surprising that the subject of war should feature so prominently in his work. It was clear from the experience of 'The Unavoidable Subject' that the government was not going to allow Shaw to speak freely on radio about *the* war, but in one way or another, directly or indirectly, substantively or peripherally, the subject features in several of Shaw's plays. The BBC was aware, of course, that it was subject to government restrictions on its programming, but Ogilvie and his colleagues did not take the position that consultation was necessary about plays that raised moral or philosophical questions about war in general. Indeed, as we have seen in the case of *Too True to be Good*, Shaw was sometimes more cautious than the BBC itself in this regard (see above, p. 106).

Soon after the start of the war, BBC radio broadcast some excerpts from *Saint Joan*, but only from the Trial Scene, a scene that draws attention more to Joan's plight as an individual than to the political and military causes she espouses (see above, p. 86). The Trial Scene was broadcast again on 15 September 1940, but by the following summer a full production of *Saint Joan* – the BBC's first since 1929 – was being considered, with Constance Cummings as Joan. Cummings had played Joan in an Old Vic production at the Buxton Festival in 1939. Shaw didn't know her work, but he had met her and discussed Joan with her when she visited him in his Whitehall flat before the Buxton performance.[47] Shaw still asked the BBC, however, if she had 'the right voice' for Joan.[48] There is no record of a response from the BBC, but after Shaw had listened to the broadcast on 15 September (in two parts, 7:10–9:00 and 9:20–10:40 pm), he wrote (24 September 1941) to Gielgud, who had directed the play, to express his satisfaction with Cummings's 'strength and great intelligence.' Shaw thought she lacked 'music and artistry in the touches of dialect,' but 'if she has a good ear she will get that and go far.' He had some other criticisms ('The pages must not be played by girls. It turns the performance into a XIX century opera bouffe'), but he was well enough pleased to offer to 'adapt it a little to an audience which cannot see it' if the BBC decided to broadcast the play again.[49]

Saint Joan was, as the BBC put it, 'the biggest thing the Drama Department have attempted since the [outbreak of] war' (RT, 29 August 1941). In an essay about the play commissioned by the BBC to accompany the broadcast, critic Desmond MacCarthy argued that this 'play of many and splendid merits' is, above all, 'a religious play,' in which Shaw makes the point that 'God does not speak through tradition or organised religions, but through the hearts and minds of individuals' (RT, 12 September 1941). There is nothing in MacCarthy's essay that makes any connection between Saint Joan and war, and certainly nothing to suggest that there might be any connection between Joan's war in Europe and the European war that listeners were hearing about every day on the BBC. But how could listeners not make the connection? That was certainly the view of Grace Wyndham Goldie, who recognized and understood the connection. In one sense, she agreed with MacCarthy, at least to the extent that Saint Joan 'is not about war.' 'Yet,' she continued in her review of the production in The Listener (25 September 1941), 'since Joan's inspiration is connected with war and the expulsion of invaders from France,[50] here we have a play of profound vision with war as part of its vision.' This made Saint Joan, said Goldie, 'more relevant and more desperately necessary' than it ever was in times of peace, in comparison to which 'the Lears and Hamlets and Macbeths, being concerned with human experience which transcends war, appear too remote from the present danger.' The BBC made the connection more explicit when it selected Saint Joan for discussion in a series called 'The Living Image,' the first part of which, broadcast on 31 October 1942, dealt with 'The Image of War.' Extracts from the play were read by Lucie Mannheim and Marius Goring.[51]

The BBC also considered *Saint Joan* to be suitable for wartime schools broadcasts, and Shaw went out of his way to be helpful with them. Some extracts from scenes 1 and 3 were broadcast for schools on 10 February 1942, for which Shaw revised the BBC script for introductory and linking passages sent for his approval.[52] He also listened again and thought the narrator 'quite successful' in speaking the passages – as was Joan, 'who got every word across in its full meaning.'[53] The concluding section of the narrator's commentary refers to the statue of Joan in Winchester Cathedral, 'and though she has no altar there you may pray to her if you will.' When Mary Somerville, Director of School Broadcasting, subsequently wrote to Shaw to seek approval for a repeat of the broadcast, she reminded him that this line caused 'a spot of bother' among 'our "no popery" friends,' who thought that Shaw was 'encouraging children to pray to saints.' 'Would you like to re-phrase the passage?' Somerville wondered (by deleting 'you may pray to her if you will'). 'Go ahead,' Shaw replied, clearly in one of his more benign moods.[54]

Though nothing came of plans for a production of Shaw's first war play, *Arms and the Man*, towards the end of the war,[55] excerpts from it were repeatedly on the air during the war. As we have seen (above, p. 104), Shaw was upset by the BBC's plan to cut parts of act 1 for a broadcast on 14 March 1940, but in the event the full text of the opening act was broadcast, with all of its barbs against romanticizing war. The Midland Region of the BBC got away with broadcasting a five-minute excerpt from the same act of *Arms and the Man* on 26 July 1941 simply by neglecting to ask Shaw's permission. Shaw received an apologetic letter asking for 'retrospective authority for the broadcast'; he agreed ('No harm done'), but charged a fairly steep 5 guineas.[56] Another short excerpt from *Arms and the Man* was broadcast on 4 February 1944 in a talk by critic John Palmer on 'Life and the Theatre,' for which Shaw did not charge a fee, the excerpt (unspecified) being 'within Mr Palmer's statutory right of fair quotation.'[57] Shaw took this position as well with an overseas broadcast of an excerpt from act 3 on 24 January 1945 in a program called 'British Show Business at War,' with Laurence Olivier and Ralph Richardson.[58]

The wars in *Saint Joan* and *Arms and the Man* have a European setting; the war in *The Devil's Disciple* is the American revolutionary war against Britain. Shaw sets the play in 1777, the year *in which the passions roused by the breaking-off of the American colonies from England ... boiled up to shooting point, the shooting being idealized to the English mind as suppression of rebellion and maintenance of British dominion, and to the American as defence of liberty, resistance to tyranny, and self-sacrifice on the altar of the Rights of Man' (CP* 2:53–4). Broadcasting a play about the United Sates and Britain at war at a time when Britain was in growing need of U.S. support in the war against Germany seems like an aberration, but there was no government intervention when the BBC announced that it would broadcast excerpts from the play on 17 May 1940 (just a few days before the Dunkirk evacuation). Nor did Shaw seem to find it a problem, arguing only with the BBC about the selection of the excerpts. The BBC wanted excerpts from the first two acts, 'with a very short connecting link,' but Shaw insisted on 'the whole first act or none.'[59] He seems to have got his way (as he usually did), including an extra ten minutes for the broadcast. While the *Radio Times* listing (10 May 1940) allows twenty-five minutes (3:35–4:00 pm), the BBC's in-house records show that the program actually ran until 4:10 pm. The BBC's promotion in the *Radio Times* of the broadcast of *The Devil's Disciple* focused on the star, Robert Donat ('Listeners ... will remember him in *The Dark Lady of the Sonnets* a short while ago' [22 April 1938]), who was touring *The Devil's Disciple* in the provinces in an H.M. Tennent company production. The BBC also pointed to the melodramatic nature of the play, but added that it also has 'a true Shavian touch, not only in its substance, but in its conclusion of villainy triumphant.' There is no mention anywhere of war.

Another Shaw play with a war theme and European setting is *The Man of Destiny*, one of the most frequently broadcast of his plays,[60] but its only appearance during the war was in a program called 'Vaudeville of 1944,' featuring 'famous stars of Variety, music, and drama,' one of whom, Esmé Percy, performed one of Napoleon's speeches from *The Man of Destiny* – the one about the English, 'a race apart.' The program was broadcast on 1 April 1944, just a few weeks before the Allied invasion of Europe on 6 June (D-Day), so Napoleon's compliments (albeit, in the context of the play, ironic compliments) about the English would have been more appropriate than at less successful periods of the war. 'Every Englishman,' declares Napoleon, 'is born with a certain miraculous power that makes him master of the world'; the Englishman is 'the great champion of freedom and national independence,' whose 'watchword is always Duty.' Never mind that Napoleon also says that this great champion of freedom 'conquers and annexes half the world, and calls it Colonization,' and that his sense of duty is indistinguishable from self-interest.[61]

The Millionairess, 1942

Next to *Saint Joan*, the most ambitious radio production of a Shaw play during the war years was *The Millionairess*, broadcast in two parts on 28 and 29 June 1942. The idea for the production – the radio premiere of the play – was raised by Val Gielgud in March 1942, when he had also apparently raised with Shaw the possibility of a 'Shaw Festival' on BBC radio. Shaw rejected any notion of production of 'a special group of his plays,' but approved *The Millionairess* project.[62] And he did so with unusual enthusiasm.

Shaw wrote *The Millionairess* in 1934–5 with Edith Evans in mind as Epifania for a premiere at the Malvern Festival, but she turned down the part, and the Malvern production was delayed until 1937, when Elspeth March played Epifania. In the meantime *The Millionairess* had opened in Vienna (in German) in January 1936 and in Melbourne (in English) in March 1936. The first production in England was in the unlikely confines of the seaside resort of Bexhill in Sussex in November 1936. Edith Evans finally agreed to play the part in a provincial tour in anticipation of a West End opening in September 1940, but the production was cancelled because of the Blitz. It was June 1952 before *The Millionairess* got to the West End (at the New Theatre, with Katharine Hepburn as Epifania).[63] But it was Edith Evans who was in the role for the radio premiere.

Shaw had joked with Malvern Festival director Barry Jackson in September 1936 that he was banking on *The Millionairess* 'to make me a millionaire' (Conolly, *Bernard Shaw and Barry Jackson* 92), but all he asked from the BBC was 35 guineas,[64] and he worked unusually hard for his fee. Through the *Radio Times* (19 June 1942), the BBC informed listeners that 'Shaw has taken a great interest in the broadcast, and has not only written a new narrative but has prepared a special radio script complete to the last sound-effect.' Shaw had written narratives for previous broadcasts of his work (e.g., for a television production of *Geneva* in April 1939), but he had never prepared a full broadcast script. He had also agreed that the production could be split between two successive evening broadcasts, the first (28 June) running from 9:30 to 10:40, the second (29 June) from 9:20 to 10:10 (for a total broadcast time of two hours). The script for the broadcast[65] (confirmed by the program listings in the

Radio Times) shows that the break between the two parts was at the end of act 2, the final speech of which (by the Doctor, after Epifania's exit) Shaw slightly rewrote (with obvious allusions to Sergius's final 'What a man!' line in *Arms and the Man*) as 'What a woman! There is no might and no majesty save in Thee, O Allah; but, oh! most Great and Glorious, is this another of Thy terrible jokes?' The speech is followed by Shaw's directions for sound effects to make the transition to Part II: *'Turkish music, accented with big drum and cymbals, to indicate change of scene, suddenly dropping to a few slow sinister chords in the bass to prepare for the atmosphere of the sweaters' cellar.'*

If Shaw's script for the production shows keen sensitivity for creating the right mood and atmosphere for listeners, his script for the Narrator[66] in the production shows equal concern for providing listeners with adequate information about the setting and characters of the play. Whereas the stage direction in the published text of the play for Epifania's entrance into Sagamore's office at the beginning of act 1 merely says, *'A tragic looking woman, athletically built and expensively dressed, storms into the room'* (CP 6:883), radio listeners got a little more insight into what Shaw had in mind:

> *The door is thrown open by the solicitor's clerk, who is evidently frightened out of his life. He tries to announce the visitor; but before he can stammer a syllable he is pushed out of the way and the room is stormed rather than entered by a tragic looking lady with a very white face contrasting with a very black dress and lustrous black hair. She is handsome in an athletic way, and very dictatorial; and she comes to the solicitor's table in a sort of whirlwind that sweeps the clerk out of the room and downstairs presumably into the dustbin. The solicitor is not afraid of her: he is amused and keeps his end up valiantly. He rises to receive her.*

And to make sure that listeners to Part II were either reminded of what had happened in Part I (or had missed Part I) Shaw wrote a plot summary for a BBC announcer as well – 'Listeners will remember ...' – before moving on to the Narrator describing the setting at the beginning of Act 3.

During an interview with the *Radio Times* (26 June 1942), Edith Evans showed the interviewer (C. Gordon Glover) her copy of *The Millionairess*, inscribed by Shaw – 'Written with an eye (and heart) to thee, Edith, to thee' – and left Glover, at least, with the impression that of all the Shaw parts she had played 'there is no part in which she more wholeheartedly revelled than that of Epifania.'

For once, then, all boded well for a successful production of a Shaw play by the BBC: active and constructive collaboration between Shaw and the BBC, no tension between director (Barbara Burnham) and playwright, and the actor for whom Shaw wrote the lead role playing it. Shaw's own enthusiasm – even excitement – about the production is evident in a letter he wrote to Edith Evans on 20 April 1942, when he expressed his determination that the production 'must be a big occasion for both of us.' He outlined his plans for the script and the narration, and told Evans that she would be 'splendid,' and that he would listen to the play 'in my slippers at my fireside, without shocking you by the spectacle of a dotard 33 years older than you, whom you can remember when he was young and beautiful' (Forbes 203–4).

But something went badly wrong – at least from Shaw's perspective – and the problem seems to have been in large part Edith Evans herself.

The *Listener*'s drama critic (now Alan Dent) was impressed by the production, but went to great lengths in his review (2 July 1942) to qualify his admiration. The production was, Dent said, 'a triumph,' but it was also 'a trial'; 'a treat,' but 'a severe one.' He thought the play 'long' when he saw it at Malvern in 1937 'without Miss Evans,' and it is still 'long on the radio, even with her.' Dent reminded readers that Shaw had subtitled *The Millionairess* 'A Jonsonian Comedy,' but for Dent 'the play's characters are far more curious than humorous, and the play itself is neither witty nor rich enough to be called Ben-Jonsonian.' It is, on the other hand, Dent continues, 'an 'indisputably, unremittingly, unendingly larkish' play, and the performance of Edith Evans was a 'wonderful romp.' Dent declared that 'both playwright and actress are obviously delighted [and] millions of listeners are no doubt satisfied – and I had better change the subject.'

Dent may have been right about the listeners, and he may have been right about the actress; but he was wrong about the playwright. Shaw listened to Part I on Sunday 28 June, and told Hugh Beaumont (who was interested in the possibility of producing *The Millionairess* in London) two days later that it was 'such a horrible mess' that he 'gave it up for dead.' However, a '1000lb bombshell' (which, unhappily, has not survived) that Shaw sent to the BBC on Monday 29 June made Part II 'quite decent.' Alan Dent thought that Edith Evans was having a 'wonderful romp' in the production. Shaw saw it differently. He told Beaumont that she 'played farce instead of tragedy,' and that she 'slurred all her keywords so carelessly' that obviously 'she has not really caught on to the part' – so much so that Shaw told Beaumont that he was 'not keen on a London production.' *The Millionairess*, he said, 'will not bear underplaying or half playing.'[67]

Shaw didn't spare Edith Evans his wrath, though he distributed the blame more evenly than he had in his letter to Beaumont. Shaw had never directed a radio play, and never would, but the letter he wrote to Evans on 7 July 1942 showed that he wasn't short of ideas on how it should be done. The 'fiasco' of *The Millionairess*, he said, 'was not your fault.' The fault lay with 'the production, or rather the absence of any production.' And then, sounding like Hamlet giving advice to the Players, he explained the problem:

> For broadcasting, the players, being invisible, must be specially careful not to imitate one another, nor to take their speed and pitch from one another, nor to race or rival one another, nor to pick up a cue and return it as a cricketer fields a ball as smartly and quickly as possible, betraying what should be concealed at all costs: that is, that they knew all along what the previous speaker was going to say and were not for a moment in doubt as to what to reply to it. An actor should always be surprised at what is said – delighted, disgusted, alarmed or what not as the case may be, but always a bit surprised, or taken aback enough to make the audience believe that it is unexpected.

The cast for *The Millionairess* 'did all it could to avoid these essentials,' creating a performance that was 'utterly unintelligible, discordant, noisy, until at last Epifania was lost among half a dozen people trying to be more Epifanian than she, and being all mistaken for one another by the distracted listeners. I never heard anything quite so damnable as that first act.'

And then Shaw had some harsh words for Edith Evans herself. He told her that she had played Epifania 'with your farce mannerisms and curiously without the music in your speech that came out so beautifully in your Millamant.'[68] 'I believe you were bored by it,' he said. 'You were certainly not in the least tragic; and Epifania is soulless if she is not tragic.' Moreover, 'you were dreadfully careless about your key words: you slurred all of them and scored some misses in consequence.' Evans may have made Epifania funny, but if she 'is not interesting as well as funny the play is not quite worth listening to except by an audience of political economists.' And Shaw concluded by telling her what he had told Beaumont regarding a West End production – 'We had better chuck it, for some years at any rate' (Forbes 204–5).[69]

On 22 July 1942 the BBC wrote to Shaw to ask his permission to keep a recording of the production of *The Millionairess* in the BBC library of recorded programs 'for possible future use.' 'I object violently,' Shaw replied. 'The broadcast on the first night was not good enough to be recorded and repeated. Put the record into the garbage heap.'[70]

Other Shaw Plays

Shaw's distress over *The Millionairess* did not deter him from approving a broadcast just a few weeks later (28 August 1942) of *The Village Wooing*, with Leslie Banks as 'A' and Ellen Pollock as 'Z.' The BBC promoted it as 'a brilliant trifle' and á 'channel of escape' from current events (*RT*, 14 August 1942), but Alan Dent in *The Listener* (3 September 1942) found Banks's performance dull and Pollock's otherwise 'comparatively lively performance' ruined by arbitrary pronunciation quirks. Shaw – if he heard the broadcast – was silent on its qualities.

He seems to have been silent as well about an earlier broadcast, this one of *Androcles and the Lion* on 23 March 1941, but Grace Wyndham Goldie found it 'the saddest piece of Woolton pie that we have had from the microphone for many weeks' (*The Listener*, 27 March 1941). (Readers would have known that a Woolton pie – named after the wartime Minister of Food, Lord Woolton – was a nourishing but uninspiring vegetable pie.) Peggy Brandon from Aylesbury begged to differ, requesting 'more of Shaw's plays,' please. 'After all, he is our greatest living playwright and a little of his wit is very acceptable nowadays' (*RT*, 11 April 1941). And in the same issue of the *Radio Times* a listener from Newcastle-on-Tyne wondered why the play's epilogue, 'which is appropriate to our own times,' was not included. He probably had in mind Shaw's view (expressed in the epilogue, published in 1916) that 'the most striking aspect of the play at this moment is the terrible topicality given it by the war,' particularly on the subject of religious hypocrisy among Christians. The irony of broadcasting the play on a 'National Day of Prayer' (called by the king and reflected in special BBC programming that day) seems to have been lost on the BBC. A later production of *Androcles* with substantially the same cast and the same director (John Cheatle) was broadcast on 11 January 1942.

The only other full production of a Shaw play during the war was of *Candida* on 16 October 1943, the third on BBC radio. There would have been an earlier production, but Shaw's insistence on casting Phyllis Neilson-Terry as Candida delayed the production by at least two years.

Neilson-Terry, a leading West End actor (who also toured extensively overseas) from the early years of the century, had played Candida at the Malvern Festival in 1939, directed by H.K. Ayliff, with help from Shaw himself. Shaw told the BBC in June 1941 that he would agree to a broadcast production of the play if Neilson-Terry could be cast as Candida, 'with your best heavy man for Morrell.'[71] That didn't work out, so the BBC tried again in May 1943, suggesting that it might be done to mark Shaw's eighty-seventh birthday. Blanche Patch relayed Shaw's view that 'he has always loathed celebrations of his birthday,'[72] but agreement was eventually reached for a production later that year, with Neilson-Terry, as Shaw wished, playing Candida, and the experienced American-born actor Godfrey Tearle as Morrell. Neilson-Terry had by then given up acting for war work with the Ministry of Information, speaking around the country about 'Laundry, and Book Drives, and British Restaurants, and Vegeculture, and Making Do and Mending' (*RT*, 8 October 1943) – intriguing preparation for one of the most domestic of Shaw's heroines.

In promoting *Candida*, the BBC noted the 'rarity' of a broadcast of a Shaw play (*RT*, 1 October 1943), but in truth Shaw plays and excerpts from his plays could fairly be described as a regular feature of BBC wartime programming. Weekly series such as 'Everybody's Scrapbook' ('An album of things worth remembering in these present days'), 'Curtain Up!' (a 1941 series of talks on 'the art of drama'), and 'The Living Image' (a 1942 series on 'the relationship between life and art') frequently included performed scenes from plays such as *In Good King Charles's Golden Days*, *Back to Methuselah*, *The Doctor's Dilemma*, *Getting Married*, *You Never Can Tell*, and *Man and Superman* (see appendix 1 for details).

Adventures of the Black Girl, 1941, 1944

Dramatic adaptations of Shaw's prose works were also broadcast during the war, the most notable being his 1932 narrative *The Adventures of the Black Girl in Her Search for God*. This was first adapted for broadcast on 3 March 1941 in a version by Hugh Stewart, with Fay Compton (a white British actor) as the Black Girl under the direction of John Cheatle. For Grace Wyndham Goldie it was a huge success, 'a radio-dramatic masterpiece which was at once more adult, more stimulating, more vivacious and more appealing than anything the microphone has given us for months.' Goldie also drew connections (as she previously had with the September 1941 broadcast of *Saint Joan*) with the war:

when Shaw wrote *Adventures*, she suggested, the 'pre-Nazi' problem was 'how to find a God who will help men to develop their natural taste for goodness,' now the problem is 'how to check men's natural taste for evil once they have discarded the guiding ropes of an accepted religion' (*The Listener*, 13 March 1941).

The BBC seemed to share Goldie's view of the broadcast, and on 22 May 1941 asked Shaw if the broadcast could be repeated. Shaw's reply was a curt 'NO. Ask Val Gielgud why.'[73] Gielgud let it be known to his BBC colleagues that Shaw wanted a 'coloured actress' to play the Black Girl, but when B.H. Alexander asked Shaw directly about this he explained that 'the color of the skin does not matter.' It was again an issue for Shaw of appropriate *voices* for the microphone. 'Some [white] American actresses who are good speakers, and have rich contralto voices, are familiar with the soft speech of the darkies [*sic*]. Also there are real colored dark beauties on the American stage (singers mostly; but all my parts should be sung) if only we could get at them.' Shaw wondered if Paul Robeson might have some suggestions.[74] With or without Robeson's help, Gielgud came up with the idea of casting the black American actor and singer Elisabeth Welch, who had settled in London in the 1930s (and had co-starred with Robeson in the 1936 British film *Song of Freedom*). Elisabeth Welch, however, meant nothing to Shaw; 'I am too far out of date,' he told Alexander. 'Gielgud must use his artistic judgment. If the woman has a sharp ultra-English voice and accent, and barks all through like an Old Bailey barrister cross-examining God, the effect will be horrible and blasphemous. If she has a softly rich warm *lovable* voice and the slightest possible negro lisp, the broadcast will have a success of the right sort.'[75]

But – for reasons unknown – plans fell through for another 1941 production of *Black Girl*, and it was not until April 1944 that the idea was revived, with Elisabeth Welch still the choice for the Black Girl. After Shaw had vetted the script and admonished the BBC not to 'tomfool with a Stravinsky orchestra' for the music – 'every bar must be primitive African *not* BBC'[76] – the production was scheduled for 19 June 1944 as a 'starred' program, a new designation of programs recommended as 'the personal choice of the BBC' (*RT*, 9 June 1944). Starred or not, the current critic for *The Listener* (Herbert Farjeon) was far less enthusiastic than his predecessor, complaining that Elisabeth Welch's voice, while 'American,' was 'not noticeably coloured.' Other criticism – of a religious, not artistic nature – was less muted. Two days after the broadcast, the BBC's Director of Religious Broadcasting, the Reverend J.W. Welch, alerted his colleagues to 'complaints that are beginning to come in and more may be expected.' Some listeners, Welch reported, 'are shocked when they hear us broadcast what they think is tearing up the Bible page by page, ridiculing the Word of God, God himself, and Christ.' Welch's own view was that 'only in the superficial sense' is *The Black Girl* 'irreligious and blasphemous, and in a deeper sense it is definitely religious,' especially in its 'slaughter of erroneous ideas.' Welch urged the BBC to 'stand by our guns,' which they did – at least until August 1953, when another broadcast of *Black Girl* occasioned vigorous complaints led by the Free Church Federal Council, followed by BBC capitulation not to broadcast the play again.[77]

Shaw Abroad

The BBC expanded its overseas services throughout the war, broadcasting in English and, by the end of 1943, in 45 other languages (Briggs, *BBC* 225). Producers responsible for overseas programming often turned to Shaw. In December 1942, for example, George Orwell, a producer with the Eastern Service from 1941 to 1943, approached Shaw for permission to include an extract from act 1 of *Arms and the Man* in a series on English Literature for university students in Calcutta. Shaw rejected the request, but told Orwell that the scene between Raina and Bluntschli in act 3 would be acceptable. Shaw's preference, however, was for something from his prose works, or 'a piece of oratory such as Caesar's first soliloquy, or the Devil's speech on death from the third act of Man and Superman, or the prologue to Caesar and Cleopatra spoken by the god Ra,' all of which, Shaw told Orwell, are 'deliberately rhetorical,' while *Arms and the Man* 'has no special literary pretensions.'[78] Orwell decided instead to use a four-minute extract from a recording of Sybil Thorndike as Joan in the trial scene of *Saint Joan*, which Shaw approved (for 4 guineas),[79] but when Thorndike's fee turned out to be 'prohibitive,' Orwell went back to Shaw's suggestion of the Raina-Bluntschli scene from *Arms and the Man*, broadcast on 22 January 1943.[80]

Full-length productions of Shaw's plays were normally broadcast overseas only if there was a domestic broadcast as well. More typically, there were 'snippets by soloists,' as Shaw once dubbed them, which he thought 'deadly dull.'[81] That was in October 1941, and by February 1943 his aversion to snippets was such that he banned them 'absolutely.' This was after B.H. Alexander had sought permission for a 'programme of excerpts' from his works for the African Service. 'Quite out of the question,' Shaw replied. 'All Africa would write in to demand what you meant by unloading a budget of senseless highbrow rambling on them ... It must be entire plays or lectures or nothing.'[82] And he could be as prickly about cuts to his plays for overseas broadcasts as for domestic broadcasts, once telling B.H. Alexander – apparently in response to a request to cut a play for transmission to Germany – to 'strike me out of possibilities for your German service, or any other service that mutilates works of art to fit your Procrustean clock.'[83]

For overseas broadcasts, economic and cultural issues came into play as well. Shaw didn't much like the idea of a two-part 2000-word summary of *Everybody's Political What's What?* on the Chinese Service in October 1944 because 'it may stop the sales of my book in China.'[84] And he positively forbad the broadcast of an Arabic translation of his 1913 playlet *Beauty's Duty*, which concerns the impending separation of a conservative husband and a sexually freethinking wife. In its wisdom, the BBC had decided that 'programmes for the unsophisticated Arab audience have to be plain and simple,' so 'we thought the best way of ensuring that our listeners grasped the point of the story [sic] would be to write an introduction and conclusion to it.' A 'rough English translation' was sent to Shaw for his approval. That was on 7 December 1943.[85] By early February 1944 Shaw hadn't replied, so the BBC sent a reminder. Shaw's explanation in a postcard he wrote on 12 February 1944 was that he 'must have been speechless with amazement.' 'How anyone with the faintest conception of the difference between Arabia and Bloomsbury could contemplate throwing B's D at the head of a Bedouin passes my understanding. B's D is not good enough even for Bloomsbury, and you may strike it out of your list of broadcasting possibilities once for all.'[86] The BBC remained convinced that *Beauty's Duty* 'would have most admirably beguiled the Bedouins,' but reluctantly agreed to abide by Shaw's eminently sensible interdiction.[87]

7 Television Returns, 1946–1950

Resumption of Television Broadcasting

Plans for the reintroduction of television broadcasting in Britain – suspended on the outbreak of war in 1939 (see above, p. 97) – began well before the end of the war with the establishment in September 1943 of a government committee (chaired by Lord Hankey) mandated to 'prepare plans for the reinstatement and development of the television service after the war' (Paulu 52). Even though the Allies had begun several important military offensives by the autumn of 1943 (including the invasion of Italy), the government decision to pay attention to the future of television when the outcome of the war was by no means certain showed an admirable combination of foresight and optimism. The Hankey committee report – released in December 1944 – made a number of important recommendations, including planning for colour television and for achieving national coverage for television broadcasting as soon as possible. It recommended also that television remain a BBC monopoly, and that there be a big increase in the broadcasting licence fee (from ten shillings to two pounds) to help cover the costs of television development.

Much to the satisfaction of the BBC, the government accepted the recommendations, and by 1 February 1946, less than a year after VE Day, television was back in business, though only with the broadcast of test patterns to get mothballed equipment back in good working order. The BBC was able to announce, however, just a few weeks later (*RT*, 12 April 1946) the resumption of regular television broadcasting, beginning on 7 June with Shaw (*Dark Lady of the Sonnets*) and Mickey Mouse (see below, p. 133). In addition to getting the service back on the air, the BBC also undertook an active promotional campaign for television. A long article in the *Radio Times* ('What is this Television?') on 17 May 1946 celebrated television as a distinctive 'new art form' – it 'isn't cinema, it isn't a peep-show, it isn't a toy' – one that had to be considered the equivalent of a 'feast, not a snack.' It wasn't to be treated trivially. 'You sit down to it. You leave letters unwritten. You forget the income-tax form. If people ring up, you are out – in another world.' Studio productions of plays, the BBC boasted, had 'the deftness and finish of West-End productions,' while a spectator at a live event would need 'the eyes of a hawk, the neck of a giraffe, and the legs of an antelope' to match the speed and versatility of the television cameras. That was the good news; the bad news was that, for now, only those living within a thirty-mile radius of the studios at Alexandra Palace in north London could receive a television signal.

Three weeks later (*RT*, 7 June 1946), Director of Programmes Denis Johnston (Irish playwright and former Director of the Dublin Gate Theatre) continued to whet the appetite of prospective television viewers with a description of what he had in store for television programming: continued outside broadcasts 'at regular intervals,' but also a wide range of studio productions of 'variety, studio sporting items (such as wrestling), cookery and fashion shows, ballet, star instrumentalists, quizzes, talks and maps illustrating the news, dance bands, and gardening demonstrations,' not to mention interviews with 'visiting celebrities' and 'all sorts of other items of interest,' including full-length plays.

And so plans moved forward, until the momentum was temporarily halted by the harsh winter of 1946–7 and resultant fuel shortages that caused a government-ordered suspension of television services from 10 February to 11 March. Gradually reintroduced from the middle of March (*Fanny's First Play* was one of the first productions), television continued to attract viewers, prompted by BBC promotional efforts, but still hampered by the limited range of the Alexandra Palace transmitters and, according to Val Gielgud, an attitude among senior management that regarded television as 'the Cinderella of the BBC' – it was 'thrust away out of sight ... neglected ... starved' (Gielgud, *Years in a Mirror* 127). In an article in the *Radio Times* on 3 June 1949 Sir William Haley, who had succeeded Robert Foot as Director-General of the BBC in 1944, predicted that about 200,000 television licences would have been issued by the end of 1949, a long way from the twelve million radio licences anticipated by then. But in the same article Haley announced that the government had approved the construction of a new television transmitter for the Birmingham area, which would bring television within reach of several million additional homes. The new transmitter went into service on 17 December 1949, and was hailed by the BBC as a major step in the plan to bring televison service to some 80 per cent of the population of Great Britain by the end of 1954 (*RT*, 9 December 1949). The BBC reported in September 1950 that the number of television licences issued had passed the half-million mark, representing over a million potential viewers for any given program. The number was not quite that high on 21 March 1950, when *The Man of Destiny* was televised – the last Shaw play to be televised during Shaw's lifetime – but the audience (in the hundreds of thousands) was almost certainly the largest single audience at that time ever to have seen a Shaw play – a far cry from the small audience that gathered in the Royalty Theatre (capacity about 650) in London on 9 December 1892 to see *Widowers' Houses*, Shaw's first play.

'I will have no television and no more broadcasting'

Shaw's fascination with television – as evidenced by his visit to Alexandra Palace in July 1937 to watch the broadcast of *How He Lied to Her Husband* (see above, p. 92) – was not sufficient to convince him to buy a television set (he could have got a good one, with a 10" x 8" screen, for about £60), and although he authorized television productions of a dozen or so of his plays (none of which he saw) between the resumption of television service in February 1946 and his death in November 1950, he remained sceptical about the value of television to playwrights and the theatre. He had two major concerns. One – already referred to in chapter 5 (p. 90) – was that as the quality of televison improved and as living rooms became more comfortable, theatregoers would stay at home to watch plays rather than 'pay guineas for theatre stalls and taxis,' thereby killing the box office 'from which I get my living.' He made that point on 5 May 1950 in a letter to Val Gielgud, and had said much the same thing a few days earlier in a note on 27 April 1950 to one of Gielgud's BBC colleagues when rejecting a request for permission to televise *Major Barbara*: 'Television would destroy ordinary theatrical business, and should be limited to plays theatrically dead.' His own plays, he not surprisingly insisted, 'are alive and still growing.'[1] Shaw's other concern about television productions – a familiar Shavian refrain – was that the BBC simply wasn't up to the job of doing justice to his plays. That was his concern about the proposed television production of *Major Barbara*, which he believed the BBC would cut and 'undercast' (even though they were proposing Wendy Hiller or Phyllis Calvert to play Barbara).[2] And when in May 1949 the BBC asked Shaw if he would authorize a television production of *The Devil's Disciple*, he initially flatly rejected the idea because the previous December's radio production of the play (a repeat of the 21 January 1947 broadcast, see below, p. 136) had so upset him. 'I will have no television and no more broadcasting,' he declared, until the BBC can show that they 'get the idea' of how to do his plays.[3] That outburst prompted a response from the Head of Television Drama, Robert MacDermot, who argued that the radio production of *The Devil's Disciple* was no indicator of what could be achieved on television. Radio and television, MacDermot said, 'are as different as chalk and cheese – or Shaw and Shakespeare.' MacDermot wanted to do the play on Shaw's birthday (26 July) and promised that 'the best available stage actors' would be used for the production. MacDermot even offered to instal a television set in Shaw's home 'for the occasion,' if only Shaw would give the BBC 'the chance of proving that we *have* got the idea.' Shaw returned the letter to MacDermot (through the Society of Authors) with a large NO against the offer of a television set, but with instructions that the play be licensed for the broadcast.[4] But if MacDermot thought he had got Shaw onside as far as television was concerned, he was wrong. Only a few weeks before his death Shaw was laying down firm conditions again about not allowing any cuts to his plays 'to suit [the BBC's] timetables.' And that, he made clear, applied to television as well as radio.[5]

Televised Plays, 1946–1950

But Shaw, ever the pragmatist, knew full well the value of television for spreading the Shavian creed. He welcomed film and television crews to his home at Ayot on 24 July 1946 to record his ninetieth birthday greetings to the world, and, judging by his highly theatrical and jovial performance before the camera, he thoroughly enjoyed himself. It was also a self-deprecating performance in which he introduced himself as 'an old man who was once a famous playwright,' but now 'only an old dotard.' That didn't stop him giving advice, however, on how to be 'prosperous and happy' – become a 'shopkeeper or a stockbroker,' or marry one, he said. His final words, though, had a ring of sincerity about them: 'the way to have a happy life is to be too busy doing what you like all the time, having no time left to you to consider whether you are happy or not ...' The film was shown on BBC television on his birthday (26 July) and the sound tape was broadcast on British and

American radio.[6] And despite his reservations about the capabilities of the BBC to do credit to his plays, Shaw was frequently cooperative and accommodating when specific proposals were put to him.

The first post-war television production of a Shaw play was of *The Dark Lady of the Sonnets* on 7 June 1946, the first day of the resumption of television broadcasting after the war. The production was announced by the BBC in the *Radio Times* on 26 April (with a photograph of rehearsals for a 'test performance' of television), but it had to share the opening ninety-minute program with a range of other performances, including the Mickey Mouse film, a Canadian comedian (Jackie Hunter), a pianist ('Kay on the keys'), an impressionist (Beryl Orde), and ballet dancer Margot Fonteyn. For his next televised play, however, Shaw had the full evening's programming to himself. But the play was *Saint Joan*, the most ambitious television production of a play yet essayed by the BBC, and one evening wasn't enough. The play was split into two parts, with scenes 1–4 showing on Sunday 23 June 1946, scenes 5 and 6 and the Epilogue showing the following Sunday evening, 30 June. The production was brought into the Alexandra Palace studios from the King's Theatre, Hammersmith, starring Ann Casson (daughter of Sybil Thorndike, the first English Joan) as Joan.[7] Maurice Gorham, Controller of BBC Televison, judged the production 'brilliant' (Gorham 224).

Saint Joan was followed on 20 July (repeated on 27 September) by the less challenging (and much less expensive) *Village Wooing*, with Michael Golden and Philippa Hiatt. A Shaw play was then on television each of the next three months: *Candida* on 6 October (repeated on 11 October), *Androcles and the Lion* on 3 November (repeated 5 November), and *Arms and the Man* on 22 December (repeated 24 December). The pace slowed down in 1947, with only *The Man of Destiny* on 16 January and an abbreviated *Fanny's First Play* on 16 March. *Fanny* was produced without the framing Induction and Epilogue on the grounds, as explained by the director, Stephen Harrison, that 'Shaw's lampooning of the critics,' while 'topical' when the play premiered in 1911, would no longer be 'amusing' in 1947 (*RT*, 14 March 1947). Shaw seems not to have objected to this reasoning.

Early in 1948 (*RT*, 9 January), the BBC announced 'an important event' – a television production of *Pygmalion* (the first), with 'film star' Margaret Lockwood as Eliza. After studying at the Royal Academy of Dramatic Art (RADA) in London, where she may well have encountered Shaw, who served as a member of its Governing Council from 1911 to 1941, Lockwood acted in London in the 1930s before turning to films, soon becoming famous acting alongside Michael Redgrave and

Rex Harrison. Eliza was her first BBC acting role, and the BBC gave her star billing. A front-page photograph of her being fitted for 'the bedraggled costume of the sluttish flower girl' appeared in the *Radio Times* on 6 February 1948, while an article in the same issue stressed that viewers would get *Pygmalion*, 'in its entirety and exactly as it was in the original stage version.' It would also be the longest television production (still live, of course) ever attempted by the BBC. Lockwood herself confessed to being nervous about learning such a big part – 'I have been in films for so long, having to remember bits at a time, that I've almost forgotten the art of memorising long speeches.' Another article (by critic Ivor Brown) in the same issue of the *Radio Times* (and with another picture of Lockwood, this time trying on an elegant gown) gave a brief history and some analysis of the play (a 'conflict between the person and the social machine, the individual and the organisation'). Following two performances on 8 and 10 February 1948 (two-and-a-half hours, with one intermission), the BBC claimed to have received 'many letters' of appreciation, some of which were published in the *Radio Times* on 27 February, including one from a Mrs Shern in Hertfordshire, who had invited seven friends to watch the play, all now 'determined to instal television sets at the earliest possible moment.' And an enthusiastic F.C. Poulett ('a viewer since 1938') from Harrow declared that *Pygmalion* 'excelled anything previously broadcast.' Not to let such praise fade away too quickly, the BBC published yet another photograph (*The Listener*, 4 March 1948), but this time with Margaret Lockwood sharing the set with fellow actors Ralph Michael (Higgins), Arthur Wontner (Pickering), and Beatrice Varley (Mrs Pearce).

Shaw did not see the *Pygmalion* television production, but he was becoming increasingly aware of the vast potential of the medium, especially after another famous actor – Gertrude Lawrence – had alerted him to the possibility of an international television broadcast of *Pygmalion*. Nothing came of the idea, but it caused Shaw to reflect on the 'fabulous' fees that a playwright could charge, with 'audiences of many millions paying nothing at the doors, and next to nothing for their licenses and receivers.' 'Has anything been done' about this, he wondered in a letter to the Society of Authors?[8] The answer was no to that particular question, but the Society assured Shaw that it was 'closely in touch with recent televison developments,' and that there had been 'discussions on the subject with the BBC and with Equity.'[9]

Which was just as well, because buoyed by the success of *Pygmalion*, the BBC was on the lookout for other big names for Shaw plays. Margaret

Leighton – Raina in a television production of *Arms and the Man* (20 and 24 June 1948) – certainly did not yet have the star appeal of Margaret Lockwood, but film stardom wasn't far in the future for her, and she had already attracted attention as Raina to Laurence Olivier's Sergius and Ralph Richardson's Bluntschli with the Old Vic Company at the New Theatre in London in 1944–5. (She also happened to be married to Max Reinhardt, who was to become a major publisher of Shaw's letters and plays.) This new BBC production of *Arms and the Man* was directed by Harold Clayton, who elicited from Margaret Leighton a performance that, according to *The Listener* (1 July 1948), had 'greatly increased in subtlety and delicacy of effect' since her appearance at the New.

Like Margaret Lockwood and Margaret Leighton, Ellen Pollock appeared in several films (from 1928 through to the early 1990s), but she never achieved their fame. Pollock was, however, an accomplished stage actor who had toured the United States, Australia, and South Africa, and had extensive experience in Shaw, including producing a Shaw season at the Lyric, Hammersmith, in 1944. She had also appeared (as Catherine) with Margaret Leighton in *Arms and the Man* ('an outstanding performance,' said the *Radio Times* on 6 August 1948), and was now cast (with Walter Hudd, also an experienced stage and film actor) in the BBC's second televison production of *Village Wooing* on 10 August 1948. The production pleased one viewer enough to prompt the comment, 'What's the difference whether we win an Olympic title or not – we've still got Shaw – brilliant, witty, amusing' (*RT*, 3 September 1948).[10]

The 1948 Shaw televison productions were rounded out by an afternoon performance of *Androcles and the Lion* on 10 October by the Glyndebourne Children's Theatre Company and excerpts from *Heartbreak House*, in a program called 'Sigh no More, Ladies' on 19 October.

Things did not get off to a good start in 1949, when Norman Collins, new Controller of BBC Television, wrote to Shaw – undoubtedly with the best of intentions – to invite him to submit a new play for a proposed television 'Festival of New Plays.' A new Shaw play, Collins said, 'would give real importance' to the event. 'Is it possible that you would be ready to consider either writing such a play or if there is any play which you have which has not been presented, making it available for this purpose?' Perhaps it was Collins's tortuous prose that irritated Shaw, perhaps it was his insensitivity to Shaw's age and reputation. Whatever it was, Collins got a caustic response. 'Say that there are about 50 plays of mine that have not been televised,'[11] Shaw wrote. 'I can only treat a request for a new one as evidence that the applicant lists me as a recent beginner. This is a mistake. I am in my 93rd year, and am fairly well known.' That was the end of that discussion. It was followed in May by another prickly exchange. For this one, the BBC kept Collins behind the scenes, replacing him in the first instance with R.G. Walford, Head of Copyright.

The issue was simple enough. The BBC wanted to recognize Shaw's ninety-third birthday with the television premiere of *The Devil's Disciple*. The problem was that Shaw remembered the radio production of the play the previous December, which – he told Walford – was so bad that he wanted the recording destroyed. In the meantime there would be no television production of the play. So Walford gave way to Robert MacDermot, Head of Television Drama, whose plea to Shaw (described above, p. 132) was successful, and *The Devil's Disciple* duly appeared on television on 26 July 1949.

Two more Shaw television premieres were produced in 1949: *Widowers' Houses* (6 and 10 November) and *Buoyant Billions* (14 November). *Widowers' Houses* was the BBC's own production, but *Buoyant Billions* – on Shaw's insistence – was the production ('same cast and as far as possible same scenery,' said Shaw)[12] that had only just closed (12 November) at the Princes Theatre, where it had opened (10 October) following its English premiere at the Malvern Festival on 13 August 1949. Given Shaw's sense that a television production was likely to damage, if not destroy, the theatrical life of a play, it is surprising that he allowed the televising of *Buoyant Billions* after only one West End run. And the BBC's own promotional piece in the *Radio Times* (by Lionel Hale) on 11 November 1949 gave mixed messages. It's a play, said Hale, 'about nothing and about everything,' but there is 'talk, talk, talk – about life and death and the hereafter and politics and economics and money and the present chaos of the world.' Hale also quoted Alan Dent from the *News Chronicle*, who described the play as 'footling, brilliant, and wise.' After he had seen the television version, Hale told *Radio Times* readers (25 November) that he had found the play 'often infuriatingly trivial,' but he conceded that 'the sheer guile of the old maestro's tongue kept the screen continuously alive.'

There was just one television production of a Shaw play during the last year of his life. It was *The Man of Destiny* (21 and 27 March 1950), one of the most frequently broadcast of his plays (five previous productions on radio, two on television). Concerned about quality to the last, Shaw gave permission for the new production on condition that 'two stars of the very first rank play Napoleon and the Strange Lady' –

and 'are approved by me.'[13] In the event, Napoleon was played by Hugh Burden, who had had a steady but unspectacular West End career and no Shaw or broadcasting experience, while the Strange Lady was played by Valerie Hobson, who might be said to have achieved 'star' status (and certainly fame) in films such as *Great Expectations* (1946), *Kind Hearts and Coronets* (1949), and *The Rocking Horse Winner* (1949), but who had appeared in only a handful of West End plays, none by Shaw. It was a strange coupling, one that didn't impress *The Listener*'s critic, who found it all 'indifferent stuff.' Valerie Hobson 'fluttered pleasantly,' while Hugh Burden – apparently an actor of modest physical stature – 'wasted some of his few inches on a Napoleonic stoop.' There were some compensations, including Burden's occasional delivery 'with conviction and attack,' but nothing could conceal 'the melodramatic absurdity of the plot' (*The Listener*, 6 April 1950). If there were any positive viewer reactions they were not recorded in either the *Radio Times* or *The Listener*.

The production of *The Man of Destiny* did not mark the end of Shaw's deliberations with the BBC about televising his plays. In the spring of 1950 he rejected requests for a production of *Major Barbara* (see above, p. 131), despite a strong personal appeal from Val Gielgud – 'In asking you to reconsider your decision I am sure I am justified to the extent that the other plays of yours which have been televised have been outstandingly popular with the audience, and have not, I think, done their producers discredit'[14] – and as late as mid-August 1950, just three weeks before the fall in his garden that led to his death on 2 November, he wrote to Cecil McGivern, Head of Television Programmes, rejecting the proposed casting for a new television production of *Saint Joan*.[15]

Of the seventeen Shaw plays (or extracts) that were televised by the BBC during Shaw's lifetime Shaw saw only one – the first, *How He Lied to Her Husband*, in 1937. But despite his grumbles and reservations about the medium, it served him well in the years between the end of the war and his death in taking accomplished productions of his plays into the homes of hundreds of thousands of viewers, many of whom would otherwise never have seen a Shaw play. Meanwhile, aided in 1946 by the new Labour government's extension of its charter (and its monopoly) for another five years, the BBC had embarked on an ambitious restructuring of its radio services that would also serve Shaw well.

8 Radio Finale, 1945–1950

Between a broadcast on 19 June 1944 of *The Adventures of the Black Girl in Her Search for God* and a schools broadcast of excerpts from *Caesar and Cleopatra* on 6 July 1945 there was a profound Shavian silence on BBC radio – no plays of his, no talks by him, and no talks about him. There had never been such a Shawless period in the whole history of the BBC. And then there was another hiatus of almost six months before the next Shaw broadcast on 16 December 1945 – a sound excerpt from the film version of *Caesar and Cleopatra*.[1]

The Shawlessness coincided with the beginning of a period of uncertainty within the BBC about the future of radio drama. Val Gielgud, still the key drama figure within the BBC, was beset with misgivings. On the one hand, and somewhat paradoxically, he believed that the austere circumstances of wartime radio production had been beneficial in that they had forced producers and directors to focus on the plays themselves, rather than being distracted by 'the dangerous fascination of merely mechanical means.' Acting, too, had improved during the war, he believed, to the point where it might now be said that radio acting had become 'an acknowledged professional craft' and had reached 'a new high level of microphone performance.' Moreover, with limited public entertainment options during the war, radio drama had also increased in popularity, achieving the status, in some people's minds at least, of Britain's de facto 'national theatre' (Gielgud, 'Policy and Problems' 19–21). But what, Gielgud and others wondered, would be the effect of *televison* on radio drama? Would people still be interested in merely *listening* to a play in their living room if they had the option of experiencing a play in its more natural medium – sound *and* vision? In the early years of television after the war Gielgud was frustrated by what he saw as the BBC's neglect of television – 'not enough resources, inadequate technical facilities, lack of rehearsal time' – but it still seemed to him that in the long run 'the seeds of death for the play broadcast in sound were inevitably sown' by television and that the radio play would have to contemplate 'fighting a rear-guard action, depressed by the knowledge that in the long run its defeat must be assured' (Gielgud, 'Drama in Television and Sound' 200–3).

Gielgud was writing about what he called 'a crisis in development' in drama broadcasting in 1950, by which time there was plenty of evidence to show that whatever the nature of the crisis Shaw had not suffered from it. The period of neglect in 1944–5 seems not to have been a matter of BBC policy, and in any event there was soon to be more than adequate compensation for the silence. Two crucial factors were involved in the Shaw resurgence – his ninetieth birthday on 26 July 1946 and the post-war restructuring of BBC Radio into three distinct programs: Light (for 'light' entertainment), Home (a middlebrow mix of news, talks, music, features, and drama), and Third (a highbrow mix of classical music, lectures, and drama).

Birthday Celebrations, 1946

Having told William Maxwell that July 26 'has not the smallest importance beyond that of any other day in the year,' and that he would 'spend the day as usual in solitary work and meditation,'[2] Shaw actually had a very busy ninetieth birthday in London. He visited an exhibition of his work mounted by the National Book League, became an Honorary Freeman of the City of Dublin at a ceremony in his Whitehall flat, and visited the BBC studios to listen to a recording of the birthday speech that he had made at Ayot St Lawrence on 24 July, telling BBC engineers in London, according to a report in the *New York Times* (27 July), that they had 'ruined' his voice. Nonetheless, that was the recording broadcast on British radio and television on his birthday (and also in the United States via shortwave on the NBC network).[3] Shaw returned to Ayot on the 26th (still grumbling, apparently, about the recording [*NYT*, 27 July]), and almost certainly listened to the radio that evening. He featured prominently on both the Home Service and the Light Programme. It is unclear at what time the birthday speech itself was broadcast since it is not included in the *Radio Times* listings, but Blanche Patch, on holiday in Cheltenham, listened to it in her hotel that evening, reporting to Shaw that 'if the "Wireless" here was a better instrument, I should say that it came over very well.'[4] Apart from his birthday speech (which he may not have wanted to hear again), Shaw could have listened to Eric Portman and Jeanne de Casalis in a Light Programme production of *The Man of Destiny* from 8:10 to 9:15 pm, and then quickly switched to the Home Service to hear a 'birthday tribute' from playwright Denis Johnston. In the spirit of a fellow Dubliner who, like Shaw, has 'an ear trained to recognise blarney,' Johnston – no doubt much to Shaw's relief – eschewed 'sycophantic praise,' but hailed Shaw for his courage, 'the courage that speaks the inopportune truth at the awkward moment.' We need Shaw, Johnston said, 'to remind us that in the long run it's worthwhile to recognise the truth even if it's inconvenient and some rascal may use it against us.'

Johnston's tribute was published in *The Listener* (1 August 1946), the previous week's issue of which (25 July) had carried an editorial tribute to Shaw by way of preparation for the birthday broadcasts. While respectfully conceding that 'the time for assessing Shaw's place in life and letters is happily not yet,' the editorial nonetheless hazarded (in the purplest of purple prose) that Shaw's 'true place is securely with those writers for the high comic stage who, from Plautus through Molière to Sheridan, have taught the human biped to forget its malodorous nakedness in bursts of antiseptic laughter.'

The birthday programs and articles themselves had been preceded by a gradual renewal of BBC interest in Shaw in the first half of 1946. The afternoon schools broadcast on 29 January included scenes from *Saint Joan*, and Shaw's own voice – an extract from his 'Whither Britain?' talk of 6 February 1934 (see above, pp. 64–5) – was heard on a program broadcast on 24 February to celebrate the BBC's reaching ten million radio licences. This was followed on 20 April by a production of *Candida* (the BBC's fourth radio production of the play), this one again starring Phyllis Neilson-Terry, who had played Candida in the October 1943 production. The *Radio Times* devoted a full-page article to the play in its 12 April issue, in which Beverley Baxter described *Candida*, written when 'the Irishman's genius was at full tide,' as 'Shaw's best play.' 'Never before or since,' according to Baxter, 'has Shaw shown such understanding of a woman.'[5] Philip Hope-Wallace, who commented on the production in *The Listener* (25 April 1946), concurred with Baxter's 'best play' judgment of *Candida*, but also offered (a bit eccentrically) *Arms and the Man* and 'parts of' *Saint Joan* as *Candida*'s equal. Hope-Wallace welcomed from the production the 'rare sense ... of a first-class mind at work,' and wondered ('yet again') why 'we do not hear more Shaw on the air' (a wish amply fulfilled in the coming months). In fact, Hope-Wallace had to wait only a couple of weeks for another Shaw play, albeit a slighter one. *Village Wooing* (like *Candida*, the fourth BBC radio production of the play) was given a Sunday afternoon slot on 5 May, following a Haydn and Brahms concert that came immediately after a gardening program on 'Why Vegetables Are Vital' – a proposition that Shaw would certainly have endorsed. Having urged more Shaw, Philip Hope-Wallace was, fortunately, pleased with the production of *Village Wooing*, a play that 'maddened' him in the theatre ('which somehow seemed the wrong place for it'), but one that 'took to the air like a lark' (*The Listener*, 9 May).

There remained just a radio snippet from *Major Barbara* (a Wendy Hiller recording) on 19 June 1946 (as well as television productions of *The Dark Lady of the Sonnets*, *Saint Joan*, and *Village Wooing*) before the birthday celebration broadcasts and articles described above. And there the mini-Shaw resurgence might have fizzled out (or at least flattened out) had it not been for the major restructuring of BBC radio services that was implemented in 1945 and 1946.

The Third Programme

During the war, BBC radio had operated with two programs: the Home Service for domestic listeners, and the Forces Programme (beginning on 7 January 1940) to entertain British armed forces serving overseas. The Home Service (with regional services supplementing the London base) continued after the war, but the Forces Programme was replaced by a new domestic service called the Light Programme (for 'light' entertainment, beginning on 29 July 1945). Shaw's natural fit was with the Home Service (although the Light Programme sometimes carried extracts from the plays and, occasionally, a complete shorter play). But Shaw's presence on BBC radio received a prodigious boost by the creation of a third radio service, known (somewhat unimaginatively) as the Third Programme (and, since 1967, as Radio 3), which began broadcasting on 29 September 1946, not long after Shaw's ninetieth birthday. Prosaically described by one BBC historian as a service 'for the intellectual' (Paulu 158), the Third Programme prompted a more enthusiastic assessment from writer Edward Sackville-West, who flamboyantly described it as 'the greatest educative and civilising force England has known since the secularisation of the theatre in the sixteenth century' (quoted in Briggs, *BBC* 250). The BBC's own characterization of the Third Programme, as explained by Director-General Sir William Haley, was that it was a kind of 'great works' service that would 'seek every evening to do something that is culturally satisfying and significant,' which meant, he said, 'the great classical repertoire in music and drama, and – so far as they are broadcastable – in literature, and the other arts.' There will also be talks, he promised, 'from the great European thinkers,' everything being directed 'to an audience that is not of one class but that is perceptive and intelligent' (*RT*, 27 September 1946). G.R. Barnes, head of the Third Programme, promised that 'a principal item of considerable length, demanding sustained attention' would be broadcast every night (*RT*, 26 September 1946). That 'principal item' was frequently musical, but plays – Shaw's prominently among them, as we shall see – became a mainstay of the new service as well.

The Third Programme – then and now – had its detractors as well as enthusiasts. While Edward Sackville-West might gush about the civilizing influence of the service, Max Beerbohm (drama critic – Shaw's successor at the *Saturday Review* – caricaturist, and BBC broadcaster – on topics in a lighter vein) thought it a good incentive to emigrate (Briggs, *BBC* 250). And why, one listener wanted to know, was the Third Programme so committed to 'dull, dreary, mournful, never-ending symphonies and ... wailing operatic singers, apparently in pain of the most terrible kind' (*RT*, 11 October 1946). During the 1947 fuel crisis in Britain, the then Minister of Fuel and Power – Emmanuel Shinwell – ordered the temporary suspension of the Third Programme (as well as television services) because its transmitters consumed more power than could be justified: it was ridiculous, Shinwell reasoned, 'when people couldn't cook a bit of haddock, to listen to Beethoven or Bernard Shaw' (Carpenter 53).

Even with transmitters at full power, the Third Programme could initially reach only about half the population of the country (Carpenter 24), but the Third's listeners were serious and dedicated, so that, for example, the broadcast of *Saint Joan* on 29 September 1948 had an audience of around a half million (ibid. 92). After the introduction of the Third Programme, nearly all broadcasts of Shaw plays were aired in that service, though some were still occasionally heard on the Home Service, where the potential audience was considerably larger. The Home's biggest drama audience was its weekly *Saturday Night Theatre* series, which began on 3 April 1943 with about five million listeners, increasing to an average of about seven million by the autumn of 1945 (*RT*, 28 March 1947), which is probably about the number who listened to *Candida* (20 April 1946) and *Androcles and the Lion* (28 December 1946, repeated 30 December) when they were included in the series. The BBC also had a Monday night drama series called *World Theatre* on the Home Service, a series, Val Gielgud explained, that was 'very different' from the Saturday night plays: 'Canvasses will be found wider; characterisation more complex; while subjects will be the ultimate realities of the life of man rather than its more entertaining superficialities' (*RT*, 21 September 1945 – it is interesting that, by Gielgud's reckoning, then, *Candida* and *Androcles*, not to mention other *Saturday Night* plays by writers such as Somerset Maugham and John Galsworthy, were judged to be dealing with 'entertaining superficialities'). *Saint Joan* was heard in the *World Theatre* series on 2 June 1947, but given the wide appeal of Shaw's plays it is not surprising that the BBC found it hard to fit them into the straitjacket of segregated categories of perceived listener interests and capabilities (lowbrow, middlebrow, highbrow). So even the Light Programme got occasional Shavian offerings – *The Man of Destiny* on Shaw's ninetieth birthday, for example (repeated on the Light on 14 July 1947).[6]

The advantage of the Third Programme, however, was that it gave producers and directors the opportunity to focus on major works – music or drama – free from the demands of structured evening schedules (e.g., news broadcasts), and free from the necessity of appealing to large audiences (large, that is, by broadcasting standards). Thus, one of the greatest of Shaw's annoyances with the BBC – the need to cut his plays to make them fit a pre-arranged schedule – was removed (or at least reduced). The BBC could also argue that both the technical and artistic quality of radio productions was on the rise after the war as studio facilities improved and as its resident Repertory Company (numbering about fifty by 1947 [*RT*, 19 September 1947]) gained in experience, its casts being supplemented by guest appearances by leading actors from the professional theatre. Technical advances now also permitted routine and high-quality recorded programs. Most plays were still broadcast live, but the *Saint Joan* production aired on 2 June 1947 had been pre-recorded, mainly to accommodate the schedule of star actor Constance Cummings (*RT*, 21 March 1947).

Man and Superman, 1946

An immediate and impressive example of what could be accomplished on the Third Programme was provided by a production of the full version of *Man and Superman* on 1 October 1946 (repeated on 2 October). The BBC gave virtually the whole of only the third evening of Third Programme transmissions, which initially ran from 6:00 pm to midnight, to the play. On 1 October the performance began at 6:00 pm for acts 1 and 2. There was an intermission at 7:50 (thirty minutes of Bach organ music), and act 3 (*Don Juan in Hell*) ran from 8:20, non-stop, to 10:30. A fifteen-minute cantata for tenor and piano (by Michael Tippett) was aired during the second intermission, and act 4 (a mere forty-five minutes) concluded at 11:30. The evening transmission ended with a thirty-minute performance by the Galimir String Quartet of a lyric suite by Alban Berg. If anyone doubted the Third Programme's commitment to high culture, here was ample evidence to reassure them. (The same pattern was used for the second performance on 2 October, the intermission music consisting this time of a violin and piano recital, Italian madrigals, and Bach's Cantata 211.) And just for good measure, act 3 was aired again on the Third on 7 October and on 14 November 1948 (billed in the *Radio Times*, 12 November 1948, as 'one of the most stimulating torrents of talk in all modern drama'), and acts 1, 2, and 4 on 1 November.

Listeners had been prepared for this longest-ever broadcast play by an enthusiastic introduction to *Man and Superman* ('one of the peaks in Bernard Shaw's dramatic works') in the *Radio Times* (27 September 1946) by Desmond MacCarthy, and by a broadcast talk on Shaw ('Bernard Shaw: Socialist or Rebel?') by W.R. Inge, former Dean of St Paul's and longtime BBC broadcaster, on 30 September. Inge's talk (published in *The Listener*, 10 October 1946) didn't say much about *Man and Superman*, but generally praised the individualistic and humanitarian instincts of this 'born rebel.'

Shaw listened to the broadcast. If he were pleased that the BBC had undertaken such an unprecedented production, he was at pains not to show it when he wrote to the director, Peter Watts, on 3 October 1946. For a start, Shaw wasn't happy with the absence of music in the hell scene; it was needed, he said, 'as a blessed relief to the cackle [i.e., the dialogue!] as well as for its proper effect.' Shaw thought he detected 'a faint moaning' in the broadcast, but judged it to be 'probably an interference from another wave length.'[7] He then gave explicit directions about what should be done with music for the repeat broadcast:

If you cannot add it to the record you must get the theatre orchestra to stand by. At the entrance of the statue the first two chords of the overture to

Don Giovanni must crash out fortissimo in the broadest measure. When the devil appears the opening staves of Le Veau d'Or, the song of Mephistopheles from Gounod's Faust, rattles out. At the end, when Ana cries 'A father for the Superman' the band bursts out with 'unto us a child is born' from Handel's Messiah, and makes a resounding and triumphant finish.

Alas, the BBC seems not to have acted on Shaw's advice, and listeners to the repeat performances of *Man and Superman* did not benefit from the bold musical bravura Shaw wanted. (The cost of having a full orchestra and choir in the studio may have had something to do with it.)

Shaw was also annoyed that all the stage directions for the play were read aloud, 'a damnably stupid' thing to do, he told Watts, 'an intolerable interruption, intrusion, and distraction.' Shaw agreed that 'descriptive passages' at the beginning of each act were necessary, but 'even ... they should be drastically cut.' He recommended that Denis Johnston, the narrator in the production, do the cuts, and then, when reading what was left, Johnston should not 'speak them as if they were part of the play,' but 'interpolate them sharply and authoritatively so as to make it clear that he is an announcer, not a character in the drama.'

Pausing to tell Watts that his 'credit as a producer [director] is bound up with these changes, damn you,' Shaw then launched into two more complaints. It was a mistake, Shaw charged, to do the whole play in one evening. Better to do it as a matinee and evening performance. If that is not possible (and, given, the Third's starting hour of 6:00 pm, it wasn't), then do it on separate days 'with the hell scene all by itself.' And, finally – no doubt to Watts's relief – Watts was enjoined not 'to treat my printed text with blindly superstitious reverence.' The text, Shaw said, 'must always be adapted intelligently to the studio, the screen, the stage, or whatever the physical conditions of performance may be.' Sound direction – though previous BBC directors who had attempted such adaptations knew the risks involved in trying to adapt a Shaw play to Shaw's satisfaction.

There is no record of a response from Watts to Shaw's barrage of complaints, and in any case, since repeat performances were recordings of the first (live) performance, there wasn't much he could do about them – short of scrapping the recording and starting again. (Shaw had not demanded such action, though he had on a previous occasion when he was distressed by a performance – and would again.)[8] It is unlikely that Watts could have got such a large cast together again anyway, nor is it clear that they would have been eager to do another live broadcast. Sebastian Shaw (Tanner), for one, seems to have been exhausted after the live performance. Etienne Amyot, a program planner for the Third Programme, recalls the actor 'breathing heavily towards the end and undoing his shirt' (Carpenter 32).

Tired though he might have been, Sebastian Shaw acquitted himself well, Philip Hope-Wallace thought, 'playing with point and sensibility' (as did, Hope-Wallace said, Grizelda Hervey as Ann Whitfield). Unlike Shaw, Hope-Wallace also appreciated Denis Johnston's stage directions, and generally found the whole production 'a splendidly spoken, exhilarating excursion for the mind.' 'And what a relief,' he said, 'not to have the laughs which in the theatre splinter up this crystalline witty, but deeply serious play' (*The Listener*, 10 October 1946).

The production of *Man and Superman* was an early hallmark program for the Third Programme, and promised well for continuing serious attention to Shaw by the BBC. And it wasn't long before there was further – and very substantial – evidence of the importance of Shaw to the Third Programme.

The Shaw Festival, 1947

The first appearance of Shaw on radio in 1947 was a repeat (recorded) production on the Third Programme on 5 January of a Home Service dramatized version (19 June 1944, see above, pp. 126–7) of *The Adventures of the Black Girl in Her Search for God*. Philip Hope-Wallace quickly dismissed *Black Girl* in his *Listener* column (16 January 1947) – 'Shaw wrote a lot of plays; why dramatise his pamphlets? On the ideas I decline to comment and as for the entertainment value, I will kindly refrain' – but Hope-Wallace wasn't about to refrain from listening to and commenting on the next Shavian offerings on the Third.

There have been several Shaw Festivals over the years, from that at Malvern in 1929 (Conolly, *Bernard Shaw and Barry Jackson* xxiv–xxxi) to the longest-running one (founded in 1962 and still going strong), in Niagara-on-the-Lake, Ontario. There were four plays in the Malvern Shaw Festival – *The Apple Cart*, *Back to Methuselah*, *Heartbreak House*, and *Caesar and Cleopatra* – running from 19 to 24 August 1929 for a total of six performances (including three nights for the full *Methuselah* cycle). The opening season of the Shaw Festival in Niagara-on-the-Lake ran from 29 June to 11 August 1962 (four weekends) with the *Don Juan in Hell* scene from *Man and Superman* and *Candida* (four performances each). The BBC's Shaw Festival ran from 19 to 29 January 1947 (with repeat performances from 4 to 8 February), with productions of *Mrs Warren's Profession*, *The Devil's Disciple*, *The Doctor's Dilemma*, *The Shewing-up of Blanco Posnet*, and *The Apple Cart* (two broadcasts for each play). Audience figures can only be estimated, but it is safe to say that while the Malvern and Niagara-on-the-Lake audiences could be measured in the hundreds, the BBC audiences could be measured in the millions.[9]

There was a preliminary announcement of the 'Shaw Festival' (the BBC's term) in the *Radio Times* on 20 December 1946 – a simple listing of the plays to be included and the dates of production. An identical announcement was published in the *Radio Times* on 3 January 1947, and then in the following week's issue Val Gielgud gave some preliminary information on casting for *Mrs Warren's Profession* and *The Devil's Disciple*. The name that would have caught most readers' attention was that of Esmé Percy who, Gielgud rightly pointed out, 'has been connected with Shaw's work over so many years with such distinction, both as actor and producer.' Gielgud might also have mentioned that Percy had appeared in previous radio productions of Shaw's plays, including one as early as March 1928 when he played Napoleon in *The Man of Destiny*. Percy was to play Praed in *Mrs Warren's Profession* (and, it was subsequently announced [*RT*, 24 January 1947], Proteus in *The Apple Cart*). Any readers of the *Radio Times* who might have missed these relatively low-key announcements would have been alerted to the big event as soon as they saw the *Radio Times* for 17 January, which carried a front-page sketch of Shaw (head and shoulders) with a prominent 'Shaw Festival' heading, a list of plays and dates to be included in the Festival, a promise of repeat recorded broadcasts of the plays, and reference to two articles on Shaw in the same issue by W.R. Matthews and Esmé Percy.

W.R. Matthews was W.R. Inge's successor (in 1934) as Dean of St Paul's. Like Inge, Matthews admired Shaw. In his *Radio Times* article, 'Pamphleteer of Genius,' Matthews praised Shaw's 'masterly use of rhetorical English,' placing him in the tradition of Swift as 'pre-eminently a great pamphleteer,' whose 'most important dramas are conflicts of ideas.' For Matthews, Shaw's prefaces 'are generally more interesting than his plays' – only *Saint Joan* is 'certain of immortality.' Matthews ended his article with a resounding 'word of gratitude' to Shaw: 'no one,' declared the incumbent of one of the most senior positions in the Church of England, 'has done more than Bernard Shaw to awaken us from complacency and to force us to realise the intolerable imbecilities of our civilisation.'

'For the best part of thirty years,' Esmé Percy told *Radio Times* readers in his contribution ('Supreme Dramatist'), 'I have dedicated myself to acting and producing the plays of that dramatic genius, Bernard Shaw,' and went on to explain what Shaw had meant to him as an actor. Like Matthews, Percy lauded Shaw's prose, not the prose of the pamphlets and the prefaces, but the prose of the plays, 'the most noble, crystal clear and rhythmic prose the English theatre has ever known.' And it was prose, Percy argued, that served Shaw's 'supreme' 'instinct of the theatre' in creating a host of memorable characters. 'I emphatically deny,' Percy wrote, 'that Shaw's characters are mere puppets set-up to spout Shaw. They are just as real as Ibsen's.'

And then came the plays: *Mrs Warren's Profession* on 19 January (repeated on 6 February); *The Devil's Disciple* on 21 January (repeated 4 February); *The Doctor's Dilemma* on 23 January (repeated 7 February); *The Shewing-up of Blanco Posnet* on 28 January (repeated 8 February); and *The Apple Cart* on 29 January (repeated 5 February).[10] It was an eclectic grouping, but the rationale for the selection seems to have been (there is no extant documentation) that there had never been a full BBC production (radio or television) of any of the five. Extracts from *The Devil's Disciple*, *The Doctor's Dilemma*, and *The Apple Cart* had been heard from time to time, but in the case of *Mrs Warren's Profession* and *The Shewing-up of Blanco Posnet* the Shaw Festival productions were the first time that any or all of the texts had been broadcast by the BBC.

Philip Hope-Wallace used most of his *Listener* column on 23 January 1947 to welcome the whole idea of the Shaw Festival, noting again 'how wonderfully well this dramatist takes to the special conditions of radio drama.' He thought this particularly true of *Mrs Warren's Profession*, its dialogue 'so clear, so explicit, so vital,' making it one of those plays that radio 'enhances.' The irony of this once-banned play now making 'a Sunday-evening sermon for a million family circles'[11] did not escape Hope-Wallace, but then again, he pointed out, the play 'is as profoundly moral as any play, or any sermon either, well could be.' Two weeks later, having by now heard all of the Shaw Festival plays, Hope-Wallace again applauded Shaw for giving radio drama 'its chief want' – 'ideas wrapped up in good talk.' His example this time was *The Apple Cart*–'not a good play,' but 'as a piece of sustained conversation it suits radio splendidly.' *Blanco Posnet*, on the other hand, merely 'passed the time agreeably' (*The Listener*, 6 February 1947).

It is hard to imagine that Shaw did not listen to at least some of the Shaw Festival plays, but if he said or wrote anything about them not much has survived. His most substantial extant reaction is a letter to the Society of Authors (partly quoted above, p. 132) in which he excoriated the production of *The Devil's Disciple* (in a recorded version re-broadcast on 13 December 1948). Voices were wrong, characterization was misguided, the music was 'horribly messed,' and it all came across as a 'farcical comedy' rather than the 'full blooded melodrama' that it is. The recording of 'that damned broadcast' should be destroyed, Shaw implored (but did not demand).[12]

'I will not grouse about it': Shaw and the Radio

It might have surprised the many BBC directors and producers who had been on the receiving end of such complaints and withering criticism, but in the course of an interview with the *Radio Times* on the occasion of the twenty-fifth anniversary of the BBC in 1947 Shaw, in response to a question about the quality of BBC services, said that 'to an old man like myself the difference between wireless and no wireless is so colossal that I cannot measure it and will not grouse about it' (*RT*, 7 November 1947).[13] Since acquiring his first radio receiver in 1925, Shaw had become a regular listener. He quipped, 'When I want to hear a good play, I listen to one of my own' (*RT*, 7 November 1947), but his listening tastes were eclectic – music, news, even children's programs. The lover of Wagner and self-identified 'high-brow third-liner' (*Daily Telegraph*, 22 July 1947) could still tune in to the Light Programme to listen to the popular Music Hall broadcasts in the 1940s, once claiming that his 'strongest musical impression' in 1948 was the 'amazing virtuosity' of the saxophonist Aubyn Rayinski playing 'demi-semiquavers prestissimo' on the radio (*RT*, 25 November 1949). He must have found some of the BBC's effeteness irritating ('It has steadily been the BBC's aim to win appreciation for the true, the beautiful, and the good'),[14] but his appreciation of founding Director-General John Reith's achievements at the BBC was deep and genuine. Among other things, Shaw admired Reith for his generous support of the ailing Edward Elgar when, at Shaw's urging, he commissioned Elgar's Third Symphony ('magnificent on your part'), and, above all, Shaw saw Reith as 'an able man of action,' indeed, a potential prime minister – 'though nothing but another war will ever make you a P.M.,' Shaw wrote in 1948.[15] By the time that Shaw wrote that to Reith (February 1948), radio had become an indispensable part of Shaw's daily routine. Even before the death of his wife, Charlotte, in September 1943, listening to the radio was a priority, even more so than talking to Charlotte, according to Blanche Patch. 'He and Charlotte never seemed to speak to each other much,' Blanche Patch told Nancy Astor in a letter on 2 June 1947 – 'he preferred the racket of the wireless!' (Wearing 266). And in another letter to Nancy Astor (4 July 1947), Blanche Patch complained about 'the deadly little village' of Ayot – 'No means of getting out of it, no shops, & absolutely no one with whom one can be friends in the real sense' – and grumbled that even when she saw Shaw, which was usually only at mealtimes, he preferred to eat in silence – 'or with the radio blaring' (Wearing 267). And Shaw was by no means a *passive* listener. He had never been reticent about letting the BBC know what he thought of their broadcasts, and not just those of his own plays. One of the programs he listened to in 'deadly' Ayot in July 1947 was a Third Program description of a bullfight, which prompted him to write to the *Daily Telegraph* (22 July 1947; Shaw, *Agitations* 339–40) to call for 'a public enquiry into the mental condition of the BBC.' 'In my early days,' he said, 'England was proud of having abolished bear baiting and all such savageries, and made bullfighting a national reproach to Spain. But now!!!' One of Shaw's last reactions to a BBC broadcast was a long letter published in *The Listener* on 1 December 1949 in which he dismissed a lecturer's call for an international language in favour of his well-known campaign for a phonetic alphabet.[16] It's hard to reconcile this picture of Shaw as an active listener to the BBC with Hesketh Pearson's description of the elderly Shaw falling asleep by the radio. 'I wanted to know,' Pearson said in a program about Shaw's home at Ayot in March 1951, 'why he turned on the wireless when it so often sent him to sleep. "That's why," he replied.'[17]

Shaw remained keenly aware as well of the financial aspects of his various involvements with the BBC. For many years he had dealt directly with the BBC himself in negotiating fees for the broadcast of his plays, but after the war he authorized the Society of Authors to act on his behalf. The Society informed the BBC of this by letter on 27 March 1946 – 'in future, all enquiries relating to broadcast performances of Bernard Shaw's plays should be addressed to the Society of Authors.'[18] This followed an exchange of correspondence between Shaw and the Society of Authors a few days earlier, which had concluded with the Society's assurance to Shaw that they would 'certainly get better terms' for him from the BBC.[19] The arrangement worked well, with the Society keeping in touch with Shaw about any significant developments – for instance, when the BBC increased its scale of fees in May 1948 to £97.0.0. for the performance of a full-length play[20] – but otherwise not bothering him with what they judged to be routine requests from the BBC. The system worked well enough for about three years, during which the Society of Authors 'always licensed broadcast and television performances of Shaw's plays without reference to him except when obviously necessary' (e.g., when the BBC wanted to make cuts to a text).[21] That changed after – for Shaw – the disastrous radio production of *Candida* in March 1949 (see below, pp. 156–7). Thereafter Shaw insisted on being consulted about all proposals to broadcast his plays. He continued, however, to seek guidance from the Society of Authors on broadcast fees, including offers from abroad. He wrote, for example, on 10 October 1949 to ask the Society if an offer of $1000 for a broadcast of *Candida* in the United States was 'enough.' The reply was that although the Society had not negotiated any standard fees in the United States, $1000 was 'in the neighbourhood' of what could be expected, though 'under pressure' the broadcaster (unspecified) might increase the offer to $1250 or $1500.[22] The Society also helped Shaw by keeping him well supplied with copies of the standard licensing forms for authorizing productions of his plays; they sent him a dozen, for example, on 2 August 1949.[23]

In truth, the Society of Authors may not have minded too much being relieved of the authority to license Shaw's plays for broadcasting because he was becoming increasingly unpredictable. 'Never let a play be broadcast until it is so hackneyed that all playgoers have seen it in the theatre,' he counselled Malvern Festival producer Roy Limbert in August 1948,[24] but a year later he licensed a television production of *Buoyant Billions* after just one short London run of the play (see above, p. 136). And a resounding 'NO' to a request to license a television production of *The Devil's Disciple* in July 1949 quickly softened into approval for the production after some gentle cajoling from the BBC (see above, p. 132). Another capital letters 'NO' was initially given to a request from the BBC (via the Society of Authors) for some brief excerpts from *Pygmalion* and *Saint Joan* to be performed by Gertrude Lawrence in a radio program about her life – 'I bar these excerpts,' said Shaw, though he had approved many excerpts over the years. 'Turn down all applications for them. My plays must be broadcast in their entirety or not at all.' But when Gertrude Lawrence asked Shaw herself, he changed his mind: 'Miss Gertrude Lawrence is hereby licensed to include Act III of *Pygmalion* or anything of mine she likes in the broadcast of her Success Story.' The fee? Knitting Shaw a pair of mittens, 'for my personal use next winter.'[25]

Shaw's Final Broadcasts

As part of the ongoing celebrations of Shaw's ninetieth birthday, the Borough of St Pancras, where Shaw had served as a vestryman and councillor from 1897 to 1903, conferred on him the Freedom of the Borough. Shaw agreed to attend a ceremony to receive the Certificate of Freedom in the Council Chambers on 9 October 1946, but a fall in his London flat the day before the ceremony prevented his attending. Arrangements were quickly made for the BBC to make a recording of Shaw's remarks that could be played, in Shaw's absence, at the formal ceremony, and also broadcast later that day for listeners nationwide. The occasion of the recording was one of the most extraordinary in the history of Shaw's relationship with the BBC. Because of his injury, Shaw spent the day (9 October) in bed, where he received the mayor and the town clerk, who arrived with the BBC crew to assist with the recording. They arrived just as a medical team – at the direction of Shaw's osteopath – were setting up a portable X-ray machine to check for any fractures that Shaw's fall might have caused. As Blanche Patch explains it, the X-ray machine had to be connected via coils of wire through the bedroom window to equipment in the street below. In the meantime, Patch supported the town clerk as he climbed a stepladder to check the flat's voltage system for the BBC recording equipment (Patch 233),[26] equipment that could operate only with 'yards of rubber tubes being thrown from the windows to the apparatus in the street,' Patch explained in a letter to Lady Astor (Wearing 194). The BBC staff in the flat included an engineer named Skip Arnell and the project supervisor, Max Robertson, who later became well known as a BBC radio and television tennis commentator. Robertson has left an account of the occasion in which he describes being cautioned by Patch 'not to tire him [Shaw] too much, as he is in a great deal of pain.' Robertson, somewhat overawed by the prospect of meeting Shaw, was then taken into his bedroom, where he saw Shaw 'sitting up in bed, wearing, my trembling eye noted, an old fashioned striped pyjama jacket, out of the top of which his huge cranium obtruded.' While Arnell was setting up the equipment, Robertson plucked up enough courage to ask Shaw if he could interview him after the recording was over. 'No, certainly not,' was the response, and Robertson was again rebuked when he attempted to hold the microphone for Shaw, being told 'in commanding tones,' to 'Give it to me.' Before they started the recording Robertson had to tell Shaw that he would have to pause after three-and-a-half minutes since that was all that could be stored on one disc. And so they began, with Robertson anxiously attending on Shaw in his bedroom while Arnell monitored the rudimentary and unreliable recording equipment in the BBC recording van in the street below.

> As I listened, my awe for this venerable old man of letters became tinged with professional respect. Here he was, at the age of 90, in pain with a broken leg, talking forcefully and clearly and without any hesitation, expressing himself in beautiful spoken prose and showing no exasperation when after a minute Skip (no doubt making his own authority felt) whistled a raspberry up from the depths below and told us through the talk-back that he had 'swaff problems' and that we would have to start again. Shaw took it all in his stride and gave a breathtaking 11 minute performance, having to stop twice more for a new disc, picking up each time the thread of his thought and speech as if there had been no interruption and generally giving the impression of an actor/writer at the peak of his powers.[27]

In his talk Shaw spoke positively of his experience of municipal politics, saying that he rejected opportunities to stand for election to the House of Commons ('The Government offered me a choice selection of seats which I could not possibly win and they could not possibly win') in favour of a political arena where 'things could be done.'[28] The talk was broadcast on the Home Service on 9 October, immediately following the six o'clock news. Shaw 'tottered from his bed' to listen to it, Patch reported to Lady Astor, and 'thought it very good' (Wearing 195).

Shaw wasn't so pleased with his next – and last – radio broadcast, which he described in a letter to S.K. Ratcliffe as a 'pitiable effort, but good enough' (CL 4:805). It was an unusual piece: a few minutes of dialogue between Shaw and theatre impresario C.B. Cochran, who had over a long career produced Ibsen, Brieux, O'Casey, Coward, and Shaw himself – and had further endeared himself to Shaw as a promoter of boxing matches at London's Royal Albert Hall. Shaw wrote the dialogue for a program put together by St John Ervine as part of the BBC's twenty-fifth anniversary celebrations. Called 'A Pageant of Plays and Players 1922–1947,' the program also included Edith Evans, John Gielgud, Sybil Thorndike, Lewis Casson, Emlyn Williams, and other stars, supplemented by members of the BBC repertory company. It was broadcast on

12 November 1947 in the Light Programme, and repeated (also on the Light) on 23 November. Shaw recorded the dialogue at Ayot on 5 November (*CL* 4:805), reading both his own and Cochran's part, as well as that of the BBC announcer. Cochran and the announcer subsequently recorded themselves, however, for the broadcast itself.

Lasting about eight minutes, the dialogue takes a few digs at Shakespeare ('he never invented a plot: he only touched up old plots'), but Shaw's main point is to argue that the art of the theatre 'never changes.' Cochran tells the announcer, who wants to discuss 'the revolution' that Shaw started in the theatre, that 'Mr Shaw made no revolution,' and Shaw supports him. 'I tell you the theatre has its changing fashions,' he says, 'but its art never changes.' 'When I began,' Shaw tells the announcer,

> the London stage was crowded with French dramatizations of police and divorce cases spoilt by the translators in deference to British prudery. No character in them had any religion, any politics, any profession, any relation to life but the charm of the young players and the bugaboo of the middle aged heavy villains. Speeches of more than twenty words were considered impossible and too long: I knocked all that into a cocked hat by giving my characters religions, politics, professions and human nature. In my first play [*Widowers' Houses*] I made the heroine commit a violent assault: a thing thought unwomanly on the stage. [B]ut it was only a mild return to Euripides, whose heroine murdered her mother with an axe. So much for your revolutions!

After which the exchange comes to a limp conclusion with the announcer complaining (Brutus-like) to Shaw, 'You do me wrong,' to which Shaw responds, 'I am sorry. I am too old: I oughtnt to be here.' Shaw then calls on Cochran to leave with him, and says 'Goodbye, everybody.' Cochran says his own 'Goodbye,' and as they leave other voices are heard: 'Goodbye, goodbye, goodbye.'[29]

Not Quite Goodbye

There was a sense of finality about those goodbyes from the ninety-one-year-old Shaw, but although Shaw never recorded anything again for the BBC it wasn't for want of trying on the BBC's part. Shaw turned them down several times – for a broadcast in a 'series of famous authors reading their own works' (Carpenter 52); for a talk on the medical profession;[30] for 'a three hundred to four hundred word postscript' to a program on dialects ('These dialect tomfooleries are not in my class. When I address the public I do so as *primo assoluto* and not as an extra');[31] for a talk on 'The Ideas and Beliefs of the Victorians';[32] and (for the Far Eastern Service) 'on any subject' (in a series called 'I Speak for Myself').[33]

Shaw also rejected requests from various overseas departments of the BBC in the post-war years. The Latin-American Service asked him for a talk on Beatrice Webb in November 1945, but at Fritz Loewenstein's suggestion Shaw offered instead his 'History of a Happy Marriage,' recently published (20 October 1945) in *The Times Literary Supplement* (a review of Margaret Cole's *Beatrice Webb* [1945]). When, however, the BBC sought permission to broadcast a Spanish translation of the article 'in a fifteen-minute period' Shaw refused: 'These 15' broadcasts are no use to me.'[34] At about the same time (25 November) Shaw received an invitation from the French Service to give a talk (in French) on Welsh writer Arthur Machen, which he declined because 'this literary stuff is quite out of my line; and nothing will induce me to touch it. I should be out of date anyhow.'[35] Shaw was also parsimonious about granting permission for overseas re-broadcasts of his BBC talks. 'DAMN the Overseas!' he wrote about a request to re-broadcast his 'As I See It' talk, originally broadcast on 2 November 1937. 'I demand 50 guineas, but recommend the easy alternative of dropping me out. I am not keen on stale bread.'[36]

But if Shaw wasn't prepared any longer to give talks himself, there was no shortage of people eager and willing to give talks about him. Desmond Shawe-Taylor gave two thirty-minute talks in December 1948 on the Third Programme on 'Bernard Shaw as Music Critic'; Alys Russell gave some 'Recollections of the Young Fabians' ('a personal picture of them when they were still young and obscure men and women' [*RT*, 14 January 1949], Shaw among them) on the Third on 21 January 1949; H.N. Brailsford reviewed Shaw's *Sixteen Self Sketches* on the Third in April 1949 ('And now at last, full of years and of glory, by far the greatest living figure in literature, the old man has published an autobiography'); and in August/September 1949 William Maxwell, a director of Shaw's printers, R & R Clark, gave a talk on the Scottish Home Service about his experiences with Shaw (summarized in *The Listener*, 10 September 1949).

There were broadcasts as well of not just the plays, but of Shaw's correspondence – a dramatized reading, for example, of extracts from the Shaw–Ellen Terry correspondence on the hundredth anniversary of Ellen Terry's birth (27 February 1947).[37] And on 13 February 1950, in a program about James Joyce, a letter from Shaw to Sylvia Beach (11 June 1921), pro-prietor of the Shakespeare and Company bookshop in Paris, was read, in which Shaw declines to purchase a copy of *Ulysses* ('a revolting record of a disgusting phase of civilization; but it is a truthful one').[38] Another out-of-the-ordinary Shaw broadcast was a reading of his short story *Aerial Football* (first published in 1907) by Cyril Cusack on 12 September 1948 (repeated on 14 September and 26 December).

But the plays were still the mainstay of Shaw broadcasts in the 1940s. The flurry of activity around the BBC's Shaw Festival in 1947 was fol-lowed by a new production of *Arms and the Man*, broadcast in the Home Service on 17 May 1948. While conceding that 'half the theatrical effect' of the play was lost in a radio performance, *Listener* critic Philip Hope-Wallace was grateful that 'much remains,' and welcomed as well the 'mus-cular and nervously taut' language of the dialogue (*The Listener*, 20 May 1948). Shaw's views on the production – assuming he heard it – are not known, but if the BBC thought that he was too old and tired to muster the energy needed to launch his acerbic attacks when he was displeased by their efforts they were much mistaken. Witness, for instance, his reaction to the production of *Candida*, aired on 30 March 1949 on the Light Pro-gramme (repeated on 2 April in the Home Service) with a stellar cast that included Andrew Cruickshank (Morrell), Emlyn Williams (Marchbanks), and Edith Evans (Candida). Philip Hope-Wallace (*The Listener*, 7 April 1949) didn't think Edith Evans was quite right for Candida – 'one keeps hearing in that unique voice Millamant [in Congreve's *Way of the World*] rather than Mrs Morell' – and Emlyn Williams 'sounds too calculating for the boy-lover.' Still, even with reservations, he welcomed the play. Shaw begged to differ. Vociferously. A few days after the second broadcast, Shaw wrote (on 8 April) to Val Gielgud. The letter is worth quoting in full as an example of Shaw's still acute – he was nearing his ninety-third birth-day – critical sensibilities, and his ability to express them, especially about his own work. It was routine practice now for the BBC to record its pro-grams, but in this instance Shaw took strong exception to the practice:

Please destroy the Candida record: it is a hopeless failure; its broadcast-ing has probably killed the play for the next few years.[39] It is underplayed all through; and the end completely sacrificed by Morell's casual remark of 'D' you mean me, Candida?' instead of the thunderstruck 'Do you mean ME, Candida' which is the climax of the play, and the explanation of the finish. Such a blunder shews that neither the actor nor the producer [director] has the least notion of what the play is about.

The announcer omits all the entrances and exits; and as Lexy's voice is undistinguishable from Morell's, no listener can make out which of them is speaking or who is on the stage and who not.

E.E. [Edith Evans] is badly miscast: she was very clever in the second act; but the part makes nothing of her, and she cannot make enough of the part: it is not in her line.

You must not broadcast my plays until you get an experienced producer. You have one at hand in Esmé Percy.

Emlyn did not change from the colloquial to the hierarchic when he stood revealed as the stronger of the two: 'Out, then, into the night with me!' sounded like 'I think I will go out for a bit of a stroll.'

The tapping of the typewriter does not sound like the rattle of a machine gun or the banging of a weaver's loom. It was half way between.

You really are a pack of duffers.[40]

Shaw did, however, let the duffers have another go later in 1949, this time with *In Good King Charles's Golden Days*, but only after a firm assurance from the BBC that there would be no alterations to the text. 'My plays must be broadcast in their entirety or not at all,' he stipulated (not for the first time).[41] Uncut, the play ran on radio for two hours and fifteen minutes on the Third Programme on 18 September 1949, repeated on 23 September and 11 October (both on the Third), with no recorded adverse reaction from Shaw. A new production of *Village Wooing*, BBC radio's fifth (as well as two television productions), also passed uneventfully in one broadcast performance on 18 February 1950.

Full Circle: *Saint Joan*

While *Saint Joan* was certainly among the best known of Shaw's plays, its length and large cast – not to mention Shaw's reluctance to sanction cuts – inhibited frequent full-scale productions of the play, though broadcasts of excerpts were fairly common throughout the 1930s and 1940s (see appendix 1). It was over a decade after the 1929 landmark production (see chapter 2) before the next radio production of the play in 1941, starring Constance Cummings (see above, p. 117). *Saint Joan* was not included in the BBC's Shaw Festival in January 1947, but amends were made later that year when Constance Cummings again appeared as Joan in a production directed by Val Gielgud (who had co-directed the 1941 production). This new production took up virtually the whole evening on the Home Service on 2 June 1947, running in two parts, the first (immediately following a thirty-minute music program of 'Rhythm, Romance, and Rhumba') lasting an hour and three quarters, the second an hour and twenty minutes. The fifteen-minute intermission was occupied by the nine o'clock news. The production again convinced Philip Hope-Wallace of Shaw's greatness as a radio playwright ('our greatest,' he said in his *Listener* review) – 'it is as if, by some unconscious sensitivity, he had sensed when writing the play how well it would lend itself to the intimate voice of the radio' (*The Listener*, 5 June 1947). The production must have given 'widespread pleasure and satisfaction,' Hope-Wallace thought, a view apparently shared by the BBC since the broadcast was repeated (this time on the Third) on 26 July 1947. (The intermission this time – as befitted listeners to the Third – was a Mozart duet for violin and viola.) Shaw, however, did not join in the 'widespread pleasure and satisfaction.' He expressed his disappointment in the production to Gielgud, and apparently instructed him not to use the recording for any future broadcast. 'As you say,' Gielgud conceded to Shaw (whose letter has been lost), 'we must do better next time.' Gielgud defended the performance of Constance Cummings on the grounds that 'she was rather below par at the time'; her performance this time, he thought, 'was nothing like as good as the one which she gave about two years ago.'[42]

As if making up for lost time, BBC radio quickly returned to *Saint Joan*, this time in a production starring a Swiss actor, Maria Becker, in a production that ran on the Third on 29 September 1948 from 8:00–11:15 pm, with a fifteen-minute intermission (music of François Couperin). The Third's audience got another opportunity to hear Becker's 'wonderfully intelligent and touching performance' (Hope-Wallace, *The Listener*, 7 October 1948) on 8 October – with more Couperin during the intermission.

There is no record of Shaw's reaction to either the 1947 or 1948 broadcast of *Saint Joan*, and by the time of the next one – in September 1950 – he was only a few weeks away from the end of his life. A fall in his garden on 10 September 1950 fractured his thigh and he was hospitalized the next day for surgery. Complications kept him in hospital until 4 October, and it was from his hospital bed that on 18 September 1950 he listened (*CL* 4:881) to the last Shaw play broadcast by the BBC during his lifetime. The last Joan he heard was a strange choice by the BBC, an actor named Joan Hart, who had been an extra in the BBC's 1947 production, though she subsequently had a named role (Louise de Kéroualle) in the 1949 broadcast of *In Good King Charles's Golden Days*. The *Joan* broadcast again occupied a full evening's programming on the Home Service, 7:20–10:45 with a break for the nine o'clock news. It was repeated on

24 September (Part 1) and 1 October 1950 (Part 2) in Sunday matinées. Again – and hardly surprisingly – there is no record of Shaw's reaction to the production, though *The Listener*'s critic (Hubert Griffith, standing in for Hope-Wallace) found much to praise in 'an important and moving experience,' including Joan Hart's 'wonderfully well-sustained and modulated performance' (*The Listener*, 28 September 1950). Shaw may or may not have felt the same way, but he would surely have been pleased by the decision of the *Radio Times* (22 September 1950) to publish an article by his old friend and colleague Barry Jackson to accompany the production. Jackson's 'Memories of *St Joan*' included reminiscences of both the first English performances of *Saint Joan* at the New Theatre in 1924 and the Malvern Festival production (with Wendy Hiller) in 1936, which Shaw had a hand in casting and directing (though the nominal director was Herbert Prentice).

The 6 October 1950 issue of the *Radio Times* carried two readers' letters about Joan Hart's performance. One (from J.L. Powell, Norwich) asked, 'Why must Joan Hart be made to speak with a Yorkshire accent, which anyway was neither convincing nor maintained throughout?' The other (from H.W. Little, Colwyn Bay) asked, 'Why did the BBC have to give her a broad Lancashire accent? Joan was supposed to be a French country girl, not one from the outskirts of Wigan.' Shaw would surely have chuckled at the confusion about the accent – and perhaps blamed the duffers at the BBC for causing it. But by now he had returned to his home in Ayot St Lawrence to die, and the next burst of BBC Shavian activity was the broadcast of news of his death on 2 November 1950 and the obituaries that quickly followed.

Epilogue

Shaw died just before 5:00 am on Thursday 2 November 1950. BBC news broadcasts carried the announcement of his death at the earliest opportunity – 7:00 am on the Home Service, 9:00 am on the Light. (The Third Programme did not begin transmissions until 6:00 pm, and did not, in any case, broadcast news bulletins.) Obituaries and tributes were broadcast later in the day on the Home Service (by Peter Bingham) after the 9:00 pm news, followed immediately by a tribute by St John Ervine. On the Light Programme a tribute was given by Hesketh Pearson in the daily 'News and Radio Newsreel' program that ran from 7:00 to 7:25 pm. The tribute on the Third Programme took the form of a recording of act 3 of *Man and Superman* (first broadcast on 1 October 1946), which replaced a scheduled production of Christopher Fry's *Venus Observed*. On Sunday 5 November the regular Home Service weekly program 'The Critics' included an appreciation of Shaw, and, after some delay because he was living in California, an appreciation by Thomas Mann was broadcast on 8 January 1951 on the Third Programme.[1] It was a dignified and well orchestrated farewell to Shaw, which was really quite an achievement, because behind it lay five years of planning that can more appropriately be described as shambolic than dignified.

The BBC had, as one might expect, been preparing for Shaw's death for some time, though an obituary file on him seems not to have been opened until April 1945, surprisingly late in view of Shaw's advanced age by then (just over a year shy of his ninetieth birthday). The story thereafter is a bizarre catalogue of internal BBC rivalries about selection and control of Shaw's obituary writers, bureaucratic wrangles about process and content, long periods of inactivity, bruised egos, interdepartmental rivalry, outright rejections, and conditional acceptances –

all played out while other departments in the BBC were doing their level best to persuade Shaw to keep on broadcasting for as long as possible (see chapter 8).

The BBC's first candidate for a Shaw obituary was Max Beerbohm, Shaw's successor as theatre critic for the *Saturday Review* in 1898 and frequent caricaturist of Shaw. Beerbohm was contacted by C.V. Salmon, Assistant Director of Talks at the BBC, on 12 April 1945:

> Though the words wear a most mournful and unwarrantable aspect there is no help from supposing that Bernard Shaw must one day die. May that day be still very far off, but when it comes we shall be wanting to do his memory honour. We have decided to ask you whether you would undertake to prepare an appreciation of Bernard Shaw which we could use on the occasion. We should expect to place it after the Nine o'clock News and should be able to devote fourteen minutes to it, or a length roughly of eighteen hundred words.
>
> We should hope if you would do it for us that you would speak a little about Shaw the person, a little about his work, and a little about what you think he stood for, and will appear to those who come after us to have stood for ... We should ask you to come here at your convenience when you had written it and record it for us so that we should be able to use it at short notice when we had to.[2]

One could hardly wish for a more discreet and respectful (albeit lugubrious) approach on what was clearly a sensitive issue, but Beerbohm would have none of it. 'I am very sorry, but – No, I couldn't possibly think and write (and *speak*!) in the past tense about a man who is living,' he responded on 15 April. 'And quite apart from that,' he added, 'how are we to know that the buoyant Bernard won't survive me?' (He didn't; Beerbohm did not die until 1956.)

A few weeks went by until Donald Boyd, Talks Editor for the Home Service News programs (a different department from Salmon's), wrote to Hesketh Pearson, one of Shaw's biographers, on 28 June. Boyd's approach was much more businesslike than Salmon's, and he seems to have been unaware of Salmon's earlier initiative:

> My colleagues in the Talks Department will no doubt plan to broadcast various critical talks on Shaw's importance after his death. Our business in the news bulletins would be immediate and much more factual. We should hope to remind people of Shaw's long career, and indicate its salient points,

and recall the controversies which his work has aroused, with some personal picture of the man if it does not arise from the sketch.

Boyd told Pearson he could have twelve minutes, or roughly 1300–1400 words. Pearson replied immediately (1 July) to accept the offer, and agreed to record his talk later in July. 'If anything happens to Shaw in the meantime,' Pearson assured Boyd, 'you can depend on me to do an obituary at short notice.' Ten days later Pearson sent the script to Boyd, who took his time reading it, before responding on 23 August that he wanted some revisions, especially some toning down of 'extreme claims' about Shaw's influence in helping the Liberal Party win the 1898 election[3] and the role of the Fabian Society in creating the Labour Party. Pearson immediately agreed (26 August) to discuss Boyd's concerns, but nothing much then seems to have happened until Norman Collins, Controller of the Light Programme, began to think about what the Light Programme should do on the occasion of Shaw's death. He circulated an internal memo (18 February 1946) recommending a plan that would provide for 'a number of short pieces by those who have been associated with his work in one way or another.' He suggested St John Ervine, Pearson ('though he is terribly small calibre'), *Daily Telegraph* critic George Bishop, and F.E. Loewenstein, Shaw's self-appointed bibliographer (who was also now dealing with much of Shaw's correspondence with the BBC).

By now, word was out – at least in BBC circles – that plans were being discussed for Shaw's obituary, and someone whose name had not yet been mentioned decided to put his oar in. This was critic Desmond MacCarthy, who since 1930 had been talking and writing about Shaw on BBC programs and in BBC publications. MacCarthy phoned the BBC on 25 March 1946 to let them know that he was interested. But another memo that circulated two days later still omitted MacCarthy. New names, however, appeared – critic James Agate, film producer Gabriel Pascal (*Pygmalion, Major Barbara, Caesar and Cleopatra*), film director Anthony Asquith (*Pygmalion*), and Cecil Lewis, closely associated with Shaw during the early years of the BBC (see chapter 1).

The tentative plan now was to have a formal obituary arranged by the News Department (for the Home Service), an appreciation 'two or three days later' (also on the Home Service), and a symposium on the Light Programme. For the rest of 1946, as Shaw approached and then passed his ninetieth birthday, the memos flew thick and fast through the BBC labyrinth, one (28 March 1946) adding Harley Granville Barker's name to the mix and also proposing a full-length production of *Saint Joan*. Many of the memos, though, addressed the perceived deficiencies of Pearson's obituary, which he had now recorded, and which remained the only script so far commissioned and submitted. Another part of the BBC bureaucracy, the Literary Advisory Committee, had now got involved with the Pearson obituary. An internal memo (2 April) reported that the committee had listened to the recording, and, 'in the main,' thought the script 'competently compiled' and 'well delivered.' But there were problems. Pearson's statement that Shaw and the Fabians 'created a new political power in England and saw a policy which they accepted as their own carried out in Russia' was, in the committee's view, 'a dangerous one.' The committee also fretted about Pearson's description of *Androcles and the Lion* as 'Shaw's masterpiece.' It was left to Boyd to communicate these concerns to Pearson, which he did on 4 April. Pearson, who seemed entirely too anxious to do whatever was asked of him, very quickly made revisions and re-recorded his talk.

But now an argument broke out between the Home Service and the Light Programme when the Light said they wanted to use Pearson (but not necessarily the script he had recorded) and the Home (which had originally commissioned Pearson) should find someone else – MacCarthy, perhaps, whose name was now on the active list. Some inter-departmental angst went on, until the Light Programme decided that perhaps they should read the Pearson script. It was sent to Collins, who told Boyd (17 April) that 'though I take my hat off to it as a thoroughly well done formal obituary, I am afraid it is absolutely hopeless for the Light Programme.'

At some point during all this kerfuffle Pearson had been to see Shaw in his London flat to discuss his obituary. Initially nettled by being written about in the past tense – 'But, damn it, I'm not dead yet!' he told Pearson (and later repeated the same irritation in writing on the script of the obituary) – Shaw then, Pearson says, 'warmed to the theme,' and made several suggestions, including one that Pearson 'must say that I have provided for the greatest players a modern grand repertory comparable only to that left by Shakespeare.' But Shaw's only 'real complaint,' according to Pearson, 'was that I had made little of his contributions to science and sociology,' an omission Shaw proceeded to rectify by dictating to Pearson three long paragraphs on those contributions, paragraphs that Pearson included in the revised script he subsequently sent to Shaw (marked 'Private and Confidential'). Shaw kept the script 'for several weeks,' and when Pearson 'demanded' it back, Shaw returned it 'with so many corrections and additions' that Pearson 'rebelled' and recorded his own version, which was in any case never used by the BBC.[4]

Discussions about the obituaries and tributes had now been under way for twelve months, and all the BBC had in hand was Pearson's contribution, though it was not at all certain how – or even if – it would be used. A new plan was then put into place (17 April 1946), consisting of a MacCarthy obituary for the Home Service News, a Pearson tribute (but not the obituary he had written) for the Light Programme (perhaps paired with one by St John Ervine), a more formal tribute for the Home Service ('fifteen minutes on the Sunday following death') by Max Beerbohm (who had already said no) or Granville Barker, and a full production (Home Service) of *Saint Joan*. At this stage the Third Programme, which had invested so heavily in Shaw since its launch in 1946, was excluded.

During May, more names emerged: fellow-Fabian Sidney Webb, Shavian actor (and first wife of Granville Barker) Lillah McCarthy, philosopher C.E.M. Joad ('who could have his say about Shaw the Fabian and about all the Life-Force and Superman stuff in the plays, and more particularly in the prefaces'), and founding member of the Fabian Society E.R. Pease ('probably too old to do it well' – he was eighty-nine in 1946). And then C.V. Salmon, who, having started the process over a year before, must have been getting increasingly frustrated by the floundering, had a new idea (24 June) – why not ask Shaw to write his own obituary? 'It would be very characteristic of the man,' Salmon suggested to his colleagues, 'and might, I think, strike listeners as a stroke of genius.' Pearson had in fact privately had much the same idea, but Salmon's colleagues didn't even think it worth discussing.

And then there was some action, quite decisive action in the context of a year of thrashing about. N.G. Luker, Assistant Director of Talks, sent out three invitations (all dated 8 July 1946) to participate in a Light Programme symposium on Shaw following his death. The letters were sent to George Bishop (who was invited to speak on Shaw 'from your personal experience of him as a man'), St John Ervine (Shaw 'as a dramatist'), and – a new figure in the discussions – Lord Lindsay, Master of Balliol College, Oxford ('Shaw's philosophy'). Bishop and Ervine accepted, Lindsay declined ('I am much too occupied with other things'). Fabian writer and editor Raymond Postgate – another new name – was suggested as an alternative to Lindsay, and on 2 August Postgate was sent the same letter that had previously gone to Lindsay. He quickly accepted, but was upset when he later discovered (23 October) that the fee was a mere 7 guineas. Postgate didn't know it, but the BBC, never wedded to the concept of equality, had already offered fees of 12 guineas to Ervine and 8 guineas to Bishop (describing them in both instances as 'special fees'). Postgate (30 October) wanted 21 guineas, a request met with incredulity by Luker (1 November): 'I can hardly believe that he would seriously have suggested that we should pay him 21 gns for a seven-minute script.' Postgate subsequently settled (22 November) for 9 guineas, plus 3 guineas if circumstances permitted him to do the broadcast live.[5]

So that, for now at least, looked after the Light Programme. The Home Service had held on to Pearson for the obituary, but still felt the need for an appreciation as well. Veteran broadcaster and novelist J.B. Priestley – still another new name – was approached on 17 October 1946. He took little time to decline the invitation, replying on 20 October that he 'would rather not do the talk on Shaw, partly because I did two articles about him in connection with his 90th birthday, and also because although I have a vast admiration for his mind, personality and outlook, I have never been able to accept him as a great dramatist.' Priestley recommended Joad, 'who adores every word Shaw has written.' For reasons unknown, Joad was not pursued, but the Home Service came up with yet more names, this time spreading the net internationally – American playwrights Thornton Wilder and Elmer Rice, and Czech diplomat Jan Masaryk. Closer to home, Irish playwright and BBC executive (Director of Programming for Television since 1945) Denis Johnston was also suggested. Irish novelist and poet James Stephens was yet another suggestion.

By early 1947 nothing had been resolved for the Home Service, and the Talks people were clearly – and understandably – getting fed up. The Talks Department circulated a request on 5 March, wearily one suspects: 'Do you think that before making further suggestions we can ask for some guidance about the sort of speaker that would be acceptable – for example, is there a preference for someone from the world of literature, or of the theatre, or of socialism – a young man or an old man, an Englishman or an Irishman?' (Talks might also have asked, but didn't, if a *woman* would be acceptable; all the suggestions so far had been for male speakers.)

The memo had an immediate, though perhaps unanticipated, effect: silence. Unless a section of the Shaw Obituary file has simply disappeared, there was no further discussion – at least in writing – of the issue for almost two years, by which time Shaw had passed his ninety-first and ninety-second birthdays. And then, abruptly and decisively, the Talks Department, in the person of a new Assistant Director, W.M. Newton, phoned Bertrand Russell, perhaps by 1949 almost as famous (and, in some respects, as notorious) as Shaw (and soon to be awarded the Nobel Prize for Literature). Russell was also a frequent BBC broadcaster, and was known to have been sympathetic with Shaw's views on subjects such as the First World War. They had also collided on their bicycles near Tintern Abbey in September 1895 (see Russell's obituary in appendix 4). Russell immediately agreed to do a ten-minute talk on Shaw, and Newton quickly spread the news of his conversation, including an important proviso imposed by Russell (7 February 1949):

> He told me, with a great horse-laugh, that if the BBC was gambling on his being alive to read the GBS obituary, it was making a wild bet,[6] as Shaw is clearly immortal. He also made, with another burst of laughter, a proviso that GBS should not be invited to do his (Russell's) obituary, and pointed out that he (Russell) had already done his own obituary (back in the thirties) for the BBC in some series which appeared in the Listener.[7]

Russell followed up two weeks later (22 February) with the script ('the stuff on Shaw,' he called it), worrying that the BBC 'might think it not sufficiently complimentary,' asking that the script be treated as confidential, and reminding them of his condition that Shaw 'is not to do my obituary!'[8]

Russell's agreement meant that the BBC now had confirmed arrangements for the Light Programme symposium (Ervine, Bishop, Postgate), for the Home Service obituary (Pearson), and for the Home Service tribute (Russell). There was still no plan for the Third Programme, though if that were to be a broadcast of a BBC recording of a Shaw play (in whole or in part), it could fairly easily be arranged at the last minute.

There was still no sign, however, that the 'last minute' was approaching since Shaw was still giving every appearance, as Russell put it, of being 'immortal.' Some eighteen months went by, then, without any significant activity in the Obituary file. That situation changed dramatically on 10 September 1950 when Shaw fell in his garden and was hospitalized the next day with a fractured thigh – a life-threatening injury for someone of Shaw's age (now ninety-four). In checking with Russell, the BBC learned that he would be leaving England for a visit to the United States 'on or about October 22nd.' A copy of Russell's script was sent to him in case he wanted to make any revisions, but the dilemma faced by the BBC now was what to do if Shaw died while Russell were in or en route to the United States and therefore unable to do the broadcast.

It was decided that there should be a reserve speaker who could be brought in if Russell had left the country by the time of Shaw's death. There was also the possibility of the situation that Russell had mentioned to the BBC – that Russell might die before Shaw. An internal memo (19 October – Shaw was now out of hospital but suffering from kidney failure and not expected to recover) succinctly expressed the problem thus: 'we have to have another piece ready in case of Shaw's demise during Russell's imminent absence in America, or in case of the demise of Russell himself!' A possible solution emerged through John Morris, Head of the BBC's Far Eastern Service, and a personal friend of E.M. Forster. In many respects Forster was an entirely inappropriate choice, never close to Shaw socially, politically, or intellectually. But he was eminent and could easily get to BBC studios in London from his Cambridge College (King's) at short notice. And the personal connection with Morris might just work. It was, though, a sensitive situation because Forster would have to play second fiddle to Russell, and whatever talk he prepared might not be broadcast. Morris was asked to write to Forster, and did so, gingerly, on 19 October 1950:

My dear Morgan,
I have been asked to approach you privately on a matter which our News Division finds it slightly embarrassing to write officially. I also find it slightly embarrassing, but I nevertheless feel sure you will understand the circumstances. The point is this: Bertrand Russell has agreed [to write] (and has indeed written) an obituary talk to be used after the nine o'clock news in the event of Bernard Shaw's death. Meanwhile, Russell leaves tomorrow for the United States where he will be for the next few months. Now comes the embarrassment. In the event of Shaw's death during Russell's absence, would you be prepared to take on the job? What is required is a tribute of from 1500–1800 words of personal appreciation, comment and, if you wished, criticism. Biographical details would be covered in the news bulletin which would precede the talk and should therefore be omitted from anything you might feel inclined to say.

It may well be, of course, that you would have felt disinclined to talk about Shaw in any circumstances, in which case there is nothing more for me to say. If, however, you would agree to take on this job, I for one would

certainly use your piece in my own Service even in the event Bertrand
Russell should be available to do the tribute for the Home Service.

It was a delicately framed letter, and Morris's ability and willingness
to guarantee at least an overseas broadcast of any talk that Forster
might write was a nice touch. But it didn't work. A pencil note on the
BBC copy of Morris's letter indicates that Forster declined (probably in
a telephone call to Morris).

What next? The circulation of a memo (undated, but probably late
October or early November 1946) with some thirty names on it
(friends, neighbours, critics, actors – almost anyone BBC staff could
think of who had had *some* kind of relationship with Shaw) suggests
something close to panic. Then Denis Johnston's name came up again,
which seemed an easy (and appropriate) solution. Peter Bingham
(from the BBC's Obituaries Department) prepared a letter to Johnston,
but it was never sent. (The original typed copy, dated 25 October 1950,
is marked in blue pencil, 'not approached.') That seems to have been
because St John Ervine was favoured, despite his previous commitment to the Light Programme symposium. The situation was explained to Ervine in a telephone call in which Ervine agreed to be
Russell's back-up. This was followed by a letter (27 October) from
Bingham to Ervine thanking him for his willingness to 'fill in the
breach,' since the BBC 'is anxious to tie this matter up as soon as possible.' 'One cannot tempt fortune too much,' Bingham said, 'even with
the nonagenarian vegetarian of Ayot St Lawrence.' There was, however, a problem, Bingham confessed. Ervine would have to send in a
new script because 'our Record Department cannot find the recording
you did in 1946.' Since Ervine lived in Devon, it was, however, agreed
that he could do the actual broadcast from the Exeter studios of the
BBC. This was agreed in a letter from Bingham to Ervine dated 1 November 1950, a letter in which Bingham also said, 'It looks as though,
after all, Shaw is not going to die on us just for the moment.' By the
time Ervine received the letter Shaw was dead.

Despite over five years of planning and discussion the arrangements
for the Shaw obituaries and tributes were all last-minute. Peter Bingham
ended up writing the formal obituary himself for the Home Service
News. St John Ervine had at most two or three days' notice to write the
Home Service tribute. The Ervine-Bishop-Postgate symposium for the
Light Programme was forgotten about (the 1946 recordings and scripts
seem to have been lost anyway). Pearson's script (revised by Shaw) for

the Home Service was never used, and at some point late in the day Pearson prepared an entirely new script for the Light Programme's 'News and Newsreel,' while last-minute adjustments were made to 'The Critics' program on the Home Service on 5 November to include Shaw in the discussion. The Third Programme did not announce any plans, even internally, until the very day of Shaw's death. A memo (2 November) gave details of the switch from Fry's *Venus Observed* to act 3 of *Man and Superman*, and also revealed that Thomas Mann had been approached 'for a talk about Shaw, which, if it materialises, we expect to place in about a fortnight from now.' (It was actually broadcast nearly ten weeks later, on 8 January 1951.)[9]

And that might have been that, except that Raymond Postgate – now running a team of restaurant critics in preparation for the first edition of *The Good Food Guide* in 1951, which Postgate edited, and the most prickly of the trio hired in 1946 for the Light Programme symposium – was not amused by the BBC's indifference to its commitments. As soon as Postgate heard of Shaw's death – probably on the BBC News! – he telephoned the BBC to enquire what was happening with the symposium plans. The duty officer who took the call reported that Postgate was 'obviously hurt' by the BBC's forgetting him, but Peter Bingham didn't think it was a problem for his Obituary Department to deal with. 'He is obviously Talks' baby,' he said, claiming that there was no mention of Postgate in 'the correspondence we inherited' from Talks. So Eileen Milloy from Talks tried to explain. She wrote to Postgate on 6 November, telling him that despite the 1946 agreement there had been 'several revisions' of initial plans, and that 'it was finally decided by the Controller of the Home Service on the occasion of Shaw's death to commission an entirely new script by Mr St John Ervine' and replace the 'programme originally planned' (i.e., the symposium) by the discussion in 'The Critics' program, 'which, as you may have heard, took place last Sunday.' The letter concluded with an apology for 'any misunderstanding in the matter.' Eileen Milloy's summary gave a false sense of coherence to what in truth had been five years of muddle. In one of his last communications with the BBC Shaw had called them 'a pack of duffers' (see above, p. 157). He was referring to production and creative staff on that occasion, but had he known about the obituary shambles he would surely have applied the phrase to administrators as well.

But the BBC duffers, to their credit, retained their faith in Shaw in death as in life. In 1951 alone there were radio or television productions of *Candida*, *Heartbreak House* (the radio premiere), *Saint Joan* (a television production starring Constance Cummings), *Pygmalion, The Devil's Disciple, John Bull's Other Island, The Doctor's Dilemma, Androcles and the Lion, Cymbeline Refinished* (another radio premiere), *Widowers' Houses, Arms and the Man,* and *Mrs Warren's Profession.* The production of *Widowers' Houses* on 11 November 1951, directed by Esmé Percy, marked the beginning of a cycle of Third Programme broadcasts of Shaw's work, arranged by St John Ervine, that stretched well into 1952. As Shaw's reputation has fluctuated since then, so has the BBC's commitment to his work, challenged as the BBC has also been by the loss of its monopoly in both radio and television broadcasting and its inevitable and increasing sensitivity to audience ratings. Anniversary dates have, however, occasioned major BBC tributes to Shaw – in 1956 (the hundredth anniversary of his birth), 2000 (the fiftieth anniversary of his death), and even 2006 (the sesquicentennial of his birth). Part of the 2006 tribute was the release of a set of DVD recordings of ten television productions of Shaw's plays from the 1970s and 1980s,[10] and (in collaboration with the British Library) a set of CDs of his radio broadcasts from 1931 to 1947.[11] These publications serve as a valuable reminder in the early years of the twenty-first century of one of the most important cultural collaborations of the twentieth, a collaboration that was perpetually volatile, but consistently creative, and one that worked not just for the benefit of the BBC and Bernard Shaw, but for the benefit of millions of radio listeners and television viewers in Great Britain and around the world.

Appendix 1
Shaw's Broadcast Plays and Talks, 1923–1950

Full details of Shaw's plays broadcast on the BBC (director, designer, cast, etc.), talks on Shaw on BBC Radio, articles by and about Shaw in BBC publications, and dramatic sketches, readings by and about Shaw, and information about sources can be found at www.utparchives.com/9780802089205_appendix.pdf.

Plays and Adaptations on BBC Radio

1 December 1923	*Man and Superman* (excerpts)
20 November 1924	*O'Flaherty V.C.*
13 January 1926	*Passion, Poison, and Petrifaction or The Fatal Gazogene*
28 March 1928	*The Man of Destiny*
25 April 1929	*Saint Joan* (Part 1, Scenes 1–3)
26 April 1929	*Saint Joan* (Part 2, Scene 4–Epilogue)
16 October 1929	*Captain Brassbound's Conversion* (repeated 19 Oct. 1929)
15 May 1930	*The Man of Destiny* (repeated 16 May 1930)
17 June 1933	*Back to Methuselah* (excerpts)
7 September 1934	*Back to Methuselah* (excerpts)
3 December 1934	*Village Wooing* (repeated 4 December 1934)
2 January 1935	*Back to Methuselah* (Part 1 only; repeated 3 Jan. 1935)
22 December 1935	*Candida*
27 May 1936	*Saint Joan* (excerpts)
11 January 1937	*The Man of Destiny* (repeated 12 Jan. 1937)
29 January 1937	*John Bull's Other Island* (excerpts)
27 February 1937	*Too True to be Good* (excerpts)
3 March 1937	*Saint Joan* (excerpts)
3 May 1937	'The Emperor and the Little Girl' (short story: repeated 5 Sept. 1937; 7 Nov. 1938)

1 August 1937	*The Apple Cart* (excerpts)
17 October 1937	*Saint Joan* (the Cathedral Scene)
17 October 1937	*Candida*
22 March 1938	*Village Wooing*
22 April 1938	*The Dark Lady of the Sonnets*
31 May 1938	*Saint Joan* (Scenes 1 and 3)
21 July 1938	*The Dark Lady of the Sonnets*
14 August 1938	*Saint Joan* (excerpts from Scene 6)
6 October 1938	*How He Lied to Her Husband*
25 January 1939	*Geneva* (excerpts from Act 3)
28 March 1939	*Saint Joan* (Scene 5)
14 April 1939	*Arms and the Man*, Part 1 (Act 1)
18 April 1939	*Arms and the Man*, Part 2 (Act 2)
21 April 1939	*Arms and the Man*, Part 3 (Act 3)
12 November 1939	*The Apple Cart* (excerpts)
13 November 1939	*Saint Joan* (Trial Scene)
31 December 1939	*Saint Joan* (Trial Scene)
10 February 1940	*In Good King Charles's Golden Days* (last Act)
14 March 1940	*Arms and the Man* (Act 1)
17 May 1940	*The Devil's Disciple* (excerpts)
29 August 1940	*In Good King Charles's Golden Days* (excerpts)
15 September 1940	*Saint Joan* (Trial Scene)
24 October 1940	*Back to Methuselah* (excerpts, Eve's speech)
17 January 1941	*Man and Superman* (excerpts)
7 February 1941	*The Doctor's Dilemma* (excerpts)
21 February 1941	*Getting Married* (excerpts)
3 March 1941	*The Adventures of the Black Girl in Her Search for God*
23 March 1941	*Androcles and the Lion*
18 April 1941	*The Adventures of the Black Girl in Her Search for God* (excerpts)
26 July 1941	*Arms and the Man* (excerpts)
15 September 1941	*Saint Joan*
11 January 1942	*Androcles and the Lion*
10 February 1942	*Saint Joan* (excerpts from Scenes 1 and 3; repeated 22 Feb. 1944)
19 February 1942	*You Never Can Tell* (excerpts from Act 1)
24 June 1942	*The Devil's Disciple* (excerpts)
28 June 1942	*The Millionairess* (Part 1: Acts 1 and 2)
29 June 1942	*The Millionairess* (Part 2: Acts 3 and 4)
28 August 1942	*Village Wooing*
31 October 1942	*Saint Joan* (excerpts)

25 January 1943	*Candida* (excerpts)
16 October 1943	*Candida*
4 February 1944	*Arms and the Man* (excerpts)
1 April 1944	*The Man of Destiny* (excerpts)
19 June 1944	*The Adventures of the Black Girl in Her Search for God*
6 July 1945	*Caesar and Cleopatra* (excerpts)
16 December 1945	*Caesar and Cleopatra* (excerpts)
29 January 1946	*Saint Joan* (excerpts)
20 April 1946	*Candida*
5 May 1946	*Village Wooing*
19 June 1946	*Major Barbara* (excerpts)
26 July 1946	*The Man of Destiny* (Act 3 repeated 7 Oct. 1946; full play repeated 14 July 1947)
1 October 1946	*Man and Superman* (repeated 2 Oct. 1946; Acts 1, 2, and 4 repeated 1 Nov. 1946; Act 3 repeated 14 Nov. 1948)
28 December 1946	*Androcles and the Lion* (repeated 30 December 1946)
5 January 1947	*The Adventures of the Black Girl in Her Search for God*
19 January 1947	*Mrs Warren's Profession* (repeated 6 Feb. 1947; 4 Aug. 1947; 2 June 1948)
21 January 1947	*The Devil's Disciple* (repeated 4 Feb. 1947; 11 Aug. 1947; 13 Dec. 1948)
23 January 1947	*The Doctor's Dilemma* (repeated 7 Feb. 1947; 15 Aug. 1947)
28 January 1947	*The Shewing-up of Blanco Posnet* (repeated 8 Feb. 1947)
29 January 1947	*The Apple Cart* (repeated 5 Feb. 1947; 20 Sept. 1948)
2 June 1947	*Saint Joan* (repeated 26 July 1947)
17 May 1948	*Arms and the Man*
3 August 1948	*Pygmalion* (excerpts)
29 September 1948	*Saint Joan* (repeated 8 Oct. 1948)
30 March 1949	*Candida* (repeated 2 Apr. 1949)
18 September 1949	*In Good King Charles's Golden Days* (repeated 23 Sept. 1949; 11 Oct. 1949)
2 February 1950	*The Fascinating Foundling* (excerpts)
18 February 1950	*Village Wooing*
13 March 1950	*The Apple Cart* (excerpts)
18 September 1950	*Saint Joan* (Part 1 repeated 24 Sept. 1950; Part 2 repeated 1 October 1950)

Plays on BBC Television

| 8 July 1937 | *How He Lied to Her Husband* |
| 4 July 1938 | *Androcles and the Lion* (repeated 13 July 1938) |

26 February 1939   *The Dark Lady of the Sonnets* (repeated 6 March 1939)
10 April 1939   *Candida* (repeated 19 April 1939)
23 April 1939   *Geneva* (Act 3)
2 May 1939   *Annajanska, The Bolshevik Empress* (repeated 7 May 1939)
9 June 1939   *Passion, Poison, and Petrifaction* (repeated 15 June 1939)
20 July 1939   *The Man of Destiny* (repeated 28 July 1939)
7 June 1946   *The Dark Lady of the Sonnets*
23 June 1946   *Saint Joan* (Part 1, Scenes 1–4)
30 June 1946   *Saint Joan* (Part 2, Scenes 5–6, Epilogue)
20 July 1946   *Village Wooing* (repeated 27 Sept. 1946)
6 October 1946   *Candida* (repeated 11 Oct. 1946)
3 November 1946   *Androcles and the Lion* (repeated 5 Nov. 1946)
22 December 1946   *Arms and the Man* (repeated 24 Dec. 1946)
16 January 1947   *The Man of Destiny*
16 March 1947   *Fanny's First Play*
8 February 1948   *Pygmalion* (repeated 10 Feb. 1948)
20 June 1948   *Arms and the Man* (repeated 24 June 1948)
10 August 1948   *Village Wooing*
10 October 1948   *Androcles and the Lion*
19 October 1948   *Heartbreak House* (excerpts, Act 1)
26 July 1949   *The Devil's Disciple*
6 November 1949   *Widowers' Houses* (repeated 10 Nov. 1949)
14 November 1949   *Buoyant Billions*
21 March 1950   *The Man of Destiny* (repeated 27 March 1950)

Talks and Debates by Shaw on BBC Radio

9 June 1925   'What Is Coming?' (debate between Hilaire Belloc and Bernard Shaw)
27 January 1927   'The Menace of the Leisured Woman' (debate between the Viscount Rhondda and G.K. Chesterton, chaired by Bernard Shaw)
28 October 1927   'Do We Agree?' (debate between Bernard Shaw and G.K. Chesterton)
7 December 1928   'How It Strikes Me'
14 October 1929   'Points of View'
31 January 1930   'The National Theatre'
28 October 1930   'Toast to Einstein'
30 May 1931   'Saint Joan'
11 October 1931   'Russia'

11 July 1932	'Rungs of the Ladder'
28 October 1933	'Playwrights and Amateurs'
6 February 1934	'Whither Britain?' (repeated, excerpts only, 24 Feb. 1946)
20 January 1935	'Film Censorship'
18 June 1935	'Freedom'
17 August 1935	'In Town Tonight'
11 June 1937	'School'
2 November 1937	'As I See It: This Danger of War'
26 July 1946	Birthday broadcast
9 October 1946	Freedom of St Pancras Speech

Appendix 2
Texts of Selected Shaw Broadcasts

A. 'Rungs of the Ladder.' Broadcast 11 July 1932. Published in *The Listener,* **20 July 1932**
[See chapter 3, pp. 63–4. The five paragraphs set off in square brackets are in the typescript of the talk in the British Library, but are marked, in Shaw's hand, 'Discarded pages of Rungs of the Ladder broadcast' (Add Ms 50705, ff. 68–72). They are published here for the first time.]

Rungs of the ladder! What does that mean to you? The climb from obscurity to success. What would it have meant to my grandfather? Well, in his time the ladder was not the beginning of the career of a good and great man, but the end of the career of a bad one. He went up it to be hanged. Don't you think there is an idea in that for the BBC? Why should we not have a set of talks, not from the people who have made good but from the people who have made bad? Not from the upstarts, but from the downstarts. Of course, we cannot have talks from people who have been hanged, though we might have some from people who ought to have been hanged. But we could hear the unlucky people, the down and out, the unsuccessful, and the criminal. Perhaps they wouldn't tell us the truth; but do any of us tell the truth about ourselves? If you imagine that I am going to tell you the truth about myself you never were more mistaken in your life. I couldn't if I tried. I don't know what it is. I believe you would get more truth from the bad lots than from the good. Good people are apt to be modest about their achievements, because they know how small they were really. But bad people are always so vainglorious that they cannot help bragging about their exploits even to the police. Only the other day a man killed the President of the French Republic for the sake of having his portrait in all the papers and being the most famous man in Europe just for one week.[1] He has even passed into history; for, as Richard the Third used to say on the stage when I was a boy, when Richards were really Richards,

Th'aspiring youth that fired th'Ephesian dome
Outlives in fame the pious fool who raised it.

You have already had some Ladder talks from highly respectable friends of mine. Well, have you noticed how very little you got out of them about their success? All the things they told you might have happened to quite unsuccessful and disreputable people. Jim Thomas, now a Cabinet Minister, cleaned engines.[2] Well, what of it? Lots of people have cleaned engines and are cleaning them still without the faintest chance of becoming Cabinet Ministers. If you come to that, I have cleaned dirtier things than engines; but that is not how I became famous. William Davies, our most authentic and unadulterated poet,[3] told you he began his public life as a juvenile gangster and was birched by the west country police for stealing. Well, I, in my modest way, was a juvenile gangster; but as the police did not catch me, and I was not birched, clearly it was not birching that made Davies a great man.

So I will not waste your time by telling you things that happened to me and might have happened to anybody. You think I am a great man; and so does the B.B.C.: that is why I am here at the microphone with countless millions of my fellow creatures hanging on my words to find out how to become great or to put their children in the way of becoming great. You know from the picture of me in the *Radio Times* that, to look at, I am just like any other old man with a beard. What you want to get at is the difference between us, the mysterious something that has made me a great man whilst you are a nobody. Let me assure you to begin with that the mysterious something is not any moral superiority on my part. I can write plays; and you can't: that is all. I can write anything. If I couldn't I should probably be a tramp. As it is, I am so well off that everybody pretends I am much more respectable than I really am; and the newspapers back them up. Never believe what the papers say of me. Even the *Radio Times*, in the few lines about me announcing this talk, has two mistakes and two romances. I was never in a surveyor's office; and I was never a commercial traveller. That romance isn't even romantic.

The truth is there are no such things as great men and women. People believe in them just as they used to believe in unicorns and dragons. The greatest man or woman is 99 per cent. just like yourself. In fact I may be insulting you by saying so, because the so-called great people have often been, as to that 99 per cent. of common humanity, downright bad lots. Even the best of them are apt to be a bit spoilt if that odd 1 per cent. is made too much of during their lifetime. Mind, I say *if* because it is dangerous to be different from other people: if you carry it too far in certain directions you will not be a hero or heroine: you will be a martyr.

There are plenty of martyrs about. We are apt to think only of those who are imprisoned, crucified, stoned, scourged, burnt at the stake, or killed in some other sensationally unpleasant manner; but most martyrs suffer persecution and poverty until they die what are called natural deaths, and pass away unwept, unhonoured, and unsung. It all depends on the nature of that 1 per cent. If you are a very attractive woman, for instance, or a man with a beautiful tenor voice, you will be indulged in selfish misbehavior to an extent that would never be tolerated from an unattractive woman or a man with no ear for music. If you have a genius for making money, you may do anything you like, from pitch-and-toss to manslaughter, provided you keep technically within the law. But if your 1 per cent. of genius threatens to make poor people rich or rich people poor, or to destroy superstition by exposing it in the light of genuine religious truth, or to win votes for the good of the community against private vested interests, you will be very lucky if you escape martyrdom. So take care. If you want your children to be safe and respectable you must bring them up to do nothing except what everybody does, right or wrong. The moment they depart from that well trodden, straight, and simple path, they are in danger. Their way may be a better way; but it will be just as dangerous as if it were a worse way. For instance, should you bring up your children to wear starched collars? Starched collars are not only unhealthy and uncomfortable and troublesome: they are dirty; for starch in wearing apparel is a matter in the wrong place, which is the classic definition of dirt; and the fact that the dirt is white and glossy does not alter the case. No matter: all you have to consider is whether ladies and gentlemen wear starched collars. You find that gentlemen do and ladies don't. Therefore, if you wish your children to be ladies and gentlemen you will teach your daughters that it is wrong to wear starched collars and your sons that it is right to wear them. That is to be their morality.

For the same reason you must accustom your children to go to church, but to be very careful not to think too deeply about religion. Thinking about religion made George Fox, the founder of the Quakers, a great man; but it also led him to walk by his inner light instead of by the golden rule of walking where other people walk; and the end of that was that he raged against churches; called them steeplehouses; went into them with his hat on and interrupted the services by contradicting the clergy; and was finally thrown into prison. And the result of his setting women thinking about religion was that many most respectable ladies became Quakeresses and were publicly flogged for it, though if they had just done what everybody else in their class did and gone to church regularly, nobody would have dared to lay a finger on them.

Now this makes things easy for parents; for instead of having to make little saints of their children, all they have to do is to inculcate one single simple precept

'When in Rome do as the Romans do.' The model you must hold up to them for imitation is not any of the saints or heroes nor any of the great and good, but simply that very sensible and successful clergyman the Vicar of Bray.

Thoughtless people will tell you that children are a great responsibility. That is nonsense: children are a great expense until they are able to support themselves; and parents should not have to bear that expense; but the notion that parents are responsible for the conduct of their children, or for their character and future, is rubbish, and often very mischievous rubbish. Our children come into the world whether we like it or not, with characters which we have not made and cannot unmake. Some of their characteristics are survivals of savagery, so troublesome to us that they often infuriate us into clouting them at one end or smacking them at the other. Wordsworth tells us that they also come trailing clouds of glory; and this is true; but these intimations of immortality, as he called them, are sometimes even harder to bear than the savageries, because they put our worldliness to shame. Anyhow, whether the child's inborn characteristics are good or bad, the parents are not responsible for them: all they can do is to defend the family against them when they are unbearable, and let them have their way when they are not too mischievous. The expense is the worst part of it. Of course the world must be peopled; but it is the business of the State to see to that, and to see that the parents are well paid for it. At present our statesmen neglect this duty scandalously. They know that Nature will drive enough people to have children haphazard to keep the race from perishing; and unless you are an income-tax payer you get no allowance. But what is the result? The whole expense of replacing the dead falls on the actual parents, and the pain and risk on the actual mothers, whilst the old bachelors and old maids and the married couples who practise birth control contribute nothing but their share of the education rate, which does not cover the crushing cost of the schooling of the professional and business classes. Yet the renewal of the population is just as vital a necessity for the bachelors and old maids and the willfully sterile as for the actual parents. If our women had any sense they would threaten the Government with birth control, and refuse to become mothers unless the education and support of their children were State-guaranteed, and they themselves properly compensated for their pain and risk and trouble. Women who bear children for us are not in a condition to support themselves by climbing ladders.

My parents fed me and schooled me and lodged me as well as they could afford to. They paid a governess to teach me to read and write and do a few sums in simple arithmetic. The arithmetic did not get beyond simple addition and subtraction, because the poor old lady was incapable of explaining the nature of division; and as to the reading, I could never understand why she kept bothering me with a spelling and reading book; for I must have been born able to read – or else I acquired the power along with my first set of teeth: at all· events I can remember no time at which a printed page was not as intelligible to me as it is to-day; and I could not understand why I should be made to draw pothooks and hangers when I knew perfectly well how to write. To her dying day this old lady no doubt believed that she had taught the most famous of her pupils to read and write; but she really only confronted me with the problem of what the spelling book meant by the word *ab-ba, abba*. I wondered what it meant; and I am still wondering.

But she did teach me one very curious habit. She taught me to feel ashamed and to cry whenever she gave me a little slap on the shoulder that would not have hurt a fly, and to feel so pleased when she gave me a good mark that I rushed downstairs to boast to the servants about it when she left. I believe she regarded this as a triumph of moral training; but if so she was completely mistaken; for the truth is that I was such a ridiculously sensitive child that almost any sort of rebuff that did not enrage me hurt my feelings and made me cry; and I was also so imaginative that I boasted not only of the childish things I had actually done but of impossible fictitious adventures and exploits which were all the more heroic because I was in a fact a most disgraceful little coward. Poor Miss Hill – that was the lady's name: why should she not have it inscribed on the roll of fame with my own? – had no suspicion that she should have been knocking both the excessive sensitiveness and the silly boastfulness out of me instead of practising on the one and encouraging the other. She was terribly poor; and as she had been brought up as a lady and was therefore helpless without an independent income, she had to earn her scanty shillings by teaching genteel infants her ladylike accomplishments and her appalling limitations. The Miss Hills are supposed to be an extinct species nowadays; but it is surprising what a lot of people you meet still who seem to have been educated by them, even at the universities. You beware of Miss Hill. Never let yourself be persuaded that you are enjoying yourself, no matter how much you have paid for it, when you are really only being bored and over-charged for something you don't really like. And never let yourself be bluffed into feeling ashamed and disgraced when there is nothing really wrong with you. Look at me! I say and do and think lots of things that you let yourself be bluffed out of saying and doing and thinking. Am I any the worse? Not a bit: I make a good living by it.

My parents took no moral responsibility for me. I was just something that had happened to them and had to be put up with and supported. I never suf-· fered the meddlesomeness of those morbidly conscientious parents who are so busy with their children's characters that they have no time to look after their own. I cannot remember having ever heard a single sentence uttered by my mother in the nature of moral or religious instruction. My father made an effort or two. When he caught me imitating him by pretending to smoke a toy pipe he advised me very earnestly never to follow his example in any way; and his sincerity so impressed me that to this day I have never smoked, never shaved, and never used alcoholic stimulants. He taught me to regard him as an unsuccessful man with many undesirable habits, as a warning and not as a model. In fact he did himself some injustice lest I should grow up like him; and I now see that this anxiety on his part was admirable and lovable, and that he was really just what he so carefully strove not to be: that is, a model father. Many of us who are parents go through agonies of hypocrisy to win more respect from our children than we deserve. In our virtuous resolution to do our duty as parents we become humbugs; and when our children are old enough to find us out, as they do at a very early age, they become cynical, and laugh at the affectionate respect we have damned ourselves to gain. Be advised by me: do as my parents did: live your lives frankly in the face of your children according to your own real natures, and give your sons a fair chance of becoming Bernard Shaws.

I don't believe you will have the face to tell them even to do as everybody else does. It will stick in your throat when you are face to face with a child's innocence; for the child will grow up into a world where everybody is doing wrong. In the organized working class everybody is trying to do as little as possible and get as much as possible for doing it. In the middle class everyone is trying to make as much money as possible by getting as much work out of the working class and paying them as little for it as possible. In the propertied class everybody is living as luxuriously as possible without doing any work at all at the expense of both the other classes. It is frightful to say to a child 'Go thou and do likewise'; yet what else can you say? Your honest impulse is to tell your sons and daughters to speak the truth fearlessly; but if the best you can do for them after that is to start them in life as salesmen and shop assistants, or in the publicity industry of advertising, or in diplomacy, you are checked by the reflection that only as shameless liars can they hope to succeed. When Polonius said honestly to his son 'Neither a borrower not a lender be,' the son might very well have replied 'Father: no doubt you mean well; but nothing pays like lending provided you lend other people's money; and, as to borrowing, you can do nothing in big business nowadays without borrowing millions. Please do not give me any more good advice: I shall take the advice of the ancient Greeks, which was to first secure a handsome income and then practise virtue.'

I am afraid we must make the world honest before we can honestly tell our children that honesty is the best policy. At present the world is so dishonest that the bankrupt Bank of England is paying fourteen shillings in the pound though an honestly organized country could easily pay thirty. You had really better give your children no advice at all, but go your own way and leave your children to go theirs and form their own conclusions. Let us hope their conclusions will be wiser than ours.

The worst of it is that when you have resolved not to meddle with your children's souls and characters other people will. Schools and universities will do their best to stuff them with barbarous traditions, and make them believe that knowledge can be acquired by memorizing a set of obsolete answers to obsolete questions. Yet, if you can afford it, you cannot deny to your son or daughter the social training by which the communal life of the university rubs off the bad manners of the private house. If I were sending a son of mine to a university I should play Polonius to this effect. 'Go to the university, my son, but do not take a degree. When you are able to say that your university was Oxford or Cambridge and your college such and such a college, nobody will dream of asking whether you took a degree or not. Neglect the official curriculum of study as far as possible without being kicked out. Learn all you can; but never study anything that does not interest you. Take care of your mental health; for you cannot have a healthy body unless you have a healthy mind; and never forget that our traditional competitive British sport produces bad manners, bad feeling, brainless pugnacity, lust for doing the other fellow down, and almost everything that is contrary to the instincts of a true gentleman. Remind yourself continually that the conventional public school and university man is a walking calamity. In short, my son, if you react against your university it may make a social being of you; but if you let it impose on you do not expect to be mentioned in my will.'

[But you may now feel obliged to inform me that your son is not a Bernard Shaw; that if he is not supplied with an artificial character and equipped with a ready made set of traditions he will have no character and no traditions at all; that he is no more capable of reacting against his environment than a cork is capable of swimming upstream; and that if he is not a university man he will be a nobody. Well, in that case, he will be happy anywhere and you may congratulate yourself on having a son who will never give anybody any trouble provided he is reasonably goodhumored. If you send him to Oxford he will be a good Oxford man; and if you send him to Moscow he will be a good Communist. Such men make for social stability, and are nuisances only at moments like the present, when it is urgently necessary to get a move on.

But perhaps you are not yet a parent and are an ambitious young person. You think that my position is a highly desirable one; that I have world wide fame, immense influence, and a hundred thousand a year or so; and you want to know how I got there so that you may follow in my footsteps. I am sorry to disappoint you; but nothing that you can do or not do can advance you a step on my path. I owe my position, or rather what you imagine to be my position, solely to certain accidental abnormalities with which I was born, just like a giant or a dwarf or a two headed sheep at a fair. I can write plays. I can write anything. All the real live words in the English language are instantaneously at my command without thinking. I have an imagination which includes a sense of character. I have the analytic faculty which makes a critic and the comprehensive faculty which makes a political philosopher. I have a strong natural taste for fine art and an inexhaustible interest in science. I have the artist's passion for perfection which makes it intensely disagreeable for me to finish a piece of work until I have made as good a job of it as I can. Good work, sound reasoning, and intuitions that carry one forward at a bound to goals that are ahead of reasoning, are not dismal highbrow affectations to me: they are comfortable satisfactions and delightful luxuries. I cannot have them unless I am fed, clothed, lodged, and artificially warmed in winter; but I grudge the time and energy I have to spend on these common necessities, and have devoted much of my life to the study of Socialism because it would be quite easy to provide as much of them as any reasonable person wants at the cost of, at most, four hours work a day for everybody. If you add to the four hours work eight hours for sleep, two for meals, and two for locomotion, all of which are necessities as much as the work, we should have eight hours left in which to indulge our noblest aspirations and desires and to kill any thief or slacker who should try to shirk his four hours duty or put it on to someone else. I am not only a good Socialist by nature but I have a healthy natural scorn for all artificial and external substitutes for natural health and happiness. If you cannot keep healthy without pills and potions, cannot be happy without beer or champagne, cannot sleep without drugs, cannot kiss a woman unless she paints her lips scarlet, and cannot slay or reform a disease bacillus by your blood unless it is gingered up by inoculation, then you are a human mistake and had better go and drown yourself; for you are not really enjoying life: you are only letting your [word missing] persuade you that you are a most important and fortunate person, or at least that you will be someday when you win the Irish Sweep and can buy all the things you see in their shop windows. I have money enough now to buy anything I want in those shop windows; but I walk daily past miles of them and buy no more than I did when I walked past them without a penny in my pocket. I often stop to stare at them and wonder how anybody outside a lunatic asylum could be demented enough to imagine that he or she could possibly want them or find any place at home for them excepting a dust bin. I like the children's toyshops best; for I can understand the children wanting the toys and not knowing how soon they will get tired of them and smash them and throw them away. But the grown up people's toys! It is hard

to contemplate them without feeling that the late heavy rains may be the beginning of a new deluge without any ark. If I were God, I should certainly
lose patience.

However, let us get back to the point, which is, whether my position can be
attained by any ladder climber who makes up his mind to follow my example.
The answer is in the negative. Unless you are born with my natural endowment and capacity any attempt on your part or on that of your son to become
another Bernard Shaw would produce failure, disappointment, humiliation,
prostration, and possibly suicide, precisely as any attempt on my part to excel
in the thousand things that I cannot do – I have tried some of them, by the way,
and proved a hopeless duffer at them – would ruin my life.

I do not mean, by the way, that my professional qualities are unique, and
that you are probably destitute of them. Everyone has them in a certain degree.
Lots of amateurs can write a little, play a little, sing a little, garden a little, play
cricket and football, golf and bridge, dabble in chemistry and physics and pho-
tography, cut a figure in debating societies, drive motor cars: in short, find
great interest and satisfaction in doing for fun what others do for a living. I do
some of these things myself. But the arts by which I have become famous cannot be acquired by cultivation: they are either easy and natural or they are impossible. I forget how many plays I have written: probably between forty and
fifty. My first play, performed in 1892, is a much less cultivated work of art
than my last; but it will hold an audience just as well, and in fact, had its greatest success within the last year or so in Germany.[4] For all commercial purposes
the work of the novice is as good as the work of the veteran, if not better. Unless Nature has done ninetynine hundredths of the work before you are born
the utmost cultivation will never make you anything more than an amateur. If
Nature has made that contribution, and you are reasonably healthy and indus-
trious, hardly anything can prevent you from fulfilling your destiny in your
natural vocation. Mind: I do not mean that you will necessarily make money.
On the contrary, your vocation may keep you poor. One of England's greatest
poets told me that the income from his poems amounted to about a hundred a
year. He was living partly on his inherited means and partly by keeping a shop
in Oxford Street. Einstein is the greatest genius now living: we have to go back
three hundred years to Sir Isaac Newton to find anyone comparable to him.
But both these great men would have starved if jobs had not been found for
them that could have been done by quite commonplace men. Mozart was bur-
ied in a pauper's grave; and Beethoven could have earned more money as a
bootmaker than as a composer, though these two were great even among the
greatest in their profession. I was over forty before I could afford to marry, and
nearly thirty before I could live on what I earned by my pen.

In short, you may rule genius out of your calculations. If you are not born with it you cannot acquire it; and it is an extremely improbable accident of birth in any case. And even when you are born with it, it is a toss up whether it condemns you to infamy, starvation, and death on the scaffold or makes you a millionaire. The normal assumption must always be that you are not a genius, and that you may thank your stars for your escape as far as material wealth and fashionable successes are concerned.]

And now you will tell me that all this may be just what a queer fellow like myself would say to his son, but that as you are not a queer fellow nor a playwriting genius, and neither is your son, what you want to know is how the dear boy is to make more money than his neighbours; for I take it that making more money than one's neighbours is what is meant by climbing to the top of the ladder. Well, the simplest way is to inherit it; but that is very poor fun, because if you are born at the top of the ladder you can do nothing but cling giddily to it or else fall down it; and if you are brought up to be supported by other people instead of by your own exertions you are apt to lose the use of your legs. The parents who leave their children provided for in this way are doing them a very bad turn. It should be forbidden by law, and it will, presently. However, so few can afford this, and death duties and taxation of unearned incomes are making it so precarious, that I need not waste more of your time on it than to say that the lady and gentleman business is a bad business, with a worried present and a worse future.

How then, are you to raise yourself above the level of your neighbours if you have neither special talent nor inherited property? If you are a good Trade Unionist you will tell me indignantly that no one should try to rise above the level of his fellow workers: he should try to raise that level and rise with it. But this is too high a morality for the people turned out by our middle-class schools and universities, who are all trained morally to regard life as a race for eminence, every man for himself and devil take the hindmost. These poor dupes don't know that this sort of race is a donkey race, in which you are the donkey, carrying a landlord and capitalist on your back as well as their hired jockey, who holds a carrot in front of your nose which you never can overtake; so that though you and the other donkeys strain every nerve none of you can win. Your riders have all the fun and you all the labour. This is the inevitable lot of nine out of ten ordinary decent fellows under our system of property and competition. And now what about the tenth donkey, whose success persuades you that you, too, have a chance? Well, the tenth donkey is a specially fast one. He manages to jump on to the donkey in front of him and finish the race as one of the riders instead of one of the ridden.

You see, most of the propertied riders ride so badly that they would be thrown off in no time if they were not held on by jockey solicitors, jockey agents, jockey business managers, and jockey financiers. Besides, they have to be waited on by servants, physicked by doctors, amused by actors and singers; and kept in a good opinion of themselves by clergymen, who also keep the donkeys well persuaded that the donkey race is true religion. These professional and business men carry the propertied people on their backs; and the donkeys carry the lot. The race must also be kept in order by soldiers and policemen to see that the donkeys do not purposely lie down and roll over on their riders. The technical word for this sort of rolling over is revolution.

Is there any way to the top of the ladder for people without property who are not born with exceptional qualities? None. Nobody can get exceptional wages for what other people do just as well. However, there is one rule that breaks through all the other rules. Any of us can get almost anything that is humanly and legally obtainable if only he or she values it sufficiently to sacrifice every other consideration to it. If only you love money so much that you are prepared to seek it with all your heart, all your soul, all your mind, and all your body, letting nothing stand in your way except the police; if in gaining it you find your supreme satisfaction and delight: in short, if you are crazy about money, you will get heaps of it. Such devotion is a very unusual gift, to say nothing of its being one of the seven deadly sins. Its possessor is always haunted by the dread of poverty: the money maniac runs madly in pursuit of riches because he thinks the wolf is always at his heels. Every day now we read of some poor man, beaten by the vain search for employment, found dead with his head in the stove. But what is his despair compared to that of the famous South African millionaire who committed suicide because he had lost a couple of millions and had only four millions left? You may say he must have led a dog's life; but my dog is much happier than he can ever have been. Better be a poor man and be able to sing 'My mind to me a kingdom is'[5] than to see nothing in the world but money. I enjoy life quite sufficiently, though making money is to me such an unpleasant interruption of my work that I am not half as rich as I should be if I attended to my business properly. But I do not complain. My bodily wants – those that money can supply – are modest. Give me a comfortable flat in the West End of London, a pleasant little house with a few acres of ground in the country, a couple of good motor cars, and four or five thousand pounds a year pocket money, and there is not a more contented man in England than George Bernard Shaw. Only, as I believe in equality of income, I should feel much safer if everybody else had them as well; and I assure you there is nothing but your own political stupidity, and your silly notion that happiness is to be found at the top of a ladder, that make such an excellent arrangement impossible. The moral of my career is Down with the ladder! Let us all keep our feet on the ground and see to it that the footing is good. Good-bye. Always glad to come and wake you up and set you thinking.

B. 'Whither Britain?' Broadcast 6 February 1934. Published in *The Listener,*
7 February 1934
[See chapter 3, pp. 64–5.]

Whither Britain? What a question! Even if I knew, and you all know very
well that I do not know, could I tell you in half an hour? Now put a reasonable question, say a little bit of the big question: is Britain heading straight
for war? That's what you want to know, isn't it? Well, at present Britain is
not heading straight for anywhere. She is a ship without a pilot, driving before the winds of circumstance; and as such she is as likely to drift into war
as into anything else, provided somebody else starts the war. All the statesmen in Europe agree that another war would be a deplorable catastrophe;
and every country in the world is willing to disarm if all the others will disarm first, very much as I might safely offer to subscribe one hundred million
pounds to the Society for the Prevention of Cruelty to Children if twelve
other philanthropists would do the same; and so the League of Nations has
set up a Disarmament Conference which, after two years of fooling, has virtually ended in the confession of our Foreign Secretary, Sir John Simon, a
clearheaded lawyer, that the Disarmament Conference is really an armament
Conference, vainly trying to regulate armaments; and the Chairman of the
Conference, Mr. Arthur Henderson, has threatened to resign, because not
one of the Powers has, or ever had, the very slightest intention either of dis-
arming or of refraining from pursuing its researches into the newest and
most frightful methods of slaughter with all the diligence that terror can inspire. Only they would all like to do it as cheaply as possible; for the war taxation is very heavy. So they spent months discussing whether, if England
promises never to kill a German with a 16-inch shell, but always to do it with
a 10-inch one, Germany will make the same promise as to killing Englishmen. Now I cannot bring myself to take an interest in this. If I am to be killed
by a shell, I prefer it to be as big as possible, as it will give the occasion importance and make a bigger noise. Besides, I am still of the opinion I expressed in 1914, that the slaughter of a German lad by an English lad is as
great a loss to England as to Germany, and that the slaughter of an English
lad by a German lad is just as much a loss to Germany as to England. The notion that what is devilment for one army is heroism in another won't wash.
That is why so many of you – shall I say the most amiable of you? want to
prevent war altogether. Well, so do I. But we must not allow ourselves to be
put off by humbug about disarmament.[1]

Disarmament will not prevent war. Men fought just as fiercely as they do
now before a single one of our modern weapons was invented; and some of the

greatest naval battles were fought when fleets were moved by oars instead of by turbine engines. I have no doubt that, in the African tribes, when it was first proposed to use poisoned arrows instead of plain ones, there was just the same cry of horror about it as we had in England when the Germans attacked us with poison gas. Only fiends, we said, would use such a weapon! But at the end of a fortnight, when Lord Kitchener told us not to fuss, as we were going to use it ourselves, we settled down to it just as the African tribes settled down to the poisoned arrows; and we may as well settle down to the fact that in the next war all the most diabolical means of spreading death and destruction will be ready for use. We are at present working hard at them, and so are all the other Powers; so let us face it. We have got to, whether we like it or not.

Are we, then, to be exterminated by fleets of bombing aeroplanes which will smash our water mains, cut our electric cables, turn our gas supplies into flame-throwers; and bathe us and our babies in liquid mustard gas from which no masks can save us? Well, if we are it will serve us right; for it will be our own doing. But let us keep our heads. It may not work out in that way. For what is it that happens when a single soldier finds himself fact to face with a dozen of the enemy? He puts up his hands and demands quarter. What is it that happens when a body of troops finds itself hopelessly outnumbered and surrounded? It surrenders. What will London do when it finds itself approached by a crowd of aeroplanes, capable of destroying it in half an hour? London will surrender. White flags and wireless messages: 'Don't drop your bombs: we will give in,' will fill the air. But our own air squadrons will have already started to make the enemies' capitals surrender. From Paris to Moscow, from Stockholm to Rome, the white flags will go up in every city. All the navies will strike their colours; ransoms and reparations and indemnities will cancel each other after a squabble in Geneva; and the most disgraceful and inglorious war on record will peter out in general ridicule.

Therefore let us not join the present foolish protest against the multiplication of bombing aeroplanes. They are angels of peace. If the airmen gas the earth there will be no place for them to land and get their dinners. Besides, wars like the last one in 1914 involve the mobilization of vast assemblages of men and munitions in such numbers that the mobilization almost immobilizes itself by its own weight and mass. Such mobilization is impossible with an enemy in the air going at speeds of one hundred miles per hour and upward, and equipped with means of destruction and death that put big assemblages at its mercy. Mobilization will come to mean not the concentration of troops, but their rapid dispersal. Very small armies, highly trained to run away at the first report of an approaching enemy, will supersede the big battalions of Napoleon and those stupid imitators of his that do not know that Napoleon is deader than Queen Anne. So do not let yourselves be scared into perfectly useless attempts to keep war on its old Napoleonic footing. If you are a humanitarian, like myself, appeal to the chemists to discover a humane gas that will kill instantly and painlessly; in short, a gentlemanly gas, deadly by all means, but humane, not cruel. Even if we have to stop fighting we shall find a use for it at home.

There is another snag in war. It gets us into money troubles. Now this is curious, because wars cannot be fought on credit: they must be paid for on the nail: Englishmen and Germans cannot kill one another with Exchequer bills and War Loan scrip; nothing but hard shot and shell and high explosive, handled by real men, wearing real boots and clothes, and eating real meals, are of any use on the battlefield. The men and women who are making the boots and the guns and the explosives must be fed and clothed and housed; and this also cannot be done on credit. Promises of next year's boots and of food to be grown twenty years hence will not keep a war going for five minutes, much less five years. By hook or crook, Governments which go to war must be able to lay their hands on actual provisions and munitions. When the war is over there is nothing of them left: they are all consumed, or worn out, or fired off; and all that there is to shew for it, even by the victors, is a little glory and a great deal of death and destruction and disablement and desolation. But it is then discovered that the belligerent States obtained a great deal of their supplies and munitions, not by paying for them, but by promising to let the owners and their heirs live freely on the labor of their countries until the Government of the States buy back their promises or cancel them by taxing free incomes. They also try to repay the owners and enrich themselves by plundering the defeated enemies; but this does not work, because enemies are not defeated nowadays by old-fashioned decisive battles, but by blockade and starvation. Battles are useless: they last for months and then peter out as the last waves of the offensive are shot down by machine guns on the barbed-wire entanglements. Consequently, when the enemy is starved out, there is nothing to plunder. All that can be done is to make the defeated enemy pay an annual tribute year by year out of his earnings, and calling it reparations and indemnities. It sounds all right; but when we tried it on Germany it nearly ruined us. You see, there are no gold mines in Germany, so that when the Germans began paying us the tributes, they could not pay in gold money, they could do it only by supplying us with ships and steel and coal and the like.

Now before letting them do this we should have turned all our shipbuilders and steel smelters and coal miners into makers of chocolate creams and Christmas crackers, our shipyards into lawn tennis courts, our steel works into palace hotels, besides closing down all the coal mines. But our statesmen had never thought of this; and when they found that living on German labor meant that all our own labor was thrown out of work, they had to put tariffs to keep German goods out. This meant refusing to let the Germans pay in the only way they could pay: that is, refusing to let them pay at all. Of course, our statesmen didn't say so, because they didn't understand what they were doing. They said that the Germans must pay in gold, and get it by selling their goods to other nations for gold. But the other nations did just what we did, and for the same reason. They put on prohibitive tariffs and refused to admit German goods. The Germans could get no gold and had to keep their goods to themselves: it was a complete deadlock. Yet we managed to make it worse. To carry on the war, all the victorious allies had borrowed their supplies recklessly from America; and England had not only borrowed largely herself, but guaranteed the borrowings of several of the others. When the war was over, the borrowers defaulted or repudiated in all directions, leaving England owing an enormous tribute to the United States to pay for what they borrowed in addition to what she herself had borrowed. But the United States would not ruin their industries by accepting English goods in payment; they, too, wanted gold. Well, England has no gold mines; and when she tried to buy gold for her goods from other nations, up went their tariff walls to keep her goods out. When England and France had scraped together all the gold they could lay their hands on and sent it to America, America was bursting with gold that it would not sell for goods, and Europe was bursting with goods that it could not sell for gold. So trade in gold was brought to a standstill. Yet both Continents were perfectly solvent, and had nothing to do but wipe the slate and be happy.

Unfortunately, this simple solution got muddled up with the money question. Money is nothing but a title deed to goods. A penny is exchangeable for a pennyworth of goods. A pound is a title deed to a pound's worth of goods. There is only one sort of goods that is both handy and readily exchangeable for any sort of goods that its owners prefer to have, and that is gold. Accordingly, all the nations had to make their money entitle the owner to its value in gold. Anybody who had an English five pound note could go into the Bank of England and demand and receive five golden sovereigns for it. This was called being on the Gold Standard. But when the war tributes drained all the gold in Germany into England and France, and then drained all the gold in England and France into the United States, the Gold Standard became impossible in Europe. When you presented your five pound note at the Bank of England, the Bank had to say: 'Sorry: no gold today. You can have it in British coal or steel, or in British fried fish and chips; or would you like a British bicycle? You will not be allowed to take the bicycle into the United States, but it will be all right here.' Now this meant that England had gone off the Gold Standard. It was a great surprise to our voters, because the Government had just won an election by an impassioned appeal to the voters to save the country from utter dishonor and bankruptcy by saving the Gold Standard at all costs. The truth is, neither the voters nor the statesmen understood a thing about it. If they had, some voter would have asked the Prime Minister 'Have you any gold to back our money with; or if not, can you buy any? Because if not, we must go off the Gold Standard whether we like it or not; and the only things that can happen will be that if the United States will not take their tribute in goods, they must go whistle for it, just as we have had to go whistle for our tribute from Germany.' But nobody said anything of the sort, because nobody knew what the Gold Standard meant. So Democracy, through its voters, swore to maintain the Gold Standard to the last drop of its blood; and its political leaders promised to die rather than haul down that sacred emblem. But the first man who presented a five pound note at the Bank of England brought all that nonsense down with a crash. The election shouting was hardly over when we came off the Gold Standard like a hen off a hot griddle.

Now you would have thought that after this the nations would have seen that they must write off their debts and wipe the slate all round. But they were prevented by their insane Syndicalism. Syndicalism is well known on the Continent in a crude revolutionary form, as the doctrine that all our industries should be owned and managed and financed by the workers actually engaged in them – the mines by the miners, the railways by railwaymen, the factories by the factory hands, and the theatres by the actors and scene-shifters. Now everyone with two pennyworth of sense and knowledge of business knows that mines cannot be managed by miners, nor factories by factory operatives, nor railways by porters, plate-layers, locomotive-drivers and stokers. It is not their job. They know no more of the financing and managing and marketing of their trades than a cabin-steward knows about navigation. We can see this very clearly when Syndicalism is proposed for poor men who work for weekly wages; but we swallow it like children with our eyes shut and our mouths open when it is applied by Boards of Directors, bankers, and industrial and financial bosses generally. Yet these people are as ignorant of the difficult science of high politics as a coal hewer or cotton weaver is of office business. Their job is not to promote the welfare of the nation, but to make profits for themselves and their shareholders. They think that the nation is prospering when they are making profits, and is being ruined when their trade comes to a standstill. The shipping companies think that the country lives by its overseas trade, and that if every pound of cheese we make had to go three times round the world before we were allowed to eat it, we should be three times as rich as we were before. If you told them that the real interest of every country is to have as little overseas trade as possible they would think you had gone stark raving mad. If we had been able to produce everything we consumed during the war, there would have been no submarine campaign. But then the ship-owners would not have made enormous fortunes out of the war. The war was a godsend to them. But it was not a godsend to the rest of us.

But never mind the shippers. Now let us come to the very worst example of Boss Syndicalism. The most important trade in the country is the trade of money, because, as I have just reminded you, money consists of title deeds to all sorts of goods, from diamonds to baked potatoes. The trade in money is conducted by the bankers, who make enormous profits by keeping our spare money for us and lending it to us again at interest. They are always looking for borrowers, just as bakers and tailors are looking for customers, and they don't care a rap whether the borrower is a Britisher or a foreigner: they lend to whoever will pay the highest interest on the best security. And just as the cobbler comes to think there is nothing like leather, and the ship-owner that there is nothing like overseas trade, the bankers come to think that the whole business of the world consists of borrowing, and that we are all being ruined when we are not up to our eyes in debt. Now you know as well as I do that nations should be cash nations, just as the late Sir Jesse Boot[2] was a cash chemist. If a Government lets itself be guided by money-lenders, the money-lenders will guide it by the shortest way to bankruptcy, exactly as they guided the prodigal son. When we found out that the plundering of Germany, ordained by the Treaty of Versailles, had ended in one pound notes being worth only twelve-and-sixpence, we should have stopped it, and wiped the slate all round, but for the money-lenders. How did they prevent us? Very simply. They said 'All your difficulties arise from the fact that you think that Germany cannot pay her tribute to you. But you forget that she can if you lend her the money. We can arrange that quite easily.' Instead of sending them to the nearest lunatic asylum, our Boss Syndicalist Government said: 'Splendid! Why didn't we think of that before?' Of course, the German industrialists eagerly borrowed all the money they were offered, and used it to try to flood the markets of their creditors with German goods. Then up went all the tariffs again higher than ever, to keep out the German goods, and the old deadlock was worse than ever. Practically all the States stopped paying war debts. We were too honest to repudiate our debt to the United States: we acknowledged it handsomely and fully; but as we send only a few pounds now and then, to shew our good faith by what is politely called a 'token payment,' the United States will lose nothing worth mentioning when she takes the advice I gave her last April in New York,[3] and magnanimously writes off her unpayable debt. The plundering game is up, and the money-lending bubble is burst. The late Sir Jesse Boot and his Woolworth competitors turn out to have been much sounder financiers than the bankers; and the likelihood of another war is all the less because the last one, instead of doing all the glorious things it promised to do, and was intended to do, only smashed up the three Empires that began it; broke the Bank of England; and left the European belligerents, victors and vanquished alike, in the position of undischarged bankrupts, whilst their American creditor, with her banks broken in all directions, is cursing her Boss Syndicalism more heartily than any of them.

And now what will the United States do to us in England when they realize that we cannot pay them in gold and that payment in commercial goods will ruin their industries? Will they ask for payment in territory: say by handing over Jamaica to them? Will they offer to take the Codex Sinaiticus, the Elgin Marbles, and their pick of the choicest works in the British Museum Library, the Bodleian, and the National Gallery? We should reply that we will pay only what we borrowed; and what we borrowed was not territory, nor art treasures of incalculable value, but food and munitions. There is no job that we could do for the United States that her millions of unemployed would not clamor for if it were proposed to let us do it; and so the deadlock would come again, as hopeless as ever. There is really nothing for it but to wipe the slate, the sooner the better.

And now comes the question – when we have wiped the slates, what then? Are we to continue to live under a dictatorship of bankers and ship-owners, with cabinet ministers as their puppets and scapegoats? If so, what will happen? The ship-owners will keep on clamoring for more overseas trade, and filling the newspapers with their alarms of national ruin whenever there is a decrease in our exports. Manufacturers and farmers will want to keep out foreign goods and supply our own necessities by our own labor. But the two sets will agree on one point. They will both want to force English goods on foreign nations. If a country that has been wearing British stockings begins, very sensibly, to knit its own stockings, and puts a duty on British stockings to keep them out, the newspapers will echo the cries of our stocking merchants and ship-owners for what they openly call retaliation: that is, the Government is bullied into putting a vindictive duty on some product of the other country, to force it to give up knitting its own stockings. Nothing more senselessly stupid from the point of view of both nations could be imagined; but the ship-owners and the home manufacturers are quite well pleased, because the vindictive duty keeps out foreign goods. This silly squabbling used to end in wars; but war, as I said before, is becoming impossible, because instead of merely killing young soldiers, mostly unmarried, in the old style, it now kills women and men indiscriminately, and this means not glory but extermination. So we can no longer count on war to make us sit up and take our public business seriously. The disappearance of war seems such a relief at present that nobody thinks of looking beyond it; but as the waste of life under Boss Syndicalism is much worse than the slaughter in old-fashioned war, civilization may be in greater danger from peace than from war. I cannot go further into this now.

But there remains a very important point which I have not touched. When you ask 'Whither Britain?' what exactly do you mean by Britain? Do you mean the British Isles or the British Empire; for there is all the difference in the world. Ask a Cockney soldier to die for Camberwell, and he will think the demand a very proper one, though he won't die if he can help it. But ask him to die for Calcutta, and his reply will be unprintable. Therefore, we shall have to be very careful about this Empire business. I should be very glad indeed to see our Imperialist Englishmen regarding the Hong Kong Chinese, and the Singalese and the Malays, the Maoris, the Hindus and Zulus and Bantus as their compatriots, their fellow-Britains, their own Imperial flesh and blood, instead of lumping them all contemptuously together as niggers and Chinks. But if this touching extension of the brotherhood of mankind is to be effected at the cost of repudiating all our nearest European neighbors as foreigners and enemies, to be harassed with tariffs, and threatened by big armaments, then instead of giving three cheers for the Empire I feel inclined to say simply 'Don't be silly.' I grant you that nationalism and patriotism have to be reckoned with when there are friendly human instincts and ethnological facts at the back of them; but there are no friendly instincts at the back of Imperialism. On the contrary, the instinct not only of the distant Indian, but even of the nearby Welshman, the Irishman and the Scot, is to resent and repudiate Imperial dominance, so that if we are to preserve the connections, we must make it appear flattering and advantageous to all the parts of the Empire, giving them Home Rule, calling them dominions instead of colonies, and putting them on the same footing as what we call the Mother Country, or even on a better one. But think what that may lead to. There is only a handful of English-speaking people with pink skins in the dominions. The Indians outnumber the rest of the Empire, including England, five to one. Consequently, the effect of making India a dominion, in the Canadian sense, would be that England would become, in effect, a dominion of India, and England might not like that. England might break off from the Empire, as the United States did. Now think over this. I cannot feel sure of the permanence of any intimate political combination that is not based on homogeneity: that is, on the people in the combination being reasonably like one another in their tastes and religious faiths, their traditions and hopes. Now it is as plain as a pikestaff that a combination of the northern states of Europe with the United States of America, and with Australia and New Zealand, would be far more homogeneous than any possible combination of Europeans with Asiatics. In the war, when the French let loose their negro soldiers and the British their

Asiatic soldiers to slaughter our German neighbors, I felt, and I hope you did too, that this was not playing the game of Western civilization. When the question 'Whither Britain?' is put to me, I am quite prepared to make cheerful guesses as far as 'Britain' means British ideas and British stock; but if means a miscellaneous crowd of Chinese, millions of different sorts of Indians, a handful of Malay head-hunters and Fijian cannibals, and masses of dark-coloured native contingents from North and South Africa, then I can only shake my head. If I were a stranger from another planet I should say that an attempt to combine England with India before England was combined with the United States on the one side and with all her Western European neighbors on the other, is a crazy reversal of the natural order of things, and cannot possibly last. I could understand an Asiatic combination, with Japan as its most aggressive organizer, frightening the West into a European and American combination; but I could not back the permanency of the present combination.

I repeat, if we do not make the constituents of the Empire so independent of England that England will have nothing to do but support an enormously expensive navy to protect them, they will break off as the American colonies did; yet if we grant them that independence, the tail will wag the dog, as it did very vigorously at the Ottawa Conference.[4] As between the present arrangement of forty-five million pink men sitting on the heads of three hundred million brown and yellow men, and the international co-operation insisted on by Mr. Wells, I am on the side of Mr. Wells; and Wells and I are both much cleverer and more disinterested than the Boss Syndicalists. It is true that the Parliamentary gentlemen pay no attention to us, just as their grandfathers paid no attention to Dickens and Ruskin, Carlyle and Marx and the Fabians of the nineteenth century; but that did not in the least prevent things turning out as Dickens and the rest said they would, and as the Parliamentary gentlemen said they would not. So look out, dear listeners, look out. So long.

C. 'Film Censorship.' Broadcast 20 January 1935. Published in *The Listener*, 30 January 1935
[See chapter 3, pp. 57–8.]

The Prime Minister is quite right in hinting that though everyone desires wholesome theatres and picture houses, censorships are the very devil. Mr. MacDonald did not use these blunt words; but you may take it from me that they represent his meaning precisely. The Archbishop speaks of undesirable films. There are no undesirable films. No film studio in the world would spend fifty thousand pounds in making a film unless it was a very desirable film indeed. Possibly not desirable by an Archbishop, but certainly desirable by that very large section of the human race who are not Archbishops. Still, as Arch-bishops are very like other respectable gentlemen except that they wear gaiters instead of trousers, any film corporation which devoted itself to displeasing Archbishops would soon be bankrupt. In short, nobody wants to produce un-desirable films. Therefore let us stop talking about desirable and undesirable, and consider whether we can weed out from the great mass of desirable films those which are detrimental to public morals. The censorship method, which is that of handing the job over to some frail and erring mortal man, and making him omnipotent on the assumption that his official status will make him infal-lible and omniscient, is so silly that it has produced the existing agitation; and yet some of the agitators are actually clamouring for more of it. Others are ob-sessed with sex appeal. Now sex appeal is a perfectly legitimate element in all the fine arts that deal directly with humanity. To educate and refine it is one of the most sacred functions of the theatre. Its treatment under the censorship is often vulgar; yet I believe that, on balance, the good that has been done by the films in associating sex appeal with beauty and cleanliness, with poetry and music, is incalculable. It is in quite other directions that the pictures are often mischievous; and if a new public enquiry is set on foot, people who consider sex as sinful in itself must be excluded from it like other lunatics; and its busi-ness must be to ascertain whether, on the whole, going to the films makes worse or better citizens of us. As to the remedy, the most successful one so far has been the licensing of places of public entertainment from year to year by representative local authorities, accessible to complaints from individuals or deputations, and with powers to withdraw licences from ill-conducted houses for what are called judicial reasons by a majority vote. The subject is difficult, delicate and complicated; but so far, licensing has proved the most effective ex-pedient for keeping decent order pending the time when theatres and picture houses will be public institutions under the control of a Ministry of Education and the Fine Arts. This is my considered opinion; and I am an old hand and know what I am talking about. Sleep on it before you join the outcry.

D. 'School.' Broadcast 11 June 1937. Published in *The Listener*, 23 June 1937 [See chapter 3, pp. 61–2.]

Hallo, Sixth Forms! I have been asked to speak to you because I have become celebrated through my eminence in the profession of Eschylus, Sophocles, Eu-ripides, and Shakespeare. Eschylus wrote in school Greek; and Shakespeare is 'English Literature,' which is a school subject. In French Schools I am English literature. Consequently all the sixth forms in France shudder when they hear my name. However, do not be alarmed: I am not going to talk to you about

English literature. To me there is nothing in writing a play; anyone can write one if he has the necessary natural turn for it; and if he hasn't he can't: that is all there is to it.

However, I have another trick for imposing on the young. I am old: over eighty in fact. Also I have a white beard; and these two facts are somehow associated in people's minds with wisdom. That is a mistake. If a person is a born fool, the folly will get worse, not better, by a long life's practice. Having lived four times as long as you gives me only one advantage over you. I have carried small boys and girls in my arms, and seen them grow into sixth form scholars, then into young men and women in the flower of youth and beauty, then into brides and bridegrooms who think one another much better and lovelier than they really are, then into middle-aged paterfamiliases and anxious mothers with elderly spreads, and finally I have attended their cremations.

Now you may not think much of this; but just consider. Some of your schoolfellows may surprise you by getting hanged. Others, of whom you may have the lowest opinion, will turn out to be geniuses, and become one of the great men of your time. Therefore always be nice to young people. Some little beast who is no good at games and whose head you may possibly have clouted for indulging a sarcastic wit and a sharp tongue at your expense may grow into a tremendous swell, like Rudyard Kipling. You never can tell.

It is no use reading about such things or being told about them by your father. You must have known the people personally, as I have. That is what makes a difference between your outlook on the world and mine. When I was as young as you the world seemed to me to be unchangeable; and a year seemed a long time. Now the years fly past before I have time to look round. I am an old man before I have quite got out of the habit of thinking myself as a boy. You have fifty years before you, and therefore must think carefully about your future and about your conduct. I have no future and need not care what I say or do.

You all think, don't you, that you are nearly grown up. I thought so when I was your age, and now, after eighty-one years of that expectation I have not grown up yet. The same thing will happen to you. You will escape from school only to discover that the world is a bigger school, and that you are back again in the first form. Before you can work your way up into the sixth form again you will be as old as I am.

The hardest part of schooling is fortunately the early part when you are a very small kid and have to be turned into a walking ready reckoner. You have to know up to 12 times 12, and how many shillings there are in any number of pence up to 144 without looking at a book. And you must understand a printed page just as you understand people talking to you. That is a stupendous feat of sheer learning: much the most difficult I have ever achieved; yet I have not the faintest recollection of being put through it, though I remember the governess who did it. I cannot remember any time at which a printed page was unintelligible to me, nor at which I did not know without counting that 56 pence make four and eightpence. This seems so magical to me now that I sometimes regret that she did not teach me the whole table of logarithms and the binomial theorem and all the other mathematical short cuts and ready reckonings as well. Perhaps she would have if she had known them herself. It is strange that if you learn anything when you are young you remember it for ever. Now that I am old I forget everything in a few seconds, and everybody five minutes after they have been introduced to me. That is a great happiness, as I don't want to be bothered with new things and new people; but I still cannot get on without remembering what my governess taught me. So cram in all you can while you are young.

But I am rambling. Let us get back to your escape from your school or your university into the great school of the world; and remember that you will not be chased and brought back. You will just be chucked out neck and crop and the door slammed behind you.

What makes school life irksome until you get used to it, and easy when you do get used to it, is that it is a routine. You have to get up at a fixed hour, wash and dress, take your meals and do your work all at fixed hours. Now the worst of a routine is that though it is supposed to suit everybody, it really suits nobody. Sixth form scholars are like other people: they are all different. Each of you is what is called an individual case, needing individual attention. But you cannot have it at school. Nobody has time enough nor money enough to provide each of you with a separate teacher and a special routine carefully fitted to your individual personality, like your clothes and your boots.

I can remember a time when English people going to live in Germany were astonished to find that German boots were not divided into rights and lefts: a boot was a boot and it did not matter which foot you put it on, your foot had to make the best of it. You may think that funny; but let me ask how many of you have your socks knitted as rights and lefts? I have had mine knitted that way for the last fifty years. Some knitters of socks actually refuse my order and say that it can't be done. Just think of that! We are able to make machines that can fly round the world and instruments that can talk round the world; yet we think we cannot knit socks as rights and lefts; and I am considered a queer sort of fellow because I want it done and insist that it can be done. Well, school routines are like the socks and the old German boots: they are neither rights nor lefts, and consequently they don't fit any human being properly. But we have to manage with them somehow. And when we escape from school into the big adult world, we have to choose between a lot of routines: the college routine, the military routine, the naval routine, the court routine, the civil service routine, the legal routine, the clerical routine, the theatrical routine, or the parliamentary routine, which is the worst of the lot. To get properly stuck into one of these grooves you have to pass examinations; and this you must set about very clear-headedly or you will fail. You must not let yourself get interested in subjects or be overwhelmed by the impossibility of anyone mastering them all even at the age of five hundred, much less twenty. The scholar who knows everything is like the little child who is perfectly obedient and perfectly truthful: it doesn't exist and never will. Therefore you must go to a crammer. Now what is a crammer? A crammer is a person whose whole life is devoted to doing something you have not time to do for yourself: that is, to study all the old examination papers and find out what are the questions that are actually asked, and what are the answers expected by the examiners and officially recognised as correct. You must be very careful not to suppose that these answers are always the true answers. Your examiners will be elderly gentlemen; and their knowledge is sure to be more or less out of date. Therefore begin by telling yourself this story.

Imagine yourself a young student early in the fifteenth century being examined as to your knowledge of the movements of the sun and moon, the planets and stars. Imagine also that your father happens to know Copernicus, and that you have learnt from his conversation that the planets go round not in circles but in ellipses. Imagine that you have met the painter Leonardo da Vinci, and been allowed to peep at his funny notebook, and by holding it up to a mirror, read the words 'the earth is a moon of the sun.' Imagine that on being examined you gave the answers of Copernicus and Leonardo, believing them to be the true answers. Instead of passing at the head of the successful list you would have been burnt alive for heresy. Therefore you would have taken good care to say that the stars and the sun move in perfect circles, because the circle is a perfect figure and therefore answers to the perfection of the Creator. You would have said that the motion of the sun round the earth was proved by the fact that Joshua saw it move in Gibeon and stopped it. All your answers would be wrong; but you would pass and be patted on the head as a young marvel of Aristotelian science.

Now passing examinations today is just what it was in the days of Copernicus. If you at twenty years of age go up to be examined by an elderly gentleman of fifty, you must find out what people were taught thirty years ago and stuff him with that, and not with what you are taught today.

But, you will say, how are you possibly to find out what questions are to be asked and what answers are expected? Well, you cannot; but a good crammer can. He cannot get a peep at the papers beforehand; but he can study the old examination papers until he knows all the questions that the examiners have to keep asking over and over again; for after all their number is not infinite. If only you will swot hard enough to learn them all you will pass with flying colours. Of course you will not be able to learn them all; but your chances will be good in proportion to the number you can learn.

The danger of being plucked for giving up-to-date answers to elderly examiners is greatest in the technical professions. If you want to get into the navy, or practise medicine, you must get specially trained for some months in practices that are quite out of date. If you don't you will be turned down by admirals dreaming of the Nelson touch, and surgical baronets brought up on the infallibility of Jenner and Lister and Pasteur. But this does not apply to all examinations. Take the classics, for instance. Homer's Greek and Virgil's Latin, being dead languages, do not change as naval and medical practice changes. Supposed you want to be a clergyman. The Greek of the New Testament does not change. The creeds do not change. The Thirty-nine Articles do not change, though they ought to; for some of them are terribly out of date. You can cram yourself with these subjects and save your money for lessons on elocution.

In any case you may take it as a safe rule that if you happen to have any original ideas about examination subjects you must not air them in your examination papers. You may very possibly know better than your examiners; but do not let them find out that you think so.

Once you are safely through your examinations you will begin life in earnest. You will then discover that your education has been very defective. You will find yourself uninstructed as to eating and drinking and sleeping and breathing. Your notions of keeping yourself fit will consist mostly of physical exercises which will shorten your life by twenty years or so. You may accept me as an educated man because I have earned my living for sixty years by work which only an educated man, and even a highly educated one, could do. Yet the subjects that educated me were never taught in my schools. As far as I know, my schoolmasters were utterly and barbarously ignorant of them. School was to me a sentence of penal servitude. You see I was born with what people call an artistic temperament. I could read all the masterpieces of English poets, playwrights, historians and scientific pioneers; but I could not read schoolbooks, because they are written by people who do not know how to write. To me a person who knew nothing of all the great musicians from Palestrina to Edward Elgar, or of the great painters from Giotto to Burne Jones, was a savage and an ignoramus even if he were hung all over with gold medals for school classics. As to mathematics, to be imprisoned in an ugly room and set to do sums in algebra without ever having had the meaning of mathematics explained to me, or its relation to science, was enough to make me hate mathematics all the rest of my life, as so many literary men do. So do not expect too much from your school achievements. You may win the Ireland scholarship and then find that none of the great business houses will employ a university don on any terms.

As to your general conduct and prospects, all I have time to say is that if you do as everyone does and think as everyone thinks you will get on very well with your neighbours; but you will suffer from all their illnesses and stupidities. If you think and act otherwise you must suffer their dislike and persecution. I was taught when I was young that if people would only love one another, all would be well with the world. This seemed simple and very nice; but I found when I tried to put it in practice not only that other people were seldom lovable, but that I was not very lovable myself. I also found that to love anyone is to take a liberty with them which is quite unbearable unless they happen to return your affection, which you have no right to expect. What you have to learn if you are to be a good citizen of the world is that though you will certainly dislike many of your neighbours, and differ from some of them so strongly that you could not possibly live in the same house with them – that does not give you the smallest right to injure them or even to be personally uncivil to them. You must not attempt to do good to those who hate you: for they do not need your officious services, and would refuse to be under any obligation to you. Your difficulty will be how to behave to those whom you dislike, and cannot help disliking for no reason whatever, simply because you were born with an antipathy to that sort of person. You must just keep out of their way as much as you can; and when you cannot, deal as honestly and civilly with them as with your best friend. Just think what the world would be like if everyone who disliked you were to punch your head.

The oddest thing about it is that you will find yourself making friends with people whose opinions are the very opposite to your own, whilst you cannot bear the sight of others who share all your beliefs. You may love your dog and find your nearest relatives detestable. So don't waste your time arguing whether you *ought* to love all your neighbours. You can't help yourself; and neither can they.

You may find yourself completely dissatisfied with all your fellow-creatures as they exist at present and with all their laws and institutions. Then there is nothing to be done but to set to work to find out exactly what is wrong with them, and how to set them right. That is perhaps the best fun of all; but perhaps I think so only because I am a little in that line myself. I could tell you a lot more about this; but time is up; and I am warned that I must stop. I hope you are sorry.

E. 'As I See It.' Broadcast 2 November 1937. Published in *The Listener*, 10 November 1937
[See chapter 3, pp. 66–7. The three paragraphs set off in square brackets are in the typescript of the talk in the British Library, but are marked, in Shaw's hand,

'Discards from Broadcast "As I See It"' (Add Ms 50705, ff. 103–5). They are
published here for the first time.]

What about this danger of war which is making us all shake in our shoes at
present? I am like yourself: I have an intense objection to having my house de-
molished by a bomb from an aeroplane and myself killed in a horribly painful
way by mustard gas. I have visions of streets heaped with mangled corpses in
which children wander crying for their parents and babies gasp and strangle in
the clutches of dead mothers. That is what war means nowadays. This is what
is happening in Spain and in China whilst I speak to you;[1] and it may happen
to us tomorrow. And the worst of it is that it doesn't matter two straws to Nature, the mother of us all, how dreadfully we misbehave ourselves in this way,
or in what hideous agonies we die. Nature can produce children enough to
make good any extremity of slaughter of which we are capable. London may
be destroyed; Paris, Rome, Berlin, Vienna, Constantinople may be laid in
smoking ruins and the last shrieks of their women and children give way to the
silence of death. No matter: Mother Nature will replace the dead. She is doing
so every day. The new men will replace the old cities and perhaps come to the
same miserable end. To Nature the life of an empire is no more than the life of a
swarm of bees; and a thousand years are of less account than half-an-hour to
you and me.

Now the moral of that is that we must not depend on any sort of divine
providence to put a stop to war. Providence says 'Kill one another, my children:
kill one another to your heart's content. There are plenty more where you came
from.' Consequently, if we want war to stop we must all become Conscientious
Objectors. I dislike war not only for its dangers and inconveniences but because
of the loss of so many young men any of whom may be a Newton or an Einstein,
a Beethoven, a Michelangelo, a Shakespeare, or even a Shaw. Or he may be what
is of much more immediate importance, a good baker or a good weaver or
builder. If you think a pair of combatants as an heroic British St. Michael bring-
ing the wrath of God upon a German Lucifer, then you may exult in the victory
of St Michael if he kills Lucifer, or burn to avenge him if his dastardly adversary mows him down with a machine-gun before he can get to grips with him.
In that way you can get intense emotional experience from war. But suppose
you think of the two as they probably are: say, two good carpenters taken away
from their proper work to kill one another. That is how I see it; and the result is
that whichever of them is killed, the loss is as great to Europe and to me. In
1914 I was as sorry for the young Germans who lay slain or mutilated in No
Man's Land as for the British lads who lay beside them, so I got no emotional
satisfaction out of the War. It was to me a sheer waste of life.

I am not forgetting the gratification that war gives to the instinct of pugnacity and admiration of courage that are so strong in women. In the old days when people lived in forests like gorillas or in caves like bears, a woman's life and that of her children depended on the courage and killing capacity of her mate. To this day in Abyssinia a Danakil woman will not marry a man until he proves that he has at least four homicides to his credit. In England on the outbreak of war civilized young women rush about handing white feathers to all young men who are not in uniform. This, like other survivals from savagery, is quite natural; but our women must remember that courage and pugnacity are not much use against machine-guns and poison gas.

The pacifist movement against war takes as its charter the ancient document called the Sermon on the Mount, which is almost as often quoted as the speech which Abraham Lincoln is supposed to have delivered on the battlefield of Gettysburg. The Sermon is a very moving exhortation; and it gives you one first-rate tip, which is, to do good to those who despitefully use you and persecute you. I, who am a much-hated man, have been doing that all my life; and I can assure you there is no better fun, whereas revenge and resentment make life miserable and the avenger hateful. But such a command as 'love one another,' as I see it, is a stupid refusal to accept the facts of human nature. Pray, are we lovable animals? Do you love the rate-collector? Do you love Mr. Lloyd George? And if you do, do you love Mr. Winston Churchill? Have you an all-embracing affection for Messieurs Mussolini, Hitler, Franco, Ataturk and the Mikado? I do not love all these gentlemen, and even if I did, how could I offer myself to them as a delightfully lovable person? I find I cannot like myself without so many reservations that I look forward to my death – which cannot now be far off – as a good riddance. If you tell me to be perfect as my Father in Heaven is perfect, I can only say that I wish I could. That would be more polite than telling you to go to the Zoo and advise the monkeys to become men and the cockatoos to become birds of paradise.

The lesson we have to learn is that our dislike for certain persons, or even for the whole human race, does not give us any right to injure our fellow creatures, however odious they may be. As I see it, the social rule must be Live and let Live. And as people who break this rule persistently must be liquidated, even pacifists and non-resisters must draw a line accordingly.

When I was a young man in the latter half of the nineteenth century, war did not greatly concern me personally, because I lived on an island far away from the battlefields and because the fighting was done by soldiers who had taken up that trade in preference to any other open to them. Now that aeroplanes bring battle to my house-top and governments take me from my proper work and force me to be a soldier whether I like it or not, I can no longer regard war as something that does not concern me personally. You may say that I am too old to be a soldier; but if nations had any sense they would begin a war by sending their oldest men into the trenches. They would not risk the lives of their young men except in the last extremity. In 1914 it was a dreadful thing to see regiments of lads singing 'Tipperary' on their way to the slaughter-house; but the spectacle of regiments of octogenarians hobbling to the front and waving their walking-sticks and piping up to the tune of 'We'll never come back no more, boys; we'll never come back no more,' wouldn't you cheer that enthusiastically? I should. But let me not forget that I shall be one of them.

It has become a commonplace to say that another great war would destroy civilization. Well, that will depend on what sort of war it will be. If it is to be like the 1914 war, a war of nations, it will certainly not make an end of civilization. It may conceivably knock the British Empire to bits and leave England as primitive as she was when Julius Caesar landed in Kent. Perhaps we should be happier then; for we are still savages at heart, and wear our thin uniform of civilization very awkwardly. But, anyhow, there will be two refuges left for civilization. No *national* attack can seriously hurt the two great federated republics of North America and Soviet Russia. They are too big, the distances are too great. But what could destroy them is civil war; war like the wars of religion in the seventeenth century. And this is exactly the sort of war that is threatening us today. It has already begun in Spain, where all the big Capitalist powers are taking a hand to support General Franco through an Intervention Committee which they think it more decent to call a Non-intervention Committee. This is only a skirmish in the class war, the war between the two religions of Capitalism and Communism which is at bottom a war between labour and land-owning. We could escape that war by putting our house in order as Russia has done, without any of the fighting and killing and waste and damage that the Russians went through; but we don't seem to want to. I have shewn exactly how it can be done, and in fact how it must be done, but nobody takes any notice. Foolish people in easy circumstances flatter themselves that there is no such thing as the class war in the British Empire, where we are all far too respectable and too well protected by our parliamentary system to have any vulgar unpleasantness of that sort. They deceive themselves. We are up to the neck in the class war.

[I daresay you are neither a Capitalist nor a Communist because most people have no capital and don't understand Communism. Now I am both a Capitalist and a Communist. I have what you would consider a lot of money invested in securities of one sort or another, giving me a comfortable income for which I don't work, though other people have to work hard to produce every penny of it. Naturally that suits me very well, though I cannot conscientiously recommend it to those other people. So far, I am a Capitalist. But there is another side to it which is not so pleasant for me. I must have a house to live in. A quite decent house with two living rooms and three bedrooms can be built for £400. The interest on £400 at ten per cent is £40 a year; and I shouldn't object to paying that for it. But for two living rooms, a workroom and two bedrooms I have to pay £700 a year or thereabouts. I have been paying on that scale for the last forty years. If I refuse I shall be pitched into the street neck and crop.

You tell me I am lucky to be able to afford it. But think of the people who can't afford it. Think of the girl in the city with a clerk's wages having to pay fifteen shillings a week for ninepence worth of accommodation before she spends a penny on herself. Think of the women whose underfed children are clamouring for more food having to give the money that would buy another loaf to somebody who has the whole police force at his back when he says 'Pay me first, or out you go into the street, you and your brats.' Think of her husband, who cannot bring her home a shilling more because he has to provide the shareholders with fifty horse power motor cars before he touches a farthing of the colossal wealth his newspapers tell him his labour is producing.

My own trumpery grievances do not stop at my ground rent. I sometimes need the services of a professional man. I am obliged to occupy his time for half an hour or less. For this I have to pay him three guineas. Yet by taking a bus to the suburbs for two-pence I can obtain the same service for five shillings, although the suburban gentleman has a house all to himself whilst the three guineas man has only two rooms. He does better, somehow, out of his five shillings – or shall I say out of my five shillings – than his fashionable colleague does out of my three guineas. And that is because he has not to hand over so much of it for permission to live in the suburbs as his colleague has to live in the west end. Now what provokes me is that I have to work for the three guineas, and then the professional man has to work for it, and finally it nearly all goes to somebody we never saw who pockets it without ever having had to work at all. That is to say, he inflicts on me and on the professional man exactly the same injury that a robber does; but we must not call him a robber because he has somehow managed to get laws passed which make his proceedings quite legal, besides enjoying a high social position and perhaps a seat in the House of Lords. All sorts of clever excuses are made for this queer arrangement; but it is fundamentally dishonest.]

What is it that is wrong with our present way of doing things? It is not that we cannot produce enough goods. Our machines turn out as much work in an hour as ten thousand hand-workers used to. But it is not enough for a country to produce goods: it must distribute them as well; and this is where our system breaks down hopelessly. Everybody ought to be living quite comfortably by working four or five hours a day with two Sundays in the week, yet millions of labourers die in the workhouse or on the dole after sixty years of hard toil so that a few babies may have hundreds of thousands a year before they are born.

As I see it this is not a thing to be argued about or to take sides about. It is stupid and wicked on the face of it; and it will smash us and our civilization if we do not resolutely reform it. Yet we do nothing but keep up a perpetual ballyhoo about Bolshevism, Fascism, Communism, Liberty, Dictators, Democracy, and all the rest of it. The very first lesson of the new history dug up for us by Professor Flinders Petrie[2] during my lifetime is that no civilization, however splendid, illustrious and like our own, can stand up against the social resentments and class conflicts which follow a silly misdistribution of wealth, labour and leisure. And it is the one history lesson that is never taught in our schools, thus confirming the saying of the German philosopher Hegel. 'We learn from history that men never learn anything from history.'

Think it over. So long.

F. 'The Unavoidable Subject.' 1940 (not broadcast). From Shaw, *Platform and Pulpit* **286–92**
[See chapter 6, pp. 106–12.]

The other day a young man from Scotland told me that he was going to be a conscientious objector. I asked him why. He replied, 'Because this is a silly war.' I quite agreed with him. All wars are silly wars nowadays between civilized peoples. I pointed out, however, that this will not stop the onset of Mr Hitler's tanks, nor turn his bombs into picnic baskets. I took it that my conscientious friend did not desire a triumphant victory for us. Not he; he thought that such a victory would go to our heads and we should abuse it. But did he desire a triumphant victory for Mr Hitler? Certainly not; for that would be still worse, because the English would only come into the streets and maffick for a fortnight and then forget all about it; but the Germans would make a philosophy of it and try to follow it up by a conquest of Europe. We agreed that our business is to reduce Mr Hitler and his philosophy to absurdity. So I asked, is there any other way of doing this now except putting up such a devil of a fight that Germany will at last say to Mr Hitler, What hast thou done with my legions? And turn on him as the French turned on Napoleon.

The young Caledonian was open to reason. He immediately borrowed £2 from me, and joined up. If he had been an Englishman he would have quoted the Scriptures to me or said he did not hold with Churchill and that lot. I should not have argued with him. I should have taken a hint from my friend Priestley and just reminded him that the Germans have sunk the Gracie

Fields.[1] That would have sent him to the front like a thunderbolt. I have not forgotten the sinking of the Lusitania.[2]

We always lose the first round of our fights through our habit of first declaring war and then preparing for it. And then we find that our troops are short of shells as they were in 1914, and short of planes and tanks as they are just now. We waste precious time squabbling about whose fault it is, and declaring that all the members of the Government whom we happen to dislike should be shot. We must stop that. The nation which is always preparing for war is like a hypochondriac who is always making his will: a dismal occupation which prevents him from doing anything else.

Mr Hitler did wonders for his country by his National Socialism, and then threw it all away to prepare for war by turning his workers into soldiers and his factories into munition works when they might have been making themselves happy and comfortable as sensible welfare workers. Heaven defend us from Governments who can think of nothing but the next war and do nothing but prepare for it! So again I say, stop squabbling about it. We are guilty of our unpreparedness; and quite right we were too. It was worth it.

But we must not give ourselves moral airs as a peace-loving people because we have been deliberately careless. Mr Hitler did not begin this war; we did. It is silly to revile him as a treacherous wolf pouncing on a nation of innocent lambs. We are not innocent lambs; we are the most formidable of all the great European Powers, claiming command of the sea, which is nothing more or less than the power to blockade and starve to death any of our rivals. Having that terrible power we are under the most sacred obligation to use it to defend, not ourselves alone, but common humanity.

When Mr Hitler reconquered Poland, and had half his conquest immediately taken from him by Russia, there was peace for the moment, because Europe was terrified by his victory. The nations trembled and said, What will he do now? Who will be the next victim? Which of us dare bell this wild cat? Thereupon we, the British Commonwealth, on our own single responsibility deliberately punched Mr Hitler on the nose and told him in the plainest terms that his notions of humanity are not compatible with ours, and that we are going to abolish his rule by shot and shell, bayonet and blockade; and what had he to say to that? What could he do but take off his coat and come on? As to what he had to say he was explicit enough. He assured us that our view of the Hitleristic German Reich was exactly his view of the Imperialist British Empire; and that though *he* would be fighting with a rope round his neck, he would give us ten shots and shells for our one, and sink, burn, and destroy until he had done unto us what he had already done to Poland. And so we are at it hammer and tongs; and as it was we who asked for it, it is up to us to make good. I have no patience with the journalists and the tub thumpers who are breaking our spirits by sniveling about our being victims of a foul and treacherous aggression. We are the challengers and the champion fighters for humanity.

The British people, the real British people, feel this instinctively. But they are puzzled by the intellectuals and the politicians and journalists. They want to know exactly why we hit Mr Hitler on the nose, when he had his hands in his pockets – and in some of his neighbors' pockets as well. And they are told officially what fine fellows we are, and that we are sure to win because God is on our side, and that a trumpery scrap in which three British warships drove one German one into the River Plate was a greater victory than Jutland or Trafalgar or Lepanto.[3] That is not good enough. God has rebuked it in Belgium promptly and sharply. The people still ask, What exactly is the Big Idea that we must risk our lives for?

Until our people get a clear answer they will not know where we stand against the German legions and the Fifth Column.

What makes it so puzzling is that nine-tenths of what Mr Hitler says is true. Nine-tenths of what Sir Oswald Mosley[4] says is true. Quite often nine-tenths of what our parliamentary favorites say to please us is emotional brag, bunk, and nonsense. If we start hotheadedly contradicting everything Mr Hitler and Sir Oswald say, we shall presently find ourselves contradicting ourselves very ridiculously, and getting the worst of the argument. We must sift out the tenth point for which we are fighting, and nail the enemy to that.

Let us come down to brass tacks. What am I, a superannuated non-combatant, encouraging young men to fight against? It is not German national socialism: I was a National Socialist before Mr Hitler was born. I hope we shall emulate and surpass his great achievement in that direction. I have no prejudices against him personally; much that he has written and spoken echoes what I myself have written and spoken. He has adopted even my diet.[5] I am interested in him as one of the curiosities of political history; and I fully appreciate his physical and moral courage, his diplomatic sagacity, and his triumphant rescue of his country from the yoke the Allies imposed on it in 1918.[6] I am quite aware of the fact that his mind is a twentieth-century mind, and that our governing class is mentally in the reign of Edward the Third, six centuries out of date. In short, I can pay him a dozen compliments which I could not honestly pay to any of our present rulers.

My quarrel with him is a very plain one. I happen to be what he calls a Nordic. In stature, in color, in length of head, I am the perfect blond beast whom Mr Hitler classes as the salt of the earth, divinely destined to rule over all lesser breeds. Trace me back as far as you can; and you will not find a Jew in my ancestry. Well, I have a friend who is a Jew. His name is Albert Einstein; and he is a far greater human prodigy than Mr Hitler and myself rolled into one. The nobility of his character has made his genius an unmixed benefit to his fellow creatures. Yet Adolf Hitler would compel me, the Nordic Bernard Shaw, to insult Albert Einstein; to claim moral superiority to him and unlimited power over him; to rob him, drive him out of his house, exile him, be punished if I allow a relative of mine to marry a relative of his; and finally to kill him as part of a general duty to exterminate his race. Adolf has actually done these things to Albert, bar the killing, as he carelessly exiled him first and thus made the killing impossible. Since then he has extended the list of reprobates from Semites to Celts and from Poles to Slavs; in short, to all who are not what he calls Nordics and Nazis. If he conquers these islands he will certainly add my countrymen, the Irish, to the list, as several authorities have maintained that the Irish are the lost tribes of Israel.

Now, this is not the sort of thing that sane men can afford to argue with. It is on the face of it pernicious nonsense and the moment any ruler starts imposing it on his nation or any other nation by physical force there is nothing for it but for the sane men to muster their own physical forces and go for him. We ought to have declared war on Germany the moment Mr Hitler's police stole Einstein's violin. When the work of a police force consists not of *suppressing* robbery with violence but actually *committing* it, that force becomes a recruiting ground for the most infernal blackguards, of whom every country has its natural-born share. Unless such agents are disciplined and controlled, their heads are turned by the authority they possess as a State police; and they resort to physical torture as the easiest way to do their work and amuse themselves at the same time. How is that discipline and control to be maintained? Not by an autocrat, because, as Napoleon said when he heard about Nelson and Trafalgar, an autocrat cannot be everywhere. When his police get out of hand and give his prisons and concentration camps a bad name, he has to back them up because he cannot do without them, and thus he becomes their slave instead of their master.

And this reminds me that we must stop talking nonsense about dictators. Practically the whole business of a modern civilized country is run by dictators and people who obey their orders. We call them bosses; but their powers are greater than those of any political dictator. To prevent them abusing those powers we have Factory Acts which have made short work of our employers' liberty to sacrifice the nation's interest to their own. It is true that we cannot get on without dictators in every street; but we can impose on them a discipline and a code of social obligations that remind them continually that their authority is given to them for the benefit of the commonwealth and not for their private gains. Well, one of our aims in this war is to impose a stiff international

Factory Act on Mr Hitler, one that will deal not with wages and hours of labor, but with the nature of the work done, for peace or war.

When I say that we must stop talking nonsense about the war what I mean is that we must be careful not to go on throwing words about that we do not understand. Could anything be more ridiculous than people who were terrified the other day when Sir William Beveridge very properly used the word 'Socialist' to describe our war organization?[7] They flooded the B.B.C. with letters asking whether all their property was going to be taken away from them. Whilst they were writing, the Government in two hours and twenty minutes placed the country under the most absolute Military Communism. Everything we possess – our properties, our liberties, our lives – now belong to our country and not to ourselves. To say a word against Socialism or Communism is now treason. Without them we should soon have no property or liberty at all, and would be lucky if we were alive. Therefore I beg you, if you must talk, to confine yourself to what the lawyers call vulgar abuse, which will relieve your feelings and hurt nobody. I hope you are too much of a gentleman (or a lady) to call the Germans swine; but if you want to blow off steam by calling Mr Hitler a bloodstained monster do so by all means: it won't hurt him, nor need you worry if it does. But be careful; if you call Stalin a bloodstained monster you must be shot as the most dangerous of Fifth Columnists; for the friendship of Russia is vitally important to us just now. Russia and America may soon have the fate of the world in their hands; that is why I am always so civil to Russia.

Remember that the really dangerous Fifth Column consists of the people who believe that Fascism is a better system of government than ours, and that what we call our democracy is a sham. They are not altogether wrong; but the remedy is for us to adopt all the good points of Fascism or Communism or any other Ism, not to allow Mr Hitler and his Chosen Race to impose it on us by his demoralized police. We are fighting him, not for his virtues, but for his persecutions and dominations, which have no logical connection whatever with Fascism and which I hope we will not put up with from Mr Hitler or anyone else. He is as sure that God is on his side as Lord Halifax[8] is that God is on ours. If so, then we shall have to fight God as well as Mr Hitler. But as most of us believe that God made both Mr Hitler and Lord Halifax, we must reasonably believe that God will see fair. And the rest is up to us.

Appendix 3
German Wartime Propaganda Broadcasts about Shaw, 1940

[On 29 July 1940 the Director-General of the BBC, Frederick Ogilvie, instructed BBC staff to provide him with information on 'references to Bernard Shaw on the German wireless' so that he could 'draw ministerial attention' to them. This was in the context of the ban imposed on wartime broadcasts by Shaw by the Minister of Information, Duff Cooper. BBC staff provided the following transcripts of German broadcasts in the spring and summer of 1940 that referred to Shaw. Broadcasts in languages other than English were translated by BBC staff. For further context see chapter 6, pp. 106–14.]

A. 28 May 1940 (in German)

[Quotes Shaw]: '"When a Briton requires new markets for his rotten Manchester goods, he sends out a mission to preach the gospel to the natives. These natives then kill the missionaries. Then the Briton takes up arms to defend Christianity. For defence of his home coasts he takes a parson aboard his ship, hoists a flag with a cross at the masthead, and sails to the end of the world, crushing, burning, and destroying everything that stands in the way of his domination of the seas." The world can see in this mirror the true unmasked face of the Englishman. Time-bombs and church garments, hired murderers and hangmen, or Pharisees in ecclesiastic surplice, all of these are again and again the mere tools of British civilisation, which is alleged to be sponsored by God.' (BBC File 315 1A iv)

B. 30 May 1940 (in German)

'On May 30, 1431, in the market square at Rouen, the English burnt Joan of Arc at the stake. The Secret Service did not exist in those days, but its methods were already familiar to the English, and whoever got in the way of their self-ish and brutal policy was destroyed. What can the feelings of France be on the occasion of this anniversary? We could quote Anatole France and Bernard Shaw, whose ironic descriptions of his fellow countrymen are well known but we shall quote only Schiller and through him Joan of Arc herself.' [Quotations from Schiller follow.] (BBC File 317 1A ix)

C. 5 July 1940 (in French)

'The well known writer Bernard Shaw prophesied long ago that the greatest menace to Britain was Churchillism, with its crimes and misdeeds; it will fi-nally engulf the country in its ultimate defeat. This prophecy is on the point of being fulfilled.' (BBC File 353 1C ii)

D. 18 July 1940 (in Norwegian)

'Unless the United States of America enters the war, things will be pretty bad for England, Bernard Shaw has declared to a London paper, the "Star," accord-ing to a German report from Lisbon.' (BBC File 367 1M i)

E. [?] July 1940 (in Spanish, for South America)

'The London Press, hostile to Duff Cooper since the shipment of his children to the USA, describes him as incapable of carrying out his duties. His latest effort is an order to the London Press prohibiting the publication of articles by Bernard Shaw, who is thus to be gagged.' (BBC File 371 1K xi)

F. 25 July 1940 (in English)

'George Bernard Shaw at his brightest made the witty remark that it was the privilege of the working classes in capitalist countries to be betrayed by their leaders and their parties. In making this sweeping statement, Mr Shaw must have been thinking of the history of the last three decades of the British Labour movement.' (BBC File 373 1B i)

G. 26 July 1940 (in English for North America)

'England's Bad Boy No.1 is George Bernard Shaw. Just when Duff Cooper thought he had everyone so quiet and muffled that he could cram large pieces of propaganda down their throats, up spoke George Bernard Shaw. His remarks were as natural as those of any Englishman who has reached a certain state of maturity. Someone asked Shaw how he thought the war would end. He said he thought England would lose. Duff Cooper went into a fury. He called a conference. What could the Ministry of Information do to keep the English people from hearing such frank admissions of the truth? Send Shaw to gaol? No, that would do only for less popular offenders. Forbid all Shaw publications? No, replied Duff Cooper, I like to do things on the quiet and avoid a fuss. Just look at how I shipped my boy to the USA. No one found out about it for a long time, and then it was just bad luck ...

Then Duff Cooper sent out his agents to Shaw's friends, to his publishers, to journalists and musicians, urging them not to speak the truth or to say anything about politics at all. Even H. G. Wells, who obediently stopped expressing his opposition to the war, wrote a letter. In this, so they say, were the words "Pipe down on this losing the war stuff, Bernard. The people will find out soon enough without you telling them."' (BBC File 374 1K x)

H. 27 July 1940 (in French)

'The British Ministry of "False News" stated that there was no prohibition in force respecting the publication of Bernard Shaw's works. This statement was intended to refute a report of neutral journalists in London. In England however there is no need to achieve such ends by a blunt prohibition. There are more subtle methods at the disposal of the Government and they have probably been made use of in this case.' (BBC File 375 1C i)

I. 28 July 1940 (in Portuguese for Brazil)

'[After the first World War, Britain] continued to live in the dream-world that she had created, and persisted in sticking to her antiquated methods. She did not see that time marches constantly on, and that new conditions call for new methods. This method of thought had often been criticised by Bernard Shaw. But in spite of all Shaw's sarcasm, in spite of the way he showed up the desperate situation of the working class, the Government continued to take half-measures always, promising, as in 1914, that they would better the lot of the workers, and on the other hand forbidding Bernard Shaw to pour any more ridicule on what they called democracy. In one of Shaw's works, he has a character called Necker who spends so much time looking in the mirror that he has none left to wash his face. Exactly so did England behave; instead of modernising her political and social life, and cleaning up the dirt in the national organisation.' (BBC File 376 1K iiia)

Appendix 4
BBC Obituaries of Shaw

[For discussion of the BBC's planning for broadcast obituaries see Epilogue, pp. 160–70.]

A. Hesketh Pearson [1946]
[The text printed here is a revised draft of Hesketh Pearson's obituary, originally commissioned by the BBC in 1945. Pearson discussed his first script with Shaw, and incorporated some of Shaw's suggestions into a revised script, which he then sent to Shaw. Shaw made substantial revisions, which are reflected in the version given here. The obituary was not, however, used by the BBC. An entirely different obituary by Pearson was eventually broadcast (see E, below). The script reproduced here is in HRC, Shaw 74/1.]

The great career which has just entered its ninth decade began when Charles Dickens was writing *Little Dorrit*. Bernard Shaw was born in Dublin on July 26th, 1856. The schools he attended taught him nothing; but at home and in the National Library of Ireland he acquired a considerable culture in operatic and religious music, and in literature and painting. From his father he inherited a vein of humorous anti-climax, and from his mother a love of serious music. His father, unsuccessful in business, could not afford him a university education;[1] and after five years in a land agent's office, he left Dublin for London at the age of twenty and joined his mother, who, after a career as an amateur, had gone there to teach singing professionally. His vocation overcame his pretences of seeking further business employment, and for years, from 1876 to 1883, he lived at his mother's expense, teaching himself how to write by steadily producing one novel a year, each of which was sent to every leading London publisher and rejected by all of them. They got into print in obscure shortlived magazines, and were published in America in pirated editions; but he always hated them because they reminded him of his immaturity, impecuniosity, and repeated failures. His mental development, however, can clearly be traced in them; for the rationalist freethinker of the first two had read Marx and become a socialist in the last.

Writing novels did not absorb his energy, which was perhaps increased by his being a vegetarian, a teetotaller and a non-smoker. Unusually diffident and even timid by nature and lack of social training, he sought to overcome these defects by attending meetings at which he suffered agonies in his earliest attempts at public speaking. But from the moment that he was converted to socialism, he became a man with a mission; his nervousness vanished; and he became a platform virtuoso. In 1884 he joined the newly born Fabian Society, and with Sidney Webb worked hard to make socialism respectable, practical and constitutional. He flung himself into all the controversies of his time, scientific, religious, political, medical, becoming an eloquent speaker and a brilliant debater; and though he preferred working-class audiences, he was soon a star orator in fashionable quarters. As he never charged a fee for public speaking, the demand for his services was considerable. Though he could be depended upon to deal with every subject under the sun, socialism remained his chief topic, and he and Webb, after much discussion and intrigue, managed to persuade the Liberal Party to adopt 'the Newcastle programme' of social reform and win the 1892 election on it.[2] It was dropped when it had served its turn at the polls, as Shaw and Webb foresaw, and were ready with their fierce 'To Your Tents, O Israel,' followed by their 'Plan of Campaign for Labor' calling for the formation of the Labour Party, which made its first appearance in the House of Commons in 1906.

Meanwhile, with the assistance of his friend William Archer, Shaw was earning a living as a critic, at first of books and pictures, though his reputation was made as a critic of music in *The Star* and *The World* from 1888 to 1894, and consolidated as theatre critic to *The Saturday Review* from '95 to '98, when the initials 'G.B.S.' became equally famous and infamous, his work giving much gratification to the iconoclast and entertainment to the orthodox.

Meanwhile the bouleversement in his social and political outlook effected by the shock of Marx's treatise on Capital was succeeded by the impact of Henrik Ibsen on the European theatre. It reached Shaw betimes through William Archer, and produced the most staggering of all his critical blasphemies, his attack on the supreme reputation of Shakespeare, which not only scandalized the literary world, but caught it out through the Bardolators (as Shaw dubbed them), [who] echoed Shakespeare's praises without reading him while Shaw knew him through and through, and, as in music, remained fundamentally a sound classic. None the less he turned all his guns on Shakespeare,[3] championed Ibsen, who was being execrated, ridiculed Brahms, then regarded as the successor of Beethoven, and eulogised Wagner, then believed to be a madman. As his most deeply considered judgments were expressed with a humorous levity, grave professors tried to dismiss them as the sallies of a buffoon but could not compete with him in irresistible readability.

While criticising the production of others he was busy proving his own ability as a dramatist, though nearly everyone, including his friends, and of course the critics, thought that he had mistaken his vocation. His first play, *Widowers' Houses*, was received with violent disapproval; his second, *The Philanderer*, was refused by every manager who read it; his third, *Mrs Warren's Profession*, was censored as it dealt with a subject which the Victorians thought unfit for discussion. Turning his attention to more pleasing themes, he wrote *Arms and the Man*, *Candida*, *You Never Can Tell* and his one frank melodrama *The Devil's Disciple*. These four became the outstanding successes of the repertory theatres in the early decades of the present century, and two of them had long runs in America and Germany.

In 1898 Shaw's health broke down, but this did not deter him from marrying Charlotte Payne-Townshend and producing his Shakespearian history play,[4] *Caesar and Cleopatra*, in which, by rescuing a full dress stage chronicle from the artificiality of traditional blank verse he had a marked effect on modern drama and biography. His reputation as a playwright in this country was made between 1904 and 1907, when J.E. Vedrenne and Harley Granville-Barker leased the Court Theatre, London, with Shaw's plays as their stock in trade. London Society, led by King Edward VII, flocked to see *John Bull's Other Island*, *Man and Superman*, *Major Barbara*, *The Doctor's Dilemma*, *Captain Brassbound's Conversion*, and, indefatigably, *You Never Can Tell*.[5]

The experiment at the Court Theatre in the possibilities of artistic management was [text illegible] to breaking point: its winding-up left the management solvent but penniless, and obliged Shaw, whose credit was involved, to disgorge some of his royalties, but left him a leading figure in the commercial theatre through a series of highly lucrative successes and long runs beginning with the productions in America of *The Devil's Disciple* by Richard Mansfield and of *Man and Superman* by Robert Loraine, of *Candida* in Germany with Agnes Sorma in the title part, and culminating with the London triumph of Mrs Patrick Campbell in *Pygmalion* and the record run of *Fanny's First Play*. These, and the later successes of *Saint Joan* with Sybil Thorndike and *The Apple Cart* with Cedric Hardwicke and Edith Evans, proved that Shaw could not only bring money to the box office but had provided for the greatest players a modern grand repertory comparable only to that left by Shakespeare. In his latest years he was commonly ranked as the undisputed successor of Shakespeare. When reproached for having challenged this comparison his comment was that as he had lived forty years longer than Shakespeare and was standing on his shoulders he had all the advantages, but that no human writer could surpass Shakespeare at his best on his own ground.[6]

When questioned about his reputation Shaw amused himself by injecting 'Which reputation? I have made fifteen.' He quite seriously and emphatically claimed to be a pioneer in science, though he had never worked in a laboratory, and contemptuously dismissed laboratory experiments as 'put-up jobs.' His laboratory, he said, was 'the wide world, in which I can control nothing except to a very limited extent my own mind.' He classed politics as a science and denounced popular democracy as the government of the ignorant by vulgar adventurers foolish enough to imagine that government is a voluptuously omnipotent sinecure, civilization having always to be rescued from the messes they make by military geniuses. Genuine practicable democracy, he contended, means government in the general interest by rulers chosen from panels of the five per cent or so of tested qualified rulers. The assumption underlying Adult Suffrage that at the age of twenty one everybody becomes infinitely wise politically, and that the voice of the people is the voice of God, he regarded exactly as Coriolanus does in Shakespeare's most mature chronicle play. What Democracy needs, he declared, is a scientific anthropometrical test. Finally, to secure genuine democracy by proportional representation of men and women, he invented and advocated the Coupled Vote, obliging the elector to vote, not for a single representative but for woman as well as man, thus securing the presence of men and women in equal numbers on all elected authorities. But he would not admit that any electoral reform could secure good government unless and until the span of human life was extended sufficiently to make political maturity possible, and this he estimated at three hundred years, allowing a century for non-adult scholarship, another for practical administration, and a third for oracular voteless senatorship. In *Back to Methuselah* he placed no limit to human life except the statistically certain fatal accident which must occur to everyone sooner or later.

In this apparent extravagance he claimed to be a scientific biologist, or, as he sometimes called himself, a metabiologist. Official biology in his day was completely dominated by the Mechanists and neo-Darwinists; and he fought them tooth and nail as a creative neo-vitalist evolutionist, taunting them with their failure to account for the difference between a live body and a dead one, and postulating a creative Life Force or Evolutionary Appetite, proceeding experimentally by trial and error, with mankind as its most elaborate instrument. There is consequently no problem of evil: the evils we suffer are the mistakes of the experimenting Life Force, which aims always at increased power and deeper knowledge. He did not disparage the Baconian observation of facts, but insisted that anyone (any fool, as he puts it) can observe, but only the relevantly gifted few can rationalize their observations, a criticism which culminated in his attack on Pavlov,[7] then at the height of his reputation, dismissing him as an intellectual blunderer and moral imbecile. He steadily denounced the claims of laboratory researchers to be exempt from moral law in their pursuit of scientific knowledge. As he put it, 'to boil your mother merely to find out at what temperature she would die would be an addition to knowledge; but people who forget that there are things that no man ought to know are better dead.' Inhuman experiments by inhuman persons moved him to abhorrence. He maintained that humane experiments could always be devised by scientific workers who were not too lazy, callous, or stupid for high science. Popular and official Darwinism he discounted as nine tenths nothing but anticlerical reaction against the Bible.

It is not possible to summarize the controversy in an obituary notice, nor is it now necessary, as it has, on the whole, gone Shaw's way, and metabiology has come to its own again. The Russian political experiment begun in 1917 has tried crude catastrophic Socialism only to be forced back by inexorable facts into the Fabian methods prescribed by Shaw and Webb. Many of his Shavian suggestions that seemed subversively revolutionary or fantastic when he first put them forward are now commonplaces, though the old view of their author still persists long after its basis has dissolved. In any case they interest and are understood by few, whereas there is a relatively enormous publicity for his exploits as a playwright. How he will stand in future centuries cannot be foreseen. He himself was fond of saying that reputations that are not for an age but for all time mean world stagnation, and that the sooner he is forgotten the better. It remains to be seen whether the memory of the man who survived five reigns will survive fifty.

B. Bertrand Russell [1949]

[This obituary was commissioned by the BBC in February 1949. Because Russell was in the United States at the time of Shaw's death, however, the obituary was never broadcast. The BBC copy has been lost, but a carbon copy, reproduced here, is preserved in the Russell Archives at McMaster University, Ontario (box 3.25, file 220.019000). With minor variations, the obituary was published in the *Virginia Quarterly* 27.1 (Winter 1951): 1–7. A modified and abbreviated version was published in Russell's *Portraits from Memory and Other Essays* (New York: Simon and Schuster, 1951) 75–80.]

Shaw, considered psychologically, was an almost perfect example of the shy man with an inferiority complex. When I first knew him his shyness was still obvious. He came to my flat on one occasion to read a new play of his, then still unpublished and unproduced, to about twenty friends.[1] He was pale and trembling with stage fright, in spite of the audience being so small and well-disposed. I think his wit was developed entirely as a sensitive man's armour against an intrusive world. The stories that he used to relate about his family rather bear out this view. I do not vouch, in any way, for the truth of the stories, only for the fact that he related them. He used to aver that nearly all his family had been drunkards who, as a result of drink, had ultimately become insane and retired to a private lunatic asylum which, according to him, existed mainly for the benefit of the Shaw family. The most remarkable of these relatives was the uncle who committed suicide by putting his head into a carpet bag and then shutting it. This uncle's fate almost invariably made its appearance at Shaw's excellent luncheons.

For the first forty years or so of Shaw's life he was poor and struggling, admired by a small élite, but regarded as a mountebank by the larger public. His admirable novels were read by hardly anybody, and such success as came his way was as a musical critic. His friendship with Webb, which was very deep and sincere, gave him a more articulate and rational gospel than he would otherwise have had, and an intellectual outlet for his sympathy with the underdog. After he became a dramatist, the activities of the Fabian Society took up a smaller amount of his attention than they had done earlier, but he still remained active in connection with this work. The Webbs used to divide mankind into the A's and the B's. A's were artists, anarchists, and aristocrats, the B's were bourgeois, bureaucrat, and benevolent. They always used to add that Shaw was an A and they were B's. Shaw, however, was only temperamentally an anarchist. Intellectually, he had a belief in strong government – too much belief, I should say, since it inclined him to sympathy with dictators.

I think the greatest service Shaw did was in dispelling humbug by laughter. We all talk in a different way from that in which people talked before Shaw, and even our emotions hardly allow themselves such delicious exhibitions of concealed egoism as were customary in Victorian times. No one nowadays tells a boy: 'It hurts me more than it hurts you,' and few people have the face to speak of 'a fate worse than death.' It is no longer necessary to assume that all parents love their children and all children love their parents. We can admit to feelings of vanity, which, though just as common formerly as they are now, were for some reason thought to belong only to all the rest of the world and not to oneself. There is certainly much less insincerity in family relations and in people's estimate of themselves than there used to be. The later stages of the change perhaps owe most to Freud, but the earlier stages, so far as England is concerned, were brought about by Shaw. This was a great work, and one for which we should all be grateful.

I am afraid, however, that since humbug changes its character from time to time, attacks on humbug must also be dated. There is in one of Shaw's plays one advanced lady who comes back from Madeira, after living there for 30 years, with the same advanced opinions with which she went there, and is astonished to find that they are no longer advanced.[2] Something of the same fate is liable to befall Shaw. His themes are of their time, not eternal. Like Restoration Comedy, they will be to future historians a valuable historic record, but they are not, like Shakespeare's tragedies, capable of remaining appropriate through all changes of manners and social systems. Shakespeare says:

As flies to wanton boys are we to the Gods,
They kill us for their sport.

Although all the mad kings have been dethroned, these lines from Lear have not ceased to be appropriate. I do not think that anything as perennial will be found in the writings of Shaw. He was, in fact, though incredibly clever, not wise. However, we cannot expect any man to possess all the virtues, and we are very grateful to Shaw for his wit, without demanding anything more profound. And it must be said that his wit does sometimes light up absurdities in a manner which is quite astonishing; for example, in Arms and the Man, the Bulgarian boasts of the number of his horses and his houses, and the Swiss hotel-keeper starts on a catalogue: 'I have 12,000 forks' and so on.[3] I do not myself enjoy Shaw so much when he is wholly serious, as in St Joan. I become worried by wrong history and by the reading of a Shavian manner of thought and feeling into an earlier age.

Shaw had developed to a very fine point the art of making his opponents in controversy look silly. Sometimes, as is apt to happen to adepts in this art, knowledge of his own virtuosity made him careless. During the first world war it appeared, in something that he published, that he believed Alaska still belonged to Russia. Naturally, somebody wrote to correct this, but Shaw managed to reply in such a manner as to make it seem that the corrector was a fool. The same characteristic showed in more serious ways. He thought himself entitled to positive opinions on scientific matters about which he knew very little. He ardently endorsed Samuel Butler's criticism of Darwin, and, from this starting point, came to agree with everything that Samuel Butler had said. I was once present at an 'Erewhon Dinner,' at which about a dozen admirers of Samuel Butler were gathered. Shaw was among them, and made a speech giving his support to all that was most disputable in Butler's many opinions. The same belief in vitalism which led Shaw to agree with Butler against Darwin led him later to admire Bergson, whose élan vitale he popularised in Back to Methuselah. His whole attitude in biological matters was anti-scientific and led him to a profound scepticism about medicine. (There is reason to believe, however, that he could not have attained his great age without the help of medicine at certain critical times.) It is interesting to observe that the inheritance of acquired characters, which was preached by Butler and Bergson and adopted by Shaw, is now the official doctrine of the Soviet Union, of which Shaw in his later years was a passionate admirer. In all these various supporters of the inheritance of acquired characters the psychological source is the same, namely a belief in the omnipotence of will and an unwillingness to admit any boundaries set by nature to what man can achieve. This doctrine is wholesome in so far as it is true, since it encourages hopefulness and effort, but when it is pushed to extreme it becomes an incitement to futile schemes and authoritarian arrogance.

Shaw's plays are, in one respect, a reversion to a much earlier type, for his characters do not aim at being complete rounded human beings, but are each an embodied point of view in an argument. His plays, in fact, are dialogues in dramatic form. They make one laugh, because one is accustomed to the absurdities they show up, but I am afraid that, in proportion [sic], as they are successful in causing people to abandon the various kinds of humbug displayed by all the characters except the hero, their mirth-provoking quality will diminish. The final judgment upon Shaw will be, I think, that he was enormously useful as a reformer, but that his effectiveness as an artist was, to a large extent, temporary.

[So far I have been speaking of Shaw as a public character; I will add a few words as regards my personal contacts with him.][4]

I first heard of Shaw in 1890, when I was a freshman at Cambridge. I heard of him from another freshman, who became my life-long friend and who had been reading him on 'The Quintessence of Ibsenism.' Ibsen, in those days, was still more or less of a novelty in England. I did not meet him [Shaw], however, until the International Socialist Congress in 1896,[5] where the German delegates, no doubt much to his satisfaction, concluded that he was a reincarnation of Satan. I later came to know him well owing to my friendship with the Sidney Webbs. He and I stayed with them in Monmouthshire at a time when he was just learning the technique of playwriting. He used to have a sort of chess board, with the names of the characters instead of pieces, and when writing a scene he would have the characters who were present in position on the chess board. He showed already some of the toughness which secured him such a long life. He had just been learning to ride a bicycle and had not yet thoroughly mastered the art. Coming to a fork in the road at the bottom of a hill, I dismounted and he ran full tilt into my bicycle. He was precipitated twenty feet through the air and landed on his back on the hard road. He jumped up at once and went on with his ride, whereas my bicycle was buckled and unusable and I had to go home by train. At every station where the train stopped, he on his bicycle had already arrived and put his head into the window and jeered.[6]

Like the man in *The Hunting of the Snark*,[7] I will now skip forty years, to a time when the Shaws and the Webbs together came to visit me at my house on the South Downs. The house had a tower, from which there was a fine view, and we induced them all to climb the stairs. Shaw was in the van, Mrs Shaw in the rear. During the whole of the ascent, Shaw talked without ceasing, and Mrs Shaw, from behind, ineffectually called up: 'Don't talk while you're going up stairs G.B.S.'

When I was young, it was considered clever to suggest that the vanity which he displayed was a pose. This however was to do injustice to his wit. It was, in fact, just as great as he pretended, but he knew how to exhibit it in such a manner that it would seem shrewd to suppose he was putting it on. I was present on two occasions which I think will prove my point. On one of these occasions, Bergson, who was in London, had been invited to a luncheon to meet a number of philosophers and Shaw. Before Bergson's professional colleagues, Shaw began expounding the visitor's philosophy, and, as was to be expected, gave an exposition which by no means recommended it to his professional auditors. Bergson mildly intervened to say: 'Ah no, it is not qvite zat,' but Shaw swept aside his intervention, saying, 'My dear fellow, I understand your philosophy much better than you do.' Bergson clenched his fists and became white with anger, but just succeeded in not making a scene. The second occasion was when the elder Masaryk[8] was on an official visit to England. He invited Shaw, Wells, Swinnerton[9] and myself to come and see him unofficially at 10 o'clock in the morning. With the exception of Shaw, we all arrived punctually, but Shaw marched in late, began at once: 'Masaryk, the foreign policy of Czechoslovakia is all wrong,' held forth on this theme for ten minutes, and then marched out of the room, without waiting for Masaryk's reply.

On one occasion Wells allowed himself to say in print that if in a shipwreck he had to choose between saving Shaw and saving Pavlov, he would let Shaw drown. After this, there was no limit to the abuse that Shaw would heap on Pavlov.

Shaw could be very cruel when his vanity was involved, but on other occasions, his kindness and generosity were equally remarkable, especially when he was still young. [His kindness and his cruelty were equally essential parts of his incredibly vigorous personality.][10]

C. *The Listener*, 2 November 1950 [unsigned editorial]

With the passing of George Bernard Shaw we mourn the death of a great man, a loss not merely to our nation but to the whole of the civilised world. His influence, direct and indirect, on at least three generations of thinking men and women has been deep. He was a playwright, iconoclast and a social reformer; and although he is best known for his plays, which are unfailingly entertaining, it was perhaps over the English theatre that he exerted the smallest power. Tolstoy rebuked him once (the letter was quoted in a recent broadcast by Mr J. Isaac) for treating the great mysteries of life in a frivolous spirit,[1] but that was just the jam that covered the powder, and the criticism measures a contrast in outlook between the Russian and the Irishman. Only stupid people ever treated Shaw as a clown. Of course he was ambitious – and he needed a platform. Born in Dublin, he came to London to make his fortune and for a time he almost starved. Having failed as a novelist and eked out a living as a musical critic, he owed to William Archer his first chance. Thus he discovered his metier, but did not find it entirely congenial.

> The fashionable theatre [he wrote afterwards] prescribed one serious subject: clandestine adultery: the dullest of all subjects for a serious author, whatever it may be for audiences who read the police intelligence and skip the reviews and leading articles. I tried slum-landlordism, doctrinaire Free Love (pseudo-Ibsenism), prostitution, militarism, marriage, history, current politics, natural society, husband hunting, questions of conscience, professional delusions and impostures, all worked into a series of comedies of manners in the classic fashion ...[2]

But it was not until he wrote *Man and Superman* in 1901 that he found a means of preaching his own religion of creative evolution, later expanded in *Back to Methuselah*, his most significant play.

But the practical application of his religion was to open the road to State socialism. The Irish in him made for the rebel and when compounded with his fundamental puritanism and the progressive atmosphere he breathed in his younger days formed the militant social reformer. One of the earliest members of the Fabian Society, he laboured with his friends, the Webbs, Graham Wallas, Sidney Olivier and others, to permeate society with revolutionary political and economic ideas. These early Fabians were not at heart democrats – they believed in improving the standards of the mass of the people even against their own wishes for their own good, and Shaw, like the Webbs, was sometimes attracted by communism.

Vast differences distinguish the life and thought of our own times from the spirit of the age, the *fin-de-siècle* cynicism, when Shaw was a young man. G.K. Chesterton, who, though a friend of his, shared few of his ideas, recalled in his superb essay on Shaw something of the atmosphere of the days when they were both young:

The years from 1885 to 1898 were like the hours of afternoon in a rich house with large rooms; the hours before tea-time. They believed in nothing except good manners; and the essence of good manners is to conceal a yawn ... I meet men who when I knew them in 1898 were just a little too lazy to destroy the universe. They are now conscious of not being quite worthy to abolish some prison regulations.[3]

But Shaw was a worthy faction of that Life Force which he worshipped. At times wrong-headed and even cranky, as an exposer of superstitions, of greed, and of hypocrisy he was unequalled. Many of the ideas for which he fought are now woven into the fabric of society; much of the nonsense he laughed at is now confined to a few pockets of resistance. He died, rich, successful and admired. All that matters little. What is important is that he did something that few individuals achieve – he helped to change the face of a community.

D. St John Ervine, BBC Radio (Home Service), 2 November 1950. Published in *The Listener*, 9 November 1950

When your friend dies part of you dies too; and the death of Bernard Shaw, whom I have known and loved for more than forty years, leaves me with the feeling that I have lost a large part of my life. You will not, therefore, expect me to talk of him tonight with cold detachment: one does not attempt appraisals under a sense of bereavement.

I was a very young man when I met him for the first time, and, like all who were young then and came into his company, I fell instantly under the influence of his powerful and compulsive personality. There are times when the young feel despondent but they forget that there has always been ample cause for despair. We had plenty when I was young. A small nation, mainly inhabited by uncouth and reactionary farmers, had held up the greatest Empire in the world for about four years and had deeply humiliated us who felt that we were unshakably strong; and in the midst of this distressing turmoil the old Queen who had seemed immortal had died in grief at so much slaughter of her soldiers. The world had broken away from its moorings like a rudderless ship and was adrift on a dark and sullen sea. It was at this time that Shaw began to be prominent, and the swiftness of his sure and abundant wit and the courage with which he proclaimed his optimistic opinions brought the discouraged youth of my generation running to his side. He was a valiant man, and because he treated us as if we were valiant too, we felt valiant. The flower girl in his play *Pygmalion*, you will remember, behaved like a lady when she was treated like a lady.

He was a great laugher, and he laughed with his whole body. He threw his shoulders about while the laughter ran up his long legs and threatened to knock his head off. That is how I remember him, and like to remember him, as a great laugher. But he was a kindly laugher. There was not a sneer in his whole composition.

Shaw's chief occupation was to stimulate thought; and he set you thinking even when he was wrong in a great and magnificent manner. Your mind when you came into his company could not lie down and quietly rust. He compelled you to turn over your beliefs and furbish them afresh. You could not in his presence take yourself or your faith for granted. You had to know not only what you believed but why you believed it. Does this make him sound an uncomfortable person to know? If it does I have done him deep injustice for he was a good companion. The public impression of him, like that of all people who are known mainly through press reports or platform appearances, was largely false. His affectation of conceit upset dull-minded, routine people who failed to observe that he laughed at it more than anybody else.

He told me once that when he was running down the stairs to Charing Cross underground railway station he slipped and completed the descent on his mouth and nose. 'And what did you do then, GBS?' I asked; and he replied, 'I got up as if that were my normal way of descending stairs!' And as he spoke his shoulders began to shake and he was trying to shatter himself with his own laughter.

His appearance was impressive. He had what the film people call a photogenic face, and he was long and lean, over six feet in height, slim and well-built. His hands were beautiful and his light blue eyes were at once full of fun and of that brooding look sometimes seen in men with a high sense of humour. But his most noticeable feature was his famous red beard. Teasing him one day I said: 'GBS, you're such a socialist that you go about with the red flag nailed to your chin!' And that set him laughing with his whole body so heartily that I feared the flag would fall off his face. All his movements were light and easy, the movements of a man in fine fettle; and when he walked through a street his strides were long. He looked fit even when he wasn't. He told me many years ago that he had a severe and almost blinding headache about once a month, but this, he said, merely proved what abundant energy he had; he could not get rid of it in the normal manner. There was a period shortly before the outbreak of the second world war when he was heavily disabled by pernicious anaemia. That was the only time in his life when I saw him under the weather, and I shall never forget my surprise when, entering my drawing-room in Devon, I found him fast asleep on a sofa. He was the last man in this world whom I should have expected to take a nap in the afternoon. But he was over eighty then. Even in his worst illnesses he could put up a good appearance and it was part of his pride to look well.

He was a shy man. People always laugh when I tell them that. But all those platform tricks and displays of comic conceit were the devices a shy man used to help him to assert himself. Once when I was young I saw him enter a room which he had expected to find empty. There were about a dozen people in it and Shaw, who was then reaching the height of his renown, blushed like an embarrassed young girl. I mention this shyness because it is the least known of his characteristics and because it explains things he said and did which offended people and made them think he was callous and even cruel when, in fact, he was only clumsy through shyness. He was not callous or cruel, he was infinitely kind and generous. He would do more for his friends than his friends would do for themselves. It was his strong sensitivity in other people's troubles which sometimes made him seem awkward and unkind. He could keep control of himself when he was distressed only by uttering the first flippancy that came into his head.

He was a solitary-minded man who had little need of other people. He had nearly all he needed in his own mind. But like all great writers he had an abiding love of people. The most casual survey of Shakespeare and Dickens is sufficient to prove how much they loved humanity. An author who seems to have all the elements of greatness and yet fails to become great almost certainly falls short in love of people. Shaw sometimes criticised the follies of mankind with a candour that seemed to be very harsh, but he liked people and had their welfare close to his heart. It was his eagerness to promote the general welfare which made a socialist of him, although no man known to me was more individualistic in his nature. He hated untidiness, and he regarded ill-health and ignorance and poverty and unmerited suffering as part of a slovenly world which he wished to abolish. There was no rancour in him. He bore no malice, nor did he withold his hand even from his most bitter enemies.

His beginnings were hard and there were times when he was poor. I do not know any writer who had to fight for his life in literature so fiercely as he had. The whole temper of his time when he was young was opposed to his outlook on the world, and he had not only to create an audience for his work but to create actors and actresses who could understand his work. He was over forty before he gained a foothold in the theatre. In April 1897 the tide of adversity seemed as if it were about to ebb. Henry Irving had agreed to produce his short play *The Man of Destiny* with himself and Ellen Terry in the principal parts; and Mr Cyril Maude accepted *You Never Can Tell* for a performance at the Haymarket Theatre, which was then, as it still is, the leading comedy theatre of London. In less than a fortnight he sustained two blows that might have knocked out a less valiant man for ever. Irving refused to produce *The Man of Destiny*, and the managers of the Haymarket after a fortnight's rehearsal decided that *You Never Can Tell* was hopeless. Two players had walked out on the ground that there was not a laugh in the play, which had no 'exits' of the sort that old-fashioned actors liked. Shaw faced this bitter experience with gay courage, and did not let it daunt or even depress him. It seems incredible to us that anybody could ever have believed that there was not a single laugh in this charming comedy, which has been acted thousands of times all over the world. Yet such was the fact.

In his old age he was a very lonely man. He had lost his wife Charlotte [on 12 September 1943], a most dear and lovable woman, and nearly all his contemporaries, including Sidney and Beatrice Webb, were dead. The loss of Charlotte was irremediable, far greater than even he had imagined it would be. His behaviour to her was full of what is called old-fashioned courtesy. He never broke the slightest promise he made to her. Once when he and I were talking together he turned to me when she was out of earshot and said: 'If Charlotte were dying, I know an infallible way to restore her health!' 'How?' I asked. He began to shake his shoulders: 'I should simply go to bed and say I was dying,' he replied. And indeed Charlotte would have come out of the grave to help him. I do not doubt that she was waiting for him this morning when he went away.

He was a noble man, of unbounded charity, who won and kept the deep affection and love of many dissimilar men and women. To know him was to know a genius in its most fragrant form. His serenity of mind endured to the last; he faced his end without fear. I said to him one day that Thomas Hardy had told me that death meant no more to him than removal from one room to another. Shaw nodded his head. 'That's how I think of it,' he said. I loved him this side of idolatry, and I thank my God that I had the honour and privilege of knowing this brave and great and noble man who brought glory to our stage and enriched the world by his presence in it.

E. Hesketh Pearson, BBC Radio (Light Programme), 2 November 1950. Published in *The Listener*, 9 November 1950

One afternoon, just after Shaw's ninetieth birthday, I asked him if he would write his own obituary for the postscript which I was preparing for my biography of him. 'But I am not dead yet!' he exclaimed. I replied that a man could not very well write his own obituary unless he were alive. He saw the point and at once began to dictate a synopsis of his philosophy, which was equality of income and equality and truth between men, and a belief that God was in every one of us. This made him the most tolerant of men. Once during the 1914 war when he was attacked by someone who declared that he should be tarred and feathered, I expected Shaw to show annoyance. Instead, he laughed, and said good humouredly, 'Oh, he's a very amusing fellow.' This was not an attitude of superiority but pure good fellowship and tolerance of another man's views. He was essentially humble.

But the story of his philosophy as dictated to me went on for such a long time that I began to suffer from writer's cramp, and begged him, if there was much more of it, to get in a dictaphone or stenographer. He promptly cut it short with the remark, 'Well, you asked for it, and now you can finish it.' I have done my best to do so; and it was as well that I did not let him continue, because the result would have been not an obituary of himself but a summary of his teaching.

He was always like that; ready at any moment to propound his views, seldom willing to talk gossip which is the flesh and blood of biography. His explanatory nature was first manifested when as a young man he got a job in the Edison Telephone Company and had to persuade householders in the east end of London to allow insulators, poles and so forth, on their roofs in order to carry the telephone lines. But he soon threw in the job and spent the next nine years explaining himself at great length in five novels, all of which were rejected by every publisher in the country. During this period he lived at his mother's expense, flatly refusing, as he put it, to earn an honest living. Then he became a picture critic, a music critic, and a theatre critic, annoying every orthodox person in the land with his very unusual opinions. Later, he wrote plays in which his social, political and religious beliefs were all carefully explained.

He used to produce [i.e., direct] his own plays, and there never was a more popular man in the theatre. A single incident will give some idea of his free-and-easy way with actors. At one rehearsal he advised a thoroughly experienced player to pass behind the table at a certain moment; at the next rehearsal he advised him to pass in front of it. 'But Mr Shaw, you told me yesterday to go behind the table,' complained the actor. 'Oh, did I' said Shaw lightly, 'Well, that just shows the danger of paying any attention to what I say.' His light-heartedness and lack of self-importance were the distinguishing features of his character. I never knew him to be aloof or depressed, though towards the end of his life he dreaded the arrival of visitors at his country house, and once, when I asked him whether he would see someone, he answered: 'I don't want to see anybody, and I don't want anybody to see me. You don't know what it is to be as old as I am. Do you suppose I want the great GBS to be remembered as a doddering old skeleton?'

Though he achieved an international reputation, he declined honours of all kinds, including the Nobel Prize for Literature.[1] He told me that when the first Labour Prime Minister, Ramsay MacDonald, offered him a peerage, he said, 'I cannot afford to be a Duke, and you cannot decently offer me anything less.' 'In that case,' returned MacDonald, 'we must give you the Order of Merit.' 'I have already conferred it on myself,' replied Shaw. He certainly had. He revolutionised the British drama, lifted criticism to a level of intelligent entertainment it had never reached before and has not attained since, profoundly influenced the philosophy of his age, and was largely instrumental in creating a new political power in England. But apart from his achievements in so many fields, he proved that controversy can be conducted with the utmost good humour, and that singleness of purpose and un-deviating sincerity can be united with genial toleration and unfailing gaiety.

F. *The Listener*, 9 November 1950 [unsigned editorial]

We make no apology for returning to the subject of George Bernard Shaw, the news of whose death arrived just as this journal was going to press last week. Though he lived on after his powers had waned – he was in his forties when Queen Victoria died – Shaw was one of the great figures of the last half-century. It is impossible for authors of obituaries to foretell how long his plays will endure, to measure his exact influence on the English stage, or to deter-mine how far his witty advocacy of Fabian socialism contributed to forming the kind of world in which we live. The BBC in particular owed much to him. On the few occasions when he broadcast, his attractive Irish voice came excel-lently across the air, while his plays, being full of wit and argument, lost very little by being performed on the sound radio. On his side, we are told that Shaw 'was a systematic listener to the radio' and 'never failed to be home in time to hear the BBC's six o'clock news bulletin with his wife.' We also know that he was a reader of this periodical: one of his last letters, on the subject of spelling, was published in our columns.[1]

Is it not strange that after his death so many have seen fit to damn him with faint praise? Is this because he outlived his contemporaries and annoyed a younger generation? One newspaper printed a vituperative article written by H.G. Wells before he died in which he referred to Shaw's 'ego-centered, de-vouring vanity,'[2] though Mr Hesketh Pearson, in a broadcast which we publish today,[3] says that he was essentially humble. Another newspaper chose to re-produce some remarks made by Mr Churchill relating to Shaw's attitude in war time;[4] a third dealt in a somewhat involved and lengthy way with his sup-posed 'lack of human understanding.'[5] As for some of the epithets served up in Grub Street to describe this powerful thinker and man of genius, they had to be read in order to be believed; one can only hope that their authors had never read his books or seen his plays and had been told by the office boy that he was simply a great clown. It can be said that a prophet is never honoured in his own country or if that is no good excuse for vulgarity, since Shaw after all was an Irishman, that the English have never understood the Irish and for that rea-son were unable to keep the Free State within the Commonwealth. At any rate it is probable that Shaw was better appreciated in Paris and Berlin and even in

New York than he ever was in London. His plays could frequently be seen abroad, sometimes in English, when none was being performed on the London stage. Those who believe that he lacked human understanding should look for some foreign resort where *Candida* is being performed.

But perhaps the explanation of the general depreciation and sense of satisfied superiority that permeated many of the articles written on Shaw's death is that the middle generation here is unable to recognise how much the climate of opinion in which they were brought up owed to the influence of his teaching. The moving broadcast by Mr St John Ervine, which we publish today,[6] may redress the balance. Mr Ervine says that Shaw's chief occupation was to stimulate thought and that he set you thinking even when he was wrong. Certainly his part in promoting the teaching of the Fabians ought not to be underestimated. For the few dozens of educated people who mastered the arguments of the Webbs in favour of reforms which have now become the commonplaces of all political parties, thousands must have taken in the social criticisms of Bernard Shaw, from generations of university undergraduates to the patrons of worthwhile repertory theatres. Possibly some whose outlook on life he helped to shape now resent the success of his efforts. But the effectiveness of his teaching is undeniable.

G. International Radio Obituaries (as reported in *The Listener*, 9 November 1950)

Last week wireless commentators all over the world paid tribute to Bernard Shaw. In some western countries even news bulletins were interrupted, following his death, to make room for Shaw plays. Different commentators dealt with different aspects of his personality. Rome Radio spoke of him as a social reformer; the West German radio as 'a fanatical fighter for truth'; the Finnish radio as one who 'tried to educate man into a nobler being.' The French radio claimed him as the British Voltaire; the Irish as the great champion of Irish freedom. Communist commentators concentrated on him as 'the great admirer of Stalin.' Thus, the East German radio stated:

> Shaw was a great friend of the USSR, an uncompromising follower of world peace, the enemy of any reactionary hypocrisy and ecclesiastical dogmatism, a sincere fighter for world progress.

The Czechoslovak radio, however, though likewise voicing its praise, added that 'his conception based on reformist so-called Fabian socialism sometimes clouded his views':

Although Shaw based his ideology on Marx's criticism of the capitalist order, he did not penetrate to the class substance of scientific socialism. But he was an honest enough spectator to see where truth and injustice stood. It must be said to his honour that, although remote from the ideals of scientific socialism, he looked towards them with understanding.

H. Val Gielgud, *Radio Times*, 17 November 1950

So many words have been written by so many distinguished people in memory personal, affectionate, artistic, and critical of George Bernard Shaw that the present writer's contribution may well appear superfluous, though he hopes that it may not seem impertinent. But while it is undoubtedly as dramatist and social reformer that Shaw will be chiefly remembered, his contribution to Broadcasting, albeit for the most part far from deliberate, was great. And I should imagine that it is unlikely to be forgotten, at any rate by regular readers of the *Radio Times*.

It is rather for my colleagues of the Talks Department than for me to set down an adequate appraisal of Shaw as a broadcasting personality, as one of the few genuinely great talkers on the air. To all hearing he took to the new medium like the proverbial duck to water, producing an unforgettable effect of a personality entertaining, whimsical, witty and wise through the agency of a voice beautiful in itself, which he handled with the virtuosity of an accomplished musician in words and vocal tone. The individual and personal stature of H.G. Wells was inevitably lessened for the listener to his broadcasts, who was inclined to ask himself at their close if this could be the voice which had launched a thousand schemes for the Greater Future of Mankind. But Shaw at the microphone fulfilled every imaginative expectation. He spoke to the individual and not to a hypothetical mass meeting. And to listen to him was simply a joy.

But, while this personal contribution was distinguished and unforgettable, it is probable that the greatest impact of Shaw upon listeners was achieved in the performances broadcast of his plays. I have always believed – indeed I said as much as long ago as 1930 – that it was nothing less than a tragedy both for broadcasting and to the causes which Shaw had at heart, that a microphone was not at his disposal as a medium in its own right at the beginning of his career as a dramatist. For Shaw's potential audiences were far beyond the capacities of any theatre or theatres, and his particular individual approach to drama – through discussion and argument, rather than through plot and situation – would have been ideally suited to pieces written directly for presentation through the medium of broadcasting. When broadcasting had found its professional feet it was too late to wheedle or persuade Shaw to write plays specially for the new medium. His reaction was typical: a mixture of amiability, exasperating inflexibility, and acute and penetrating professionally critical interest. His plays might be broadcast – yes. They would be made available on perfectly reasonable economic terms. But they must be broadcast *as they were written*. Not a word, not a comma, must be changed. No cutting was even to be contemplated.

It is true that after one of the first broadcasts of *St Joan*, in the course of a letter rather surprisingly appreciative, he suggested that certain scenes in the play needed definite adaptation if they were to make their effect by means of sound alone.[1] But an urgent invitation that he should make those adaptations before the play was broadcast again met with no response. This lack of will to engage in active co-operation – this refusal to take into account considerations of timing and of listening saturation-point – made the Shaw problem one of the most consistent and baffling of headaches to beset the Drama Department. It was only with the advent of the Third Programme that it became possible to do Shaw justice by broadcasting a series of his plays,[2] as opposed to handling one occasionally when circumstances made it possible to do violence to other programme items in finding the time required by GBS.

In the face of this attitude of Shaw's it might have been supposed that he would take little or no interest in productions of his work on the air; that, having assured himself that the chastity of the scripts would be undefiled, he would have left it at that. Far otherwise. There is in existence a series of famous postcards – varied by one or two letters, and heightened in one or two cases by red ink – from which it was made abundantly clear that whoever might not be prepared to give up the better part of a whole evening to listening to a play of Shaw's, GBS was certain to be of the listening audience. And his comments were very much to the point. An invitation was extended to one producer to take and make use of a revolver – having assured himself that it was properly loaded – after *Captain Brassbound's Conversion* was broadcast in the early 'thirties.[3] I was myself instructed in no uncertain terms that no repeat of *The Black Girl in Her Search for God* would be permitted unless a genuine coloured artist could be found for the leading part. No European voice, Shaw maintained, could provide what he demanded in the way of vocal colour.[4] Casting suggestions – for the most part, alas, incapable of practical implementation – were by no means infrequent, and often tended to ignore the effect of the passage of the years upon artists with whose work he had been familiar in his theatrical heyday. The letter regarding *St Joan*, to which I have already referred, was worthy of his best critical period. And in this connection I hope I may be permitted a personal reminiscence.

Owing to the last-minute illness of the actor playing Warwick, I was compelled to undertake the part myself at short notice. I had never plumed myself upon my acting abilities, and I must confess that my heart sank to boot level when I realised that Shaw had actually listened to the performance. However, he treated me more kindly than I am sure I deserved, and indeed went so far shortly afterwards when we were planning the production of *The Millionairess*[5] as to suggest that once again I should be one of the cast. However, he added, with a typically realistic viewpoint, that the suggestion was only made 'in the event of the other Gielgud not being available.'

It is among the keenest of my regrets that I never met him. He passed me once at close quarters, in Berlin of all curious places, in – I think – August of 1934, leaving behind him the most startlingly vivid impression of striding knickerbockered vigour and gleaming blue eyes. We had hoped – indeed we still hope – to include among the special Television Drama plans for the period of the Festival of Britain a production of *St Joan*.[6] Shortly before his accident Shaw had made his consent to the deal contingent upon our reaching mutual agreement over casting, and Esmé Percy, whose links with GBS were so intimate and so long-standing, had been kind enough to say that he would do his best to arrange for me to visit Ayot St Lawrence. I console myself with the reflection that I was still the responsible head of the Drama Department when the Third Programme initiated its play policy with a series of Shaw plays; and in particular for the fact that it essayed what was considered quite impossible – yet more than justified itself in performance – the presentation to listeners of *Man and Superman* at full length, including the scene of Don Juan in Hell.[7]

On his ninetieth birthday Shaw was saluted by Sir William Haley as the BBC's Grandest Inquisitor. We cannot hear again that rich humorous voice. We shall read no more of the curtly pungent postcards. But broadcasting can pay its debt to one of the greatest figures of our age by continuing to make available, by sound and vision, to an audience literally nationwide, the plays of a dramatist whose welcome home by Shakespeare must have been assured.

I. Thomas Mann, BBC Radio (Third Programme), 8 January 1951, repeated 14 January 1951 [recorded in California]. Published in *The Listener*, 18 January 1951

LES DIEUX S'EN VONT – 'The gods pass.' With George Bernard Shaw another of Europe's old guard has departed, the Nestor of that great saturated generation, gifted with enduring vitality, productive to the last, leaving behind what must be called in comparison, a race, not without interest but frail, sombre, endangered and withered before its time. He was preceded in death by Gerhart Hauptmann, of whom G.B.S. scarcely took note, though plays like *The Weavers* and *The Rats* should have greatly pleased him, and by Richard Strauss, whom he knew quite well and in whom he admired the great tradition as well as the brash, revolutionary efficiency of a man born under a lucky star.[1]

Still among us are the octogenarians André Gide, Shaw's kinsman in capricious genius and protestant morality, and the aged Knut Hamsun,[2] now merely vegetating, a man broken by politics, though still the quondam creator of highly discriminate narrative works that yield nothing in richness and charm to Shaw's dramatic works. Shaw, judging by his writings, was sublimely unconcerned with this compeer and it is true that in many respects the two of them were counter-poets, especially in the matter of socialism. The brunt between them in the personal sphere was a sense of obligation towards Germany, well founded in either case, though it spelt Hamsun's political doom, while in the more intelligent Shaw it maintained the character of a well-tempered gratefulness, which, for the rest, laid little claim to any very extensive intimacy.

There is a certain meaningfulness in allowing a German to speak in Shaw's honour, for Germany – and more particularly the Austrian cultural dependency of Germany, in the person of Siegfried Trebitsch,[3] who, with curiously unerring instinct, staked his cards on translating Shaw's plays into German – Germany recognised his importance to the modern stage, indeed to modern intellectual life as a whole, earlier than the English-speaking world. His fame actually reached England only by way of Germany, just as Ibsen and Hamsun conquered Norway, and Strindberg Sweden, by the same roundabout route, for London's independent theatre fell short of doing for Shaw's reputation – soon to grow to world-wide dimensions – what men like Otto Brahm and Max Reinhardt and their actors, and with them Berlin's dramatic criticism, were able to accomplish, for the simple reason that at that time the German stage was ahead of its British counterpart. Moreover, [Germany was] less frozen in the bourgeois mould, more receptive to new things, better prepared to view the Anglo-Celt as the new spear-shaker, the great dramatic, intellectual and mischief-maker, the mighty wielder of words, twinkling with exuberance, the creative critic and dialectician of the theatre of the age. He never denied his indebtedness to Germany, and repaid it in a highly amusing essay, 'What I Owe to German Culture,'[4] going so far as to declare that his own culture was to a very considerable degree German. This is a vast exaggeration, at least regarding the influence of German literature on him, which was meaningless. He himself very humorously described the fragmentary and casual nature of his knowledge of this sphere, which indeed enjoys a great popularity anywhere. In his childhood, he relates, he had once read a story by a certain Jean-Paul Richter and *Grimm's Fairy Tales* as well, adding that he still regarded Grimm as the most entertaining German author. Strange that he should not have mentioned Heine or Hoffmann, usually

accounted the most entertaining Germans. Stranger still that he should have regarded Grimm as a single individual, possessed of the un-Germany quality
of being entertaining. He seems to have been unaware that this Grimm consisted
of two persons – the brothers Jakob and Wilhelm, romantically inspired lovers of
German antiquity, who listened to their fairy tales from the lips of the people,
and collected them conscientiously. This, apart from the fact that the two
planned a gigantic etymological dictionary of the German language, with which
they were never done, and which German scholars are now again engaged in
rounding out. In point of fact, this work of many volumes makes the most entertaining reading in the world for anyone interested in the German tongue as
Shaw was in the English.

'Everyone ought to learn German,' Shaw said, and he himself was determined to do so. But since he was only fifty-five there was no hurry. He never
did learn it, and when Germans who knew no English visited him he would let
them talk until they ran out of breath. Then he would put his hand to his heart
and say, '*ausgezeichnet*.'[5] He did not quite know what this word meant, he said,
tongue in cheek, but it always made the Germans happy. I myself would have
been quite apt to speak a little English with him, but I never visited him, for
purely humanitarian reasons, for I am convinced that he never read a line of
mine and this might have been a source of some embarrassment to him. True,
we might have avoided that plight by shunning literature altogether and turning at once to a subject that concerned us equally – music. It was German music Shaw had in mind, and nothing else, when he spoke of German culture and
his debt to it. He made that very plain, and declared frankly that all the western culture he had acquired was as nothing compared to his intuitive grasp of
German music from its birth to maturity.

Shaw, the son of a mother who was a singer and singing teacher, left a body of
dramatic writing that is the epitome of intellectuality. Yet the music of words is
part and parcel of it, and he himself stressed that it was constructed on the model
of thematic development in music. For all its sober brilliance, its alert and deri-
sive critical judgment, it strives deliberately for musical effect. No reaction to it
pleased the author more than that of a British colleague whom he held in high
esteem – Harley Granville-Barker – who exhorted the actors at a Shaw rehearsal:
'For God's sake bear in mind that this is not a play but an opera – deliver every
speech as though you expected to give an encore.' In truth, Shaw, like every important dramatist before him, created his own idiom. The language of the theatre
at bottom, [is] as unrealistic as the chanted passion of the opera – exalted, exaggerated, pointed, terse and striking, no wit less rhetorical than Corneille's verses
or Schiller's iambic measures, and, strange as it may sound, no less pervaded
with pathos, a term not here meant to imply unctuousness and bombast, but the

ultimate in expression – an eccentricity of speech, steeped for the most part in humour, full of *esprit*, challenge, effrontery, the reigning paradox.

In his preface to *Saint Joan*, which is so good that it almost makes the play superfluous, he stripped bare the scientific superstition of our times, insisting that the theories of our physicians and astronomers and the credulity with which we accept them would have dissolved the Middle Ages in a roar of sceptical merriment. That sets the style. Yet not only does Shaw, the essayist, speak in this way. He often, indeed for the most part, has his characters speak in similar fashion, and it should be noticed in passing that his figure of speech about 'dissolving an audience in a roar of sceptical merriment' precisely describes his own effect on spectators.

When William Archer, in 1885,[6] first met the young Dubliner, only recently come to London, in the library of the British Museum, he found Shaw preoccupied with two works which he studied in turn for weeks on end. They were *Das Kapital* by Marx, and the score of Wagner's *Tristan und Isolde*. Here you have the whole of Shaw – here is Shaw, the radical socialist, zealously addressing meetings, going beyond the teachings of Henry George, who aimed only at the reform of land holding, demanding the nationalisation of capital in every form; Shaw, the guiding spirit of the Fabian Society, who wrote *The Intelligent Woman's Guide to Socialism and Capitalism*, a book Ramsay MacDonald went so far as to call 'the world's most valuable next to the Bible'; Shaw, beginning his career as a playwright with *Widowers' Houses*, a tract about middle-class pseudo-respectability, about the social evils of slum ownership; Shaw, who remained for ever a man of social contentions, who called his plays, sometimes a little condescendingly, 'dramatic conferences'; and Shaw, the born Thespian utterly lacking Wagner's sultry eroticism, with its out-heavening of Heaven, yet Wagner's true pupil as a maker of intellectual music and also as his own apostle and tireless commentator. He wrote a book about Wagner, *The Perfect Wagnerite*, a work of shrewd lucidity that compares most favourably with the burrowing flim-flam of German Wagner exegetists, nor is it mere coincidence that close beside this book stands another treatise of critical gratitude and homage, *The Quintessence of Ibsenism*, for Ibsen, about whose trait, his kinship to Wagner, I once attempted to write, was Shaw's other teacher and his case is an interesting demonstration of the extent to which an altogether different temperament can utilise, for its own purposes, like-minded experiences, once they had been fully encompassed; creatively melting them down into something totally new and personal.

Ibsen is supposed to have said once that each of his plays might just as well have become an essay. Shaw, for one, never forwent the essay, which inhered in his every play – letting it stand beside the play, or rather embodying it in a preface often as long and as eloquent as the play itself, calling things by their names with a critical directness unfitting in the play proper. I, for one, find fault, for example, with the unhappy scrambling of essay and drama that allows Cauchon and Warwick, in the fourth scene of *Saint Joan*, to concoct the terms 'protestantism' and 'nationalism' in definition of Joan's heresy and of heresy in general. Factually, these terms may not have been anachronisms in the fifteenth century, but as formulations they have an anachronistic effect which breaks up form and style. They belong to the essay, where indeed they are to be found. The play should have shunned them, should have been content with an interpretative formulation. Neither this, nor even the fact that in *Saint Joan*, as in other plays of Shaw, the aria sometimes turns into an editorial, can keep this dramatic chronicle from remaining the most fervent thing Shaw ever wrote – the play that is poetically the most moving, that comes closest to high tragedy, a work inspired with a truly elating sense of justice; a work in which the mature rationality of an *esprit fort* that has outgrown the confines of the eighteenth and even the nineteenth century, bows before sanctity; a work fully deserving its world fame.

There is but one other play I would put beside it, or perhaps even ahead of it. That is *Heartbreak House* – creative fruit of the first world war – a play of which neither Aristophanes nor Molière nor Ibsen need have been ashamed; a play that belongs in the foreground of comedy, a play of sparkling dialogue and a fanciful cast of characters, supremely humorous, yet filled with things cursed and condemned, pitched in the mood of a doomed society. When all the one-act plays are included – enter among them such as *Great Catherine* and *Shewing Up of Blanco Posnet* – it turns out that Shaw wrote more plays than Shakespeare, and if they are of uneven weight, like those of his great predecessor, against whom he liked to match himself, so gaily, if some of them have withered, their problems growing outdated, as he foresaw, they do include, beside those already named and singled out for praise, such things as *Caesar and Cleopatra*, *Man and Superman*, *Androcles and the Lion*, and the stunningly clairvoyant political satire *The Apple Cart*, things that have withstood and will long continue to withstand the onslaught of time, in part because of their wisdom and their proudly edifying message, in part because of the winged wit of their poetic idiom. When we add the floodtide of essays, commentary, and amplifying criticism, embodying an all-embracing encyclopeaedic knowledge that draws equally on the natural sciences, theology, religious and general history, and especially the social economic sphere, always artistically leavened, full of aesthetic charm and unfailingly entertaining – when we add all this we find ourselves face to face with a lifework of astonishing scope, apparently the fruit of continued aspiration, unceasing merriness, and of an indefatigable will to work.

Like Ibsen and Wagner, Shaw was first and last a hard worker. In the words of Zarathustra, 'His goal was not his happiness, but his work.' To him, idleness was, above all, a crime against society and utterly foreign to his nature. He said once that he had never been young in the sense that the average person sows his wild oats. For that very reason he remained everlastingly youthful in his work, frisky as a colt, even in his old age. Anti-bourgeois to the core, a Marxist fond of a revolutionary slogan, 'Enemies of the bourgeoisie – unite,' he was yet in his own moral convictions and mode of life middle-class through and through, indeed puritanical. He could have retired from literature tomorrow, he said, and become a respectable cheesemonger, without changing one iota of his domestic habits. For him, the counterpart of the bourgeois was not the bohemian, but the socialist. The world of people, he said, who spent their evenings over champagne suppers, with actresses, models and dancers – that world was unknown to him, and he wondered how its hapless victims endured it, indeed, he often doubted that it actually existed, for all the actresses and dancers he had known were decent, hard-working women. He himself was a man of rigorous and sensible work habits. He did not burn the midnight oil, tossing off his plays on the spur of inspiration: he performed his intelligently planned literary labours between breakfast and the noonday meal, and he went to bed regularly before midnight, so that he might tackle them in the morning with freshness, lucidity and poise.

Dissolute bohemianism revolted him – he simply had no practical use for it. Vice bored him, and as for intoxication, he put these words into the mouth of the old captain in *Heartbreak House*: 'I dread being drunk more than anything in the world. To be drunk means to have dreams; to go soft; to be easily pleased and deceived; to fall into the clutches of women.' Clearly, intoxication was meant to include pre-eminently erotic ecstasy, an experience unknown to Shaw. This does not mean that he was a misogynist. On the contrary, like Ibsen, he may well be described as an extoller of women. The women in his plays are generally superior to the men, in common sense and sense of humour, usually at the expense of the men. But he was fond of quoting Napoleon, who said that women were the business of idlers, adding, on his own, that no man with any serious mission in the world could spare time and money for affairs with women. St Anthony he was not, for that saint was beset by temptations, while Shaw, with his virtuous nature, evidently found continence of the flesh as easy as abstention from meat. He made no dogma of vegetarianism; one man's meat, he said simply, was another man's poison. But, the rebellion against the tyranny of sex – his own expression – was part of his social, moral and aesthetic credo, and there is nothing in his plays of passion, infatuation, sensual abandon, that *Come può esser ch'io non sia più mio* of Michelangelo,[7] and indeed these qualities would seem strangely out of place there.

One is tempted to ask him, as the prince importunes the queen in Schiller's *Don Carlos*, 'Sie haben nie geliebt?' ('Have you never loved?'). The answer would probably have been a laughing 'No' – laughing, but a 'No,' none the less. Of that same virtuous character, a Marienbad elegy, with its passion-brimmed sorrow – indeed, anything like the experience the septuagenarian Goethe underwent with Ulrike von Levetzow would have been unimaginable in the case of Shaw,[8] and he prided himself more on it than do we on his behalf. His was a magnificent durability, yet it somehow lacked full-bloodedness, so much so that, despite the grandeur of his life, it detracted from his stature.

I am quite fond of the massive meals that delighted Luther, Goethe and Bismarck, and I rather fancy Churchill's drinking and smoking as well. In the picture of Shaw, not merely his physical presence, but also his intellectual stature, I find a certain quality of gauntness, vegetarianism and frigidity that somehow does not quite seem to fit my idea of greatness. That idea implies a degree of human tragedy, of suffering and sacrifice. The knotted muscles of Tolstoy bearing up the full burden of morality, Atlas-like. Strindberg, who was in hell; the martyr's death Nietzsche died on the cross of thought; it is these that inspire us with the reverence of tragedy; but in Shaw there was nothing of all this. Was he beyond such things, or were they beyond him? He called one of his own plays 'A Light Play about Difficult Things' – he might well have given that title to all of his writings, and I am not so certain whether this very definition will not apply to all art to come, and whether Shaw may not turn out to have been the smiling prophet of generations, emancipated from tragedy and gloom. Yet I ask myself whether his facility was perhaps not a little too facile; whether he was ever the man to take grave matters with their full gravity. Let the future determine his weight in the scales to the last ounce. This much is certain – his sobriety, like his diet of greens, was necessary to his particular brand of clear-headedness and constraint and liberating ebullience, and nothing could be more erroneous than to mistake his coolness for an actual incapacity for love. He may have laughed at everyone and everything, but he was anything but a Mephistophelian nihilist – thrusting the Devil's chill fist in the face of the powers of creation.

Again, it is his Captain Shotover in *Heartbreak House* to whom he gives these words to say: 'Old men are dangerous: it doesn't matter to them what is going to happen to the world.' Shaw did care what was to become of the world, right down to the age of ninety-four. The clergyman who intoned the prayers at his death-bed was quite right when he said, 'This man was surely no atheist.' He was no atheist, for he reverenced the vital force that is conducting so noble an experiment with man on earth, and was sincerely concerned lest God's experiment become a failure.

Convinced that the aesthetic element, creative joy, is the most effective instrument of enlightened teaching, he tirelessly wielded the shining sword of
his word and wit against the most appalling power threatening the triumph of
the experiment – stupidity. He did his best in redressing the fateful unbalance
between truth and reality, in lifting mankind to a higher rung of social maturity. He often pointed a scornful finger at human frailty, but his jests were
never at the expense of humanity. He was mankind's friend, and it is in this
role that he will live in the hearts and memories of men.

Notes

Preface

1 17 November 1950. For an engaging and extensively illustrated history of the *Radio Times* see Currie.
2 See appendix 1 for a calendar of productions. Among the major plays that were not produced by the BBC in Shaw's lifetime are *Widowers' Houses*, *The Philanderer*, *Caesar and Cleopatra*, *John Bull's Other Island*, *Major Barbara*, *Misalliance*, *Heartbreak House*, *Back to Methuselah*, and *Too True to be Good*.
3 Comments to a symposium on 'the Drama and the Microphone,' *The Play-goer* (Liverpool Playhouse), 25 March 1925. Typescript copy, Burgunder 4617/3. Published in Dukore 4:1408.
4 Ten shillings was the annual cost of the licence (legally required) to listen to BBC broadcasts. The BBC is still funded through a licensing system. It is necessary to buy a licence to receive television broadcasts (both BBC and commercial), but not radio broadcasts.
5 Pegg 7. These calculations do not reflect the number of illegal listeners, i.e., those who did not purchase a licence. Shaw told Herbert Thring, Secretary of the Society of Authors, on 12 May 1923 of a report he had seen in the *Daily Mirror* that estimated the number of unlicensed radios at 200,000 (*CL* 3:826).
6 Internal BBC memo, 6 March 1928, BBC Archives, COP/SCR 1924–35, file 1a.
7 Broadcasting in Britain was initially controlled by the British Broadcasting *Company*, a consortium of radio manufacturers operating under government licence. Established by royal charter on 1 January 1927, the British Broadcasting *Corporation* was independent of any commercial interests.

Chapter 1

1 Burgunder 4617/29.
2 Burgunder 4617/13. Parts of this letter are published in Bonham-Carter 2:207–8.
3 Burgunder 4617/24.
4 Burgunder 4617/13.
5 BL Add Ms 56628, f. 88.
6 Burgunder 4617/13
7 And the copyright issue remained a problem throughout Shaw's life as un-authorized broadcasts of his plays in other countries, including the United States, proliferated. As early as the summer of 1925 Shaw was taking legal advice about U.S. radio broadcasts of his plays 'done without his consent' (internal BBC memo, 10 July 1925, 'The Organiser of Programmes' [Cecil Lewis] to 'The Managing Director' [John Reith], BBC Archives, COP/SCR 1924–35, file 1a).
    And Shaw also urged the Society of Authors to take action against such infringements of copyright. *Pygmalion*, for example, was broadcast in Stockholm (12 February) and Amsterdam (25 April) in 1928 without Shaw's approval: 'Obviously this is a matter for the Society's serious consideration. Can anything be done?' (BL Add Ms 56628, f. 212).
8 Internal BBC memo, 7 November 1950, BBC Archives, Cecil Lewis Talks 1927–62.
9 Shaw to Thring, [29] January 1924, Burgunder 4617/13.
10 Ibid. 'I told the manager to ask £50, with the result that the project fell through.' The manager was almost certainly Harcourt Williams, who had produced *The Dark Lady* at the Kingsway and Coliseum theatres in the autumn of 1923, playing the role of Shakespear himself.
11 Thring to Shaw, 21 May 1924, Burgunder 4167/31. Shaw wrote his response, dated 22 May 1924, at the bottom of Thring's letter and returned it. The return is date stamped 23 May 1924.
12 BBC Archives, COP/SCR 1924–35, file 1a, 27 May 1924.
13 BBC Archives, Incorporated Society of Authors, 1924–6, file 1a.
14 Ibid., file 3a, 9 July 1930.
15 Burgunder 4617/13. Also *CL* 3:889–90. Thring's letter to Shaw about the free broadcast has not survived, but its content is obvious from Shaw's reply. Thring no doubt recalled that Shaw had told him at the end of January that he had initially asked a hundred guineas (=£105) for a reading (Shaw to Thring, [29] January 1924, Burgunder 4617/13).
16 BBC Archives, Incorporated Society of Authors, 1924–6, file 1a.

17 Records of royalty payments, British Library of Political and Economic Science, Shaw Business Papers, section 28/1, ff. 40, 57.

18 In the theatre, however, Shaw did normally work from a set royalties formula related to the box-office returns. Given the unique circumstances of radio audiences, Shaw never attempted a similar approach to broadcasts of his plays.

19 Shaw to Lewis, 15 October 1924, HRC, Shaw 39/4. Shaw is referring to his country home in the Hertfordshire village of Ayot St Lawrence.

20 Shaw to Lewis, 1 May 1925, HRC, Shaw 39/4.

21 The occasion is recorded in Shaw's engagement diary, British Library of Political and Economic Science, Shaw Business Papers, section 26. An internal memo, 10 July 1925, BBC Archives, COP/SCR 1924–35, file 1a, notes, 'He has recently installed a Burndept 4 valve set and loud speaker.'

22 See his memoirs, *Sagittarius Rising* (London: Peter Davies, 1936).

23 HRC, Shaw 39/4. The letter is also in *CL* 3:881–2.

24 On 2 and 24 October. The visits are recorded in Shaw's engagement diary for 1924, British Library of Political and Economic Science, Shaw Business Papers, section 26.

25 My thanks to Lauren Arrington for this suggestion.

26 I have not succeeded in locating this letter, but it is quoted in the transcript of a program called 'I Loathe Being Called George,' 'The Story of Bernard Shaw and the BBC,' broadcast by the BBC (Radio 4) on 6 November 1975, with Cyril Cusack as Shaw (BBC Archives, Script Library, Programme no. BLN45TC4399H). There are five different voices in *O'Flaherty V.C.*, two of them female. Towards the end of the play the four principal characters are 'all speaking at once at the top of their voices.'

27 Shaw to Thring, 22 November 1924, Burgunder 4617/13.

28 Shaw to Trebitsch, 23 August 1925 (Weiss 260).

29 Lewis to Shaw, 12 May 1925, HRC, Shaw 51/4. Shaw's response, dated 16 May 1925, is written at the bottom of Lewis's letter.

30 BBC Archives, Talks 1924–32, file 1a, 19 October 1925.

31 Lewis to Shaw, 10 June 1925, BBC Archives, COP/SCR 1924–35, file 1a. Shaw's explanation about the unauthorized U.S. broadcasts is in an internal BBC memo (written by Lewis), 10 July 1925, BBC Archives, COP/SCR 1924–35, file 1a.

32 BBC Archives, COP/SCR 1924–35, file 1a. The 'book on Socialism' is *The Intelligent Woman's Guide to Socialism and Capitalism*, begun in 1924, published in June 1928. The BBC did not broadcast it, though they did invite Shaw to discuss it on air. He declined (see above, pp. 23–4).

33 Ibid.

34 HRC, Shaw 54/2.

35 BL Add Ms 56628, f. 106.

36 Letter to Thring, 30 November 1925, BBC Archives, COP/SCR 1924–35 file 1a.

37 Ibid.

38 Gibbs (*Chronology* 259) also gives the wrong date (15 January 1926).

39 Colgate University Archives.

40 HRC, Shaw 64/1, is a series of short notes by Shaw on his involvement with the committee, including the dates of his involvement. See above, pp. 51–4, for further discussion of Shaw's work on the committee in the 1930s.

41 My account of the Shaw-Belloc debate is based on the extensive report in the *New York Times*, 28 June 1925. The 'salient points' of the debate were also published in the *Weekly Westminster*, 20 June 1925.

42 Lewis to Shaw, 10 June 1925, BBC Archives, COP/SCR 1924–35, file 1a.

43 *New York Times*, 13 February 1927. Shaw's summing-up was also published in *Time and Tide*, 4 February 1927, with slight variations from the *New York Times*'s version. The *Time and Tide* account is reprinted in Shaw, *Platform and Pulpit* 168–71.

44 *Do We Agree?* 10. The text of the debate was also published in *G.K.'s Weekly*, 6.138 (5 November 1927): 724–30.

45 BBC Archives, Talks 1924–32, file 1a, 14 June 1928.

46 Ibid., 18 June 1928.

47 Extracts from the talk were published in the *New York Times*, 6 January 1929. They are reprinted in West 186–98.

48 *Manchester Guardian*, 17 August 1926.

49 *CL* 4:25, 15 July 1926. The BBC did, indeed, 'know very well already' that Shaw would not avoid controversy. When approached in May 1924 to give a radio talk he had been told that he must avoid the topics of politics and religion. 'Politics and religion are the only things I ever talk about. They are the only things worth talking about,' he responded (Briggs, *BBC* 66).

50 The dinner attendance figure is given in an account of the evening by T.P. O'Connor, MP, one of the speakers (and a former editor of the *Star* when Shaw wrote editorials and music criticism for the paper). See *T.P.'s and Cassell's Weekly* 6.146 (14 August 1926): 511.

51 There was extensive coverage of Shaw's speech in the *New York Times*, 15 August 1926, from which these extracts are quoted.

52 E.g., *The Observer*, 1 August 1926. The letter, written on 28 July 1926, is in *CL* 4:25–6.

53 *Manchester Guardian*, 17 August 1926. The letter is reprinted in Shaw, *Agitations* 252–5.

54 No script of the talk has been located.

55 BBC Archives, Cecil Lewis, Talks 1927–62, file 1. No script of the talk has been located.

56 Shaw's engagement diary for this date records a meeting with Eckersley at 11:00 am (British Library of Political and Economic Science, Shaw Business Papers, section 26).

57 BBC Archives, COP/SCR 1924–35, file 1a.

58 Letter to Siegfried Trebitsch, 8 May 1928 (Weiss 288).

59 BBC Archives, COP/SCR 1924–35, file 1a.

60 Ibid.

61 Shaw to Lewis, 24 June 1924, HRC, Shaw 39/4. Also in *CL* 3:881–2.

62 Val Gielgud (appointed Head of BBC Drama in January 1929) records that in 1925 'a small Repertory Company of actors was formed, though it did not survive' (Gielgud, *British Radio Drama* 21). A permanent BBC repertory company was subsequently established. See above, p. 116.

63 BBC Archives, COP/SCR 1924–35, file 1a.

64 The BBC's international 'Great Plays' series began on 11 September 1928 with *King Lear*, and ran monthly during 1928–9. There was an announcement in the *Radio Times* on 31 August 1928 that the series would 'probably' include a play by Shaw, but in the end *Lear* was the only British play included.

65 Ibid.

66 1929 was the 500th anniversary of the beginning of Joan's military career. All letters referred to in this paragraph are in the BBC Archives, COP/SCR 1924–35, file 1a.

67 The meeting (at 11:30 am) is confirmed in Shaw's engagement diary for 13 December 1928 (British Library of Political and Economic Science, Shaw Business Papers, section 26). It is probably this meeting that Eckersley recalls in his memoirs: 'I remember spending half an hour with Bernard Shaw in his flat in Whitehall Court – looking onto the river, seeing whether I could persuade him to let us use some of his plays for broadcasting. After a few days I got a postcard from him saying it would be all right, and naming a copyright fee. I replied saying I thought an extra nought had got in by mistake to which he never replied. I took this as agreed – and certain of his plays were used. He made it quite clear however that the exact script was to be observed – no cuts – no alterations' (Eckersley 154).

68 R.J.F. Howgill, BBC Programme Services Executive

69 BBC Archives, COP/SCR 1924–35, file 1a. Details of the Dutch *Saint Joan* have not been traced.

70 Shaw received a cheque from the BBC for £52.10.0 on 8 May 1929 (British Library of Political and Economic Science, Shaw Business Papers, section 28/1, f. 33).

71 BBC Archives, COP/SCR 1924–35, file 1a.

Chapter 2

1 By the end of 1928 over 2.6 million radio licences were held by households in Great Britain (Coase 199).
2 Internal memo from Eckersley to Gielgud, 4 January 1929. BBC Archives, COP/SCR 1924–35, file 1a.
3 Draft letter (carbon copy) from Eckersley to Blanche Patch, 4 January 1929. BBC Archives, COP/SCR 1924–35, file 1a.
4 Shaw to Macdona, 10 January 1929. Colgate University Archives, box 16, file 755c. Dorothy Holmes Gore had toured as Joan in 1925 and was to appear (as Amanda) in the UK premiere of *The Apple Cart* at the inaugural Malvern Festival in August 1929.
5 BBC Archives, COP/SCR 1924–35, file 1a, 14 January 1929.
6 Ibid., 17 January 1929. Shaw's fee was actually 50 guineas.
7 Internal memo, 14 January 1929, Gielgud to Cecil Graves (Eckersley's Assistant Controller; Eckersley was still on holiday). BBC Archives, COP/SCR 1924–35, file 1a. Quotations in the next two paragraphs are from this memo.
8 Internal memo from Eckersley to Reith, 17 January 1929. BBC Archives, COP/SCR 1924–35, file 1a.
9 The actual broadcast times were 7:30–9:00 pm and 9:20–12:00 pm.
10 BBC Archives, COP/SCR 1924–35, file 1a, 4 February 1929.
11 Ibid., 13 February 1929.
12 Ibid., Cecil Lewis, Plays 1929–33, file 2, 14 February 1929.
13 Ibid.
14 Ibid.
15 Ibid.
16 The full cast for the broadcast is given on p. 46.
17 The draft for this announcement (BBC Archives, COP/SCR 1924–35, file 1a) explains that the dividing of the play into two halves 'is compelled by the exigencies of programme construction,' a piece of bureaucratese that was happily replaced by plain English in the published version.
18 Alison Leggatt graduated from the Central School of Dramatic Art in 1924 (winning the Gold Medal), and was beginning to make a name for herself in the West End. She had no experience of Shaw.
19 Letter, Gielgud to Lewis, 11 March 1929. BBC Archives, Cecil Lewis, Plays 1929–33, file 2.
20 Shaw's response is written at the bottom of Limbert's letter, which was returned to Limbert. Both the letter and the response are dated 28 March 1929. BBC Archives, COP/SCR 1924–35, file 1a.
21 The figures are contained in an internal BBC memo, 2 May 1929, ibid.

22 Val Gielgud, 'GBS: His Contribution to Broadcasting,' *Radio Times*, 17 November 1950. *The Times* suspected something had happened with the casting, noting in its review on 29 April 1929 that 'there was apparently at least one change in the cast, and there may have been others.' It was not the practice of the BBC at that time to announce casts on air. According to *The Times*, Cecil Lewis also took part in the production, reading from Shaw's preface to the play. This was not announced in the *Radio Times*.
23 BBC Archives, Cecil Lewis, Plays 1929–33, file 2.
24 The lecture, 'Democracy,' was broadcast on 14 October 1929. *Captain Brassbound's Conversion* was broadcast on 16 October 1929, repeated on 19 October.

Chapter 3

1 See Conolly, *Bernard Shaw and Barry Jackson*.
2 The full letter, which also contains a gratuitous swipe at recently retired BBC Director-General Sir John Reith (who should be replaced, says Shaw, by 'someone who knows at least a little about the lives of the common people') is reprinted in Shaw, *Agitations* 305–6.
3 Shaw's letter to Reith is in the BBC Archives, Reith Enclosure Volumes S60/6/7. It is published in *CL* 4:309–10. Reith's account, in which he acknowledges Shaw's initiative, is in Reith, *Into the Wind* 163–4.
4 *The Times*, 7 February 1935. Other members included the Archbishop of York (chair), Lloyd George, and Sybil Thorndike, as well as representatives from the legal, religious, educational, and literary professions. In his letter of acceptance to Reith (20 August 1934) Shaw said that the BBC will now have 'a free hand,' since 'all complaint will be crushed by a reference to the Archbishop of York. An excellent idea' (BBC Archives, Reith Enclosure Volumes S60/6/8).
5 *CL* 4:375, 22 June 1934. The first meeting of the expanded committee was held on 20 September 1934, chaired by Shaw (*RT*, 19 October 1934).
6 Shaw's holograph letter to Reith is in the BBC Archives, Reith Enclosure Volumes S60/6/8. It is dated, in error, 3 December 1935 (for 1934).
7 These examples are taken from a report in the *Radio Times*, 19 October 1934.
8 The 'polka' and 'celeriac' examples are in a letter from Shaw to committee secretary A. Lloyd James, 2 December 1937 (*CL* 4:483–4).
9 The letters to *The Times* of 2 and 25 January 1934 are both reprinted in Shaw, *Agitations* 294–7, and in Ducat 191–4.
10 Among Shaw's rivals were composer Walford Davies, scientist Oliver Lodge, and G.K. Chesterton.
11 Shaw to Siepmann, 18 January 1934, BBC Archives, Talks 1933–7, file 1b. The letter is also in *CL* 4:361–2.

12 BBC Archives, Talks 1933–7, file 1b, 4 September 1935. Shaw's letter to Siepmann (20 August 1935) is in the BBC Archives, ibid. In a short essay on Shaw and the BBC ('The Stripling and the Sage'), Sir William Haley, one of Reith's successors as Director-General of the BBC, says that 'one must for ever regret that the 1935 project of a "Shaw-Churchill" broadcast debate did not materialize' (Winsten 167–70).

13 BBC Archives, Talks 1924–32, file 1a.

14 Ibid., 27 July 1929.

15 *Political Quarterly* 2.2 (April–June 1931): 172–85.

16 BBC Archives, Talks 1924–32, file 1a, 7 July 1932.

17 See Briggs, *Golden Age* 122. The BBC was sometimes criticized for being too conservative, sometimes for being too radical (ibid., 136–7).

18 Shaw's remarks were published in *The Listener*, 30 January 1935. They are also published in Shaw, *Platform and Pulpit* 261–2 and, below, appendix 2C. The typescript of the talk, with Shaw's holograph changes, is in HRC, Shaw 6/9. Shaw has noted on the script: 'This contains 488 counted (not averaged) words, and can be delivered *allegro con brio* by the author in three and a half minutes.'

19 Shaw's speech was reported in *The Times*, 1 February 1930. A fuller account is in *Drama* 8.15 (March 1930): 94–5. See also Whitworth 175–7. On behalf of the Shakespeare Memorial National Theatre Committee, Shaw subsequently received on 22 April 1938 deeds for a site in South Kensington for the National Theatre. Parts of the ceremony were broadcast on shortwave to the United States, but not on domestic radio; Shaw's remarks are on disc 2, track 3 of Shaw, *The Spoken Word*. Shaw died several years before the National Theatre became a reality when founded at the Old Vic Theatre in 1961 under the direction of Laurence Olivier. The permanent location on London's South Bank opened in 1976.

20 BBC Archives, Reith Enclosure Volumes S60/6/5. The letter is printed in full in *CL* 4:211–12. Shaw's complaints about the scheduling of the broadcast were evidently not resolved in time for listing it in the *Radio Times*. The issue of 24 October 1930 went to press without any indication that the event would be carried by the BBC. A BBC news release for the broadcast was published in *The Times* (and other newspapers) on 23 October.

21 'Here in London we are still a great center. I do not suppose that we shall be a great center long – all that will presently be transferred to the United States'; 'I must confess to you that there is not a single creed of an established church on earth at present that I can subscribe to.' See Bernard Shaw, 'Toast to Albert Einstein,' ed. Fred D. Crawford. Crawford also includes Einstein's response to Shaw's toast, which contained the following tribute: 'You, Mr Shaw, have

succeeded in gaining the love and the joyful admiration of mankind by a path which for others has led to martyrdom. You have not only preached to mankind morality but even dared to mock at what to others appeared unapproachable. What you have done can be done only by the born artist.' Transcripts of Shaw's speech (which was recorded and filmed) are held at the BBC Archives (Scripts 1930–56, file 921/SHA), the British Library (Add Ms 50704, ff. 229–36), and HRC (Shaw 11/12). The HRC also holds Shaw's typed notes for the speech (Shaw 29/7). See also Desmond J. McRory, 'Shaw, Einstein and Physics,' *SHAW: The Annual of Bernard Shaw Studies* 6 (1986): 33–67. The speeches of Shaw and Einstein are included on the British Library's CD, *Albert Einstein: Historic Recordings 1930–1947* (2005).

22 Shaw, 'Toast to Albert Einstein' 238.

23 The letter and the transcript are in the British Library, Add Ms 50520, ff. 76–81.

24 The BBC does not seem to have requested a copy in advance. In the published text (*The Listener*, 3 June 1931) Shaw says 'I have not got a manuscript ... I shall say anything about [Joan] that comes into my head.' He concludes his talk by telling his listeners that 'the British Broadcasting Corporation is in a state of very great impatience because I have already stolen very nearly ten minutes. I should have taken twenty minutes; I have taken half an hour. Just like me, isn't it? Goodnight.' *The Listener* says the text is 'verbatim,' but does not specify its origin. The *Herald Tribune* (New York) published a transcript of the shortwave transmission on 31 May 1931. The text has also been published in Shaw, *Platform and Pulpit* (208–16), and in Shaw, *Saint Joan*, ed. Stanley Weintraub (Indianapolis: Bobbs-Merrill, 1971). A week before the Joan broadcast, the *Radio Times* (22 May 1931) carried a short (and uninspiring) dramatic sketch about Shaw by Winifred Holtby, in which 'Miranda' (anti-Shaw) and 'Minerva' (pro-Shaw) debate his merits as a playwright. Minerva has an easy victory.

25 BBC Archives, Talks 1924–32, file 1a, no date.

26 The text of Shaw's speech ('Playwrights and Amateurs') is in West 228–36 and on disc 1, track 3 of Shaw, *The Spoken Word*.

27 The script is published as 'The Girl with the Golden Voice' in *CP* 7:643–5. Shaw's typescript is in British Library, Add Ms 50705, ff. 82–4.

28 BBC Archives, Talks 1933–7, file 1b, 5 June 1937. By 1938 – not long after Shaw's talk – BBC school broadcasts were being heard in nearly 900 secondary schools (Briggs, *BBC* 116).

29 Internal memo, BBC Archives, Talks 1933–7, file 1b, 10 June 1937.

30 *RT*, 25 June 1937. The text of Shaw's talk was published in *The Listener*, 23 June 1937 (with the title of 'School'). It is also in Shaw, *Platform and Pulpit*

275–82, and is included here as appendix 2D. The BBC typescript of the talk ('Talk for Sixth Forms') is at HRC, Shaw 4/12. Another typescript ('Broadcast to Sixth Form Scholars,' marked 'Transcript of the Original Shorthand Draft By G. Bernard Shaw') is also in HRC (also Shaw 4/12). The talk is on disc 2, track 1 of Shaw, *The Spoken Word*. Shaw was introduced for this broadcast by Lionel Gamlin, a BBC actor and announcer, who recalls Shaw being 'completely at ease,' while it was he who was 'stricken with nerves.' 'Young man,' said GBS, stroking the microphone with a warning finger, 'this is a devilish contraption. You can't deceive it – so don't try!' 'From that day to this,' Gamlin said, 'I have remembered Mr Shaw's genial warning with gratitude.' ('Inside Broadcasting House,' *Reynolds News*, 2 September 1945.)

31 The BBC's plans didn't always work out, of course. On 26 August 1932, for example, the *Radio Times* published an announcement that Shaw would participate in a series of broadcasts 'To an Unnamed Listener' (beginning on 3 October 1932) and his topic would be 'To a Politician.' Shaw's participation was confirmed in the *Radio Times* on 9 September 1932, but on 30 September he told Siepmann (letter, BBC Archives, Talks 1924–32, file 1a) that the scheduling was difficult for him and asked that his talk be delayed 'until next May or June.' And on 25 October he wrote to Siepmann again to tell him that the broadcast 'is absolutely, finally, and irrevocably off' (BBC Archives, Talks 1924–32, file 1a). Siepmann then seems to have turned to Reith for help, but to no avail. Shaw wrote to Reith on 17 November explaining that he was about to embark on a round-the-world cruise and he had done what he could 'to impress on that sanguine and irrepressible idiot Siepmann' that he wasn't available, now or the following spring' (BBC Archives, Reith Enclosure Volumes S60/6/7). The series went ahead (beginning on 17 October), but without Shaw. Shaw also declined an invitation to take part in a series called 'I Knew a Man,' on the grounds that 'I never knew anyone well enough' (letter to Siepmann, 20 August 1935, BBC Archives, Talks 1933–7, file 1b). The series began on 4 October 1934 with Wells talking about T.H. Huxley. Another series, 'Speeches that Never Happen,' a rare 'attempt at pure satire,' the BBC said, did appeal to Shaw. Shaw was invited to present a speech by 'The politician who admitted that his party's policy had always been disastrous,' or by 'The press magnate who admitted that the sales of his paper were falling,' or by 'The eminent physician who admitted that diagnosis was sheer guesswork,' or by 'The constructor who admitted that houses were jerry built and the situation appalling.' The possibilities were surely inviting, but Shaw ultimately declined, in part, because 'I must not take an actor's job.' (BBC Archives, Talks 1933–7, file 1b, 17 and 21 July 1934).

32 The talk was published in *The Listener*, 23 October 1929, and in the *New York Times*, 3 November 1929 ('Shaw Turns His Microscope on Democracy'). A typescript draft, with Shaw's holograph revisions, is in HRC, Shaw 7/4. The talk was subsequently incorporated into the preface of *The Apple Cart* (1930).

33 BBC Archives, Reith Enclosure Volumes S60/6/6. The letter is printed in full in *CL* 4:290–1.

34 BBC Archives, Talks 1924–32, file 1a, 11 June 1932.

35 The talk was published in *The Listener*, 20 July 1932, and is included here as appendix 2A. A typed transcript of the broadcast is in the BBC Archives, Scripts 1930–56, file 921/SHA. Shaw's shorthand draft is in the British Library, Add Ms 50705, ff. 39–49, as is a typescript (Add Ms 50705, ff. 50–67) and five further typescript pages marked by Shaw 'Discarded pages of Rungs of the Ladder broadcast 11 July 1932' (Add Ms 50705, ff. 68–72, included in appendix 2A). The talk was also carried by WABC and CBS in the United States, and brief excerpts were published in the *New York Times*, 12 July 1932. The recorded talk is disc 1, track 2 of Shaw, *The Spoken Word*.

36 Letter to Charles Siepmann, 18 January 1934 (*CL* 4:362).

37 Shaw was disappointed that the recording took thirty-four minutes, having read it to Charlotte in thirty-one minutes the night before. He offered to do it again, but the BBC seems to have accommodated the extra time. (See *CL* 4:361–2.) The BBC had developed reliable recording techniques (on acetate discs) by the early 1930s (Briggs, *BBC* 120).

38 'Whither Britain?' was published in *The Listener*, 7 February 1934. A typed transcript of the broadcast is at Burgunder 4617/7. Another transcript in the BBC Archives (Scripts 1930–56, file 921/SHA). Shaw's shorthand script (headed, in Shaw's hand, 'Whither England?') is in the British Library, Add Ms 50705, ff. 77–9. The talk was published by the Labour Party of Great Britain later in 1934 as *Are We Heading for War?* Extracts were published in the *New York Times*, 7 February 1934. The talk is on disc 1, track 4 of Shaw, *The Spoken Word*.

39 Listeners' letters were published in the *Radio Times*, 23 February and 2 March 1934, and in *The Listener*, 21 February.

40 Letter to Siepmann, 2 March 1935, BBC Archives, Talks 1933–7, file 1b.

41 Internal memo, 17 June 1935, BBC Archives, Talks 1933–7, file 1b.

42 'Freedom' was published in *The Listener*, 26 June 1935. It is included in Shaw, *Platform and Pulpit* 263–70. Talks from the series on 'Freedom' were published as *Freedom* (London: George Allen & Unwin, 1935).

43 The correspondence about Shaw's talk is all in BBC Archives, Talks 1933–7, file 1b.

44 Shaw, 'As I See It,' *The Listener*, 10 November 1937, and in Shaw, *Platform and Pulpit* (as 'This Danger of War') 282–6. The talk is included here as

appendix 2E. The transcript of the broadcast – with Shaw's holograph emendations – is in the BBC Archives, Scripts, file 921/SHA. There are three typescripts of the talk in the British Library: Add Ms 50705, ff. 85–95 (a working copy with numerous holograph emendations, deletions, and additions); Add Ms 50705, ff. 98–106 (a clean copy, but with a section headed, in Shaw's hand, 'Discards from Broadcast "As I See It" Empire Broadcast 2nd Nov. 1937'); and Add Ms 50705, ff. 107–12 (a clean copy, as published in *The Listener*). The talk is on disc 2, track 2 of Shaw, *The Spoken Word*. Shaw turned down another request to give an Empire broadcast (subject unspecified) on 25 November 1938 (BBC Archives, Talks 1938–50, file 2).

45 Metz 264–5.
46 Walsh's broadcast was reported in the *New York Times*, 19 October 1931. Shaw's talk was published in the *New York Times* on 12 October 1931 under the main headline of 'SHAW TWITS AMERICA ON REDS' "PROSPER-ITY."' Other partial and full versions were published, one (full text) in London by the Friends of the Soviet Union in 1931 with the title *Look you boob ... ! What Bernard Shaw told the Americans about Russia!* There are two typescript copies of the talk in the British Library: Add Ms 50705, ff. 16–27 has minor emendations in Shaw's hand; Add Ms 50705, ff. 28–38 is a carbon copy with the same emendations in Blanche Patch's hand. The talk is included in Shaw, *Platform and Pulpit* 226–34. The recorded talk is disc 1, track 1 of Shaw, *The Spoken Word*.
47 See Shaw, *Platform and Pulpit* 216–18. A translation of the version that was published in *Pravda* on 29 July 1931 (revised by Shaw before publication) has Shaw praising the Communist revolution and admonishing England 'for not having beaten you to it. And all the nations of the West ought to share that feeling of shame with England and envy you your glory.' See *CL* 4:256–8.
48 The talk was published in the *Cape Times*, 8 February 1932, and is reprinted in the *Shavian* 16 (October 1959): 2–7. Shaw's original holograph manuscript of the script is in HRC, Shaw 4/12. While in South Africa Shaw was also interviewed (in Durban) by the South African Broadcasting Authority (Laurence, *Bibliography* 2:866, F18).
49 The full text of the talk was published in the *New York Times*, 12 April 1933, and subsequently in *Political Quarterly* 4 (July 1933): 313–40, as well as in book form as *The Political Madhouse in America and Nearer Home* (London: Constable, 1933). A typescript of the talk, with Shaw's emendations and corrections, is held at Columbia University Library, MS Coll/Shaw, G.B.
50 The talk was widely reported in the New Zealand press. See, for example, the Wellington *Evening Post*, 13 April 1934, in *What I Said in N.Z. The*

Newspaper Utterances of Mr George Bernard Shaw in New Zealand (Wellington: The Commercial Printing and Publishing Company of New Zealand, 1934). Shaw made no reference in his talk to the banning of the epilogue from the broadcast of *Androcles and the Lion* in New Zealand in March 1934, New Zealand broadcasting regulations specifying that broadcasting not be used for 'the dissemination of propaganda of a controversial nature' (*The Dominion*, 28 March 1934). *The Dominion* described the epilogue as 'an outspoken criticism of the attitude of the churches to militarism and imperialism' and went on to quote from it at length.

51 Several of MacCarthy's reviews are collected in MacCarthy, *Shaw*. In his preface to this book MacCarthy writes: 'I have written more about Bernard Shaw than about any other writer living or dead' (vii).

Chapter 4

1 *RT*, 28 December 1934. The Shaw play was part 1 of *Back to Methuselah* (broadcast on 2 January 1935). The Shakespeare plays were *Troilus and Cressida*, *A Winter's Tale*, and *The Taming of the Shrew*.

2 Letter to Shaw, 11 November 1935, BL Add Ms 56629, f. 171. The fee for *Village Wooing* was approved by Shaw in a note to the BBC on 30 October 1934 (BBC Archives, COP/SCR 1924–35, file 1a) and for *Candida* in a telephone conversation (BBC Archives, COP/SCR 1924–35, file 1a, 11 November 1935).

3 Note to the BBC, 10 August 1936, Burgunder, 4617/15. Plans for the production were dropped, though there is no evidence to suggest that this had anything to do with Shaw's fee expectations.

4 Note to the BBC, 17 August 1938, Burgunder, 4617/16.

5 Note to the BBC, 3 November 1939, Burgunder, 4617/16.

6 BBC Archives, COP/SCR 1924–35, file 1a, 22 October 1929.

7 The cast list in the *Radio Times* gives Frederick Burtwell as Drinkwater. The review in *The Listener*, however, praises Ralph Richardson's performance as Drinkwater: 'a high-spirited, racy affair, which dealt faithfully with the Cockney dialect Mr Shaw has provided.' Since the cast lists were published several days ahead of the actual performance, there were frequently late substitutions, and it sounds as if Richardson replaced Burtwell at the last minute. Richardson was then an up-and-coming actor aged 29. He had played in *Back to Methuselah* in London the previous year.

8 Savoy Hill, just south of the Strand, near Waterloo Bridge, was the London location of the BBC studios.

9 BBC Archives, Talks 1924–32, file 1a, 29 October 1929. Also in *CL* 4:164–5.

10 BBC Archives, Talks 1924–32, file 1a, 30 October 1929.

11 BBC Archives, COP/SCR 1924–35, file 1a, 1 November 1929.

12 The first was on 28 March 1928.

13 Note to the BBC, 21 November 1936, Burgunder, 4617/15. One listener, however (describing Shaw as 'our modern Shakespeare'), remembered this production as 'a treat to listen to' (*RT*, 26 June 1931).

14 BBC Archives, COP/SCR 1936–8, file 1b, 24 November 1936.

15 *Village Wooing* was broadcast again on 22 and 23 March 1938.

16 See Conolly, *Bernard Shaw and Barry Jackson* 57. The broadcast from the Malvern Festival Theatre (managed by Roy Limbert) was independent of the Malvern Festival (managed by Sir Barry Jackson).

17 BBC Archives, COP/SCR 1924–35, file 1a, 8 March 1934. Lewis selected a little-known actor named Tosca von Bissing for the role of the Serpent because of her 'most distinctive and peculiar vocal quality ... a queer non human quality which is exactly what I was looking for' (memo to Val Gielgud, 12 December 1934, BBC Archives, COP/SCR, 1924–35, file 1a).

18 The script is in the BBC Archives, COP/SCR 1924–35, file 1a, 22 November 1934. It is a carbon copy in which there are two gaps. I have inserted the missing words as they appear in Shaw's original draft, now in HRC, Shaw 4/9. Shaw's original draft has a different conclusion. After 'omnipotence and omniscience,' he wrote: 'You may ask how we are to understand such creatures with our limited intelligence. The author has got over that difficulty for us very simply; for the children of these immortals are, from their birth to the end of their fourth year, just such as we are. Their infancy is like our maturity; and it is to these infants, and to the speeches in which the immortals adapt themselves to the comprehension of their children, that you are about to listen. You will please imagine these children as very lovely, very beautifully dressed, revelling in all the arts of music, dancing, and singing, and in the poetic traditions of the old romantic lovemaking. As to the immortals, they are naked, hairless, incredibly old, and utterly indifferent to their personal appearance or to what we call comfort. The children cannot understand them. They laugh at them and call them the Ancients; but they obey them and depend on them. You will be privileged to assist at the birth of one of the children; but do not be alarmed: she will be born from an egg hatched in an incubator, and will be as big and as clever at birth as our children are at sixteen. Now sit up and listen hard: the play is about to begin again.'

19 Internal memo, 5 November 1935, BBC Archives, COP/SCR 1924–35, file 1a.

20 Shaw's letter to Beaumont on this matter, 9 April 1937, is in the Hugh Beaumont Letterbook at Colgate University.

21 BBC Archives, COP/SCR 1936–8, file 1b, 17 September 1937.

22 This was the last visit by Shaw to a BBC studio (*RT*, 19 July 1946).

23 Note to the BBC, 17 March 1938, Burgunder, 4617/16.

24 The prologue was published in *The Listener*, 27 April 1938. It appears in *CP* 4:304–8. Two typescript drafts are held at HRC: Shaw 4/12, dated 8 April 1938, and Shaw 7/2, dated 22 April 1938 (with Shaw's holograph revisions), and one at the BBC Archives (Scripts 1930–56, file 921/SHA, with Shaw's holograph revisions, dated 22 April 1938). The broadcast is on disc 2, track 4, of Shaw, *The Spoken Word*.

25 Note to the BBC, 17 August 1938, Burgunder, 4617/16.

26 BBC Archives, COP/SCR 1936–8, file 1b.

27 Broadcast times were 4:20–4:55 pm on 14 April, 4:25–5:00 pm on 18 April, and 4:10–5:00 pm on 21 April. Although this was the radio premiere of *Arms and the Man*, the BBC had previously broadcast (on 19 February 1935, rebroadcast on 20 February 1935 and 30 March and 1 April 1937) Oscar Strauss's unauthorized adaptation of the play, the comic opera *The Chocolate Soldier*.

28 BBC Archives, COP/SCR 1936–8, file 1b, 14 January 1937.

29 BBC Archives, COP/SCR 1924–35, file 1a, 5 May 1932.

30 Note to the BBC, 19 July 1937, Burgunder, 4617/15.

31 Ibid.

32 Note to the BBC, 7 November 1939, Burgunder, 4617/16.

33 BBC Archives, COP/SCR 1936–8, file 1b, 25 February 1937, and *BBC Programme Records* 8:1 (London: BBC [1938]) 61.

34 BBC Archives, COP/SCR 1939–40, file 2a, 23 January 1939.

35 BBC Archives, COP/SCR 1924–35, file 1a, 5 July 1935.

36 Note to the BBC, 16 August 1936, Burgunder, 4617/15.

37 Note to the BBC, 1 September 1937, Burgunder, 4617/15.

38 See Norman Veitch, *The People's: Being a History of the People's Theatre, Newcastle upon Tyne, 1911–1939* (Gateshead: Northumberland Press, 1950) 50–1. In his approval to broadcast the scene Shaw stipulated that 'they must not cut the scene by a single second,' though the approval was given several days *after* the broadcast (Burgunder, 4617/16, 2 April 1939).

39 BBC Archives, COP/SCR 1939–40, file 2a, 20 December 1939.

40 BBC Archives, COP/SCR 1936–8, file 1b, 28 January 1938. See also Shaw's admonition that his plays should not be used as 'instruments of torture' on schoolchildren (above, p. 103).

41 BBC Archives, COP/SCR 1936–8, file 1b, 5 March 1937.

42 Information in this paragraph is from a lead article in the *Radio Times*, 20 November 1931.

43 BBC Archives, COP/SCR 1936–8, file 1b, 28 May 1936.

44 BBC Archives, COP/SCR 1936–8, file 1b, 7 July 1936.
45 BBC Archives, COP/SCR 1939–40, file 2a, 13 June 1939.
46 Burgunder, 4617/15, 23 September 1936.
47 Burgunder, 4617/16, 19 March 1938.
48 Burgunder, 4617/16, 2 December 1938.
49 A brief article in the *New York Times*, 22 January 1930, also announced that Lewis 'holds the exclusive American radio rights to all of Shaw's plays.' No listing of radio productions of Shaw's plays in the United Sates or Canada has been compiled. Shaw's account books in the British Library of Political and Economic Science record payments for American broadcasts – e.g., he received £25 for *How He Lied* (Shaw 28/1, f. 47).

Chapter 5

1 Bernard Shaw, 'The Drama and the Microphone,' *The Playgoer*, March 1925, in Dukore 4:1408.
2 So far as television was concerned, the 'negligible cost' was a long way in the future. In February 1937 the cost of a television receiver was reduced from a range of 95–120 guineas to a range of 60–95 guineas (*The Times*, 9 February 1937), a level still way beyond the reach of working-class and middle-class families (though *The Times* pointed out that sets could be bought 'on hire purchase terms which amount to only a small deposit and payments at the rate of £1 a week').
3 'GBS on Television,' *Television Magazine*, January 1947, in Dukore 4:1508–9. Shaw never saw a television production of one of his plays in his home, but he did watch the production of *How He Lied to Her Husband* on a set in the BBC studios in 1937 (see above, p. 92).
4 There had not been a major stage production of *Jitta's Atonement* since May 1939 (Embassy Theatre).
5 Extracts from the Selsdon Report are quoted from Smith 65–6.
6 Alexandra Palace was built in 1873 as 'The People's Palace,' a large Victorian leisure centre rather unkindly described by someone who worked there for the BBC as 'a great mausoleum in the most execrable taste, a legacy of Victorianism at its worst, a monument of brick and stucco that should make us ashamed that our concert-going and pleasure-seeking ancestors looked upon it with misguided pride' (Swift 72). It did, however, have the advantage of being near central London (six miles) and 306 ft above sea level, ideal for broadcasting purposes. No longer used by the BBC, Alexandra Palace is now (2007) a conference and entertainment venue.

7 The date of the telephone call is not known. The BBC wrote to Shaw on 23 June 1937 to thank him for giving permission by telephone and to confirm the fee and the date (BBC Archives, COP/SCR 1936–8, file 1b, 23 June 1937).

8 BBC Archives, COP/SCR 1936–8, file 1b, 14 July 1937. Cock was impressed enough with Shaw to invite him back to the television studios to appear on the first BBC television broadcast on a Sunday in early March 1938. 'I want to open with a "personality,"' Cock wrote to Shaw, offering him 'three to six minutes in front of the camera on any subject you care to tackle.' Shaw – through Blanche Patch – declined (BBC Archives, Talks 1938–50, file 2, 1 and 3 March 1938).

9 There is no record of O'Ferrall's request, but Shaw's response, in a letter dated 19 August 1937, is in the BBC Archives, COP/SCR 1936–8, file 1b.

10 The BBC request is in the BBC Archives, COP/SCR 1936–8, file 1b, 21 September 1937. Shaw's reply is Burgunder, 4617/15.

11 Burgunder, 4617/15, 11 and 16 April 1938.

12 Burgunder, 4617/16, 19 and 21 April 1938.

13 Burgunder, 4617/16, 16 July 1938.

14 Burgunder, 4617/16, 31 August and 15 September 1938.

15 Burgunder, 4617/16, 14 and 18 February 1939.

16 Burgunder, 4617/16, 6 March 1939.

17 Burgunder, 4617/16, 6 and 7 March 1939.

18 She had previously played Raina in *Arms and the Man* at the Old Vic in 1931, Epifania in *The Millionairess* at the Gaiety in Dublin in 1938, and had recently (March 1939) played Candida in a touring production in Holland.

19 HRC, Shaw 51/4, 29 and 30 March 1939.

20 The first play televised directly from a theatre was J.B. Priestley's *When We Are Married*, in November 1938 (Briggs, *BBC* 169).

21 The article from *The Times* is published with the text of *Geneva* in *CP* 7:170–2. The typescript of Shaw's synopsis, with Shaw's holograph revisions, is BL Add Ms 50643, ff. 194–5.

22 The 20,000 figure didn't impress the manufacturers of television sets: 'the lack of a really enthusiastic response to the inauguration of the world's first broadcast television station is causing serious concern to the manufacturer, who has spent considerable sums in the design and development of a reliable apparatus' (*The Times*, 23 August 1939). The principal manufacturers were Marconi, HMV, and General Electric.

Chapter 6

1 *CL* 4:815, 25 February 1948.

2 See 'Broadcasting Carries On!' *RT*, 4 September 1939. While radio broadcasts continued, the fledgling BBC television service was suspended (see
above, p. 97). The 'Home Service' was the BBC's main transmission, but a
separate 'Forces' programming schedule was established in January 1940.
There was 'little demand' among the troops for plays (Briggs, *BBC* 186).

3 'Broadcast Drama in Wartime,' *The Listener*, 14 December 1939. No author is
identified, though it was almost certainly Val Gielgud, Head of Drama.

4 Ernest Newman, *Sunday Times*, quoted in Briggs, *BBC* 177.

5 Shaw, *Agitations* 310–11.

6 BBC Archives, Talks 1938–50, file 2, 24 February 1941.

7 Burgunder, 4617/16, 31 December 1940.

8 Burgunder, 4617/16, 22 August 1941. Joan was played by Constance
Cummings; see above, p. 117.

9 BBC Archives, COP/SCR 1941–2, file 2b, 30 July 1941.

10 Burgunder, 4617/17, 14 January 1944.

11 Burgunder, 4617/17, 13 June 1945.

12 Burgunder, 4617/16, 23 August 1940.

13 BL Add Ms 50524, f. 292.

14 BBC Archives, COP/SCR 1943–8, file 3a, 7 February 1945.

15 BBC Archives, COP/SCR 1943–8, file 3a, 21 November 1945.

16 Burgunder, 4617/16, 5 November 1942. Shaw's reply is dated (in error)
18 December 1945.

17 BBC Archives, COP/SCR 1939–40, file 2a, 15 February 1940. The letter is
also published in *CL* 4:546. The broadcast of *Arms and the Man* took place on
14 March 1940, from 7:30 to 8:00 pm. A broadcast in three thirty-minute
parts had taken place on the National and Empire Services of the BBC on
14, 18, and 21 April 1939.

18 BBC Archives, COP/SCR 1943–5, file 3a, 11 January 1945.

19 Burgunder, 4617/17, 16 May 1945. Shaw had perhaps forgotten the thirty-
minute broadcast of *The Dark Lady of the Sonnets* on 21 July 1938 or the thirty-
five-minute broadcast of *How He Lied to Her Husband* on 6 October 1938.

20 See for example, pp. 23–9.

21 This was in a letter (6 March 1941) to Ronald Kidd of the National Council for
Civil Liberties. The government instructed the BBC to lift the ban. See *CL* 4:600.
The BBC's official position in such circumstances (as reported in the *Daily Herald*, 14 March 1941) was that the 'no one is invited to the microphone who has
taken part in public agitation against the national war effort ... The BBC does
not withold invitations or engagements from persons because of their political
views, or because their views on the conduct of affairs do not coincide with
those of the Government or of any particular political party.'

22 *CP* 6:527.
23 Burgunder, 4617/17, 28 March 1944.
24 Burgunder, 4617/17, 21 March 1944.
25 Burgunder, 4617/17, 28 March 1944.
26 BBC Archives, Talks 1938–50, file 2, 13 March and 17 April 1940. Rendall
    presumably had in mind, for example, the controversy caused by Shaw's
    article 'Uncommon Sense about the War,' published in the *New Statesman*
    on 7 October 1939, in which Shaw had advocated an immediate truce and a
    world conference to establish a 'constructive peace.'
27 Weymouth's account of his involvement in the affair is in his *Journal of the
    War Years and One Year Later* (Worcester: Littlebury, 1948) 1:254–60. See also
    Flora C. Buckalew, 'Bernard Shaw's "Unavoidable Subject,"' *SHAW: The
    Annual of Bernard Shaw Studies* 15 (1995): 211–29. Unless otherwise noted,
    my account is based on Weymouth and on documents and correspondence
    in the BBC Archives, Talks 1938–50, file 2.
28 The revised script is marked 'suggested re-submission to the author' (BBC
    Archives, Talks 1938–50, file 2), so the intention seems to have been to get
    Shaw's approval, but there is no evidence that Shaw ever saw it.
29 Cooper's only reference to Shaw in his memoirs, however, is to Shaw as a
    critic of Shakespeare: 'When Tolstoy attacks Shakespeare it is Tolstoy who
    dwindles in stature, and when Bernard Shaw attacks him it is Bernard Shaw
    who appears a ridiculous pigmy shaking his fist at a mountain' (Cooper 40).
30 'The Unavoidable Subject' was first published by Anthony Weymouth in
    Journal of the War Years, and subsequently by Dan H. Laurence in Shaw, *Plat-
    form and Pulpit*. Weymouth's version is based on the script given to him by
    Shaw and is now in the Pattee Library at the Pennsylvania State University,
    with a note, in Shaw's hand, 'Anthony Weymouth is authorized to quote in
    full' (dated 3 June 1946). A second (undated, but earlier) version, with ex-
    tensive revisions by Shaw, is also held in the Pattee Library. Laurence's ver-
    sion is based on the copy that Shaw sent to Beatrice Webb, which is now in
    the Passfield Papers at the British Library of Political and Economic Sci-
    ence. This version is also included in Michalos and Poff (245–50). Other
    copies (all undated) are held at Cornell University (Burgunder, 4617/7 –
    typescript with revisions in the hand of Blanche Patch); the British Library
    (Add Ms 5705, ff. 113–21 – typescript with revisions in Shaw's hand; it is
    marked 'Draft' 'To: Mr Anthony Weymouth,' and has the statement on the
    cover page 'After reference to the Ministry of Information we are obliged,
    in view of the critical military situation, to cancel this talk'); and the BBC
    Archives (two copies, both typescript, both in Talks 1938–50, file 2; one car-
    ries the statement 'Text as revised by the BBC for suggested re-submission

to the author'). Buckalew analyses the differences between the Weymouth and Laurence published texts. They are not as significant as the changes made in the (unpublished) version 'as revised' by the BBC.

31 Quotations are from the text in appendix 2F.

32 BBC Archives, Talks 1938–50, file 2, 2 June 1941. The suggestion that Churchill was involved is not entirely fanciful. Duff Cooper is known to have drawn Churchill's attention to German use of J.B. Priestley's broadcasts (West, *Truth Betrayed* 183).

33 BBC Archives, Talks 1938–50, file 2, 25 September 1941.

34 BBC Archives, Talks 1938–50, file 2, 14 July 1941.

35 BBC Archives, Talks 1938–50, file 2, 5 June 1941.

36 Ogilvie's letter is dated 1 September 1941 (BBC Archives, Talks 1938–50, file 2). Sweden was officially neutral during the Second World War.

37 BBC Archives, Talks 1938–50, file 2, 21 August 1940.

38 BBC Archives, Talks 1938–50, file 2, 3 October 1941.

39 BBC Archives, Talks 1938–50, file 2, 20 November 1941.

40 BBC Archives, Talks 1938–50, file 2, 16 January 1942.

41 BBC Archives, Talks 1938–50, file 2, 28 January 1943.

42 BBC Archives, Talks 1938–50, file 2, 24 February 1943.

43 BBC Archives, Talks 1938–50, file 2, 21 May 1943.

44 BBC Archives, Talks 1938–50, file 2, 22 January 1943.

45 The correspondence began with a letter from Shaw in *The Listener* on 5 November 1942 and didn't end until a letter from Anthony Weymouth (the same Anthony Weymouth who did his best to get Shaw's 'Unavoidable Subject' on the air in June 1940) on 11 March 1943.

46 The government closed all theatres on the declaration of war, a decision criticized by Shaw as 'a masterstroke of unimaginative stupidity.' The decision was quickly reversed (Conolly, *Bernard Shaw and Barry Jackson* 107), but the theatres remained hurt by the loss of personnel to war service and the reluctance of audiences to risk air-raid attacks.

47 Cummings (who subsequently played Joan on television) wrote about her meeting with Shaw – and about playing Joan and other Shaw parts – in 'Playing Joan on Radio and Television.' Cummings knew the role so well that for the radio production she played it without a script, which apparently caused some nervousness among the rest of the cast and the crew (Cummings 140–1). Gielgud recorded in his diary that she played the part 'with perfect *sang-froid* which the rest of the cast did not share!' (*Years in a Mirror* 114).

48 BBC Written Archives, COP/SCR 1941–2, file 2b, 30 July 1941.

49 Cummings did 'go far' – on both sides of the Atlantic – in film, television, and theatre. Among the flowers in Shaw's bedroom at Ayot St Lawrence

shortly before his death was a pot of cyclamen sent by Constance Cummings and her husband, writer and politician Benn Levy (*CL* 4:881). She died in 2005. Shaw's letter to Gielgud is in the BBC Archives, COP/SCR 1941–2, file 2b, 24 September 1941.

50 France had been occupied by Germany since June 1940.

51 *RT*, 31 October 1942. The BBC program records indicate that the extracts were from the scene with Joan, Dunois, and the Archbishop (scene 5). Only 759 words were used, and a note from Blanche Patch to the BBC, 24 October 1942, says that Shaw said that no permission was needed (BBC Archives, COP/SCR 1941–2, file 2b).

52 The BBC typescript sent to Shaw, and returned by Shaw with his holograph revisions, is BL Add Ms 50633, ff. 29–33. The fair copy is BL Add Ms 50633, ff. 34–41. It indicates that the narrator was played by Douglas Allan.

53 BBC Written Archives, COP/SCR 1941–2, file 2b, 13 February 1942.

54 The repeat broadcast was on 22 February 1944. Somerville's letter (9 November 1943) is BBC Archives, COP/SCR 1943–5, file 3a. Shaw's handwritten response is dated 12 November 1943.

55 Letter to Shaw, 8 January 1945, BL Add Ms 50524, f. 292. The proposed date for the production was 3 February 1945. This was confirmed by another letter, 11 January 1945 (BBC Archives, COP/SCR 1943–5, file 3a), but the production never took place.

56 BBC Archives, COP/SCR 1941–2, file 2b, 8 August 1941, and Burgunder, 4617/16, 8 August 1941.

57 Burgunder, 4617/17, 14 January 1944. The BBC's 'Programme as Broadcast' records indicate that the extract lasted four minutes.

58 Burgunder, 4617/17, 20 January 1945; BBC Archives, COP/SCR 1943–5, file 3a, 23 January 1945.

59 Burgunder, 4617/16, 1 May 1940.

60 28 March 1928, 15 May 1930, 11 January 1937, plus repeats.

61 No script has survived for the broadcast, so it is not known if the speech was edited for the occasion. Indeed, it is not even certain that it was this particular speech by Napoleon that Esmé Percy used. The evidence is a letter from the BBC to Shaw, 3 April 1944, which refers only to Percy's broadcast of 'Napoleon's speech from *Man of Destiny* in the "Vaudeville" programme last Saturday' (BBC Archives, COP/SCR 1943–5, file 3a). There are, however, only a few lengthy speeches by Napoleon in the play, and given the circumstances it seems highly probably that the 'race apart' speech was the one selected. The BBC's internal 'Programme as Broadcast' records indicate only that the speech lasted five minutes.

62 BBC Archives, COP/SCR 1941–2, file 2b, 29 April 1942. A 'Shaw Festival' was eventually produced by BBC Radio in 1947 (see above, pp. 146–9).

63 Information on this early history of *The Millionairess* is from Conolly, *Bernard Shaw and Barry Jackson*, passim, and Mander and Mitchenson 247–9.

64 Shaw's note (dated 26 June 1942) is on a letter to him from the BBC (23 June 1942), Burgunder, 4617/16.

65 HRC, Shaw 21/2. BL Add Ms 50639 is Shaw's copy of the rehearsal copy of the play (March 1940), in which he made the revisions from which the broadcast script was prepared. Marked on the cover (by Shaw) 'arranged for broadcasting – May 1942,' it reflects the care that Shaw took over the revisions. All alterations to the dialogue (black ink) and to the stage directions (red ink) are neatly and clearly made.

66 BL Add Ms 50638, ff. 27–31. Val Gielgud was the Narrator.

67 Shaw's letter to Beaumont, 30 June 1942, is in Laurence, *Theatrics* 214–15.

68 In Congreve's *Way of the World* at Drury Lane Theatre, 28 May 1935.

69 The next West End production of *The Millionairess* was the one mentioned above at the New Theatre, which opened 27 June 1952, with Katherine Hepburn as Epifania.

70 Burgunder, 4617/16, 22 July 1942.

71 Burgunder, 4617/16, 17 June 1941.

72 BBC Archives, COP/SCR 1943–5, file 3a, 25 May 1943.

73 BBC Archives, COP/SCR 1941–2, file 2b, 22 May 1941; Shaw's reply is dated 24 May 1941.

74 Burgunder, 4617/16, 26 May 1941; Shaw's reply is dated 27 May 1941.

75 Burgunder, 4617/16, 30 May 1941.

76 Burgunder, 4617/16, 12 June 1944.

77 The broadcast script in the BBC Archives for this production is marked 'NEVER TO BE USED AGAIN.' The correspondence about the 1944 and 1953 productions of *Black Girl* is in the BBC Archives, Entertainment R19/14.

78 BBC Archives, COP/SCR 1941–2, file 2b, 26 December 1942.

79 Burgunder, 4617/16. The letter to Shaw from B.H. Alexander seeking permission from Shaw is incorrectly dated 12 January 1942. Shaw's response (13 January 1943) has the correct year.

80 Burgunder, 4617/16, 15 January 1943, and BBC Archives, COP/SCR 1943–45, file 3a, 15 January 1943. Orwell's brief dealings with Shaw caused a minor contretemps between Orwell and B.H. Alexander, Head of Copyright at the BBC. Alexander thought that Orwell (whom she called Eric Blair) was trespassing into her territory by discussing fees with Shaw; Orwell accused Alexander of restricting his right to approach speakers, 'who in many cases are deeply suspicious of the BBC.' Not so, responded Alexander – and

certainly not in the case of Shaw: 'We are on very good terms with him.' The exchange is in internal BBC memos, 18–21 January 1943, BBC Archives, COP/SCR 1943–45, file 3a. Orwell never felt comfortable at the BBC, an institution he once described as 'half way between a girls' school and a lunatic asylum' (Briggs, *BBC* 194).

81 Shaw used the phrase in a letter giving permission for an overseas broadcast of Henry Ainley doing a short extract from the opening scene of *You Never Can Tell* (Burgunder, 4617/16, 24 October 1941).

82 Burgunder, 4617/16, 22 February 1943; Shaw's reply is dated 26 February 1943.

83 Burgunder, 4617/17, 12 May 1945.

84 Burgunder, 4617/17, 10 October 1944.

85 BBC Archives, COP/SCR 1943–5, file 3a, 7 December 1943. The script for the broadcast is BL Add Ms 50523, ff. 171–4.

86 Burgunder, 4617/17, 12 February 1944.

87 BBC Archives, COP/SCR 1943–5, file 3a, 18 February 1944.

Chapter 7

1 BL Add Ms 56633, f. 25. According to a report in the *Daily Herald* (16 August 1950), Shaw took the same position regarding American televison broadcasts of his plays: 'My works are not available for television,' he told an agent. 'Television kills a living work commercially. Mine are all alive and growing.' He added: 'There are thousands of first-rate plays and books commercially dead. They are your natural prey.'

2 BL Add Ms 56633, f. 23, 19 April 1950. The BBC subsequently gave assurances that 'no cuts or alterations whatsoever would be made in the text of the play,' but Shaw would have nothing to do with it (BL Add Ms 56633, f. 25).

3 BBC Archives, COP/SCR 1946–50, file 3b, 31 May 1949. The letter is published in Laurence, *Theatrics* 232–3. Shaw had previously said much the same thing to the Society of Authors, describing the radio production of *The Devil's Disciple* as 'a wretched affair' (BL Add Ms 56632, f. 142, 16 May 1949).

4 BL Add Ms 56632, f. 166, 13 June 1949.

5 BL Add Ms 56633, f. 46, 12 July [1950].

6 Shaw's talk is in Shaw, *Platform and Pulpit* 292–4 and is on disc 2, track 6, of Shaw, *The Spoken Word*.

7 The role had been created by American actress Winifred Lenihan at the Garrick Theatre, New York, on 28 December 1923.

8 *CL* 4:854, 26 July 1949.

9 BL Add Ms 56632, f. 171, 29 July 1949.

10 The 1948 Olympic Games were held in London. Great Britain won only three gold medals – even in the absence of competitors from Germany and Japan (not invited) and the Soviet Union (which chose not to attend).

11 Shaw underestimated the number of his plays that had been televised (in whole or in part). The number was fourteen, leaving closer to forty unproduced. The exchange between Collins and Shaw is HRC, Shaw 48/3, 31 January 1949.

12 BL Add Ms 56632, f. 189, 4 November 1949.

13 BL Add Ms 56633, f. 3, 26 January 1950. The director, Campbell Logan, had suggested Moira Lister and Eric Portman (BBC Archives COP/SCR 1946–50, file 3b, 31 January 1950).

14 BBC Archives, COP/SCR 1946–50, file 3b, 27 April 1950.

15 BBC Archives, COP/SCR 1946–50, file 3b, 17/18 August 1950. The proposed Joan was Constance Cummings, who did eventually play the role in the BBC television production of 6 May 1951 (repeated 10 May). See Cummings, 'Playing Joan on Radio and Television.'

Chapter 8

1 Shaw in fact refused permission for this broadcast, but his letter didn't reach the BBC until after the broadcast had taken place. See correspondence and telephone messages, 11, 14, and 21 December 1946; Burgunder, 4617/17. A request to use excerpts from the film in a European broadcast was flatly refused by Shaw: 'These scenes go for nothing on the sound track. I bar them absolutely' (Burgunder, 4617/17, 12 December 1945).

2 CL 4:769, 31 May 1946. The BBC had been trying from as early as April 1946 to get a commitment from Shaw for a birthday broadcast. A BBC official, N.G. Luker, visited him in the company of his neighbours in Ayot St Lawrence, Clare and Stephen Winsten, but was rebuffed. 'Much the best thing is for us to make no further move from this end,' Luker wrote to the Winstens on 26 April 1946, 'but if I hear from you of any likelihood of change, I will get recording gear and the most retiring engineers I can find down at short notice' (BBC Archives, Talks 1938–50, file 2).

3 Laurence, Bibliography 2:867.

4 BL Add Ms 50525, f. 358, 28 July 1946. Both the Radio Times and the BBC's 'Programme as Broadcast' list a Light Programme broadcast from 8:00 to 8:10 pm of extracts from three of Shaw's earlier radio talks ('Rungs of the Ladder,' 11 July 1932; 'Whither Britain?' 6 February 1934; 'As I See It,' 2 November 1937), but it seems unlikely that these would have been preferred to a new birthday talk. The birthday talk was probably broadcast, then, in place of the advertised excerpts.

5 Baxter also summarized his disagreement with Shaw over the origins of the play, Shaw having publicly denied in 1944 Baxter's claim that the Candida-Morell-Marchbanks triangle was based on the Ellen Terry–Henry Irving–Shaw relationship.

6 *The Man of Destiny* was also selected by WNYC, New York, for broadcast in a series of BBC recorded productions in the Fall of 1947 (*RT*, 24 October 1947).

7 In the letter Shaw says he listened on 'Monday,' but the play was first broadcast on a Tuesday (1 October). The letter (typed) is in the BBC Archives, COP/SCR 1946–50, file 3b. It is published in *CL* 4:779–80.

8 E.g., *The Millionairess* in 1942 (see above, p. 124).

9 The Malvern Theatre had a capacity of about 900. The Court House Theatre in Niagara-on-the-Lake seated about 400.

10 There were further repeat broadcasts of the plays in 1947 and 1948: *Mrs Warren's Profession*, 4 August 1947 and 2 June 1948 (both Third Programme); *The Devil's Disciple*, 11 August 1947 (Third) and 13 December 1948 (Home); *The Doctor's Dilemma*, 15 August 1947 (Third); and *The Apple Cart*, 20 September 1948 (Home). There were no further repeat performances of *The Shewing-up of Blanco Posnet*.

11 19 January was a Sunday.

12 BBC Archives, COP/SCR 1946–50, file 3b, 31 May 1949, and published in Laurence, *Theatrics* 232–3.

13 The original of the questionnaire – with Shaw's handwritten responses, dated 23 October 1947 – is HRC Shaw 2/19.

14 Sir William Haley, BBC Director-General, *RT*, 7 November 1946, on the occasion of the BBC's 25th anniversary.

15 BBC Archives, Reith Enclosure Volumes S60/6/13, 25 February 1948; published in *CL* 4:815–16. For the Elgar commission, see above, p. 149.

16 The lecturer was Robert Birley, who gave the second annual Reith Lectures (named in honour of the BBC's first Director-General) on the topic 'Britain in Europe,' broadcast in October and November 1949. The lecture that prompted Shaw to write to *The Listener*, 'Changes in Education and the Problem of a Common Language,' was given in the Home Service on 6 November (9:15–9:45 pm), repeated on 8 November (Third, 8:00–8:30 pm).

17 The talk was published in *The Listener*, 22 March 1951.

18 BBC Archives, COP/SCR 1946–50, file 3b, 27 March 1946.

19 BL Add Ms 56631, f. 115, 21 March 1946.

20 BL Add Ms 56632, f. 81, 31 May 1948.

21 Society of Authors memorandum, 14 November 1950 (Dan H. Laurence Collection, University of Guelph, vertical file, Society of Authors).

22 BL Add Ms 56632, ff. 181, 182, 10 and 11 October 1949.

23 BL Add Ms 56632, f. 174, 2 August 1949.
24 *CL* 4:827, 12 August 1948.
25 BL Add Ms 56632, f. 140; Richard Stoddard Aldrich, *Gertrude Lawrence as Mrs A* (London: Odhams, 1955) 258.
26 Blanche Patch also described the occasion in a letter to Lady Astor, 9 October 1946 (Wearing 194–5).
27 Robertson's account is an undated typsescript in the private collection of L.W. Conolly. Robertson was mistaken in thinking that Shaw had a broken leg; the X-ray revealed no fractures.
28 *The Times*, 10 October 1946. The text was printed in full in the *News Chronicle*, 10 October 1946. It is on disc 2, track 7, of Shaw, *The Spoken Word*.
29 The Shaw/Cochran script is in *CP* 7:658–61. BL Add Ms 50705, ff. 122–9 is a typescript with Shaw's holograph revisions. A typescript with Shaw's holograph revisions is also held in the BBC Archives (Talks 1938–50, file 2). The broadcast is on disc 2, track 8, of Shaw, *The Spoken Word*. Shaw had previously had an opportunity to be associated with Cochran in a BBC broadcast, but when they were both invited (along with John Barbirolli, John Gielgud, J.B. Priestley, and others) to select a piece of operatic music for a radio program in December 1944 Cochran accepted, but Shaw declined.
30 Postcard to the BBC, 24 June 1948 (private collection of L.W. Conolly).
31 Burgunder, 4617/17, 16 July 1948.
32 BBC Archives, Talks 1948–50, file 2, [?] May 1948.
33 BBC Archives, Talks 1948–50, file 2, 5 November 1948.
34 HRC, Shaw 48/3, 19 November 1945 and Burgunder 4617/17, 8 January 1946.
35 HRC, Shaw 48/3, 25 November 1945.
36 BBC Archives, Talks 1938–50, file 2, 16 and 22 July 1947. Shaw also received numerous requests for overseas broadcasts or re-broadcasts of his plays, a situation that was complicated by rights that Shaw had transferred to his translators. Thus, while he approved the broadcast of a new Italian translation of *The Dark Lady of the Sonnets* in February 1946, he referred a simultaneous request for a broadcast of *Saint Joan* in German to his authorized German translator, Siegfried Trebitsch (Burgunder, 4617/17, 23 February 1946).
37 The typescript is Burgunder, 4617/17, with a holograph note by Shaw (dated 18 February 1947) authorizing the broadcast.
38 The typescript, with holograph revisions by Shaw and a note authorizing the broadcast is HRC, Shaw 33/1. The letter is published in *James Joyce: The Critical Heritage*, vol. 1, ed. Robert H. Deming (London: Routledge & Kegan Paul, 1970) 189–90. See also Laurence, *Shaw: An Exhibit*, item 612 (where part of the letter, including a note by Shaw about the censorship of Joyce's play *Exiles*, is reproduced).

39 There was a production of *Candida* at the Theatre Royal, Stratford East, in July 1949, but no West End revival until the 1960s.
40 *CL* 4:845–6.
41 The stipulation is in a note to the Society of Authors, dated 29 September 1949, in response a letter to him dated 10 August 1949 (Shaw apologized for the delay in replying). BL Add Ms 56632, ff. 173, 181.
42 BBC Archives, COP/SCR 1946–50, file 3b, 15 August 1947. Gielgud's memory was a bit askew; he is referring to Constance Cummings's Joan of 15 September 1941.

Epilogue

1 A strike by the London Society of Compositors prevented publication of the *Radio Times* at the time of Shaw's death, but the last-minute programming changes caused by his death would not in any event have been given in the weekly publication. The schedule outlined here is constructed from *The Times*, *The Listener*, and internal BBC documents in the Shaw Obituary file (910). Peter Bingham's obituary of Shaw was not published, but there is a typescript copy in the Obituary file. Bingham was a BBC staff member. The obituary is an unenterprising factual account of Shaw's life, which even so manages to omit any mention of *Pygmalion* or of Shaw's 1931 visit to Russia or, indeed, of his relationship with the BBC. The Ervine, Pearson, and Mann scripts are included in appendix 4.
2 All material quoted in this chapter is, unless otherwise noted, drawn from the BBC Obituary file on Shaw (file 910).
3 Pearson's date was incorrect; he meant 1892.
4 The original script that Pearson sent to the BBC has been lost. The copy that Pearson sent to Shaw, heavily revised by Shaw, is HRC Shaw 74/1. It appears as appendix 4A. It is entirely different from the appreciation that Pearson eventually gave on the Light Programme on 2 November 1950 (appendix 4E). Pearson dealt with the concern expressed by the Literary Advisory Committee about the 'dangerous' comment on Russia by revising it to read, 'The Russian political experiment begun in 1917 has tried crude catastrophic Socialism only to be forced back by inexorable facts into the Fabian methods prescribed by Shaw and Webb.' Shaw did not change this statement. And Pearson changed his comment about *Androcles and the Lion* from 'masterpiece' to 'most perfect drama,' which Shaw in any case deleted. Pearson's account of his meeting with Shaw is in Pearson 438–40.
5 Ervine, Bishop, and Postgate all submitted scripts, but they have not survived. Postgate submitted his on 6 December 1946, with a covering letter

beginning 'Here is my arbitrary talk on Bernard Shaw.' The error ('arbitrary') was corrected to 'obituary.'

6 Not really; Russell was twenty-two years younger than Shaw.

7 The obituary was published in *The Listener*, 12 August 1936. Russell describes himself as 'the last survivor of a dead epoch.'

8 The BBC's copy of the script has been lost. However, a copy is extant in the Russell Archives at McMaster University, Ontario, and is given in appendix 4B. It was first published in the *Virginia Quarterly Review* 27 (1951): 1–7.

9 See appendix 4I for the text of Mann's obituary. It is also published in Kronenberger 250–7 (without context).

10 *The Shaw Collection* (BBC Video Ltd) contains *Arms and the Man*, *The Devil's Disciple*, *Mrs Warren's Profession*, *Pygmalion*, *Heartbreak House*, *The Millionairess*, *The Man of Destiny*, *You Never Can Tell*, *Androcles and the Lion*, and *The Apple Cart*.

11 *The Spoken Word* (British Library), introduction and notes by L.W. Conolly.

Appendix 2A

1 Paul Gorguloff, a Russian émigré, murdered Paul Doumer on 7 May 1932.

2 James Thomas (1874–1949) left school at twelve and as a teenager worked at cleaning railway engines. He was subsequently elected to the House of Commons and served as a Minister in successive Labour governments.

3 Welsh poet W.H. Davies (1871–1940).

4 Shaw's first play was *Widowers' Houses*, first produced on 13 December 1892. His most recent play (his forty-first) was *Too True to be Good*, first produced (in Boston) on 29 February 1932.

5 By Edward Dyer (1540–1607) and William Byrd (1540–1623).

Appendix 2B

1 The Disarmament Conference, chaired by former British Foreign Secretary Arthur Henderson, was held in Geneva under the auspices of the League of Nations, 1932–4. Hitler withdrew Germany from the talks in 1933.

2 Son (1850–1931) of John Boot, founder of the Boots retail company.

3 In his talk 'The Future of Political Science in America,' given on 11 April 1933 in New York (see chapter 3, pp. 69–70).

4 The Ottawa Imperial Conference, 21 July–20 August 1932, held to negotiate Commonwealth trade relationships. The agreements were perceived by some British political elements as being too concessionary to other Commonwealth countries.

Appendix 2E

1 The Spanish Civil War had started in July 1936, the Chinese Civil War in 1927.
2 British Archaeologist William Matthew Flinders Petrie (1853–1942).

Appendix 2F

1 The *Gracie Fields* (named after the popular singer) was a paddle steamer-cum minesweeper sunk during the evacuation of the British Expeditionary Force from Dunkirk in May 1940.
2 The *Lusitania* was a British ocean liner sunk by a German submarine on 7 May 1915 with the loss of almost 1200 passengers and crew.
3 Shaw is referring to the scuttling (by its commander) of the German battleship *Admiral Graf Spee* in the estuary of the River Plate, Uruguay, on 13 December 1939, where it had been driven by British warships. Jutland (1916), Trafalgar (1805), and Lepanto (1571) were the sites of great naval battles.
4 Sir Oswald Mosley (1896–1980), founder of the British Union of Fascists.
5 Shaw was a strict vegetarian; Hitler was an intermittent vegetarian.
6 Shaw is referring to the Treaty of Versailles (1919), which Shaw (and others) believed to be unduly punitive on Germany.
7 William Beveridge (1879–1963, economist and government minister) was referring to war measures such as the Emergency Powers (Defence) Act of 1940, which gave the government, among other things, sweeping powers over private property.
8 Halifax (1881–1959) was British Foreign Secretary, 1938–40.

Appendix 4A

1 The reference to the lack of a university education was inserted by Shaw.
2 The conference of the National Liberal Federation met in Newcastle in the autumn of 1891 to develop its platform for the 1892 general election. The platform was one of land, religious, and electoral reform. Gladstone's Liberals did not win a full majority, but formed a government with the support of the Irish Parliamentary Party. Pearson had put the election being referred to here in 1898; Shaw corrected it to 1892. The specific reference to the 'Newcastle programme' was added by Shaw.
3 The first half of this paragraph (up to 'all his guns on Shakespeare') was added by Shaw.
4 The phrase 'Shakespearian history play' is Shaw's. Pearson had written 'one of his finest works,' which Shaw deleted.

5 Shaw deleted a sentence by Pearson that came at this point: 'Perceiving that Shaw had become a money-maker, the West End managers displayed a progressive spirit, and two of his comedies, *Fanny's First Play* and *Pygmalion*, were performed before enthusiastic audiences; though *Androcles and the Lion*, his most perfect drama, was considered blasphemous and in bad taste.'

6 The rest of the script (i.e., the final three paragraphs) were dictated to Pearson by Shaw (see Pearson 438–43).

7 Pearson had written 'his slaughterous attack on Pavlov.' Shaw deleted 'slaughterous.'

Appendix 4B

1 The play was *The Man of Destiny*, read at Russell's flat on 22 March 1896 (Shaw, *Diaries* 2:1124).

2 Mrs Clandon in *You Never Can Tell*.

3 The actual line (from Bluntschli) is 'I have ten thousand knives and forks, and the same quantity of dessert spoons.'

4 This sentence does not appear in the McMaster typescript. It is inserted here from the published text in the *Virginia Quarterly*.

5 Held at St Martin's Town Hall, London, 27–31 July 1896 (Gibbs, *Bernard Shaw Chronology* 125).

6 Shaw's own accounts of the bicycle accident, which occurred on 12 September 1895, make no mention of jeering Russell in his train (*CL* 1:558, to Janet Achurch, 16 September 1895, and *CL* 1:559–60, to Pakenham Beatty, 17 September 1895).

7 Lewis Carroll's 1876 nonsense poem.

8 Thomas Masaryk (1850–1937), first president of Czechoslovakia.

9 Frank Swinnerton (1884–1982), novelist and critic.

10 This sentence does not appear in the McMaster typescript. It is inserted here from the published text in the *Virginia Quarterly*.

Appendix 4C

1 In thanking Shaw for sending him a copy of *Man and Superman*, Tolstoy criticized him for not being 'sufficiently serious': 'One should not speak jestingly of such a subject as the purpose of human life, the causes of its perversion, and the evil that fills the life of humanity today.' Tolstoy's letter is quoted in Henderson 520–2. The broadcast by J. Isaac has not been traced.

2 Preface to *Back to Methuselah* (Shaw, *Collected Plays* 5:337).

3 G.K. Chesterton, *George Bernard Shaw* (New York: John Lane, 1909) 247.

Appendix 4E

1 Shaw actually accepted the 1925 Nobel Prize for Literature, but donated the prize money to a foundation to support the translation of Swedish literature into English.

Appendix 4F

1 *The Listener*, 1 November 1949.
2 *Daily Express*, 3 November 1950.
3 Appendix 4E, p. 227.
4 Not located.
5 Perhaps a reference to *The Times*, which spoke (3 November 1950) of Shaw's 'defect of human understanding.'
6 Appendix 4D, p. 224.

Appendix 4H

1 Gielgud is referring to the radio broadcast of *Saint Joan* on 15 September 1941. Shaw wrote to Gielgud on 24 September 1941. See chapter 6, p. 117.
2 See 'The Shaw Festival,' chapter 8, pp. 146–9.
3 The production (on 16 October 1929) and Shaw's reaction are discussed in chapter 4, pp. 77–8.
4 See chapter 6, p. 126.
5 Broadcast on 28–9 June 1942. See chapter 6, pp. 120–4.
6 Broadcast on 6 May 1951, co-directed by Gielgud, with Constance Cummings as Joan.
7 Broadcast on 1 October 1946. See chapter 8, pp. 143–6.

Appendix 4I

1 Hauptmann died in 1946 aged 81, Strauss in 1949 aged 85.
2 Gide died in 1951 (on 19 February, just six weeks after Mann's broadcast) aged 81, Hamsun in 1952, aged 92.
3 Shaw appointed Austrian novelist and playwright Siegfried Trebitsch (1869–1956) his authorized German translator in 1902.
4 'Was ich der deutschen Kultur verdanke,' *Neue Rundschau* 22 (March 1911): 335–49.
5 'Excellent.'
6 More likely – 'almost certainly' – 1883 (Gibbs, *Bernard Shaw Chronology* 49).

7 'How can it be that I'm no longer mine?' (*The Poetry of Michelangelo*, trans. James M. Saslow [New Haven: Yale University Press, 1991] 76).

8 In 1822 the 74-year-old Goethe proposed marriage to the 19-year-old Ulrike von Levetzow, whom he had met in Marienbad. Her rejection inspired Goethe's *Marienbad* elegy. Mann seems to have been unaware of Shaw's affair with the American actress Molly Tomkins in Italy in 1927, when Shaw was seventy-one and Tomkins was twenty-nine.

Bibliography

Bonham-Carter, Victor. *Authors by Profession*. Volume 1: *From the Introduction of Printing until the Copyright Act 1911*. London: Society of Authors, 1978.

– *Authors by Profession*. Volume 2: *From the Copyright Act 1911 until the end of 1981*. London: The Bodley Head and Society of Authors, 1984.

Boyle, Andrew. *Only the Wind Will Listen: Reith of the BBC*. London: Hutchinson, 1972.

Briggs, Asa. *The Birth of Broadcasting*. *The History of Broadcasting in the United Kingdom*, volume 1. London: Oxford University Press, 1961.

– *The BBC: The First Fifty Years*. Oxford: Oxford University Press, 1985.

– *The Golden Age of Wireless: The History of Broadcasting in the United Kingdom*, volume 2. London: Oxford University Press, 1995.

– *The War of Words: The History of Broadcasting in the United Kingdom*, volume 3. London: Oxford University Press, 1970.

Briggs, Susan. *Those Radio Times*. London: Weidenfeld & Nicolson, 1981.

Buckalew, Flora C. 'Bernard Shaw's "Unavoidable Subject."' *SHAW: The Annual of Bernard Shaw Studies* 15 (1995): 211–29.

Burns, Tom. *The BBC: Public Institution and Private World*. London: Macmillan, 1977.

Carpenter, Humphrey. *The Envy of the World: Fifty Years of the BBC Third Programme and Radio 3*. London: Phoenix, 1997.

Coase, R.H. *British Broadcasting: A Study in Monopoly*. London: Longmans, Green, 1950.

Conolly, L.W., 'GBS and the BBC: In the Beginning (1923–1928).' *SHAW: The Annual of Bernard Shaw Studies* 23 (2003): 75–116.

– 'GBS & the BBC: *Saint Joan*, 1929.' *Theatre Notebook* 57.1 (2003): 11–24.

– 'Shaw and BBC English.' *Independent Shavian* 42.3 (2004): 59–63.

Conolly, L.W., ed. *Bernard Shaw and Barry Jackson*. Toronto: University of Toronto Press, 2002.

Cooke, Alistair. *Memories of the Great and the Good*. New York: Arcade Publishing, 1999.

Cooper, Duff. *Old Men Forget*. London: Rupert Hart-Davis, 1953.

Crisell, Andrew. *An Introductory History of British Broadcasting*. London and New York: Routledge, 1997.

Cummings, Constance. 'Playing Joan on Radio and Television.' *SHAW: The Annual of Bernard Shaw Studies* 4 (1984): 139–47.

Currie, Tony. *The Radio Times Story*. Tiverton, Devon: Kelly Publications, 2001.

Do We Agree? A Debate between G.K. Chesterton and Bernard Shaw, with Hilaire Belloc in the Chair. London: Cecil Palmer, 1928.

Ducat, Vivian. 'Bernard Shaw and the King's English.' *SHAW: The Annual of Bernard Shaw Studies* 9 (1989): 185–97.

Dukore, Bernard, ed. *Bernard Shaw: The Drama Observed*. 4 vols. University Park: Pennsylvania State University Press 1993.

Eckersley, Roger. *The BBC and All That*. London: Sampson Low, Marston & Co., [1946].

Ervine, St John. *Bernard Shaw: His Life, Work and Friends*. New York: William Morrow, 1956.

Evans, N. Dean. 'A Chance Visit with GBS.' *Independent Shavian* 39.1–2 (2001): 3–8.

Forbes, Bryan. *Ned's Girl. The Authorised Biography of Dame Edith Evans*. London: Hamish Hamilton, 1977.

Gibbs, A.M. *Bernard Shaw: A Life*. Gainesville: University Press of Florida, 2005.

– *A Bernard Shaw Chronology*. London: Palgrave, 2001.

Gielgud, Val. *British Radio Drama 1922–1956. A Survey*. London: Harrap, 1957.

– 'Drama in Television and Sound.' *BBC Quarterly* 5.4 (Winter 1950–1): 200–5.

– 'G.B.S.: His Contribution to Broadcasting.' *Radio Times*, 17 November 1950.

– 'Policy and Problems of Broadcast Drama.' *BBC Quarterly* 2.1 (1947): 18–23.

– *Years in a Mirror*. London: The Bodley Head, 1965.

– *Years of the Locust*. London: Nicholson & Watson, 1947.

Gorham, Maurice. *Sound and Fury: Twenty-One Years in the BBC*. London: Percival Marshall, 1948.

Grenfell, Joyce. *Darling Ma: Letters to Her Mother, 1932–1944*. Ed. James Roose-Evans. London: Hodder & Stoughton, 1988.

Henderson, Archibald. *Bernard Shaw: Playboy and Prophet*. New York: Appleton, 1932.

Hibberd, Stuart. *'This – is London.'* London: Macdonald & Evans, 1950.

Hobson, Harold. 'What We Want in Television Plays.' *BBC Quarterly* 5.2 (Summer 1950): 77–80.

Holroyd, Michael. *Bernard Shaw*. 5 vols. London: Chatto & Windus, 1988–92.

Inge, William Ralph. *Vale*. London: Longmans, 1934.

Kronenberger, Louis, ed. *Bernard Shaw: A Critical Survey*. Cleveland and New York: World Publishing Co., 1953.

Lambert, Richard. *Ariel and All His Quality: An Impression of the BBC from Within*. London: Gollancz, 1940.

Laurence, Dan H. *Bernard Shaw: A Bibliography*. 2 vols. Oxford: Clarendon Press, 1983.

– *Shaw: An Exhibit*. Austin: Humanities Research Center, University of Texas, 1977.

Laurence, Dan H., ed. *Bernard Shaw Theatrics*. Toronto: University of Toronto Press, 1995.

Lejeune, C.A. 'Films and Plays in Television.' *BBC Quarterly* 4.4 (Winter 1949–50): 224–9.

Lewis, Cecil. *Never Look Back*. London: Hutchinson, 1974.

Lewis, Peter, ed. *Radio Drama*. London: Longmans, 1981.

Mander, Raymond, and Joe Mitchenson. *Theatrical Companion to Shaw*. New York: Pitman, 1955.

MacCarthy, Desmond. *Shaw*. London: MacGibbon & Kee, 1951.

Metz, Robert. *CBS: Reflections in a Bloodshot Eye*. New York: Signet, 1976.

Michalos, Alex C., and Deborah C. Poff, eds. *Bernard Shaw and the Webbs*. Toronto: University of Toronto Press, 2002.

Moore, R.W. 'Television: A Cautionary Approach.' *BBC Quarterly* 5.1 (Spring 1950): 8–12.

Orwell, George. *The War Broadcasts*. Ed. W.J. West. London: Penguin, 1985.

Patch, Blanche. *Thirty Years with GBS*. London: Victor Gollancz, 1951.

Paulu, Burton. *Television and Radio in the United Kingdom*. London: Macmillan, 1981.

Pearson, Hesketh. *Bernard Shaw: His Life and Personality*. London: Methuen, 1961.

Pegg, Mark. *Broadcasting and Society 1918–1939*. London: Croom Helm, 1983.

Reith, J.C.W. *Broadcast over Britain*. London: Hodder and Stoughton, 1924.

Reith, John. *Into the Wind*. London: Hodder & Stoughton, 1949.

– *The Reith Diaries*. Ed. Charles Stuart. London: Collins, 1975.

Rodger, Ian. *Radio Drama*. London: Macmillan, 1982.

Scannell, Paddy, and David Cardiff. *A Social History of Broadcasting*. Volume 1: *1922–1939: Saving the Nation*. Oxford: Basil Blackwell, 1991.

Shaw, Bernard. *Agitations. Letters to the Press 1875–1950*. Ed. Dan H. Laurence and James Rambeau. New York: Frederick Ungar, 1985.

– *Bernard Shaw: The Diaries, 1885–1897*. Ed. Stanley Weintraub. 2 vols. University Park: Pennsylvania State University Press, 1986.

– *Collected Letters*. Ed. Dan H. Laurence. 4 vols. London: Reinhardt, 1965–88.

– *Collected Plays with Their Prefaces*. Under the editorial supervision of Dan H. Laurence. 7 vols. London: Max Reinhardt, The Bodley Head, 1970–4.
– *Platform and Pulpit*. Ed. Dan H. Laurence. New York: Hill & Wang, 1961.
– *The Spoken Word* [compact discs]. London: The British Library, 2006. Introduction and notes by L.W. Conolly.
– 'The Telltale Microphone.' *Political Quarterly* 6 (1935): 463–7.
– 'Toast to Albert Einstein.' Ed. Fred D. Crawford. *SHAW: The Annual of Bernard Shaw Studies* 15 (1995): 231–41.
– 'Truth by Radio.' *World Film News* 1 (July 1936): 24.
Smith, Anthony, ed. *British Broadcasting*. Newton Abbot: David & Charles, 1974.
Smithers, Stephen Walter. *Broadcasting from Within: Behind the Scenes at the BBC*. London: Pitman, 1938.
Sterling, Christopher H. *Encyclopedia of Radio*. 3 vols. New York and London: Fitzroy Dearborn, 2004.
Stokes, Sewell. 'Radio Drama as I Hear It.' *BBC Quarterly* 5.3 (Autumn 1950): 162–6.
Swift, John. *Adventure in Vision: The First 25 Years of Television*. London: John Lehmann, 1950.
Symington, Rodney. *The Nazi Appropriation of Shakespeare. Cultural Politics in the Third Reich*. Lewiston: The Edwin Mellen Press, 2005.
Wearing, J.P., ed. *Bernard Shaw and Nancy Astor*. Toronto: University of Toronto Press, 2005.
Weiss, Samuel A., ed. *Bernard Shaw's Letters to Siegfried Trebitsch*. Stanford: Stanford University Press, 1986.
West, E.J., ed. *Shaw on Theatre*. New York: Hill & Wang, 1959.
West, W.J. *Truth Betrayed*. London: Duckworth, 1987.
Weymouth, Anthony. *Journal of the War Years and One Year Later*. 2 vols. Worcester: Littlebury, 1948.
Whitehead, Kate. *The Third Programme: A Literary History*. Oxford: Clarendon Press, 1989.
Whitworth, Geoffrey. *The Making of a National Theatre*. London: Faber, 1951.
Winsten, S., ed. *G.B.S. 90: Aspects of Bernard Shaw's Life and Work*. London: Hutchinson, 1946.
Woolf, Leonard. 'The Future of British Broadcasting.' *Political Quarterly* 2.2 (April–June 1931): 172–85.

Index